American Exceptionalism,
American Anxiety

American Exceptionalism, American Anxiety

Wages, Competition, and Degraded Labor in the Antebellum United States

Jonathan A. Glickstein

University of Virginia Press

Charlottesville and London

University of Virginia Press

© 2002 by the Rector and Visitors of the University of Virginia

All rights reserved

Printed in the United States of America on acid-free paper

First published 2002

1 3 5 7 9 8 6 4 2

Library of Congress Cataloging-in-Publication Data

Glickstein, Jonathan A., 1948–

American exceptionalism, American anxiety : wages, competition, and degraded labor in the Antebellum United States / Jonathan A. Glickstein.

p.   cm.

Includes index.

ISBN 0-8139-2115-5 (cloth : alk. paper)

1. Labor—Northeastern States—History—19th century. 2. Working poor—Northeastern States—History—19th century. 3. Wages—Northeastern States—History—19th century. 4. Subsistence economy—Northeastern States—History—19th century. 5. Work ethic—Northeastern States—History—19th century. 6. Capitalism—Northeastern States—History—19th century. 7. Social classes—Northeastern States—History—19th century. 8. Slavery—Southern States—History—19th century. 9. Labor economics—United States—States—History—19th century. 10. Competition—United States—States—History—19th century. 11. United States—Economic conditions—To 1865. I. Title

HD8070 .G578 2002

331'.0973'09034—dc21   2002017362

For Eileen

Contents

Contents

Acknowledgments

FIRST I WOULD LIKE TO THANK the following individuals at the University of Virginia Press: acquisitions editor Richard Holway for his valuable encouragement and advice and managing editor Ellen Satrom for her good-hearted editorial assistance. I would also like to thank Jay Carlander, Gerald Carpenter, Terri J. Ortega, Stanley L. Engerman, Robert A. Margo, W. I. Rorabaugh, Randolph A. Roth, Kevin Murphy, Douglas R. Egerton, Mary O. Furner, Ann M. Plane, Patricia Cline Cohen, Catherine L. Albanese, John Majewski, David Brion Davis, Howell Harris, Carol Sheriff, Jennifer Luff, Brian Greenberg, James Folts, Lewis Perry, Karen Halttunen, Jeffrey Rogers Hummel, W. Elliot Brownlee, Otis Graham, Roger Daniels, Jonathan Prude, Francille Wilson, Christine Daniels, Joanne Pope Melish, James B. Stewart, John Stauffer, James Grossman and other participants in a May 1997 American Social History seminar at the Newberry Library, Patricia Cleary and other members of a May 1998 Early American History seminar at the Huntington Library; editors Frank Smith, David Perry, and Thomas LeBien and the outside readers for their presses; and the readers for earlier versions of chapters 1 and 2. Portions of chapter 1 are reprinted from a festschrift for David Brion Davis, Karen Halttunen and Lewis Perry (eds.), *Moral Problems in American Life: New Perspectives on Cultural History.* Copyright © 1998 by Cornell University Press. Used by permission of the publisher, Cornell University Press. Portions of chapter 1 also have appeared as "Early-Mid-Nineteenth-Century Perceptions of Labor's Extrinsic Rewards and the Methodology of American Exceptionalism," in "L'exception Américaine," *Annales du Monde Anglophone: Revue Semestrielle Bilingue,* no. 3 (Marseille: Université de Provence, Aix-Marseille I, 1996): 65–81. An earlier version of chapter 2 appeared as "Pressures from Below: Pauperism, Chattel Slavery, and the Ideological Construction of Free Market Labor Incentives in Antebellum America," *Radical History Review* 69 (Fall 1997): 114–59.

Acknowledgments

I am grateful for financial assistance provided by a University of California President's Research Fellowship in the Humanities, as well as by a University of California, Santa Barbara, Regents' Junior Faculty Fellowship. I am also thankful for additional support from both UCSB's Academic Senate and its Interdisciplinary Humanities Center.

Perhaps most of all, I am in the debt of UCSB's Davidson Library, particularly its ILL and Circulation divisions and especially Circulation's Claudia E. Jimenez, for putting up with my endless requests.

American Exceptionalism,
American Anxiety

Introduction

There are two points on which you can easily test the real extent of a man's sympathies with labor—his sense of justice with regard to the wages of labor, and his sentiments with regard to the intrinsic dignity of labor itself.

—The abolitionist newspaper *Emancipator* (New York), 1844

THIS AND THE following chapters engage American work, competition, and social justice in the era of early industrial capitalism and escalating sectional conflict over slavery. They are commensurately concerned with representations of the incentives and anticipated extrinsic rewards motivating manual labor—especially those motivating the exponentially growing waged-labor proportion of the American workforce.[1] Some of the chapters are relatively self-contained, others are more interlocking, and all, in addressing such open-ended subjects, are necessarily selective in their focus. Merely with respect to wages and their determinants and functions, as historians are discovering, nonformalized, more or less popular conceptions are far richer than the technical descriptions of economists would imply.[2]

This book grew out of an earlier one that focused on what the New York *Emancipator* referred to as American "sentiments with regard to the intrinsic dignity" of manual-labor employments.[3] By pursuing a different focus here, I don't mean to deny that antebellum commentary frequently commingled perceptions of work's intrinsic character with those of its instrumental value (either existing or potential). Chapter 1 offers several examples in which such perceptions were linked, and chapter 4 details a particularly prominent illustration whereby labor activists' embrace of anticapitalist versions of the labor theory of value embodied a sense of the unrivaled economic indispensability, and hence the intrinsic moral superiority, of manual-labor employments. Still, the different focuses of this and my earlier book represent more than an artificial convenience. Disparate social pressures, angsts, and objectives, as chapter 1 also indicates, did commonly generate the privileging of either intrinsic or extrinsic rewards in the body of Anglo-American commentary on worker motivation.

The one overriding theme that runs throughout this book's chapters is an insistence upon the pronounced antebellum disagreements, explicit and implicit, over poverty, the fear of poverty, and other negative work incentives (e.g., the slaveholder's lash) in a period of ascendant capitalist waged labor. These disagreements as to the prevalence, and the relative efficacy and morality, of such incentives coexisted with a mythology of American exceptionalism that alternatively extolled the salience and the benefits (both economic and therapeutic) of more exclusively positive labor incentives (e.g., the hope of improvement commonly held to animate northern wage laborers). The disagreements over work incentives suggest the shaky if not spurious nature of the consensus generated by the exceptionalist mythology.[4] The discord and attendant tensions were especially manifest in a range of early nineteenth-century debates over the circumstances under which cheap or otherwise servile labor trumped the superior productivity of more generously compensated, avowedly respectable free labor.

In examining such debates, this book at least indirectly engages the causes of an incredibly destructive civil war, one that was largely fought over the respective merits of social orders based on chattel and nonchattel labor systems. In the case of the North, ideological preparation for the war entailed a general antebellum tendency whereby the threat posed by southern slavery and the slave power increasingly dominated, and even dwarfed, debates and concerns over other forms of servile labor and work-degrading processes — ones that were unmistakably endogenous to the free states. This ideological development was by no means definitive and univocal: such prominent antislavery Republicans as the cleric Henry Ward Beecher and the urban parks designer Frederick Law Olmsted did at times during the 1850s reprove discriminatory and inegalitarian labor practices in the free states precisely (or largely) because such practices provided ammunition to defenders of the southern social order. And assaults on the South's peculiar form of servile labor also had a more deeply doctrinal progressive dimension. When Karl Marx (followed by later Marxist historians) welcomed the Civil War on the grounds that "labor in white skin cannot emancipate itself where black skin is branded" — because the continued existence and territorial expansion of chattel servitude imposed firm limits on the forward progress of northern free labor — he was affirming a position that various

American abolitionists and Republican free-labor ideologues had themselves earlier taken.[5]

Still, there remained that more boastful and complacent tendency in the northern nationalist ideological preparation for civil war: the tendency to minimize or altogether deny the existence of structural wage slavery in the free states and simultaneously to externalize, or "southernize," the ills of northern society—to attribute such ills to the hegemonic power of the southern slavocracy.[6] Accordingly, even as I see much merit in the abolitionist-Marxist prioritization of chattel slavery's extirpation, I also discern substantial logic in the alternative view taken by the utopian socialist and other labor-radical critics of northern wage slavery.[7] This was the position that without other pervasive and basic changes in American economic and social arrangements, chattel slavery's abolition would prove of the most problematic, marginal benefit to the nation's laboring classes, white or black, North or South. It was this general position that during the 1850s came to be largely defused and eclipsed by antisouthern, Republican northern nationalism and its often simplistic dichotomization of slave versus free labor.[8]

The Mythology of American Economic Exceptionalism

While finding great variety in the "sentiments" regarding manual labor's "intrinsic dignity," I also indicated in my earlier book that antebellum commentators found no particularly compelling reason to regard agricultural, factory, casual, and other physical labor in the free states as inherently different from—either more or less intrinsically dignified and rewarding than—its counterpart in the Old World or the slave states. Frederick Law Olmsted was perhaps only more openly insistent than most other elite Americans (or at least those in the free states; he was surpassed in this regard by numerous southern defenders of social hierarchy) in characterizing a good portion of this physical labor as everywhere naturally intellectually delimiting.

Where Olmsted better typified not only a significant strain of northern upper-middle-class thought but also, quite likely, substantial working-class sentiment as well was his faith in the exceptional material rewards and advancement opportunities of the social order of the free states. Indeed, for Olmsted and many others a primary function of those rewards and opportunities was to encourage northern workers, including the most unskilled, to make their employments more productive and correspondingly less mindless—to remedy at least partially the intrinsic deficiencies and disadvantages in those employments.[9] True enough, Olmsted like others seems also to have accepted that in the free states as elsewhere, the unskilled and "mere muscle market" tended most of all to be "overstocked"—frequently glutted with the poor and the desperate.[10] And if for no other reason than such glutting, it was most manifestly at the bottom end of the occupational scale that wage rates appeared to attach themselves naturally to the employments themselves rather than to individual workers and their capacity to engage in individual bargaining. Nonetheless, there still existed greater possibility in the free states than anywhere else, so Olmsted's exceptionalist faith held, that industrious performance in even the hardest and lowest physical labor would be decently recompensed—would experience extrinsic recognition and redemption, so to speak.[11] Above-subsistence wages and the savings therefrom permitted discernible property mobility and/or upward occupational mobility over time. "Out of twenty Irish emigrants, landing in New York, perfectly destitute, of whose history I have been intimately cognizant," Olmsted wrote in 1861, "only two, both of whom were over fifty years of age, have lived out five years here without beginning to acquire wealth."[12]

With such Irish immigrant male day laborers particularly in mind, Olmsted thus distanced himself from both the utopian socialist exaltations of the intrinsic dignity of all manual work and the southern proslavery elitist arguments that characterized the performers of the more "menial" portion of this work, in the free as well as the slave states, as permanent "mudsills." Although "labor in itself is not honorable," Olmsted summarized, "in no enlightened free community"— in the North, that is—"is labor in itself practically degrading, because hireling labor is everywhere the stepping-stone from poverty and mediocrity to comfort and a position of usefulness."[13] Olmsted thereby tied the legitimacy of capitalist wage labor in the North to the certitude of decent extrinsic rewards, including the likelihood of movement out of wage labor, for hirelings who were enterprising and industrious. And with special reference to the unemployment and deprivations experienced by New York City workers during the depression and hard winter of 1857–58, Olmsted added elsewhere: "Our system is by no means perfect; no one thinks it so: no one objects to its imperfections being pointed out." But however fierce and even "lawless" it might be, the "competitive system" in "the whole of the Free States" was marked by neither widespread material suffering nor the closing off of upward-mobility channels. "When any real suffering does occur," Olmsted rather moralistically insisted, "it is mainly a consequence and a punishment of their [the northern laborers'] own carelessness and improvidence, and is in the nature of a remedy."[14]

As much as anything else, this book explores the elaborations, permutations, and outright gainsays of Olmsted's claims—claims that were among the many contributions to the mythology of American economic exceptionalism, or the antebellum version of the American dream, to employ more popular parlance.[15] That mythology was hardly a simple function of objective material abundance and economic opportunity. As chapter 1 suggests, some of its most prominent early nineteenth-century formulations were constructed through interaction with Old World classical economic wage paradigms, which equally influenced those northern labor reformers and others who emerged as the most vociferous skeptics of the mythology's empirical grounding.

Such positive endorsements as Olmsted's of American economic exceptionalism, defined by its continued faith in widespread access to abundant material opportunity, also functioned as ideologies of success. As such, these endorsements tended to obscure the real dimensions of failure up and down the nineteenth-century American economic ladder (e.g., the bankruptcy experienced by innumerable small businessmen as well as the "suffering" of wage-earning laborers), even as they also exhibited Olmsted's inclination to acknowledge and reprove economic failure by attributing it to the individual character defects of the casualties.[16] In one important sense Olmsted's particular formulations here were also comparatively restrained, just as they were embedded in a virulent antisouthernism. For the hordes of immigrant Irish, at least, they celebrated more modest, incremental economic betterment in the free states than did the rags-to-riches variants also circulating in early nineteenth-century America, which typically "promised much more than could ever be delivered by a real society."[17] Olmsted's rather low opinion of the "habits" of the "destitute" Irish arrivals fed his fears that notwithstanding the existence of abundant, objective opportunity throughout the continental United States, they would form a "permanent lower class" in New York and other of "our large towns." He worried that the Irish might come to constitute the northern counterpart to the "majority of the whites in the plantation districts of the South" who had been morally diseased and debilitated by chattel slavery.[18]

But its underlying anxieties and relatively moderate tenor notwithstanding, Olmsted's generalized judgment regarding northern labor's instrumental value remained more celebratory than otherwise. For this reason it is unlikely that his judgment would have strongly resonated with African-American bootblacks, or widowed seamstresses, or working-class wives who cleaned up after the boarders they took in—with, that is, members of the most marginalized antebellum northern occupational groups who have left little record of their thoughts on questions of material opportunity, social fluidity, and economic justice.[19] At the same time, actual experiences in themselves do not negate the multiple intellectual reaches of the mythology of American economic exceptionalism—its capacity to generate and sustain not insubstantial expectations among a host of groups. It was largely able to do this because it encompassed both long-standing republican objectives of economic competence and productive independence (e.g., movement up the agricultural ladder) and ascendant liberal values extolling a more ambitious magnitude of wealth maximization. There was, of course, the widely recognized historic role of the mythology in pulling the Irish and other impoverished European immigrants to American shores, a circumstance that Marx and Friedrich Engels acknowledged in their scornful dismissals of the "bankrupt shopkeepers and artisans or ruined dirt farmers who strive for the good fortune of becoming petty bourgeois or farmers again in America."[20] Additionally, and with an agenda that, for the time, was hardly less contrary to existing social arrangements in the United States than scientific socialism, spokesmen at the antebellum black national conventions sought, quite unlike Marx and Engels, to make positive use of the mythology of American economic exceptionalism. They appropriated it to underscore the injustice of racial prejudice, southern slavery, and the systematic educational and economic discrimination practiced against northern free blacks. Similarly did white factory women in New England incorporate the mythology into their own efforts to discredit and resist low wages and other oppressive and unrepublican working conditions.[21]

Until recently, at least, the pronounced tendency of economic historians was to find more empirical validity than not in such celebratory exceptionalist perspectives as Olmsted's. While documenting the significant, and in some ways growing, maldistribution of wealth in the United States during the early to mid-nineteenth century, economic historians have put at least as much emphasis upon the long-term per capita increases in real incomes and living standards enjoyed by skilled and unskilled workers alike.[22] Similarly they have emphasized the sizable real wage differentials that obtained from the first between the United States and the nations of the Old World (again to the advantage of both skilled and unskilled workers in America). The uneven distribution of wealth within the United States notwithstanding, such scholars characteristically have prioritized the "rising tide lifts all boats" phenomenon, which they attribute to America's tremendous economic growth, technological and transportation advances, and productivity gains during this and other periods.[23] In support of the thesis of significantly improving working-class living standards, one economic historian has estimated that real per capita incomes in the United States were 62 percent higher in 1860 than in 1820. Two others have concluded that between these same two dates "all discernible segments of the manufacturing labor force" in the Northeast "realized substantial increases in real wages."[24]

These observations are themselves of recent vintage. But economic historians also have begun to significantly qualify their more traditional optimistic presumption of antebellum wage and income patterns. Robert William Fogel, most notably, has called attention to the fluctuations and the periodic declines in real wages and annual incomes experienced by skilled and unskilled workers alike during the antebellum years. Under conditions of widespread unemployment during both the major depression of 1837–43 and what Fogel terms the "hidden" depression of 1848–55, declines in workers' annual incomes were likely to have been particularly severe, regardless of trends in daily real wage rates.[25] Fogel adds that "indexes of real daily wages do not measure the effects of unemployment, of deskilling, or of labor speedup, all of which contributed to the economic distress of workers during the 1850s and which made the slide in the real annual income of nonfarm workers between 1848 and 1855 steeper than the slide in the real daily wage rates of particular occupations."[26] Drawing from among the most comprehensive wage databases yet developed by economic historians for the antebellum period, Robert A. Margo confirms Fogel's emphasis that aggregate long-term per capita increases in real wages concealed shorter-term stagnations, lags, and declines in real wage rates and incomes. Margo also concludes that eastern artisans fared worst of all, and that the real wage increase experienced by American skilled blue-collar workers generally was lesser rather than greater than the gains enjoyed by unskilled common laborers over the course of the 1820–60 period. This last finding of Margo's contradicts another staple of the economic-history literature, and in so doing it throws into question what that literature has also commonly inferred and acclaimed: the facility with which the growing antebellum free-market economy created demand for, and commensurately rewarded, new technical and other manual-labor expertises more than it devalued older ones.[27]

The more pessimistic arguments advanced by Fogel and Margo appear to represent a recessive position within the economic-history literature, as yet failing to overturn what Margo terms "the prevailing wisdom" positing great, largely continuous and widespread improvement in working-class living standards.[28] The quantitative scholarship on property and occupational mobility generally continues, for its part, to support Olmsted's impressionistic claims as to discernible, incremental improvement for white male common laborers in the antebellum era.[29] Margo himself does not reject all of the standard optimistic claims: American labor markets, he agrees, did respond "effectively" to guide migration from lower-wage to higher-wage geographical regions, and for the 1820–60 period overall, productivity increases did translate into real wage gains for workers of all skill levels.[30]

But as Fogel and Margo both suggest, their more pessimistic conclusions carry historiographical significance: they represent at least a limited rapprochement with the more "anecdotal" claims that social, labor, and generally left-leaning historians have been making for decades.[31] In some cases because they traditionally have been more sensitive than economic historians to artisan deskilling, and in part because they have given greater attention to the female manufacturing outworkers, black casual laborers, and other marginalized groups noted earlier, social and labor historians characteristically have been more dubious about the life chances of the American laboring population. They have been resistant to exceptionalist perspectives highlighting the degree to which economic growth and productivity gains in fact translated into improvements in those life chances, and they have been commensurately unimpressed with the evidence of American wage superiority.[32] Drawing from his finding that Irish immigrant and other unskilled canal diggers in early nineteenth-century America could look forward to the merest subsistence from their employments, the Marxist historian Peter Way concisely summarizes the latter view: "Standard-of-living comparisons among various national working classes is a matter of splitting hairs over degrees of disadvantage."[33]

My own sympathies tend to lie with the position staked out by such labor historians as Way. I am, for example, inclined as many of them are to accentuate the degree to which the splintering of antebellum labor markets along racial, ethnic, and gender lines helped create localized, overcrowded labor markets.[34] Along with inadequate and false job intelligence information and other supplementary factors, such splintering commonly acted to reduce access to economic opportunity and to keep down wage levels for many groups of workers. All acted to partially offset what is perhaps the central fact upon which the mythology of American economic exceptionalism has rested: the overall land abundance and labor scarcity that distinguished the early United States and lent plausibility to the notion that supply-and-demand forces worked to a unique degree in favor of America's free laboring population.[35]

Gresham's Law Anxieties

An inquiry into antebellum perceptions of labor's extrinsic rewards would be bizarre if it made no reference to historians' findings and debates regarding empirical patterns—hence the summary presented here of some of the scholarly literature. However, any sustained engagement with actual wage and mobility phenomena and the complicated modern scholarship on these would require a very different book from this one. I remain far more concerned in these chapters with matters of perception, and I am particularly impressed with the power of an exceptionalist mythology that, whatever the material patterns may have been, stimulated not merely optimism and complacency in elite and other quarters but also deep-seated economic and cultural anxieties throughout antebellum society. Alexis de Tocqueville and like-minded commentators captured a dimension of this phenomenon when they observed that American social values and consumption patterns, reflecting an atmosphere of egalitarianism and abundance, generated pervasive stress and "melancholy" by continually raising the definition of what constituted an acceptable competence.[36] But the anxieties to which I am referring were more than just a function of continually developing, insatiable needs and tastes. Northern free labor—above all, that which was white and male and, to a somewhat lesser extent, native-born and skilled—was commonly defined in terms of its ostensible economic well-being and privileged status. It was defined, in other words, in terms of all that it had to lose were it to be undersold and undermined by various forms of cheap and servile labor competition, either now or in the future (such concerns over respectable free labor existing quite apart from the "servile" workers' own economic insecurities and other tribulations). Olmsted, George M. Weston, and other prominent Republican defenders of dignified northern free labor notably manifested these anxieties in their confrontation during the 1850s with the southern slave power and the projected territorial expansion of slave-labor enterprises. As earlier suggested, many of these commentators vehemently endorsed the mythology of virtually boundless, widely accessible northern economic opportunity in rebuttal of the southern proslavery critiques of the northern social order.[37] But anxieties regarding servile labor competition also were expressed throughout the early nineteenth century by assorted labor activists and reformers who in basic respects challenged that exceptionalist mythology and took a less complacent, far more critical view than did antebellum Republican leaders of the endogenous openness and fairness of the northern social order.

A good number of these labor activists and reformers were expressing, preeminently, a skilled-artisan mentality. Insofar as it developed into a consciousness of anticapitalist class exploitation comparable to that emerging among European skilled workers, American artisan republicanism has been held to controvert doctrines of American exceptionalism that have denied such an indigenous history of consciousness.[38] Yet the mythology of American economic exceptionalism nonetheless exercised a certain hegemonic hold on aggrieved journeymen and their trade organizations even as these commonly characterized that mythology as an employer-generated opiate. Both as republican citizens and as among the most economically well situated of the nation's work-ers, such artisans derived their sense of entitlement in some measure from American exceptionalist mythology; at the same time, that mythology fed their anxieties over the sweated female and immigrant labor and other debased, "grinding competition" that was part and parcel of the market revolution and metropolitan industrialization.[39] Skilled workers in early industrial England and France shared similar anxieties. But where long-standing exclusionist guild tra-ditions and customs of the trade stimulated their assumptions as to their deserved—and increasingly embattled—elite status within the hierarchy of labor, the mythology of American exceptionalism served much the same role for the artisans of the new republic.[40]

Chapters 2–4 have as one of their primary concerns the American artisans' resultant sense of being squeezed. Unlike some of the recent explorations of working-class racism and whiteness, I here emphasize how much these north-ern skilled workers perceived themselves—and were also perceived by more elite commentators—not merely in terms of particular groups below them in the social scale but no less crucially in terms of those professional men and cap-italists who were manifestly above them in the competitive hierarchy. In chap-ters 3 and 4 I focus on the implications that the spectacle of elite success and the varied ideological justifications of that success had on artisan and other labor-activist responses to the most radical anticapitalist versions of the labor theory of value.

Chapters 5, 6, and 7 consider how perceptions regarding the more margin-alized and stigmatized social groups, both in the United States and abroad, played into the debates over the nature of dignified, truly free manual labor in the northern states. That labor was commonly held to include not merely work by skilled artisans and on freehold farms but the factory jobs and other kinds of semiskilled waged employments that were becoming an increasingly impor-tant part of the economic landscape. These debates constituted an important source of thematic continuity between the Jacksonian and the late antebellum periods. In essence, they express how intimately the criteria that commenta-tors employed in conceptualizing free labor were tied up with free labor's per-ceived ability—or inability—to resist infiltration and debasement from a host of forms of dishonorable, unfree labor. All of these debates shared the Gre-sham's law apprehension, stimulated by the market revolution, that the rules of economic competition are set by the morally least reputable participants, who were commonly held to include both the servile labor force and the interests that controlled and deployed them.

No less important, the same debates suggest a primary sense in which, largely owing to the market revolution, eighteenth-century American republican notions warning of the fragility of the more virtuous, altogether superior political order were now routinely applied to the economic realm. Such notions were akin to but transcended artisan-labor republicanism specifically. To the significant extent, as well, that free labor was defined in terms of its elevated material well-being and acquisitive capabilities, the anxieties expressed over its competitive resilience and possible degradation by servile labor marked a notable intersection of republican and liberal values.

Just as some recent economic (as well as other) historians have challenged the notion of a British Industrial Revolution, so they have contested the term *market revolution* for the early nineteenth-century United States, claiming, among other things, that it slights the magnitude of eighteenth-century commercial expansion and related quantitative changes. But my own position may already be apparent: on the strictly perceptual level, the market-revolution metaphor remains apt, a point that I argue at greater length in chapter 3. I would also readily acknowledge that many of the emergent perceptions were positive, even as I give greater attention in this book to those that were more hostile and alarmist. And as the case of the free-soil newspaper editor and economist George M. Weston suggests in chapter 5, some notable permutations of the more alarmist perceptions of the market revolution extended beyond the specifically working-class, plebeian distaste for capitalist innovations in free waged-labor markets.

Not only were assorted Gresham's law–like anxieties, centering on dignified labor's underselling and debasement by servile labor, expressed by individuals outside as well as within the working classes. Such anxieties might also be regarded as a prominent subset of more sweeping early nineteenth-century apprehensions over economic and financial vulnerability. In a volatile economy visited by frequent minor recessions, as well as several major ones, poverty could and did strike families of any class. "In no country of the world," Tocqueville noted, "are private fortunes more precarious than in the United States. It is not uncommon for the same man, in the course of his life, to rise and sink again through all the grades which lead from opulence to poverty."[41] Empirical studies suggest that Tocqueville exaggerated the instability of elite wealth holdings.[42] Nonetheless, the labor-centered antislavery jeremiads of a Weston and journeymen artisans' sense that they had much to lose from competition with convict or sweated labor remained part and parcel of society-wide economic insecurities and fears of downward social mobility.

A closely related and significant subtheme in these chapters is that of contagion, most particularly negative moral contagion. The missionary faith in uplift is not much in evidence in the various anxieties explored here. Free laborers cannot elevate slaves; slaves can only debase free laborers. Independent and respectable artisans cannot pass on their good character to ex-convicts who join their workshops; ex-convicts can only corrupt those artisans to their level. In such cases physical proximity and example constitute obvious conduits of pollution and degeneration.[43] But in these and other cases as well, more impersonal market-cheapening and degrading processes also prominently figure in conceptualizations of the other. At the same time, some of the themes of contagion and debasement touched on in these chapters remain less strongly related than others to the conjunction of early nineteenth-century market processes with indigenous American beliefs about republican fragility. The fundamental position of such American poor-law reformers as Joseph Tuckerman, considered in chapter 2, was that vagrants and other "undeserving" recipients of relief would demoralize independent laborers and poison the work incentives of the capitalist market.[44] But Tuckerman was avowedly derivative, and his theme originated in Old England, outside the American republican experiment.

In their attention to anxieties centering on a variety of servile laborers, chapters 5 through 7 extend the caveat to cultural studies and race scholarship that have overwhelmingly privileged whiteness. These along with other chapters throw into question the degree to which American white workers' sense of self derived with exclusive reference to the African-American component (both free and slave) of the bottom rungs of the social ladder. I am not questioning here the likelihood that most such workers, together with much of the labor press, held antiblack prejudices, and that these entered — in many cases quite profoundly — into their identity. Nor would I dispute a related principal theme, that American working-class racism, together with antiblack violence, historically has transcended and flourished disproportionately to white workers' specific fears about job competition from African Americans. Still, the particular decisiveness with which the early nineteenth-century North relegated free blacks to the economic margins — discriminated against and minimized them as competitive threats — itself helped to ensure that the scope of antebellum anxieties over labor competition would extend beyond white racism.[45] For this as well as other reasons, I join in the unease that whiteness, as the latest "master narrative" of American history, tends to oversimplify the attitudinal landscape, to obscure other bases of identity formation or axes of difference.[46]

Achille Murat

Antebellum society and its northern metropolitan centers most of all emerge in these chapters as virtual hothouses of economic competition and competitive anxieties. Even so, I would also underscore how legal proscriptions, discriminatory social norms, and the scarcity of resources that they brought to the market in the first place severely handicapped members of subordinate social groups within the competitive market.[47] In excluding northern blacks and women from the requisite training and competition for positions in professional, mercantile, and other kinds of employments, such handicapping could itself, paradoxically, contribute to the intensity of early nineteenth-century economic competition.[48] This circumstance was most notably exemplified by the thousands of desperate working-class women who found themselves crowded into seamstressing and a few other occupational fields.[49] But gender-based and other labor-market segmentation hardly alone explains why these chapters' portrait of superheated competition may not seem especially controversial. Such discrimination and segmentation may well stand out for modern critics, as it did for some antebellum ones, as among the most signal and unflattering dimensions of economic competition. But a legion of early nineteenth-century observers from the yet more deeply ascriptive societies of the Old World, only the most famous of whom was Tocqueville, had different things in mind when they marveled at the intensity of antebellum competition. Thus Achille Murat, the Frenchman turned American citizen and Florida plantation owner, offered this astonished and altogether favorable assessment in the 1830s: "Competition, — that is the secret of the American system; every thing is to be won by competition: fortune, power, love, riches, all these objects of desire are attainable; it is for the most skilful to go in pursuit of them."[50]

The treatise in which Murat offered this observation is shallow and often contradictory; as a commentator on American manners and morals, he has fallen into deserved obscurity. Yet his remarks help to introduce some of the issues treated in these chapters. Murat's celebration of the relatively uninhibited nature of American economic competition — free-market capitalist values — incorporated two of the staples of the early nineteenth-century exceptionalist mythology. First, in the absence of European-like formal barriers to equal opportunity, the competitive race was fair: "All men are born equal in rights and in chances of success. . . . All have equal chances of attaining every thing." Second, the competition remained comparatively benign: "Fortunately, however, in our land of plenty the princesses to conquer and deliver are sufficiently numerous to content all valiant knights, and even many of their squires; so that the combat is not so desperate as it might be supposed. There is room for every one at the banquet of life."[51]

One could dwell on the gendered nature of these remarks, an examination that would take in Murat's apparent obliviousness to—or acceptance of—the northern labor-market segmentation. But it may be more useful here to touch on Murat's more explicit efforts to reconcile the presence of southern chattel slavery—the most egregious denial of formal equal rights and equal "chances of success" to human beings—with his insistence on the openness of American economic competition.[52] On the one hand, Murat endorsed the view—what David Brion Davis characterizes as the more "scientific" vein of antislavery thought—that free-market competitive forces doomed slave labor.[53] Just as it was already, in 1833, expiring in Virginia and Maryland because free labor was "cheaper" there, so, Murat prophesied, would this "in time" become the case in all the states and territories.[54]

But despite this argument, and despite his related reference to slavery as a "domestic plague," Murat was hardly antislavery in even the broader sense of the term. He evidenced, for example, none of Tocqueville's revulsion for the institution (just as he exhibited none of his more celebrated contemporary's ambivalence about American economic competition and materialism). Indeed, Murat invoked black racial inferiority and several of the period's standard proslavery arguments to mount an avid defense of American bondage. The most relevant of these justifications for purposes of this discussion itself invoked competitive values. As one critical commentator remarked, in an accurate assessment of Murat's views, this was, essentially, a might-makes-right justification: "Throwing aside the principles of justice altogether, he [Murat] goes upon the principle of power alone, and argues, that a white man, by reason of his intelligence, possessing *power* over a black man, has as much right to use him for his purposes, as he has to catch a wild horse and ride him, or to kill a lion and strip him of his skin."[55] As noted, Murat trumpeted the benign nature of American economic competition for its active participants. He furthermore proclaimed the kindly treatment enjoyed by the southern chattel slaves who had fallen victim in the power struggle with whites. He favorably compared bondsmen in material condition and "happiness" to free white laborers in the Old World who were similarly denied equal liberty to compete but who were also deprived of a master's vested interest in their well-being.[56] Still, Murat's might-makes-right argument, as an effort to incorporate American chattel slavery into his celebration of a competitive system that fully rewarded "talent and merit," anticipated some of the more avowedly harsh, Social Darwinist defenses of competitive market processes that emerged later in the nineteenth century.[57]

James Freeman Clarke and Labor-Reform Discourse

Even in Murat's own time there were commentators aplenty who did not limit themselves to the case of southern slaves in finding his perspective lacking. In this as in later periods, the same premise that the native Frenchman accepted with such equanimity for the early nineteenth-century United States — that capitalism involves the unequal distribution of material goods — drew a range of markedly more adversarial constructions. A prime illustration is a friendly examination of American Fourierist, or Associationist, utopian doctrine written in 1844 by Boston's liberal Unitarian, Transcendentalist minister James Freeman Clarke.[58] "Without overlooking or undervaluing the advantages of our present civilization, without joining in any extravagant condemnation of our present social system," Clarke observed, "no thoughtful person, we suppose, will deny that there are great social evils existing among us, for which society, as at present constituted, fails to provide any remedy."[59] Clarke's elucidatory remarks merit even more extended consideration here than does Murat's treatise as a backdrop to the chapters that follow.

Against Murat's formal, legalistic notion of equal opportunity, Clarke suggested in his commentary that prevailing disparities in initial resources and endowments, in the United States as anywhere else, established the broad pattern of unequal outcomes, as well as generating harsh economic exploitation. American competition was hardly benign, nor were its only victims black chattel slaves. Clarke posited what by his time had become a virtual mantra among the Associationists and other labor reformers: the illusory voluntariness enjoyed by free laborers in the northern labor market. Such workers (most of all, as some of these reformers emphasized, wage earners without the benefit of effective unions) were ordinarily "at the mercy of capital," possessing minimal control over the commodification of their own labor. Notwithstanding the occasional "exception which proves the rule," "capital" (such as the "large clothes-dealers in the cities" who "have their agents in the countries") had the time and the capability "to look about and take advantage of all the circumstances which will enable it to reduce the wages of labor." Wage earners, in contrast, must contract their services at unfavorable and unfair terms because, unlike the employer, they lacked essential resources and "cannot wait" for better terms. "When a man must have work to-day, or go without bread for himself and family, he is not in a position to make a fair bargain." From his no-real-alternatives condition there logically ensue relationships with employers that fail to be reciprocal.[60]

Clarke's general, rather abstract assessment—what one might characterize as his male breadwinner–exploitation scenario—carried any number of implicit corollaries or assumptions. There was first his apparent assumption that as a general "rule" all "capital"—and therefore smaller as well as larger employers— possessed the resources to wait out prospective hirelings. Even more certain and central was Clarke's assumption that the more immediate needs driving wage earners necessarily eventuated in employment situations in which they were underpaid or otherwise exploited. Neither of these assumptions is immune to challenge. While already indicating that my sympathies lie with the critical perspective of labor historians that bears strong affinities with Clarke's own, I am also willing to acknowledge that the underlying material realities were complex and varied—that the antebellum economic landscape encompassed a host of examples and facts capable of sustaining conflicting narratives.[61] Or, as Robert J. Steinfeld and Stanley L. Engerman remark, what is precisely so "slippery and contestable" about market-based economic coercion, as invoked by Clarke and others, is the difficulty of evaluating "the universe of options" that the individual in fact faces.[62]

Clarke's exploitation scenario reflected some additional corollaries. First, he seemingly dismissed the American exceptionalist emphasis upon geographic mobility and the economic options it opened up to antebellum workers that reduced their position of disadvantage. Quite possibly, had Clarke been challenged at the time by Achille Murat (or by a modern-day economic historian), he would have been less dismissive. On the other hand, as critics of Frederick Jackson Turner and the western safety-valve thesis have long argued, moving oneself and one's family considerable distances in pursuit of better economic opportunities required not insubstantial monetary resources—which Clarke's male breadwinner lacked, or he would not have been so desperate for immediate employment in the first place.[63] Moving shorter distances, between local opportunity structures (from, say, New York City to Boston), was commensurately more feasible, as the evidence of rapid population turnover and large numbers of transient workers for this period might suggest. But whether or not Clarke was too quick to discount the existence of alternative possibilities for gainful employment (which would also, of course, have depended on such variables, unspecified by Clarke, as the marketable skills possessed by his breadwinner, where he was residing at the time, etc.), Clarke's portrait of wage earners driven by immediate needs entailed a further corollary. This was the absence of a system of social services and insurance to which the worker and his family might also turn as an alternative recourse to his acceptance of an "unfair bargain."

In view of the undeveloped state of the early nineteenth-century American safety net, this last corollary is less controversial than Clarke's first assumption of limited employment options. Indeed, it might hardly be worth mentioning were it not for the fact that, together with the first, it points to a third, and possibly the most central, unstated assumption undergirding Clarke's representation of the illusory voluntariness enjoyed by wage laborers in the northern labor market. This was his assumption as to the complete disagreeableness of the most likely alternative to immediate employment that awaited the worker—the alternative that pushed him into accepting employment at disadvantageous terms. A good portion of the period's labor-reform commentary, including that in the *Northampton Democrat* discussed in chapter 2, quite unequivocally painted this alternative in the stark and absolute colors of death by starvation, if not for the breadwinner himself than for one or more of his dependents.[64] Clarke was more ambiguous; he referred to those who "depend on their labor for subsistence" but later, albeit in a somewhat different context, noted that "we speak metaphorically when we talk of starving. We can live on very little. . . . In this country it is not easy for a man with two hands to starve."[65] In this as in other of his remarks, Clarke revealed something of the spiritual and ethereal bent that drew him to his ministerial calling, as well as the limited degree to which he too had imbibed the mythology of American economic exceptionalism.

Yet there remains no question that Clarke, along with others of strong labor-reform sympathies, assumed that the material deprivation confronting the worker and his family would be sufficiently unpleasant and extreme to force him (and, quite possibly, members of his family as well) into exploitative agreements with capital. And here one encounters another of Clarke's implicit but quite apparent assumptions: the initial propertylessness, or near propertylessness, of the male breadwinner that obliged him to accept an employment relation which, however disadvantageous, at least would enable him to avert a yet deeper economic crisis.

Clarke provides no indication that he possessed unusually intimate knowledge of wage levels and working-class household economies. But here, too, there were more than enough different facts to provide ample basis for conflicting narratives. Clarke's outlook, in any case, remained distinct from the oft-heard moralistic refrain that workers had largely themselves to blame for failing to save enough of their earnings from better days to tide them and their families over on worse ones. Like that of the Associationists and other labor reformers, Clark's perspective carried the assumption that male breadwinners and other wage earners had relatively few such better days in which they had earned wages more than sufficient to cover the costs of family survival. Many if not most wage earners were no more at fault for their antecedent failure to accumulate resources than they were for the most recent disadvantageous employment terms that grew out of their inability to "wait" for better terms.

Through both explicit remarks and unstated assumptions, then, Clarke conveyed a pattern of initial propertylessness and ensuing, persisting exploitation. Such a pattern would have been hardly unique to early nineteenth-century free waged labor. Indentured servitude, so central a part of the seventeenth- and eighteenth-century American labor experience, in some respects had offered yet more blatant examples. New World–bound European emigrants and native-born Americans alike, commonly finding themselves in desperate economic circumstances, voluntarily (for the most part) entered into agreements that formally reduced their freedom during the terms of service. Colonial and later state servant statutes authorized masters to administer corporal punishment and included the penalty of criminal incarceration to enforce servants' obedience and minimize their premature exits from the agreements. To the degree that employers took advantage of their positions of dominance, indentured servants experienced harsh and oppressive conditions during the duration of the contracts, after which they met with varying success in realizing their objective of economic independence.[66] It was not so very long before Clarke was writing that indentured servitude for the most part had disappeared from the northern states. This demise accompanied indentured servitude's gradual delegitimation by a mainstream opinion that had come to view the institution, like chattel slavery, as a form of involuntary labor owing to its state-endorsed compulsory and coercive features.[67]

The prominent example of adult indentured servitude possibly contributed something to the sense, exhibited by Clarke among others, of the ironies that liberty of contract—formal voluntariness—held for individuals in dire straits.[68] But more certainly, as a reform-minded person presumably outside the mainstream, Clarke could only have viewed the delegitimation and abolition of indentured servitude, along with chattel slavery, as a starting point, not an end point, for attacks on unfree practices and institutions. Definitions, degrees, and forms of coercion (physical, economic, legal) remain highly contested subjects for historians in search of meaningful distinctions between free and unfree labor.[69] But some of the most well-known nineteenth-century commentaries conceptualized the boundaries in terms of acceptable and unacceptable coercion. An important part of William Ellery Channing's 1835 attack on chattel slavery, detailed in chapter 2, was his insistence that free waged laborers in the capitalist market were indeed driven by their "masters in hunger and thirst," but that these "natural" compulsions or incentives were intrinsically ennobling. Channing's challenge to the critics of northern labor conditions was more fundamental than that of such American exceptionalist perspectives as Olmsted's or Murat's precisely because he did not, at bottom, rest the legitimacy of waged labor on the hireling's ability to commodify his labor advantageously.

Clarke wrote an admiring review of Channing's *Slavery* in the 1830s. But he confined his remarks to praising Channing for the other challenge that the nation's leading Unitarian cleric offered in his work, the one that garnered far more attention at the time. This was Channing's eagerly anticipated response to the immediate-emancipation arguments of William Lloyd Garrison and other radical abolitionists.[70] Clarke did not address Channing's ancillary celebration of the free laborer's natural sanctions of hunger and thirst. But enough has already been said to suggest that with respect to these, Clarke in the mid-1840s held a rather different position from Channing's, one more congruent with some of the existing currents of religious and philosophical idealism. The lash of hunger, the need for bread, might well be the most primordial and natural of compulsions driving market relationships. But all that was natural should not necessarily be sanctified and embedded in social norms. Whatever the larger society might accept as legitimate at the moment, Clarke suggested, such market compulsions were in fact only marginally more just when structured and exploited by private economic power without the assistance of the most blatant and direct governmental prescriptions and coercions.[71] Prevailing social arrangements and values, as northern labor reformers more generally perceived these, remained guilty of honoring and mirroring unacceptably oppressive material forces—of failing to place individuals "above the fear of *want*."[72] The persisting result was precisely those unfair employment relations that laboring people, whatever their increasing juridical rights, were obliged to choose over the freedom of starvation and material deprivation.

Clark's particular observations, then, were most conspicuously inspired by what many like-minded commentators found similarly intriguing: the more free-wheeling competition characterizing early nineteenth-century free-labor markets and the yet more deeply ironical sense in which such markets themselves conjoined formal liberty of person and voluntariness with contracted-for exploitation. Free-market capitalist values and their embodiment in unequal exchanges and property relations above all stirred Clarke: the Unitarian cleric found the prevailing, comparatively uninhibited economic competition of the antebellum period that Murat exalted to be less than liberating and in fact ethically abhorrent. Clarke did not go quite so far as had Orestes Brownson, the most famous radical thinker of early nineteenth-century America: Clarke did not explicitly insist that when individual wage earners did manage to rise out of their condition of disadvantage and join "the class of the wealthy," their success was invariably contingent upon their own transformation into exploiters in the labor market.[73] Nonetheless, Clarke characterized exploitation as basic to the capitalist wage system, most evidently of all as that system operated under the "'let alone' principle." Expressing his preference for Fourierist utopian communal arrangements over that principle, he reached for philosophic heights: "The principle of free competition is a good one for the strong, the sagacious, for those who have talent, means, energy: but it gives no choice to the weak, the poor, the friendless. It developes great energy, and produces great results: but it makes one part of society the tools and instruments by which another part may carve out their way to fortune." In the self-regulating market, Clarke furthermore insisted, the rational self-interest — the "calculating reason" — of the talented and the powerful provided but poor protection indeed for society's most vulnerable members, free and slave alike.[74]

Did Clarke intend by his free competition–exploitation scenario to denote the absolute material immiserization of those left behind? Or did he instead intend to denote, somewhat less damningly, only an increasingly uneven distribution of wealth and other social benefits — i.e., economically exploitative relationships from which the exploited may have still gained absolutely, at least materially?[75] Clarke's remarks are too general to permit an answer to this question (one that the protests of disaffected artisans also raise). Furthermore, his perspective on the "great social evils existing among us," specifically his assault on free competition, quite pointedly subordinated the myriad ways in which the legal and regulatory functions of the state in fact shaped free competition. He ignored how these functions established significant "background" conditions and otherwise contributed to differential economic power, the options available to individuals, and the ensuing market compulsions experienced by northern waged laborers.[76] Clarke's perspective — his particular challenge to the position that the capitalist market was a sphere of freedom — may not, in this connection, have been the dominant stance even within the relatively narrow confines of antebellum labor-reform circles. While similarly bemoaning society's legitimation and embedment of the lash of hunger that drove free waged workers, antimonopoly land reformers, for example, were more inclined to blame the heavy hand of government—the state's intrusive complicity with speculators and other private interests—for iniquitous and exploitative economic processes. Genuine government "let-aloneism" was for them a good part of the solution, rather than emblematic of the problem.[77]

Clarke's own aversion to capitalist individualism and its embodiment in oppressive employment relations found more developed and extensive expression in the utopian socialist literature he was commenting upon. Even here, however, there remained significant disagreements that discouraged him from becoming more than a sympathetic observer of these "constructive" socialists' anticapitalist, communal experiments. These differences extended beyond Clarke's interesting failure, which stood in pointed contrast to the rhetoric of communitarian and many other labor reformers, to use the term *wage slavery* to characterize labor-market conditions that he agreed were exploitative.[78] More basically, and true to his ministerial calling, Clarke insisted that individual sin and selfishness were the root causes of social injustice; they were the antecedent reason why antebellum Americans yielded to oppressive material forces and perpetuated these in exploitative social arrangements under conditions of free competition. The same spiritual perspective that led Clarke to relegate bad government and laws to the domain of epiphenomena prompted his criticism that the proponents of utopian social reorganization were beginning "at the wrong end" in their own common tendency to neglect "individual responsibility" and fixate on pernicious "external arrangements."[79]

These differences with the Associationists were hardly insignificant; indeed, they fueled much of the contentious debate between the disparate romantic reform impulses of the early nineteenth century.[80] I would nonetheless emphasize here some of the basic notions underlying the Associationist and other alternative social arrangements with which Clarke did signify agreement: to wit, that market-oriented meritocracies inordinately reward certain personal talents above others; that the free competition and formal equal opportunity that such meritocracies exalt enable only those individuals who possess these talents in more than ordinary degree to overcome significant, untouched disadvantages of birth and background;[81] that such competition and opportunity are by themselves of little help to people of average capacity; and that they tend, in fact, to encourage conditions of social organization that widen power discrepancies and exacerbate exploitation, inside but also outside labor processes and the labor market specifically.[82]

Clarke was also expressing, along with other middle-level reform-minded thinkers of the mid-nineteenth century, some sense of what Marx in particular more famously argued: that beyond even the matter of sheer economic disparities in people's starting-gate positions, treating individuals who have different abilities and needs the same itself eventuates in injustice. Even nominal equality and equal treatment under more fully competitive, more truly meritocratic market conditions than those actually existing in the antebellum United States (conditions shorn, for example, of pervasive social-group handicapping) amount, as Terry Eagleton notes, to a "bourgeois abstraction," one "modelled on the exchanges of the commodity form."[83] To put this point differently: Clarke was with Marx and the Associationists expressing a quite basic revulsion for the capitalist market mechanism itself. He was articulating the view that "perfect competition" (to employ neoclassical economic terminology) — economic competition that is free of monopolistic-firm market privileges and powers, and even free of disabilities imposed on social groups — may prove exploitative and unjust for particular individuals. Such competition may prove hardly less exploitative than the state-imposed "imperfect competition" singled out for attack by the period's more antimonopoly-driven labor reformers, as well as by other laissez-faire-oriented antebellum Americans.[84]

Thus far Clarke's essay on Fourierism has been considered only insofar as it compared with, and in some ways went beyond, other antebellum labor-reform critiques of existing conditions. But it merits singling out here for another reason as well. Clarke's essay contains ambiguities, and these shine a light on the equivocal and uneven manner in which many of these other labor-reform commentaries also challenged prevailing capitalist arrangements. Indeed, it is possible to come away with a different, more skeptical reading of Clarke's essay from that offered up to now. Did Clarke's fingering of northern labor exploitation and other "social evils" really amount to a fundamental questioning of early nineteenth-century American capitalism, including its system of wage labor?

Associationists themselves appear not to have thought so, if the response of their leading organ is any indication. The *Phalanx* turned away Clarke's encouraging word for the Associationists — his expressed confidence that their misguided tendency to slight individual responsibility for existing "social evils" was not truly "necessary" to their system. Instead the *Phalanx* fastened on Clarke's admonition that "if we suppose that by bringing together into an association a body of selfish, cowardly and false individuals, we can produce a generous, brave and true society, we wonderfully err."[85] The *Phalanx* concluded that the effect, if not necessarily the intent, of Clarke's "rigid assertion of individual responsibility" was to "virtually" deny "the necessity of all social reform."[86]

There is something to the *Phalanx*'s criticism. For all his evident distaste for competitive capitalist social arrangements, Clarke's prioritization of individual spiritual regeneration retained some similarity to subsequent forthright defenses of capitalism. Such defenses have dwelt on the misguided and impossibly utopian character of all alternative socialist designs, and they have ceded ground to these designs on the most dismissive of grounds: that "socialism does better with perfect people than capitalism does with imperfect people."[87] Clarke's concession to the Associationists was less damaging to their cause: their communities would fail, he indicated, not for lack of perfect people but to the extent that they remained dependent on people who were little or no better than those inhabiting the larger society. Nonetheless, Clarke's prescription — social reorganization awaiting some indeterminate degree of individual reform — might imply a certain futility in the Associationist experiments. And as the *Phalanx* indicated, Clarke's prescription taken to its extreme — the extirpation of all social "vice" through the expunging of individual "sin" and "selfishness" — would render altogether unnecessary such institutional alternatives to competitive capitalism as that offered by the Associationists.

Still, Clarke was hardly offering a defense of competitive capitalism, and the critical rejoinder of the *Phalanx* distorted his true position, which was that more communal and humane institutions — including those developed by the Associationists — could do much to help individual reform along. Yet there remains some question of how unequivocal and far-reaching Clarke's criticisms of capitalist institutions really were.

This question extends beyond the obvious possibility that Clarke's prescriptions — his appeals to an individually transformative "Christianity of love" — were hopelessly ineffectual in the face of structural capitalist forces. More to the point is that such prescriptions were likewise articulated by a host of early nineteenth-century commentators who were manifestly not anticapitalist. Joseph Tuckerman, specifically, called on employers to imbibe Christian love and soften the wage-determining market forces that he naturalized and accepted. More generally, Clarke was one among many middle- and upper-class Anglo-American public moralists whose criticisms of the cash nexus and exploitative competition constituted an early expression of concern over what scholars characterize as the "crisis of legitimation" in capitalism. This was the degree to which capitalist societies seemed to be eroding the "moral basis of their own social order" and thereby inviting social conflict through their pecuniary and calculative tendencies.[88] And of course many of these early nineteenth-century voices, such as elements of England's Tory Party, emanated from the right and not the left; these, too, could not unequivocally be placed within the anticapitalist camp, even if their antiliberal, paternalist outlooks offered more resistance to the hegemony of untrammeled free-market forces than did the equivocations of a Tuckerman.

By the same token, Clarke's critique of outstanding "social evils" bore a certain affinity with the expanding corpus of antebellum American success and prescription literature. Much of that literature also regarded as morally deficient the wealth gained by speculative enterprise and other market vicissitudes. However, by commonly isolating the more egregious instances of greedy and irresponsible behavior and by insisting, even more importantly, that this wealth was as temporary as it was morally unsound, success literature actually contributed to a more intensified commitment to the American culture of capitalist enterprise.[89]

Along with other labor reformers, Clarke was indisposed to isolate as anomalous American speculative activity or other greedy behavior.[90] Nor did he characterize the wealth gained thereby as temporary because it was unscrupulously achieved. Nor, finally, did his exploitation scenario offer much room for the converse staple of the success literature: the exceptionalist confidence that an individual's character virtues and inner worth remained a surer basis for durable, if incremental, economic ascent and success within the American social order. In short, Clarke's affinities with the corpus of success writers remained distinctly limited. But this in itself does not dispose of the larger question: the ambiguities that clouded Clarke's revulsion, and by extension the revulsion of many antebellum labor reformers, for capitalism and capitalist wage labor.

By the most simple and demanding of standards — the anti–private property standards of Marx and the Owenite socialists — Clarke along with the great majority of labor reformers was outside the anticapitalist camp. He appeared, at least, to endorse the Associationists' own position that the right of "individual property" was sacrosanct, and that the Owenites' "community of property is the grave of individual liberty."[91] But even beyond this, Clarke further indicated in his essay that he might not be so critical of wage labor under different conditions. As part of his critique of pernicious social values and the related ethos of government let-aloneism, he suggested, for example, that the exploitation of working-class females would be substantially relieved by attacking the problem of labor-market segmentation and overcrowding: "Poor women, who depend on their labor, are obliged to toil half the night at the needle for a miserable compensation, because the situations which they ought to fill, in all kinds of retail business, are taken from them by men who should be ploughing the fields."[92]

This criticism of prevailing labor-market segmentation, like many of the antebellum defenses of occupational patterns, naturalized gender differences: men don't belong behind retail counters. But aside from this feature, the radical nature of Clarke's criticism is questionable in other ways. Clarke was endorsing a labor-market reform that a host of other antebellum commentators also favored, and many of these, including Henry Ward Beecher, were clearly attempting to democratize and defend, rather than fundamentally transform or jettison, the capitalist order of the North.

In suggesting the value of merely ameliorative solutions to exploitation of female as well as male waged labor, Clarke's attitude toward wage labor also shared a significant ambiguity with many of the journeymen-dominated trade unions and other labor movements of the period, one on which several of the chapters touch. On the one hand, some of these movements intermittently endorsed anticapitalist versions of the labor theory of value, rejecting labor commodification and the capitalist profit motive as invariably disadvantageous violations of the laborer's property in his labor. Labor activists who articulated these versions (and even some who did not) viewed capitalist waged employment as wage slavery. It was deficient, and irremediably so, partly because it fell short of a manly productive, republican independence for journeymen and other citizen-workers. It was no less deficient because its dependent character virtually ensured exploitation; it obviated the possibility that journeymen and others would secure a fair and decent subsistence for their labors. But against the more uncompromising condemnations of capitalist wage labor on these grounds, the land reformer George Henry Evans and other activists did entertain another possibility: that of rectifying imbalances in resources and power and fashioning circumstances whereby American wage earners cast off their dependence on their employers. Once the sale of their labor ceased being involuntary, it would no longer entail their ongoing immiserization and degradation. This is hardly to say that Evans and like-minded individuals forthrightly embraced wage labor as a permanent status for journeymen artisans, among others. It is to say that antebellum labor activists, perhaps more than most historians have recognized, offered varied and equivocal responses to the question of whether capitalist market forces might emerge under some reordering of arrangements as a more or less nonexploitative and beneficent arbiter of the hireling's fortunes.

Clarke's critique of wage labor shared some of this ambiguity, just as his spiritual antidote to the cash nexus and its unregulated exploitations might be considered both deficient and congruent with the concerns of more conservative public moralists aiming for a more humane capitalism. It is ultimately unclear whether capitalist wage-labor arrangements, including wage labor as a permanent condition for some, would retain a place in Clarke's fully Christianized society. His considerable admiration for the Associationists' alternative social relationships might suggest that they would not. But in closing these particular introductory remarks, I would return to two fundamental senses in which Clarke's essay on Fourierism did tend toward anticapitalism. First, his support for expanded employment opportunities for women beyond the trades they presently overcrowded put him closer to Marx than to Henry Ward Beecher; it was something other than a celebration of the competitive ethos and the principle of equal competition for all. Rather, Clarke was appealing to the fact that such increased opportunities would render existing female competition for jobs and wages somewhat less brutal; they would ameliorate the economic vulnerability of women as a group. With the Associationists and other socialists, Clarke indicated that so long as an unchristian and predatory competitive capitalist ethos persisted, a more level playing field would not eliminate the exploitation and injustices perpetrated on particular individuals.

Second, there remained Clarke's hostility to that basic attribute of capitalist orders: the waged-labor incentive of poverty and the fear of poverty.[93] That hostility distinguished him from William Ellery Channing, just as it also set him apart from the many American exceptionalist commentators who like Channing valued the sanction of hunger even as they additionally insisted on both the importance and the prevalence of good wages in the northern states. By the same token, it was precisely his aversion to the compulsions of want, as an attribute of free waged-labor markets, that Clarke shared with the overwhelming majority of labor reformers and radicals of his time, however their orientations and agendas may have otherwise differed.

Poststructuralism

Although I refer to poststructural approaches throughout this study, I feel the need to add something here. Historians such as Patrick Joyce who have embraced the antifoundational linguistic turn have included among their claims the argument that "notions of the 'artisan' and 'artisan work' . . . do not reflect real social entities (which 'artisan' is so often taken to be), but are myths designed to handle economic or political situations, such as the nature of work in the mid-nineteenth century."[94] I recognize a certain validity in this argument, even apart from the demonstrations by various historians that throughout the nineteenth century the skill content of craftwork (as well as some factory labor) was inflated and socially constructed by its defenders for such purposes as preserving the trades as bastions of white male privilege.[95] There may, in fact, be no better example of the notion that artisan identity was a cultural response to emerging situations than the mechanic campaigns against state prison industry, including the complaints that the reputation and respectability of independent artisans were threatened by the contagion emanating from ex-convict laborers who joined their workshops and communities.

I am also receptive to the more general position of historians who have adopted the linguistic turn, as expressed by James Vernon: "There will always be a place for social structural approaches — like those studying population, transport, urbanization, labour processes, wage levels, and so on — for I am not arguing that society or the real do not exist, just that we can have no knowledge of them outside discourse."[96] Perhaps as good an illustration as any of Vernon's remark is the focal point of chapter 7: the antebellum trade debates between Democrats and Whigs regarding the objective, real magnitude of the Old World "pauper labor" threat. Those debates underscore how thoroughly partisan goals and discourse, and the attendant representations, mediate between us and a body of comparative wage levels and other mid-nineteenth-century empirical phenomena. Those debates illustrate, that is to say, the contested and problematic nature of economic knowledge.

Yet I remain too much of a structuralist of sorts — too much of a believer in an objective economic reality, in particular, together with the influence it wields — to be comfortable with the more extreme claims made in behalf of the linguistic turn. These include the argument that artisan work skills have no foundation in actual fact, and that such skills, along with "class" and material interests generally, amount to no more than discursively constructed phenomena.[97] In the early nineteenth century, as now, there did exist a capitalism that entailed "necessary logics of inequality and exploitation, of who gets what, and through what mechanisms," as two interrogators of poststructuralism remark.[98] Here I also tend to agree with James Epstein's criticism of Gareth Stedman Jones's influential insistence, with respect to the Chartist movement, on the autonomy of political discourse from social and economic determinants. Epstein points out that political and other language can be read in many ways, and that in the case of the Chartists, the vocabulary of "the people," "property," "industrious," and the like that they shared with other groups in early- to mid-nineteenth-century Britain in fact concealed a range of alternative, radical meanings. Some of these oppositional meanings, Epstein furthermore suggests, may have embodied more advanced, production-centered, working-class critiques of exploitation as well as the older, eighteenth-century political critiques of social relations that Stedman Jones privileges in his interpretation of Chartist language. Those oppositional meanings, at least in part, may have after all referred back to a set of preexisting material forces, economic relations, and class interests.[99] My own strong suspicion and general position is that such forces, relations, and interests (which encompass but extend beyond an individual's specific relationship to the means of production) are among the most basic components of lived experience, and as such they characteristically precede linguistic structures, however critical those structures may become to our understanding of the former.

I therefore share the skepticism toward poststructural tendencies in history scholarship that "dissolve" class "into the purely representational."[100] Yet my position remains flexible (or so I like to think), and I find particularly promising some recent sociological efforts that, drawing less from Marx than from Max Weber's looser conception of class formation, make their own qualified nod to the linguistic turn.[101] They suggest that the very mediating, contextualized power that language carries for historical actors themselves — the process of articulation, or "language-use" — gives it more than a merely epiphenomenal role.[102] Language, as one scholar has aptly characterized it, is the "stuff" of "discourse," and discourse, as "the social process of putting language in motion," remains a form of power even if power is not reducible to discourse.[103] By virtue of its contribution to the construction of consciousness and identity, language is among a complexity of cultural factors and social practices that have helped shape markets and class interests and that continue to exist in dialectical relationship with one another. It illuminates, and may also figure in, the ways that class formation intersects with race, gender, and other forms of stratification and identity.[104]

At least within the discipline of history, avid proponents of the linguistic turn have, with some notable exceptions, waged their most heated battles with scholars on the left — with the upholders of what have been called the Marxist "grand narratives" of class formation and working-class consciousness. The controversies over poststructuralism, accordingly, have centrally been about the direction of labor history and labor-oriented social history. But having outlined my own general position in such controversies, I would also stress here that this study is not primarily a labor history, and that describing working-class consciousness specifically is only one of its concerns. While blanching at so univocal a notion as ruling-class ideology, I remain even more drawn to the intellectual justifications and contortions, the rationales and self-serving postures, the complacency and the angst, that members of the American middle and upper middle classes exhibited in explicating their privileged places in the nation's social and economic structure. I remain more interested in how such individuals sought to legitimate (and in some instances, how the more radical of their number delegitimated) the fact that the most economically indispensable elements of the social order were, in the United States as in all other civilized societies, the most poorly recompensed. The feminist philosopher Nancy Fraser has observed for a more recent period that "even the most material economic institutions have a constitutive, irreducible cultural dimension; they are shot through with significations and norms."[105] More centrally at some points than at others, my focus is upon how such norms, as the particular embodiments of elite presumptions and preferences, also manifested themselves as specific public-policy choices—as in systems of state prison industry that trained and utilized convicts in nonprofessional, manual-labor employments exclusively. This study, in any case, most of all engages middle-class commentary on labor and poverty, together with the intersections of upper-middle-class values with those of artisan workers. Yet such intersections in themselves require consideration of working-class consciousness (as in chapters 2–4 especially), insofar as they raise persisting questions of ideological hegemony and compliance with market-capitalist arrangements.

Fraser's remark might be taken as another sign of the poststructuralist revulsion from the Marxist and other forms of materialist determinism or "bias" that William H. Sewell Jr. criticizes and traces to Enlightenment and even older Western intellectual traditions. Sewell notes, in a variation on Fraser's point, that "the economy" is more than the strictly material, that it is constituted as well by the "ideal or cultural or symbolic."[106] Again, I myself plead guilty to such a materialist bias, insofar as I regard the purely linguistic, at least, as more reflective than determinative of material circumstances. At the same time, some of the following chapters certainly illustrate how cultural values and prescriptions were deeply embedded in early nineteenth-century American social and economic arrangements, including relations of production and exchange, and in fact played a substantial role in shaping these. Still, while accepting up to a point Sewell's further insistence on the false dichotomy between "ideal and material," I would (in at least quasi-Marxist fashion, I suppose) simultaneously retain the characterization of many of these same values, prescriptions, and—indeed—social constructions as ideological rationales for disparate work burdens and unequal distribution of the social product.

Such antebellum commentary as James Freeman Clarke's illumines but scarcely resolves these complex and contentious scholarly issues. On the one hand, the criticisms that Clarke, Henry Ward Beecher, and others directed at dominant social values that unduly restricted women's employment opportunities, as well as influencing other unwelcome occupational patterns, would seem congruent with what I do find most valuable in poststructuralism: the reinvigorated attention it brings to the role of cultural practices and norms in shaping labor markets and property relations.[107] Yet the same early nineteenth-century commentary hardly rules out a driving role for relatively autonomous economic transformations and other structural forces (embedded as even some of these may have been with cultural values). It hardly disposes of the persisting question of how and to what extent inherited wealth differences and a battery of other economic circumstances and interests worked to help create such cultural practices and norms.[108]

The following is, in any case, a study of many texts and their multiple and overlapping discourses in economic, social, political, and religious thought. Most heavily of all, it draws on newspapers, legislative records, and other public kinds of literature, the most deliberately analytical and argumentative venues in which commentators addressed audiences. And in trying to make connections between antebellum commentary on work and the findings of social, labor, and other historians, I am inevitably drawn to what is left out as well as to what appears in the commentary. How to interpret such silences? As the willful omissions of inconvenient social and economic facts? Or as less deliberate, if perhaps equally self-serving, omissions? Or were many such silences merely reflective of the commentator's sheer ignorance of the facts? Any conclusive determination of this question is almost always impossible. But the problems and challenges posed by what is not said, as well as what is stated, are unavoidable in this kind of intellectual-history writing. And they would also seem to turn on mechanisms of individual ideological motivation—multifaceted and often highly ambiguous, operating at the unconscious as well as the conscious level—that only tangentially relate to, and in fact often run deeper than, the strictly linguistic indeterminacies highlighted by varieties of poststructuralism.[109]

It may be already apparent that these chapters offer multiple arguments as well as the single overarching one stressing discord over labor incentives in the early nineteenth-century United States. In this regard, the general subject of perceptions of labor's material incentives and rewards provides a rubric within which I stake out positions on some of the most significant issues in antebellum historiography. But if any attribute of this book does provide an additional connective argumentative thread, perhaps it is its methodology—one that, in the kind of attention it pays to forces and interests inherent in social and economic class relationships, indeed conveys a discomfiture with poststructural approaches on the various grounds noted above.

1

The World's Dirty Work
and the Wages That Sweeten It

THE VIEW THAT work was, or should be, a blessing for those who performed it was most extensively developed by the privileged classes of nineteenth-century Western societies. The members of these classes, Alasdair Clayre writes, were actuated partially by "the spectre of chaos and formlessness" raised by their own enjoyment of increased "mechanized ease" and ample leisure time.[1] But perhaps more markedly, their heightened emphasis on work's natural, intrinsic moral benefits and intellectual satisfactions was a complex and paradoxical response to the work performed by the laboring classes themselves. The "idolization" of work by the more intellectual and socially alert elements of the middle and upper classes—including Karl Marx on the left and Thomas Carlyle on the right—was stimulated by the very regimentation and trivialization, as well as by the "imminent redundancy," of growing numbers of manual-labor employments under early capitalist industrialization and mechanization.[2]

This philosophical and "increasingly agonized" insistence on the creative and other intrinsically fulfilling attributes of work blended into and drew additional force from the animus against the early nineteenth-century's purported commodification of social relationships—the tyranny of the cash nexus.[3] One manifestation of this animus was noted in connection with the discussion of James Freeman Clarke. This was the emergence of a cluster of clerical and other public moralists in England and the United States whose antagonism to capitalist processes varied widely, and who in Clarke's and other cases certainly approved of higher wages for laboring populations. Such commentators, nonetheless, remained collectively wary of justifying work primarily in terms of its market-based monetary, or extrinsic, value.[4] Among Carlyle and the other more conservative of their number, one-sided emphasis on the morally uplifting and disciplinary effects of various forms of menial labor in itself signaled a blatant exploitative mentality insofar as it reflected assumptions that members of certain social groups — such as blacks and Irish immigrants — were most naturally suited for and would derive the greatest intrinsic rewards from such labor.[5]

The early- to mid-nineteenth-century insistence on work's intrinsic value and satisfactions, either existing or potential, thus had diverse, even contradictory dimensions and impetuses, only some of which have been mentioned here. But this general insistence was often quite overwhelmed by the contrary inclination, exhibited in both working-class and middle-class circles, to accentuate the importance of manual labor's strictly extrinsic, or material, inducements and rewards. An instrumental inclination could itself encompass disparate strands: certain working-class immigrant groups, for example, may have particularly tended to prioritize occupational stability and the steady income this provided over upward mobility into better-paying, higher-status employments.[6] At the same time, the obvious fact that wage-earning manual laborers and other ordinary people needed work to survive and may thus themselves have naturally attached a practical value to their occupations may obscure as much as it illuminates, if only because the particular arrangements of private enterprise and social stratification that fostered such a need were themselves cultural constructions and by no means the only arrangements capable of developing. This is so if only because in the Anglo-American experience, at least, labor and other markets always have entailed a formal articulation of an initial legal framework to define property, contract, etc. Of relevance here is the observation that "if we had a different system than capitalism, or a system not based on private property, we would have a different distribution of income."[7] To this one might add a variation in the form of a question, one that speaks more directly to the subject here: Would manual labor carry the same instrumental value if the prevailing arrangements were somehow such that those who performed this manual labor actually employed the capitalists — those who provided the plants and other productive resources?[8] Bizarre as this scenario might appear (at least to those outside radical circles), it should still suggest that the emphasis on manual labor's material inducements and rewards in antebellum America and the ideological representations of these were not a given but require further investigation.[9]

Much of the period's commentary on labor, it is also true, simply failed either to distinguish extrinsic from intrinsic rewards carefully or to prioritize one over the other clearly.[10] Yet this failure or ambiguity was itself often studied or otherwise symptomatic of particular ideological objectives. After touting the "animal pleasure" that the "common labourer" took from his "muscular exertions," the

professor of moral philosophy Alonzo Potter added: "It is the cheering antici-
pation of some gratifying result which sweetens the toils of labour, relieves its
irksomeness, and appears to shorten its duration. . . . It is the prospect of its
reward that gives it much of its zest."[11] In Potter's case equivocal assessment
of the relative importance of intrinsic and extrinsic rewards followed from his
Whiggish vision of the harmonious, good society, which he believed was
realized to a remarkable extent by the free-labor North. In the economically
expansive, capitalist occupational hierarchy that Potter was promoting, the subordination of laborers at the bottom acquired legitimacy from both their
employments' intrinsic compensations and the system's capacity to reward them
with decent wages even as it paid out generous profits to their employers.

Nor were antebellum failures, or refusals, to clearly prioritize among intrinsic and extrinsic rewards for manual labor confined to the ideological mainstream; they also extended into radical circles that would jettison the social
arrangements cherished by Potter. An anonymous correspondent for Association, or Fourierist socialism in the United States, in 1844 addressed one of the
doctrinal contradictions of which the movement stood accused. If, as Fourier
and his followers claimed, some human beings had a natural taste or "passion"
for performing tasks that virtually all societies deemed "dirty" and "repugnant"
—if, in other words, performance of such tasks was for these individuals intrinsically pleasurable and represented no "self-sacrifice"—then why, according to
this criticism, did Association also propose bestowing on them its greatest hon-
ors and superior pecuniary rewards?[12] The correspondent's attempt to show that
this lapse in Association logic was more apparent than real was convoluted and
only intermittently convincing. But more relevant here was that the writer's
working out of the roles of intrinsic and extrinsic inducements to labor yielded
recognition of the indispensability of both to his truly harmonious society.
Within the idiosyncratic framework of Fourierist phalanx "groups" and "series,"
the writer demonstrated how the most extreme and utopian perspectives could
bring into sharpest relief concerns and tensions about work that were pervasive
in the larger society.

Yet those concerns and tensions frequently did manifest themselves in an
unequivocal privileging of manual labor's instrumental value over its intrinsic
rewards. In the extended newspaper debate that he conducted with Horace
Greeley over the merits of establishing American Fourierist communities, the
conservative Whig Henry J. Raymond advanced several arguments designed to
puncture the era's bubble of utopian enthusiasm.[13] But none was more basic
than the one he used to dismiss the claim that the phalanx would effectively

employ a variety of expedients to bring out the intrinsic "attractiveness" of hard labor:

> Working by music, plowing in uniform, conferring nominal and empty honors, &c., might do for children, but to urge it as a means of making hard labor attractive, is nonsense. The only thing that can make labor attractive to the mass of men is the stimulus of reward, the hope of recompense, and above all, the certainty of possessing and enjoying that recompense, whatever it may be. So far as these motives operate, they make labor attractive. Men now toil first to obtain a subsistence; and then to acquire the means of comfort for themselves and their children.[14]

Raymond proceeded to extol the value of such institutions as the law in "securing" an individual's "right of absolute and permanent ownership" of property—in "perfecting" his entitlement to the material rewards of his labor. But more fundamental yet was Raymond's insistence on the paramountcy of such extrinsic "recompense" in sweetening and thereby encouraging labor— they render "Labor attractive in the only sense in which it can become so."[15]

In his unequivocal privileging of work's instrumental value over its intrinsic appeal, Raymond was speaking preeminently of manual labor, and of legally free labor at that.[16] His remarks well represented those pervasive American, and especially middle-class, social attitudes that generally failed to deviate from traditional Old World attitudes and similarly failed to provide a ringing affirmation of physical labor's intrinsic dignity.[17] Recognition that hard and dirty work remained such whether it was performed in the United States or in the Old World spurred commentators across a wide ideological spectrum to frame and debate the question of American manual labor's dignity in terms of its extrinsic rewards. The characteristic tendency of the more zealous exponents of American exceptionalism was to claim that manual labor could not be "drudgery" in the United States precisely because of the material and advancement rewards to be gained thereby.[18]

Yet historians disagree over the bearing that manual labor's material rewards had on its social status during the nineteenth century. Reflecting the growing attention to the mid-eighteenth-century Anglo-American consumer revolution, one view holds that in the wake of the American Revolution, consumer and entrepreneurial impulses perceptibly raised the worth of productive manual labor, obliterating centuries-old attitudes that had disdained it as ungentlemanly.[19] A contrasting view emphasizes the stigma that republican and producerist traditions, extolling a condition of economic independence, continued to attach to wage-earning manual labor during this same period. Only toward the end of the nineteenth century did organized labor and its leaders themselves begin to accept permanent wage labor and to assert its dignity in terms of its consumerist instrumental value—in terms of the wage earner's capacity to meet material needs and wants.[20]

Both these views slight the complexity and diversity of mid-nineteenth-century ideological constructions. On the one hand, the acquisitive values of post-Revolution liberal capitalism did not so much eradicate as transmute the age-old attitudes of disdain for manual labor. During a period in which small-producer elements—independent artisans and farmers as well as wage earners—experienced increasing inequality vis-à-vis upper-middle-class occupational groups, these liberal capitalist success values suggested that the dignity of manual labor still ultimately resided in its escapability into other occupations, ones whose profit-making potential was less limited and more quickly fulfilled.[21] The most talented and deserving members of American society did not finish the "race of life" working with their hands.[22] On the other hand, the persistent ante-bellum references, within as well as outside the working classes, to the abysmal wages and living standards of Europe's "pauper" laborers reveal that an American propensity to construct wage labor's respectability around its capacity to acquire market rewards was developing well before the end of the century.[23] There is, moreover, the additional case of unmarried female wage earners, such as the first generation of New England factory women, whose newly acquired discretionary spending power assumed special symbolic meaning as a signifier of unprecedented economic independence and freedom from paternalistic controls.[24]

The antebellum era's ideological constructions of labor's extrinsic rewards were broadly defined by an ongoing series of debates, both transatlantic and interclass in nature, which turned on the existing mix of incentives that drove legally free labor, including its more unskilled and repugnant kinds, and what the proper mix should be. Were these incentives, at least in the United States, primarily of a positive nature? Did they consist, that is, of a free worker's hopes and prospects for appreciable economic and social improvement and the stimulating operation upon him or her, in bourgeois parlance, of "higher wants"? Or were the prevailing incentives for needed manual industry, even in America and, in the northern states specifically, of a negative kind? Were they dominated, in particular, by the free laborer's imperative merely to avoid starvation, reflecting the so-called utility of poverty? Incentives that are labeled positive or negative cannot in fact be readily confined to single and unambiguous meanings. But noteworthy first is that although the antebellum debates most directly addressed the material inducements and rewards obtaining for the growing northern population of free waged laborers, they were also invariably informed by perceptions of one or more of the alternative possibilities, including freehold farming, black chattel-slave labor, and even the most literally dirty work—the self-employed casual labor concentrated in the major cities. Consider as one contribution to these debates the following remarks of 1846 from the Boston *Chronotype,* edited by the social reformer and abolitionist Elizur Wright:

> Labor for nothing is not very pleasant. The muscles may rejoice in it but the mind does not. The mind wants a motive, future enjoyment, victory, praise, something to work for. . . . Let this motive be strong enough and any kind of labor becomes delightful. . . . It is the principle of property which seems to have been designed by our Creator to sweeten labor.
>
> . . . When I become a more civilized man and for some great object work on an extensive plan, the expected result sweetens every blow of the toil. . . .
>
> We may set it down as a settled principle that the right of individual property, the hope of some benefit to be gained, is absolutely necessary to secure happy industry, and of course the greatest amount of industry. The fear of the whip or of starvation cannot do it. . . .
>
> Now who can deny that there is a tendency in civilized society, with all its glorious achievements and improvements, to separate into two classes, the extremely rich and luxurious who cast off labor and betake themselves to mere consumption, and the extremely poor whose labor brings them from day to day only the provender absolutely necessary to keep the machine in motion. . . .
>
> Surely it is worth while to investigate the causes of such an evil tendency, especially in a new country, and inquire whether it may not be counteracted. Is there no plan by which the hope of humanity—that is, the hope of always growing richer and happier, may be given as the motive to every human laborer?[25]

Every one of the *Chronotype's* remarks has a long history. Moreover, the idealistic materialism that infused them, encompassing but extending beyond an ethos of rational, maximizing self-interest, ran throughout antebellum culture, notwithstanding the fact that Wright's *Chronotype* at this time was one of the leading promoters of utopian Fourierism. In our more postmodern age, where settled principles are few and far between, both the idealism and the certitude of the *Chronotype* may seem quaint. But noteworthy here are the related axioms around which this idealism and certitude gathered: that economic improvement and the hope of such improvement, centered on the acquisition of property, constituted the most efficacious of all labor incentives; that such extrinsic sweeteners of labor were most vital of all to more civilized individuals, those who had developed their ambition and wants to a particular if undefined point; and that both the negative lash of hunger driving the wage slave and the slaveholder's lash motivating the formal chattel slave were poor substitutes for the divinely inspired "principle of property." Accompanying these more widely held axioms was the special conviction that animated both middle-class labor reformers and radicals of the *Chronotype*'s ilk and some of the more thoroughly working-class movements of the period, though it was not completely confined to either of these. This was the conviction that however ethically and economically superior, however more civilized they might be, positive labor incentives were in fact disappearing from the United States — that by midcentury the free laboring population of this new country was experiencing a Europeanizing absolute impoverishment.

At other places in its commentary, it should also be noted, the *Chronotype* hedged a bit, or at least exhibited a sense of the complexity of the issues involved. In another column it first insisted, in line with the above remarks, that "we defy any mathematician to demonstrate to us that the most ingenious and industrious mechanic, even in this country, marrying and having an average family to support, can, beginning without capital and working steadily at his trade as a journeyman, die any thing but a poor man." But the paper then proceeded to observe that in the United States at least, in marked contrast to "the old countries," such poverty — such deprivation of "physical comforts" — was "at present" still only "comparative" rather than absolute in nature. Here it remained the general case that "when a man who has but five wants, and three of them supplied by a more artificial state of society and [by] the increase of wealth comes to have ten wants and four of them supplied, he has become actually a poorer man."[26]

Does a positive labor incentive remain positive when a "mechanic" is successfully motivated to satisfy a larger number of his "wants," but these realized wants also represent a declining proportion of his total wants, and he is unable, furthermore, to keep pace in this regard with individuals above him in the social scale, those who monopolize the growing capital, machinery, and wealth of society? Had this question been put to the *Chronotype*, it would likely have insisted that under such circumstances of relative immiseration, positive labor incentives transmuted into negative ones of a sort, even as it recognized the distinction between the latter and that which was genuinely compulsory: the primordial specter of starvation associated with absolute immiserization. Of course, the paper's ruminations on the nature of American poverty and inequality constituted only the most skeletal preview of modern-day sociological debates.[27] Recent historical scholarship, moreover, has thrown into doubt the empirical validity of most, if not all, of the "principles" affirmed in the first of the *Chronotype* pieces.[28] But it is the ideological constructions themselves that are the primary interest here. Can one probe more deeply the intellectual framework within which the *Chronotype*'s and other contributions to the antebellum debates over labor's extrinsic incentives were situated?

British Political Economy

In 1843 the Philadelphia *Public Ledger* editorialized how little had changed in England for all of the economic development it had undergone in "modern times." England's present commercial and manufacturing system, the *Ledger* observed, followed the feudal practice of concentrating wealth and exalting its "non-productive" owners "upon the degradation" of the laboring population. As to modern British political economy, it merited similar indictment for its governing feudal assumptions: "All its precepts, all its recommendations, are for the benefit of capital; and it treats labor, not as something endowed by God with the right to comfort, to happiness equal to that of the capitalist, but as an *expense* incidental to capital, which the capitalist cannot avoid entirely, but should *reduce* as much as possible."[29]

The *Ledger*'s criticisms of British political economy for decades had been the particular stuff of labor-activist and radical political economy in both England and the United States.[30] But the *Ledger* was a mainstream journal, and like its encomiums elsewhere to its own country's exceptionally egalitarian conditions and practices, the paper's dismissal of "the modern school of political economy" for legitimating injustices within English society was also within the American mainstream, however much America's college professors may have continued to teach from the "English classics."[31] A definitive assessment of so pervasive and open-ended a phenomenon must remain a will-o'-the-wisp. Yet the ideological construction of manual labor's extrinsic rewards in antebellum America can be characterized to a remarkable extent as a dynamic process in which the inherited conceptual framework of British classical economics collided and intertwined with, and was always selectively interpreted by, a mythology of American economic exceptionalism that was itself undergoing continuous change in the face of different pressures and challenges.

Our own dominant perception of British classical economy likely remains that of a set of gloomy propositions predicated on a society of increasingly scarce resources. In 1776, it is true, Adam Smith lent his support to a progressive and optimistic "high-wage" scenario for economic growth. That scenario markedly challenged earlier leisure-preference, utility-of-poverty mercantilist notions which had insisted that the wants of the lower classes were intrinsically limited, that these classes would not on their own initiative extend their industriousness and their productivity beyond the fulfillment of bare subsistent needs.[32] But Smith's scenario itself, in turn, came to be significantly modified and reversed by Thomas Malthus and David Ricardo. As reactions against the radical perfectionist doctrines of their era and as alarmist responses to the rising poor-relief costs and other immediate problems of the early Industrial Revolution, the most compelling paradigms of Malthus and Ricardo bleakly characterized the insuperable, "natural" laws of societies as tendencies toward overpopulation and diminishing returns. Rather than maintaining a level of wages and earnings that would permit saving and actual improvement in their condition, the great majority of the British working classes would be overwhelmingly stimulated by the negative incentive of providing the barest necessaries for themselves and their families. Nor, according to Malthus and Ricardo, should destructive governmental poor laws interfere with and blunt this most primordial, this most natural of labor incentives and market forces — the hunger that was "Nature's penalty" for laziness and inactivity. In sustaining a population of dependent paupers, those laws imposed only still further downward pressure on the wages of the independent, "virtuous" laboring poor by drawing from a "wages-fund" that at any one time was fixed and limited in size.[33]

Such were some of the most severe and dismal principles of the Malthusian-Ricardian classical economic paradigms. But scholars have also noted the tempering of those principles by Malthus and Ricardo in other parts of their writings, even as they disagree about how much weight to assign such tempering. Rather than merely inserting the utility-of-poverty notions of pre-Smithian mercantilist thinkers into their free-market vision, Malthus and Ricardo did acknowledge a bourgeois potential in the laboring population. This was the capacity of workers, through education and refinement, to develop a taste for physical comforts and conveniences that would encourage them to practice "moral restraint" and keep down their numbers. While retaining to the end an insistence on the demoralizing, labor-incentive-destroying effects of poor relief, Malthus and Ricardo expressed the recognition and hope that workers might gradually develop a welcome dependence on a level of wages above subsistence in the bare physiological sense of that term. Rising real wages could themselves, as Adam Smith had earlier suggested, accordingly serve as both an accompaniment of and as a stimulus to improved worker habits and increased industriousness and productivity.[34]

For both empirical and more strictly ideological reasons, this mellowing of the original Malthus-Ricardo economy of scarcity was carried further by later British classical economists such as J. Ramsay McCulloch, Nassau Senior, and John Stuart Mill. Not only did British population, wage, and other data from the 1820s and 1830s appear to discredit the bleakest, "inevitable misery" predictions made by Malthus and Ricardo. Their successors also recognized, in a period of continuing labor unrest, that such doctrines were too gloomy to win the allegiance of workers.[35] Nor could McCulloch and others remain comfortable with such core components of the initial paradigms as Ricardo's labor theory of value and his doctrine of the inverse relationship between wages and capitalist profits, in view of the labor-exploitation theories that Robert Owen, his followers, and other radicals were all too freely drawing from such material.[36]

From at least the time Marx dissected "bourgeois" political economy as a system of capitalist apologetics for the misery of the British laboring classes during the Industrial Revolution, historians have recognized that the wages-fund and other so-called natural laws of high political economy were themselves ideological constructions.[37] Whether or not they indeed amounted to learned rationalizations for misery, classical economic principles sought to universalize, or naturalize, market-oriented rationality and the bourgeois sense of the rectitude of competitive individualism. They were ideological in the further sense noted by Herbert Hovenkamp: the creators of these principles, "the great classical economists," were "policymakers who carried political agendas drawn from the economic disputes of their day. Their self-professed 'general' solutions were in fact pointed at very specific issues, such as the wisdom of the poor laws or the corn laws."[38] Still, the entrance of classical economy's formal economic ideas into both the British and the American "public domains" of thought, where they underwent interpretation and reinterpretation, yet furthered their metastasis as ideologies even as their technical content was diluted. The mere "transmission" of economic principles in this period significantly wrought their "transformation."[39]

The Intertwining of Classical Economics
with American Exceptionalism

In the antebellum United States specifically, a basic part of this ideological work consisted of the tendency of commentators such as the *Public Ledger* to slight or completely ignore the mellowing of British political economy.[40] That tendency — its own form of historical memory — was especially marked among the many who formed their impressions of the British paradigms secondhand or through popularized versions.[41] The American slighting is partially attributable to the intrinsic power, the salience, and the notoriety of the bleakest elements of the early Malthusian-Ricardian scenario, which even in Britain overshadowed for years all that came later. But the particular attention paid in the United States to the original harsh scenario also best suited the ideological needs of a host of commentators there, including politicians, poor-law officials, and labor leaders. Indeed, it is striking how British classical economics could be similarly interpreted — that is, agreement reached as to its central principles — by antebellum Americans who were trying to meet diverse, frequently conflicting ideological needs and often occupied widely different positions on the issue of American economic exceptionalism. While by no means exhausting the possibilities, one can identify several prominent configurations, or patterns of responses, for purposes of illustration.

There were, first, the most unequivocal American economic exceptionalists, generally commentators of a moderate and conservative bent affiliated with the Whig Party. These rejected out of hand the "fatalistic" and "dismal" Malthusian-Ricardian economy of scarcity and subsistence as completely inapplicable to the expansive, "go-ahead" American conditions.[42] The Whig polemicist Calvin Colton epitomized this tendency to define and celebrate American free labor entirely in terms of the positive labor incentives and generous extrinsic rewards that it ostensibly enjoyed. In their optimism and complacency, Colton and this configuration generally were guilty of many facile generalizations, as well as exclusions and silences bearing on gender and race. Moreover, Colton's boasting of the pervasive "freedom wages" in the United States was a simultaneous insistence on the fragility of American economic exceptionalism. With other Whigs he conducted an ongoing campaign for the high protective tariffs that he deemed essential to preventing the American wage advantage from being destroyed by competition with European subsistent, or pauper, laborers.[43]

In addition, Colton and like-minded Whigs, elaborating the *Public Ledger* editorial quoted above, conveniently fastened on the harshest, "heartless" classical economic "inevitable misery" paradigms as product and symbol of the

Old World's entrenched and corrupt class structure. Although other config-urations exhibited this same general tendency, the distinction of this moderate-conservative Whig configuration was to launch a counterhegemonic attack on British and other European societies for the primary purpose of celebrating and legitimating America's own more "openly stratified," more meritocratic society.[44] When Whigs denied the legitimacy of trade-union activities, that cel-ebration amounted to a pointed endorsement of capitalist hegemony within the United States itself. At other times the "harmony of interests" doctrines advanced by Henry C. Carey and other moderate Whigs could approach Jack-sonian Democratic ideology as a defense of the nation's communities of small-producer interests against the intrusions of large-scale corporate and other capitalist enterprise.[45] This last, more plebeian tendency notwithstanding, what generally distinguished moderate-conservative Whiggery from both Democratic and genuinely dissident commentary was its greater, more emphatic insistence on the distinctive openness of the American hierarchy. This was the Whig invo-cation of an upward and downward social fluidity to justify recognized Ameri-can wealth disparities, including the presence of economic elites. At the very least this fluidity was intergenerational: "The sons of the rich, if unworthy, become the poor of the next generation, and the sons of the poor, become its rich men."[46] Beyond even the question of its factual validity, the radical Orestes Brownson found ethically dubious such insistence on the non-European-like, meritocratic turnover in American elite membership. He lampooned it as the Whig version of the Jacksonian "Rotation in Office" credo, by which "the kickee of to-day may be the kickor of to-morrow."[47]

Lastly, in the hands of Henry Carey the Whig counterhegemonic diatribes against Europe were most fully taken to the point where the "dismal science" of Malthus and Ricardo was dismissed not because it was singularly inapplica-ble to the land-abundant, labor-scarce, high-wage United States but because it was wrong for all societies. Intrinsically and hopelessly flawed in its doctrine of overpopulation and other pessimistic principles, the classical economy-of-scarcity paradigm was to be thrown out along with the monopolistic and exploitative Old World arrangements that it sought to legitimate.[48]

A second general configuration, also Whiggish and also bolstering the mythology of American economic exceptionalism, primarily differed from the first in highlighting those elements of the severe classical economic paradigm in which it in fact found great merit. The dominant members of this configu-ration were the almshouse officials and other middle- and upper-middle-class Americans alarmed over the growing poverty and pauperism in their own nation's urban centers. It was less a matter of such officials and like-minded commentators finding any particular validity in, say, Malthus's famed ratios or Ricardo's doctrine of rent.[49] Rather, they embraced as universal and overpowering truths the more general axioms of middle-class, free-market competitive morality that underlay classical economy. These included the admonitions that the laboring poor must take responsibility for their own condition; that they could and should, with assistance from the more enlightened classes above them, internalize the bourgeois values of self-discipline, self-direction, and acquisitiveness. Compulsory outdoor relief for at least the able-bodied members of the laboring population, by insulating that population from the salutary prodding of physical want, or "Nature's penalty" for indolence, inevitably served to debilitate laborers morally and to increase the numbers of dependent poor. "Similar moral causes produce similar effects everywhere," as George Arnold, Congregational minister-at-large to the poor in New York City, warned in the 1830s regarding the spread of pauperism there. A writer for the *American Quarterly Review* bemoaned the same apparent anomaly: the increase of pauperism in a country where labor was relatively scarce, where wages were high, and where it was "impossible to imagine a state of civil society in which it would be more difficult for the Poor Laws to produce their ill effects."[50]

Nothing is more interesting in this configuration than its efforts to sustain a mythology of American exceptionalism—the belief in the unique pervasiveness of generous positive labor incentives for free labor in the United States— while also insisting that the operation of negative labor incentives remained just as valuable and vital there as in any other nation. Thus the New York *Journal of Commerce* suggested in 1848 that the "Communist" plans afoot in France to remedy inequalities of property would prove just as demoralizing and destructive in the United States, for here as everywhere "the fear of poverty and the ambition to become rich are the great stimulants to production. . . . The love of riches may impel men to labor who are secure of a provision for their wants; but no man will work, without the stimulant of want."[51] Such examples lend support to one political scientist's observation that "the idea that material security undermines work motivation and productivity holds a peculiar tenacity in American thinking."[52]

Like the first configuration, this second configuration illustrates how the belief that America offered uniquely abundant economic rewards and opportunities "to become rich" encouraged a pronounced disapproval, even contempt, for those who failed to discipline themselves, to exploit these opportunities, and in time to rise out of poverty. Yet such economic failures, even as they were disesteemed for their character shortcomings, likely performed some positive, albeit largely unrecognized, social functions for those doing the disesteeming, as well as for other antebellum Americans. More obviously, in a society where social mobility was valued and class boundaries were vague, the poor served as a means by which others could measure their own progress; poverty helped to secure the status of many who were not poor. Somewhat less obviously, the very identification of society's most egregious economic failures — the "undeserving" component of the dependent poor — helped uphold the legitimacy of dominant values. Or as the sociologist Herbert J. Gans puts this point, "Defenders of the desirability of hard work, thrift, honesty, and monogamy," if genuinely desiring in many cases to raise up the undeserving poor, simultaneously "need people who can be accused of being lazy, spendthrift, dishonest, and promiscuous to justify these norms . . . the norms themselves are best legitimated by discovering violations."[53] A moralistic view of American poverty and pauperism followed readily, in any case, from the conviction that the United States singularly lacked the unjust laws and institutions and the closed class structure that acted to "repress the ambition of the lower classes" in Old World societies.[54]

Occasionally accompanying this attitude, however, was a less moralistic note of ambivalence. In the United States as in the Old World, elite anxiety regarding the "right psychological balance between the stick of necessity and the carrot of incentives" was commonly driven by perceived distinctions between types of necessity.[55] Drawing on recent lectures by the prominent Unitarian clergyman and Whig-Republican Henry W. Bellows, the New York *Evangelist* observed in 1858 that "there is a poverty which invigorates both body and mind, which teaches the virtues of frugality and economy, and which leads to hardy industry. But, on the other hand, there is a poverty which unmans and crushes, and which sinks into the hopeless abyss of Pauperism."[56] The *Evangelist* was articulating the very uncertainty regarding poverty's actual efficacy as a labor incentive that Malthus himself had expressed years before when he noted that once poverty had "passed certain limits," it "almost ceases to operate" as a "spur to industry." Along with "the hope of bettering our condition," Malthus continued, it is "the fear of want, rather than want itself, that is the best stimulus to industry."[57] Under what circumstances, and for which individuals, do poverty and hunger indeed demoralize and crush? When and why, on the other hand, does want remain for some individuals a spur to industry, ambition, and ultimate escape from want? This question, a confession of ignorance regarding all the possible effects of poverty, embraced the poverty that was "feared" as well as "felt." It was a question passed on to twentieth-century discourse by British classical economics and by subsequent American commentators like the *Evangelist* operating in their own economic and political context, even as their uncertainty and ambivalence about poverty's effects could never truly compete with the moralistic attitudes that came more easily to them.

Little of such ambivalence toward poverty was expressed by members of a third antebellum configuration: skeptics and gainsayers of American economic exceptionalism who claimed that in emulation of the Old World, generous extrinsic rewards for legally free labor were rapidly disappearing in the northern states and had all but been supplanted there by the competitive free market's preeminent negative incentive—the exploitative and hateful "lash" of poverty.[58] This broad configuration, consisting of many of the critics of northern wage slavery and white slavery, included urban, often British-born artisan trade-union activists of the 1820s and 1830s; northern upper-middle-class utopian socialists of the 1840s; and conservative, proslavery intellectuals and politicians from the southern states. These last dominated the configuration in the 1850s as the northern criticisms tended to be dissipated and mainstreamed into the antisouthern Republican Party crusade for "free soil, free labor, free men." Many if not most of these diverse critics of American exceptionalist mythology tied the erosion and disappearance of positive labor incentives to the spread of the dependent wage-labor condition itself—to the commodification of labor power in the North. While lacking Marx's theoretical model of surplus value, a good number approached Marx's view that a truly just recompense—as distinct from temporarily high wages—was necessarily precluded by the unequal, exploitative character of the employer–wage earner relationship.

These critics of northern wage slavery were, just like Whiggish American exceptionalists on the other side of the issue, typically playing off the Old World and making use of the conventional and harsh classical economic paradigm. They were articulating their own version of the maxim "Like causes, like effects." This was not George Arnold's version, which favorably invoked classical economy in warning of compulsory poor relief's universally destructive effects on the work habits of the poor. Rather, this was a version that, to the contrary, characteristically deplored the penetration of classical economy's underlying principles and values into antebellum American culture. Thus the *Chronotype* refuted Calvin Colton's argument that classical economy was irrelevant to American conditions; indeed, it was proving all too relevant. As the *Chronotype* explained, "For the truth is that the system of things here is essentially the same as in Europe. It is not the accident of a surplus population on which Ricardo and Say reason, but the mere law of supply and demand which must regulate the price of labor every where, where it is a commodity in the market, where competition among laborers and between laborers and machinery is the prevailing fact."[59]

This third configuration's overriding image of the North as a locale of super-heated economic competition and insecurity, one that received pernicious doctrinal reinforcement from transatlantic political-economic maxims, was also fed by cultural anxieties that both encompassed and transcended white racism. Blacks and economic competition from black labor, be it slave or free, constituted a significant, but only one, form of otherness in antebellum America, and race consciousness remained only one ingredient in the many conceptualizations of wage slavery and the slavery of poverty.[60] The complaints of white male artisans who feared their own skills were being cheapened, trivialized, and even obliterated into dirty work fastened on the polluting competition, direct or indirect, that emanated from the "servile" labor of wage-earning women, juveniles, and recently arrived immigrants. This was labor which craft entrepreneurs and other employers in the free states were utilizing far more extensively than they did the labor of blacks. White working-class racism in general for this period has been recently and provocatively characterized as a form of psychological compensation that wage earners developed in tandem with their class formation and experience in the northern labor market. The construction of this racial self-identity, according to this interpretation, was never reducible to a reflexive, economic-determinist fear of job competition from blacks.[61] Yet to the extent that the labor press is a reliable guide (and it is not in all cases), then white working-class coolness to abolition, and even hostility to blacks, still commonly turned on more deliberative and methodical mental processes than attachment to a "psychic wage," though ones that similarly reflected the economic vulnerabilities and indignities imposed by competitive capitalism. A piece in the New York *Working Man's Advocate* in 1845 offered such an assessment, arguing that immediate and unprovisional emancipation would be disastrous for black slaves, for how could they, with their lack of education and general unfitness for "direct competition," hope to do even as well as the landless "white poor" of the North, who were hardly thriving.[62] The paper's editor, the printer and labor leader George Henry Evans, agreed: emancipation without land distribution would make a bad situation for northern wage earners still worse by further overstocking the labor market and reducing "black and white labor to a common level."[63]

If Evans and some other labor reformers commonly argued that southern chattel slavery was preferable to northern wage labor because of the "protection" it provided bondsman, this should not be taken to mean that they craved a comparable protection for northern wage earners.[64] Rather, they sought an approximation of wage justice and, concurrently with this, a retreat altogether from the pressures and vagaries of the capitalist wage-labor market. Although these two objectives may not have been, on a philosophical level, strictly consistent with one another, they were instrumentally tied together by the land-reform movement of the 1840s. In some of the early formulations of the western safety-valve thesis, Evans and others indicated that the increased ability of many workmen to satisfy their desire for an independent freehold would simultaneously relieve the pressure in eastern labor markets, thereby improving the bargaining leverage and lessening the vulnerability of those wage earners who remained back east. Such reform would minimize the latter's suppliance, their very need for capitalist protection.

Republican and agrarian traditions and the related yearning for insulation from the capitalist market could occasionally lead Evans and other members of this configuration actually to valorize poverty—labor for a "subsistence"—when wedded to a condition of freehold independence.[65] But more decisively, the same traditions stimulated their antipathy to poverty and even the mere fear of want as components of the competitive labor market; the salutary impact of such work incentives was limited to the capitalist's profit sheet. Indeed, the consensus among Evans and other labor reformers was that low wages and the spur of hunger, under existing labor-cheapening supply-and-demand arrangements, coerced most hirelings into being more than acceptably productive and profitable instruments for their employers—at least until they were spiritually demoralized or physically worn down, whereupon they were quite easily replaced.[66] Labor reformers held to this exploitation scenario even if they also agreed with the principle articulated by the *Chronotype* and Adam Smith: that generous rewards and the laborer's hope of appreciably bettering his condition encouraged "the greatest amount of industry."

Evans and like-minded reformers may have never completely relinquished the desire for harmonious accommodations between individual capitalists and their hirelings. Nonetheless, their movement to dismantle monopoly—specifically and primarily, the monopoly in land—still represented an attack on capitalist market processes themselves, insofar as it sought to arrest the waged vulnerabilities and the related spur of poverty that were among the principal mainsprings of those processes.[67] On this last point, above all, Evans, other land reformers, and many trade unionists of the period were in fundamental accord with the *Chronotype* and the other utopian socialist members of this configuration. The principal point of difference was that the utopians remained that much less receptive to the possibility of manipulating competitive capitalist market forces to improve the bargaining-exchange position and the social condition of waged and other laborers. Associationists and Owenites more unequivocally rejected supply and demand and labor's commodification under supply and demand as matters of principle—as among society's irremediably "false" and exploitative arrangements.[68]

There were ironies in the tendency of the *Chronotype* and other American critics of wage slavery and capitalist market processes to underscore the applicability of a European-derived supply-and-demand political-economic model that they despised. Perhaps these ironies were particularly pronounced in the case of certain southern proslavery intellectuals. These were individuals who embraced Malthusian population theory to explicate American exceptionalism's ongoing displacement in the free states by a dog-eat-dog, immiserizing competition for subsistence and yet glossed over the extent to which the same harsh Malthusian pressures logically threatened their own peculiar institution by rendering free white wage labor ever cheaper and more competitive.[69]

During the 1850s, however, northern commentators who engaged in rhetorical battle with slavery's defenders also did their part to ignore the ironies and contradictions in proslavery Malthusianism. There always had been a substantial school of thought that had found unrelenting antislavery implications in Malthus's population principle. But precisely because members of this school had predicated the dislodging of slave labor on the catastrophic, cheapening impact of "natural laws" on American free laborers—on the erosion of their high wages and other positive incentives—this antislavery Malthusianism could be of little use to the late antebellum celebrators of northern free labor.[70] They were only inspired by the intensified proslavery Malthusianism of the period to further the long tradition of demonizing classical economics. Thus a contributor to the *North American and United States Gazette* pronounced in 1858 that Thomas Carlyle had been right to characterize as the "dismal science" what were still, unfortunately, the "prevalent theories" in political economy—Malthus's population doctrine and Ricardo's theory of rent. These theories were "malignant" not merely for the death sentences that they erroneously passed on the laboring masses but also because they revealed their pernicious character by being "pressed into the service of every form of tyranny. . . . Practical application is given to it [their "faith"] in the assertion that slavery is the natural condition of the laborer, and it is otherwise still more closely applied in the declaration that our northern freemen are merely in a state of wages slavery, at some disadvantage as compared with the chattel laborers of the south."[71]

Extraeconomic Considerations in Wages'
Ideological Construction: Henry Ward Beecher

Classical economics, above all its earlier and gloomiest prognostications regarding the wage levels and general condition of laboring populations, exerted influence that was both great and largely negative in antebellum America — influence that was commonly registered through the resistance and revulsion it generated within the extensive public domain of ideas.[72] Merely by serving as a powerful weapon in the hands of both supporters and gainsayers of the mythology of American economic exceptionalism, the harsh Malthus-Ricardo scenario affected that mythology and with it the debates over antebellum labor's extrinsic inducements and rewards. Yet beyond the popular interpretation of economic principles, these debates also typically encompassed a host of "extraeconomic" considerations that were themselves continuously shaping new formulations of the mythology of American exceptionalism.

A consummate late antebellum example of such an ideological construction was offered in October 1858 by Henry Ward Beecher, the most famous minister in the United States. Beecher spoke along with several other civic leaders before an "immense audience" in New York City to raise funds for establishing a free library for New York's workingwomen similar to the city's Mercantile Library for young men.[73] Like much of the rest of the North, New York City was suffering through a period of severe depression and unemployment. Yet such transitory circumstances did not by themselves account for the plight of the one group that was being singled out for attention: in his introductory remarks the city's Mayor Tiemann noted that the meeting's particular objective was "to consider the improvement of a class which had been oppressed almost from all time — the Seamstresses."[74]

Beecher, however, began his address by suggesting that there were important social and moral lessons to be learned that extended beyond the situation of the seamstresses. He noted that

> no class could be long wronged or neglected where so large a public meeting as this could be gathered to sympathize and to aid. There are two kinds of society; one in which the Government was expected to take care of society, and the other in which society was educated to take care of itself. Doubtless it was better that the masses should be taken care of than that they should be destroyed. But it was better that individuals should be taught to take care of themselves. This was the peculiar thing that we had undertaken in America, at least in the Northern part of it.[75]

Beecher was speaking, of course, during a time of escalating sectional conflict as well as economic depression. In more prolonged attacks on the social order of the Old South, he would directly state what he only implied here: that the institution of chattel slavery collided with individual self-reliance by virtue of both the economic parasitism it granted slaveowners and the guaranteed subsistence it afforded slaves. In this last respect, to be more precise, Beecher's animus to chattel slavery reflected the same free-market competitive morality exhibited earlier in the century by Nassau Senior and other leading liberal opponents of England's Old Poor Law—to wit, that chattel slavery, like compulsory outdoor relief, was objectionable insofar as it rewarded laborers according to their wants and needs rather than according to the market value of their labor.[76]

But for all his trumpeting of the contrasting degree to which the free states "had recognized an inherent worth and divinity of the individuals, and undertaken to provide stimulants and aids to make them govern themselves," Beecher's encomiums to the northern social order were not unrestrained. His address recognized, first, at least one inevitable drawback in the northern system: "We could not have a pride of taking care of self without contempt for those who could not take of themselves"—for those New England paupers, for example, who through no fault of their own had been born "with slender endowments."[77]

Apart, moreover, from fostering such moralistic, uncharitable contempt as a by-product of its generally salutary principle of self-reliance, northern society, Beecher perceived, remained uneven and deficient in the very encouragement it gave that principle. Thus "tonight," Beecher proceeded, in turning to the subject of the meeting, "we were appealed to on behalf of a class who were weak—not by absolute weakness, but by the degradation of society"—a class of females who had been "made weak" by the mores and regulations of the northern social order. As Beecher explained, "We educate our sons to versatility" but not our women, who were educated only "to be married. . . . The things a woman may do, is taught to do well, and which are honorable and lucrative, are very few." Beecher did not intend these criticisms of the restricted economic opportunities of northern women as a blanket repudiation of the era's cult of domesticity, as an uncategorical denial of the naturalness of separate spheres for males and females. Beecher assured his audience that "a woman in her own sphere as wife or mother, was the noblest thought ever expressed by God on earth [Cheers]. But a woman, fallen and lost—a woman out of her sphere, was the saddest thing on earth. . . . There could be little said of meetings like this if all women had husbands. But many could not have them, either through their own fault or somebody else's. . . . Our wiseacres said that women must attend to her own sphere. Then let them see to it that all women were furnished with husbands; they were bound to place her in her sphere."[78]

Many of Beecher's contemporaries who joined in expressing abhorrence of single white women's oppressive working conditions may well have been acting out of a presumption of woman's inherent weakness and natural right to be protected from marketplace forces.[79] But as part of his own rhetorical strategy in his 1858 address, Beecher presented himself as a contrary voice of realism. Unnatural as it seemed, the presence of large numbers of single working-class women in the public sphere, women thrown indefinitely on their own resources for economic support, obliged northern free-labor society to extend and apply more fully its principles of self-reliance and education for self-reliance.[80] Regrettable as it might be, that presence rendered irrelevant the gendered split between home and market valorized by the separate-spheres ideology.[81] And in an example of the inconsistency for which he became notable, Beecher further assured his audience that women in the workplace need not be perceived as so unnatural after all: "A woman had the right to do anything that it was becoming in a man to do. And most things that were becoming in a man would be more so in women—for where we brought our rugged force to the work, they brought the power which lay in noble affections, in a purity which transcended anything in man."[82]

Hardly a profound or original thinker, Beecher nonetheless recognized, like others before him, that the conditions long experienced by New York's seamstresses and other wage-earning women—the segmented and crowded labor markets, the fierceness of competition, the "hard conditions and oppressive tyrannies of overseers and employers," the subsistence wages and fifteen-hour workdays—were in considerable measure social constructions.[83] They were at least in part the products of cultural biases and expectations, rooted in the idea of women as household dependents and originating outside the labor market— as well as outside conspicuous governmental activity, for that matter—which restricted women's acquisition of marketable skills.[84]

This is not to say that Beecher, on this occasion at least, acknowledged that much more pervasive antebellum phenomenon: the unpaid, "invisible" nature of wives' domestic labor. Nor did he exhibit a comparable concern with the no less onerous waged outwork within the home that was performed by many of the city's working-class women, single and married.[85] Perhaps Beecher assumed that the contributions of such women were merely economically supplementary or incidental to those of their husbands or other male household members. Neither, finally, did Beecher claim, as Paulina Wright Davis and other of his more radical feminist contemporaries did, that women's position in both the home and the marketplace derived from the same systematic denial of women's labor value.[86]

Still, Beecher did recognize in his address, albeit again to a much less sweeping extent than such feminists, that the labor market was not "a neutral arbiter of value," that it was rather "shaped by norms and practices of gender caste."[87] The rhetorical support that Beecher lent the proposed library reflected this perception:

> Women had not a fair chance in the industrial avocations of life. . . . In this city the number of women, mostly single women, employed in industrial pursuits, was incredible. . . . these 80,000 women ["directly employed in manufacturing"], or as many of them as wished, should have books to read; good books, good papers, good rooms of resort. The next thing should be, that they should have time to read. . . . Now, women, if they would not be in menial occupations, must have intelligence; and if they were born so poor as to receive no education, they must do the best they could. . . . the contemplated library must be productive of great good.[88]

Poor, uneducated women, above all single females who did not marry, Beecher insisted, should be given a chance to rise out of the "menial" and subsistent employments that entrapped them; they must have the opportunity "to overcome in later life the disadvantages of their earlier years."[89] For such women preeminently, fairer competition would make for less brutalizing competition.

Here, then, a leading spokesman of middle-class Protestant culture in the North defended a project for its tendency to empower—without aggressively or fundamentally challenging either capitalist authority or conventional notions of domesticity—a group of workers who were commonly portrayed and sentimentalized as helpless sufferers. One could more closely examine, in this connection, one of the central middle-class assumptions that Beecher shared with his cospeakers: that, were employers to actually cooperate by raising wage rates and shortening hours in their shops, young working-class women would choose to spend their leisure time reading books in libraries.[90] One should emphasize, in any case, that the proposed library was essentially a project of enlightened bourgeois philanthropy. Although one cannot assume that the seamstresses played an altogether negligible role in the occurrence of such meetings as this one, the 1850s were generally years of quiescence, even demoralization, in organized labor activity and initiatives among the city's workingwomen.[91] During this period the spread of the sewing machine tended, above all, to intensify the conditions of demoralization, expanding the pool of cheap labor, lowering piece wage rates, and necessitating workdays of fifteen to eighteen hours in the sewing trade.[92] If ensuing grievances among seamstresses over the recent technological advances did furnish some impetus for the October 1858 meeting, they were grievances that Beecher in fact sought primarily to dispel before his audience.[93]

A poststructuralist view, consistent with its disassociation of texts from single authors and its marginalization of authorial intention, might interpret Beecher's address as the product not of his individual imagination but rather of a collective antebellum culture and its language. Beecher would appear here as something like a "factory worker" who in his text has merely assembled "images, words and ideas that are the common property" of the society.[94] While putting an interesting twist on Beecher's lack of genuine profundity and originality as a thinker, such a poststructuralist perspective would also slight Beecher's truly special talent for assimilating, mixing, and packaging popular themes and images in an increasingly competitive antebellum marketplace of ideas. Beecher likely was, as suggested by several scholars before the ascendance of poststructuralist theory, the era's preeminent intellectual sponge.[95]

Beecher's address was in no way any more influential than hundreds of others bearing on economic and political topics that he and other prominent Americans gave during this period. But given his special talent, Beecher's address does constitute a particularly illuminating hodgepodge of negotiations among themes reflective of widespread social and political tensions. Beecher conceded the economically destructive effects of metropolitan industrialization and other baleful Europeanizing tendencies for the city's workingwomen. Yet he insisted that the beauty of the northern social order and its superiority over the slave South resided in its exaltation of manly economic self-help and independence. He deferred to conventions stigmatizing single status for adult women as an undesirable, even unnatural condition. But he maintained that northern women who did remain single and were forced by economic pressures out of their proper "sphere" were entitled (within reason) to increased access to masculine avenues of striving and competition and to the greater extrinsic rewards that access would bring. In contesting the "'low-wage' enthusiasts" of the eighteenth century, Adam Smith and other original "'high-wage' advocates" may well have had only the work psychology of male laborers in mind; they may indeed have perceived women merely as "part of the burden of family responsibilities" that male workers must shoulder.[96] But Beecher, for one, would enlarge such advocates' vision with respect to a particularly conspicuous and economically desperate group of mid-nineteenth-century American women. He would, at the very least, reduce that form of discrimination which impeded females from acquiring experience and skills and in so doing made them noncompetitive even to employers who held no explicit discriminatory bias. In lending his support to limited efforts both to redress the seamstresses' lack of starting-gate equality and to blunt the gender-based distortions in the labor market, Beecher was, in effect, negotiating on "the boundaries." He sought to preserve the core of dominant free-labor capitalist ideology and to render it less vulnerable to attack by altering some of its definitions of the just and the possible.[97] Or put another way, Beecher was simultaneously embracing and retreating from a completely uncritical American exceptionalist mythology.

By the same token, Beecher's address is one illustration of the morass of intellectual currents and social attitudes that informed commentary as to both the existing level of wages in the antebellum North and the reform measures needed to elevate labor's extrinsic rewards to a level consistent with economic justice. Beecher's address reflected the long-standing, fundamental debates over labor incentives, to which he referred when he spoke of the "stimulants and aids" that induced inhabitants of the free states to "govern themselves." But the address was also a response to immediate issues and pressures in the late antebellum period, and as such it illustrated how the period's representations of wages could reflect a complex amalgam of considerations. These included, but were hardly limited to, responses to escalating sectional conflict over slave labor, reactions to northern industrialization and technological change, and attitudes toward the gendering of work. Such extraeconomic considerations were pervasive in the culture, and they would ensure that not merely working-class ideological constructions but many middle-class ones as well either would contest or at least would go beyond one of our principal stereotypes for this period: that of a one-dimensional political-economic and entrepreneurial dogma that represented wages as the outcome of insuperable and impartial supply-and-demand market forces.

The Shibboleth of Supply and Demand

The early to mid-nineteenth century, in the United States as in England, is conventionally understood as the period in which the middle classes, and entrepreneurs and other capitalists most of all, began routinely and approvingly to invoke supply-and-demand conditions within the labor market as the preeminent determinant of an individual wage earner's recompense.[98] The rhetorical endorsement of supply-and-demand market rules and an attendant hostility to labor unions came all the more easily to many of the American commentators who rejected the specific axioms of the harsh Malthusian-Ricardian scenario. Invoking the mythology of American exceptionalism, they could embrace those market rules on the grounds that whatever the temporary gluts in specific local labor markets, supply and demand in the United States overall would work for an indefinite period in behalf of the laboring population that enjoyed formal freedom. Market achievement here, at least, need not exact the social costs of a brutalizing and dangerous class competition and conflict. Such a characterization of this period as one in which supply-and-demand market dogma enjoyed ascendance, if not hegemony, is of some use in broadly differentiating this period both from earlier ones, in which traditional hierarchies and customs within trades enjoyed greater prevalence and strength as regulators of labor's rewards, and from later eras in which a collectively bargained wage won increased recognition and legitimacy throughout society.

Yet the liberal capitalist supply-and-demand characterization of the wage arguments of the antebellum era remains inadequate, and not merely because it fails to encompass the assorted oppositional arguments used by labor activists and radicals, some primarily secular and others evangelical religious in inspiration. Some of these dissident arguments unmistakably regarded market capitalist—determined rewards as intrinsically and inevitably incompatible with economic justice for individual wage earners, even when they also, as in the case of American Fourierists, acknowledged a significant productive function for capitalists. Trade-union militants, among other dissidents, were often more ambiguous and equivocal. In line with their retreat from the most radical anticapitalist versions of the labor theory of value toward the end of the antebellum period, many grew more disposed to accept in theory supply-and-demand market forces as the natural basis for regulating the price of labor. But such acceptance often continued to be overshadowed, and even subverted, by their vehement insistence that a host of employer practices, including the use of laborsaving machinery, manipulated existing labor-market conditions and rendered them a hopelessly bad approximation of true, unfettered supply and demand; capitalist free-market rhetoric constituted a "miserable subterfuge" for "tyranny" and wage slavery.[99]

But the more discernibly disaffected groups and individuals aside, the inadequacy of the supply-and-demand characterization extends even to entrepreneurial and other middle-class elements that did consistently employ it because embedded in a "law" that addressed aggregate conditions in the labor market at any one time were assumptions and value judgments regarding the moral character, personal habits, and economic behavior of the market's individual participants.[100] This much itself has been obvious at least since the Reverend Malthus offered a formulation of the supply-and-demand dictum that turned principally on the laboring poor's propensity for sexual gratification. And in the United States as well as in England, the invocation of ostensibly blind supply-and-demand laws to legitimate market rewards and inequality of outcomes was closely bound up in the emergent entrepreneurial and professional success creed. As promulgated by northern Whig political economists and politicians especially (though not exclusively), that creed broke down just-price and other traditional arguments. In their place it provided a new principle of social strat-ification by its insistence that capitalist profits and professional rewards, along with wage differentials, reflected market-based, legitimate differences in indi-vidual talent, enterprise, and virtue. One of Friedrich A. von Hayek's principal arguments against distributive or social justice — that it is a meaningless concept inside a market economy because of the spontaneous or unintended and game-like character of the market — would have accordingly found little obvious appeal among the free-market defenders of an earlier era (or, for that matter, of our own era), who assumed the existence of an intimate link between material rewards and personal merit.[101]

But even more to the point, the very middle-class perception that the be-havior and misbehavior of individual wage-earning laborers were among the "thousand causes" that affected supply and demand could also act to restrain complacency regarding the distribution of market rewards.[102] There was a recur-rent sensitivity to the fact that the "law" of supply and demand, in determin-ing aggregate wage levels, would prove unjust to individual laborers. Noteworthy in this connection was the rather disjointed, and even contradictory, nature of classical economic thought itself. For if, in particular, Ricardo's influential labor-cost theory of value did indeed link an individual laborer's wages with his pro-ductive contributions, the same was less clearly true of his other doctrines: either the doctrine of natural (i.e., subsistence) wages or, more conspicuously yet, the wages-fund theory that he, Malthus, and dozens of Anglo-American political economists also advanced in one form or another.[103] Because the wages-fund was, in general, "a sum of money to be divided among the members" of the laboring class, as Herbert Hovenkamp describes it, "a worker's wages depended not merely on the amount he produced, but on the number of laborers com-peting for the fund."[104] In his reworking of the tenets of classical economics, John Stuart Mill most explicitly (if still unsatisfactorily) grappled with the result-ant free-rider problem, whereby productive and responsible laborers — those who practice moral restraint—fail to reap the full material fruits of their good behavior because of the irresponsible behavior of others who continue to multiply and drag down overall wage levels.[105] But tension arising from the inability of individual workers, for any number of reasons, to enjoy their just deserts under the operation of supply and demand is evident in more inchoate form in a multitude of the most mainstream middle-class texts, including Beecher's address.[106]

There is, finally, the most fundamental curiosity of all regarding supply and demand and the closely related dogma of free competition. And here one touches on an old and big issue that has only grown bigger in recent years. On the one hand, there is the market revolution—above all, perhaps, the pervasive rhetoric of the market revolution—in both western Europe and the United States: "Buy cheap and sell dear," and accompanying this aphorism the chronic complaints of early- to mid-nineteenth-century radical and plebeian movements that labor, especially wage labor, was indeed being commodified and cheapened through supply-and-demand market processes. On the other hand, there is the continuously mounting evidence that truly free and open competition—the unfettered operation of supply and demand—if not a chimera, nonetheless in fact was obstructed in this period in any number of ways, and more often than not, it seems, to the disadvantage of wage earners and other small producers, as some of their spokesmen (echoing one of Adam Smith's own themes) recognized.[107]

This evidence as to the myth of a truly self-regulating market comes from a variety of sources and angles. There is, for example, Louis Hartz's old finding that the antebellum activities of the Pennsylvania state government were unequivocally interventionist and promotional, and that there was, moreover, not even a fully blown laissez-faire philosophy in evidence opposing these activities. Karl Polanyi's evidence shows that the liberal proponents of England's Poor Law Amendment Act, in their devotion to the principle of a self-regulating market in labor and wages, created new almshouses and other state institutions, holding much centralized authority, that grossly violated laissez-faire practices. Free competition, in other words, did not inevitably lead to governmental laissez-faire, because many of the lower classes had to be forcibly trained to compete. There are the newer Foucaultian embellishments of Polanyi's position, which invoke Jeremy Bentham's notorious Panopticon as well as the New Poor Law to illustrate how liberal middle-class "biopower" was directed in the early nineteenth century as never before to establishing moral intervention in and surveillance over the lives of the laboring poor. Recent labor-law studies indicate that in antebellum labor-relations adjudication, either liberal competitive individualist tenets remained "abstractions," or hierarchical and restrictive master-and-servant common laws, rooted in the feudal order, privileged American employers over wage laborers in the new industrial settings, skewering the already "asymmetrical" relationships of power and exchange that existed between them in the marketplace. Continuing empirical scholarship reminds us that with particular respect to white male wage earners, collective power has mattered. Open and meritocratic free competition for employment, advancement, and better wages has historically been qualified by the extent to which transactions in the labor market have reflected not merely the abilities and performance of individual workers but their ethnic affiliation and membership in unions and other groups that have exerted control within different trades. And there are, lastly, the recent feminist studies showing that a woman's wage, above all, together with its determinants, is much more subjective and political than how economists commonly perceive the operation of individual choice in labor-market analysis; that the lower wages paid women have often, historically, been justified by reference to their supposed lesser needs, rather than to the market value of their labor.[108]

Some historians—most of all, perhaps, Marxist-oriented historians—have followed labor activists of the period with a ready explanation for many of these deviations, both ideological and actual, from the slogan of an open and meritocratic free competition: employers simply failed to observe it in situations where strict observance did not suit their perceived best interests. What Barrington Moore Jr. notes of early nineteenth-century British textile and other capitalists applies equally well to their American counterparts. In view of their preference for assured markets and suppliers, they were often hostile to competition and ambivalent about the free market with respect to their own firms and economic standing even as they dispensed advice to workers on the virtues of competition and the evils of trade unions and government assistance.[109] Such discrepancies in social attitudes and practices have proved both profound and enduring, as has their relationship to conceptualizations of labor's extrinsic rewards. With particular respect to societies in his own time, Mill noted that, generally speaking, "the really exhausting and the really repulsive labours, instead of being better paid than others, are almost invariably paid the worst of all, because performed by those who have no choice."[110] This was a material reality that was as much a part of antebellum America as it was of any other country of the time (particularly when chattel slavery is included within that reality), even as it may have been no more true for nineteenth-century market-capitalist societies in general than it was for earlier and different kinds of societies. In shibboleths such as "supply and demand" and "free competition" for capitalists and wage earners, middle-class Americans preeminently found devices appropriate enough to their early industrial-capitalist development for explaining and accepting the ages-old paradox of social hierarchy, whereby individuals engaged in society's most basic and indispensable labor—dirty and other kinds of manual-labor occupations—received the poorest material and status rewards. Employer abandonment of the shibboleths when self-interest dictated could serve as its own testimony to acceptance of the same paradoxical situation. It was left to utopian socialist and other egalitarian ideological constructions, and less decisively to a more mainstream and intermittent middle-class angst, actually to perceive the paradox as a moral dilemma.

2

Pressures from Below: Pauperism, Chattel Slavery, and the Ideological Construction of Free-Market Labor Incentives

Britain's Poor Law Commission *Report* of 1834, written principally by Nassau Senior and Edwin Chadwick, justified the Poor Law Amendment Act and its assault on the English allowance system in the following terms: "The constant war which the pauper has to wage with all who employ or pay him, is destructive to his honesty and his temper; as his subsistence does not depend on his exertions, he loses all that sweetens labour, its association with reward and gets through his work, such as it is, with the reluctance of a slave."[1] Such assertions as this have prompted historians to detail how political economists, capitalists, and other elite elements in Britain naturalized and idealized work incentives in a labor market of putatively free competition, one in which the laborer would maximize his work efforts precisely to the extent that he was rewarded according to the true market value of his labor. These historians have emphasized how this naturalization and idealization of free-market incentives was embedded in a commensurate liberal capitalist, antipaternalist animus for both pauperism within England and chattel slavery in the British West Indies. During the early nineteenth century, this elite animus configured pauperism and chattel slavery as crushing the incentive of laboring populations, thereby demoralizing them, by guaranteeing and fixing their recompense and otherwise upsetting the "natural" correspondence between performance and reward. Increasingly during this period these two institutions were represented as artificial drags on the formation of a wage-labor market that honored individual initiative, healthy competition, and "freedom of contract."[2]

My concern here is how conceptualizations of the countermodels of chattel slavery and pauperism likewise contributed to the social construction of wage incentives and extrinsic rewards generally in antebellum America, a more neglected subject of investigation. As such, the discussion extends the preceding chapter's consideration of the shibboleths of free competition and supply and demand. On the one hand, this chapter suggests ways in which moral rationales for early industrial capitalism in the United States deviated from, rather than strictly conformed to, expressions of capitalist ideology in Britain. Yet it nonetheless underscores the important role that economic necessity and the fear of such necessity—the theme of free-market tough love—assumed in the American as well as the British rationales for capitalism. Also receiving attention is the period's competing discourse of wage slavery. This is followed by consideration of antebellum labor voices that, notwithstanding their antagonism to capitalist interests, joined more elite commentators in endorsing elements of a formative free-market, free-labor ideology. In the course of these discussions, I raise questions about the salience that recent scholarship in history and cultural studies has given to white working-class racism in early nineteenth-century society.

Joseph Tuckerman and American Anti-Poor-Law Discourse

Nothing was more transatlantic than the early nineteenth-century discourse over labor incentives and pauperism. Segments of the British Poor Law Commission *Report,* including the assertion quoted above, found its way into numerous like-minded American commentaries, including *The Principles and Results of the Ministry at Large, in Boston* (1838), written by Joseph Tuckerman, the leading Unitarian clergyman and "visitor to the poor" in Massachusetts.[3] Although Tuckerman was a prominent individual in matters of poor relief, one who rode the wave of a decade-old American elite antipathy for all compulsory "outdoor" assistance (i.e., noninstitutional, home relief), he was not notably more successful than others had been in getting his proposals implemented as public policy.[4] His views are especially important, however, if only for one reason: they illustrate how an elite figure, and one who occupied a number of private and state charitable offices, could express and somehow retain a commitment to a supply-and-demand free-labor ethic and doctrine of wages in the face of an evolving capitalist labor market's manifest inability to provide subsistent wages for all who sought them.[5]

None of the early nineteenth-century American anti-poor-law commentaries, Tuckerman's included, had the English allowance system per se to berate and dismantle in their own states and towns.[6] Nor did Thomas Malthus's specter of the overpopulation of the laboring poor, which at least earlier in the century had fed much of the British antipathy toward poor relief, figure so significantly in the American anti-poor-law narratives, directed as they were to a much newer country of relatively wide open spaces. Still, the authors of these commentaries were convinced that general outdoor relief practices in the United States, above all compulsory or public outdoor assistance to able-bodied recipients, offered sufficiently demoralizing parallels with England under that nation's pre-1834 poor laws. It was not merely a case of Tuckerman and other American commentators excerpting the statements of Senior and Chadwick and invoking their economic expertise and quasi-parliamentary authority to support their own claims for a drastic curtailing of outdoor relief. Borrowing from postmodern insights into the evolution of working-class consciousness, one now more greatly appreciates how the very language castigating and linking pauperism and slavery, which was exemplified in the British commission *Report,* was itself influential. That language helped to inform and structure the very "experience" and perceptions of Tuckerman and other middle-class Americans in interpreting the behavior of their own dependent poor.[7]

The transatlantic discourse over pauperism and labor incentives was also scarcely a one-way street—the British commission *Report* itself, for example, drew on earlier contributions from such sources as the Whiggish *American Quarterly Review,* as well as from Tuckerman's own earlier writings.[8] True, the American anti-poor-law commentary was on the whole derivative and secondary to a classical economic, liberal free-market British tradition that extended from the late eighteenth-century writer Joseph Townsend, through Malthus and Thomas Chalmers, to Senior and beyond. Very generally, and particularly as this free-market tradition discarded some of Townsend's openly elitist disdain for the "brutish" laboring poor, it criticized "poor-law systems of indiscriminate relief" for their failure to morally reform and empower the recipient: "They are [but] empirical remedies, the object of which is directly to ameliorate his condition, not to render him capable of securing a better condition for himself."[9] Such attacks on indiscriminate poor relief were of a piece with a larger classical economics that, as one historian observes, owed its appeal in England less to its "internal coherence" than to its "ability to dovetail with the deeply rooted moral assumptions of the age. The market, freed from paternalistic interference by government or parish officers, would reward thrift and prudence and punish improvidence and idleness."[10]

But while the American contributions embraced the same themes, they did add at least one distinctive feature, one that put the market mechanism in a yet more beneficent light. They added a mythology of American exceptionalism that further justified the removal of demoralizing, enfeebling impediments to a competitive labor market by coupling paeans to national economic growth with persistent references to extraordinary social fluidity and unrivaled popular access to the burgeoning economic opportunities. The severest, most alarmist critics of American pauperism were Whiggish, and many of these insisted, unlike Jacksonian Democrat voices of inevitable class conflict, that economic competition in America was benignly indirect and not a zero-sum game. In the relatively fair and inclusive economic race that distinguished the United States from the Old World, prizes were both multiplying and widely enjoyed by its industrious participants. Senior trumpeted in 1841 that "the general result" of the Poor Law Amendment Act was that the English laborer, "finding himself no longer entitled to a fixed income, whatever be his idleness or misconduct, and no longer restricted to that income, whatever be his industry and his integrity, becomes, as is always the case in a state of freedom, stimulated to activity and honesty by the double motive of hope and fear."[11] The power of the mythology of American economic exceptionalism was such that the American critics of poor laws were inclined to attach still greater weight to the former motive — the positive incentive of hope of material improvement — in their own campaigns for the "emancipation" of able-bodied paupers. Few of Joseph Tuckerman's British counterparts would have been so quick to make his claim that "there are those who are perpetually passing from the ranks of the poor into those which we distinguish as the higher classes."[12]

Yet Tuckerman immediately added the warning that social fluidity in the United States, or at least in such urban centers as Boston, was also marked by the reverse movement. This was the continuous swelling of the ranks of the poor from even the affluent classes — the nether side, so to speak, of what Joyce Appleby describes as the young nation's popular culture of enterprise.[13] In the 1850s such prominent Protestant charity reformers as Robert Hartley would be more disposed to stigmatize and marginalize the poor — above all to identify the hordes of famine immigrant Catholic Irish as a recalcitrant urban "culture of poverty."[14] But one of Tuckerman's own objectives as an earlier commentator on American poverty was to diminish the otherness of the urban poor, to shock elite elements out of their sense of moral superiority and impregnable well-being. In this particular regard he hardly figures as a complacent American exceptionalist.

Nor did Tuckerman regard himself as an uncritical American spokesman for British political-economic values. Rather, he exemplified the pervasive ideological tendency of early nineteenth-century American commentators to identify British political economy with the original "inevitable misery" paradigm of

Malthus and Ricardo, and in keeping with early nineteenth-century American Unitarian "moral philosophy," he believed this paradigm to be excessively pessimistic and hard-hearted, as well as overly materialistic. Superficially regarding the working classes as wealth-producing "machinery," it slighted their moral capability to control their numbers and otherwise effect their own spiritual and material uplift.[15]

Scholars agree that the single greatest influence on Tuckerman's thinking was Thomas Chalmers, the Scottish evangelical theologian and preacher who did pioneering work among the poor in Glasgow. In his sermons and writings, Chalmers adopted an extreme version of Malthus's doctrine of overpopulation. He regarded the wages-fund as a form of providence, a means of encouraging sexual abstinence and other good behavior among the lower orders. In some respects Chalmers epitomized the gloomy fixation of British clerical economics in this period upon themes of sin and evangelical retribution. But his almost fanatical opposition to all legal assistance for the poor and his preference for voluntary charity that would bring out the best moral qualities in givers and recipients alike also anticipated the optimistic self-improvement creeds of later popular writers like Samuel Smiles and political economists such as Senior.[16] In fact, Chalmers's emphasis on working-class agency was part of his frequent apologia for the economic and social status quo. Many, perhaps, are still accustomed to thinking of the early Industrial Revolution as the age of the aggressive and masculine capitalist entrepreneur: the individual who, intuitively divining the relationship between cause and effect in the marketplace, took the initiative, created new opportunities, and seized control of the situation. Yet in a time of labor turmoil, it suited Chalmers's purposes to frequently dwell instead on capitalist impotence and innocence, an inclination consistent with political economy's general tendency to naturalize competitive market forces. Thus he insisted that "it is not in the power of master manufacturers to realize, for any length of time, any undue advantage over their workmen." Recurrent declines in profits proved that "depression in the wages of operatives" was not attributable to "the extravagant gains of their employers." Far from being "oppressors," the "capitalists are quite innocent. . . . And it is further well for the spread among . . . the working classes . . . of virtuous, and temperate, and elevated habits, that they should be thoroughly possessed with the true doctrine of wages; that they are themselves their own deadliest oppressors."[17]

It is always difficult to pin down influences with a thinker like Joseph Tuckerman who strongly reflected the intellectual ambience of a period. But Tuckerman's writings on poor relief were a typical formulation of a rather extreme position, and as such they clearly bore the imprint of Chalmers's views. Tuckerman subscribed to the common American view that eastern cities like Boston had become dumping grounds for paupers and vagrants from abroad. But he regarded as no less alarming the number of native-born dependent poor, and he accordingly regarded the persistence and spread of pauperism in the United States as symptomatic of internal malfunctions and disease.[18] To address the problem, Tuckerman argued that all legal provision for outdoor recipients in Massachusetts should be abolished because compulsory, and hence undiscriminating, charity discouraged industry, forethought, and self-denial on the part of the laboring poor and ultimately would prove ruinous to their self-support. Able-bodied paupers, who almost invariably came to view assistance as their right, were among the most grievous "victims of our poor laws."[19]

Tuckerman shared the common elite perception that the division between the undeserving and the deserving poor roughly corresponded to the current de facto division between public (or state) and private charity. He also held the conventional view that the bane of intemperance was a highly significant and even overwhelming cause, rather than merely a result, of extreme poverty and pauperism among the able-bodied.[20] Indeed, alcoholic vice led those it reduced to poverty to continuously distort their true needs. Labor activists and reformers might characterize hunger and the fear of starvation as generally effective (as well as inhumane) waged-labor incentives. But to Tuckerman and other critics of the poor laws, one mark of the undeserving, morally degenerate able-bodied pauper was the inefficacy that such motivations held for him; if given the opportunity, he was likely to expend any acquired moneys in satisfying his liquor cravings rather than in tending to the basic material needs of himself and his family. For this and other reasons, Tuckerman would compel all undeserving able-bodied paupers to earn their assistance within state workhouses.[21]

Workhouses entailing some labor regimen were also, in Tuckerman's view, the proper institutions for that murkier category of the undeserving. This consisted of the men and women who had so enfeebled themselves through drink and other "vicious" habits that they could no longer, by the most generous definitions, be considered able-bodied; they were now incapable of contributing more than "something" to their own support.[22] Voluntary, outdoor charity, informed by a discerning visiting ministry, was the appropriate mode of assistance only for deserving working-class individuals and families — those who, their good-faith efforts notwithstanding (as Tuckerman and other visitors defined such efforts), remained unable for varying periods to secure the employment and wages needed to subsist completely on their own. If these *"virtuous poor,"*

above all the aged and others requiring permanent support, proved too numerous to be relieved by private charity, then they should be accommodated in
"well-ordered" state houses of charity, or almshouses. Tuckerman would make
even each of these, "as far as it may be, a house of employment, for I would
give to this class of the poor all possible facilities for self-support. Employment
will even add much to the happiness of its inmates."[23]

Still, Tuckerman insisted on the essential distinction between workhouse and
almshouse. Inmates in the latter "have a right to support from alms when they
have been brought to poverty by causes beyond their control"—when, that is,
their poverty is not "immediately ascribable to the grossest sins." Tuckerman
drew back, then, from pressing a universal self-reliance at the expense of altruism
and of, indeed, the virtuous poor's very entitlement to relief. And in arguing that
workhouses should be reserved for those in need of "moral redemption" from
their vices, he was suggesting that their proper functions did not include penal-
izing able-bodied individuals who were willing to work but through no fault of
their own were unable to find sufficient employment.[24] In this last respect Tuckerman's views remained distinct from, and were indeed perhaps less "morally
problematic" than, the more sweeping workhouse policies formally enacted in
Britain's New Poor Law.[25]

Tuckerman nonetheless shared with the proponents of that law the unwa-
vering conviction that public outdoor relief, above all, had pauperizing tendencies, a unique capacity to reduce independent laborers to the condition of
hopeless drones. To Chalmers particularly Tuckerman owed much for this conviction, as well as for his condemnation of obtrusive human laws for eroding
the personal involvement of benefactors—for destroying the "natural" bonds
of affection between the more affluent and the poor.[26] Tuckerman furthermore
followed Chalmers and orthodox political economy generally in pronouncing
himself a believer in the ruling force of supply-and-demand market forces. In
one of the nineteenth century's innumerable illustrations of Albert O. Hirschman's "futility thesis," Tuckerman dismissed as "artificial" and "useless" various schemes to raise the wages and otherwise relieve the wants of Boston's
laboring poor. In fact, the establishment of additional "houses" to employ those
"who cannot elsewhere find employment" would perversely attract "the poor
of the country" and "increase that very excess which we should endeavor to
lessen."[27] The law of supply and demand that set wage rates in the various
trades, Tuckerman pronounced, was both inevitable and legitimate; did it not,
after all, exercise the same power over capitalist profits?[28]

But Tuckerman's writings also remain notable for the more subtle ways in which they deviated from Chalmers's more moralistic and doctrinaire pro-capitalist renderings of labor commodification and wage justice.[29] As in the case of modern-day social workers and others whose personal experience with welfare dependency—their confrontation with complex and intractable social problems—prompts them to challenge the easy negative public stereotypes of welfare recipients, so Tuckerman's extensive dealings with Boston's "deserving" poor and their circumstances reduced his comfort with free-market homilies and nostrums.[30] Along with his Philadelphia contemporary and correspondent the Irish émigré and publisher Mathew Carey, Tuckerman was among the first elite Americans to identify underemployment and structural involuntary unemployment, particularly among seamstresses and other working-class females—married, widowed, and single—as signal features of early industrial capitalism.[31] These women's meager earnings were rendered all the more inadequate by the absence of effective male breadwinners. Tuckerman's defense of voluntary charity that would supplement these earnings suggests that any lingering commitment he retained to such conventional middle-class domestic ideals as female conjugal dependence was tempered by the recognition that the male-earned "family wage" was a fiction and would likely remain so among the poorer members of the urban laboring classes.[32] Like others who were deeply hostile to poor laws and pauperism, Tuckerman exalted the virtues of economic self-support. Whatever ambivalence he felt about permanent wage labor did not, accordingly, reflect some doctrinaire early nineteenth-century republican distaste for the servile economic dependence that such labor supposedly embodied.[33] Rather, that ambivalence sprang from firsthand observation of wage labor's genuinely erratic capacity to sustain the Boston poor in their self-support.

A series of venerable propositions undergirded Tuckerman's social philosophy: that there were significant natural disparities in physical and mental capacities among individuals; that these natural inequalities, which were divinely ordained, inevitably gave rise in civilized societies to sharp economic contrasts; and that God's purpose in the appointment of riches and poverty was a Christian brotherhood of men distinguished by virtue and the absence of selfishness.[34] The most interesting of Tuckerman's writings reflect his sporadic efforts to incorporate the more modern and secular political-economic shibboleth of supply and demand into this schema. Ultimately, Tuckerman's experience with Boston's virtuous and deserving female poor would yield little more than a rather lame hedging of his support for the supply-and-demand principle.

Tuckerman insisted, in his criticisms of Malthus, that "I should esteem that to be a false and injurious principle in political economy which is not in perfect consistency with Christian morality."[35] Conceivably he believed in this connection, and in line with Adam Smith's general dictum, that paying out more generous wages would improve the productivity of Boston's sweated and other poor female laborers and was thereby in the best self-interest of employers. Nonetheless, Tuckerman also indicated that Christian morality was not strictly endogenous to political economy: justice and benevolence—words he frequently used—remained beyond the scope of political economy itself. Christian love still had an important role to play: unlike the artificial make-work schemes, it would indeed effectively blunt the harsher wage-determining effects of the supply-and-demand principle if capitalists took it to heart.[36] Tuckerman was accordingly more forthright than Chalmers in condemning as selfish and unchristian the "Buy cheap and sell dear" mentality of sweatshops and other employers. In paying out higher wages than they needed to—in observing a just price for labor—Christian capitalists would capture society's plaudits and lead the way in practicing a constructive, voluntary charity, as well, perhaps, as increasing their profits.[37] Yet as Tuckerman still perceived, the successful functioning and even the legitimacy of the modern marketplace—which merely perpetuated, after all, the ages-old disparities in property—did not absolutely require such charity and wage justice. No one better than Tuckerman illustrated the tensions, even the contradictions, that resided in Unitarian philanthropy's "twin commitments to capitalism and compassion."[38]

Tuckerman himself explicitly recognized only those contradictions and discrepancies arising from the different kinds of dependent poor—hence his efforts at a systematic classification.[39] Rhetorical strategy may also have diverted him from attending to inconsistencies and conflicts within his own social doctrine, and here one touches on the issue of Tuckerman's intended readership, which did not, it is perhaps needless to say, include the poor themselves. Far from perceiving himself as an extremist, and in his desire to marshal "public sentiment" for ministries to the poor, Tuckerman thought he was steering his own middle course: one between latitudinarian elements that would perpetuate and even extend public outdoor relief practices and a contingent of yet sterner moralists than he who disapproved of even a coordinated, systematized voluntary charity to the laboring poor and maintained that in a land of plenty the latter might always earn a livelihood if they truly wished.[40] In his writing Tuckerman may well have partially constructed this second group of critics—inflated its significance—to render his own criticisms of outdoor relief more reasonable and palatable. However, there was a real undercurrent of criticism of charitable societies here, one which raised genuine issues that fueled Tuckerman's defensiveness. Tuckerman was convinced that voluntary relief provided vital supplementary assistance to female seamstresses and other poor victimized by a market that generated inconsistent and insufficient demand for their unskilled labor. But some of Tuckerman's middle-class contemporaries, including the critics to his right, suggested that such supplemental home relief itself distorted natural market forces and imposed an additional downward pressure on wages.[41] Such relief constituted a disincentive both for employers to maintain subsistent wages on their own and for wage earners to move (either geographically or occupationally) out of glutted labor markets. And after all, could not private charity, like public relief, encourage indolence and improvidence by removing the all-important salutary "apprehension of want" from the minds of the poor?[42] No less than Tuckerman, these critics could draw on a large transatlantic discourse to support their position.[43]

But whether any form of outdoor relief—and by implication, such ministries of the poor as Tuckerman's—in fact served in some degree and in some locales to depress wages is an empirical question that carries less relevance here than the symbolic significance of the antebellum controversies over outdoor assistance. In some respects the intellectual and political currents of the time were establishing firmer distinctions between (male) wage earners and paupers dependent on public relief. During the early nineteenth century, state constitutions eliminated the property requirement for white manhood suffrage while also moving, in over a half dozen cases, to explicitly exclude from the polls all paupers, male as well as female, who had been "thrown on the town." This development, in some scholars' view, reflected the ascendant notion that independence and the capacity for self-governance resided not in property ownership per se, as traditional republicanism envisioned, but rather in the autonomous individual who could dispose of his own labor profitably and was not, in contrast to the recipient of public relief (or, for that matter, wives and children), ensconced in a legal relationship of dependence.[44] This ascendant notion of independence in turn was more congruent than the older one with notions of equal rights generated by the American Revolution, with the nation's commercial and industrial development, and with the fact that free waged laborers comprised an ever-growing proportion of the workforce of the free states. Tuckerman himself lent support to the insistent, formalized distinction between wage earner and pauper through his own efforts, in his official capacities, to ground rights and freedom in work and self-reliance. Challenging even the right of locomotion of vagrants whom he characterized as "unfit for self-direction," Tuckerman declared: "To me, indeed, it seems most absurd, to talk of the personal rights, and of the constitutionally guarantied freedom of those who not only have nothing, and who, though able, will do nothing, for self-support, but whose example is every day extending corruption to those around them."[45]

Tuckerman also was offering up here one of the guiding principles behind the New Poor Law and its attempted confinement of able-bodied paupers to workhouses: the "less eligibility" principle that sought to penalize such paupers, to ensure that their condition would be less agreeable, less desirable, than that of the "lowest class" of self-supporting, "independent" laborers.[46] This Anglo-American principle, like that of significant political and constitutional developments in the states, moved to firm up the distinction in condition and status between pauper and wage earner—to make certain that the former's situation remained unfavorable by comparison.

But there remained another basic sense in which the controversies over poor relief, and the activities and pronouncements of a Tuckerman, simultaneously acted to reinforce older patterns of social stratification. They did so by embedding and confirming in the public mind a deep and natural association between pauperism and all dependent poverty, on the one hand, and the precarious rewards earned, on the other hand, by free waged laborers specifically. This was an association that cyclical and seasonal unemployment, among other factors, did much to support, and it was one that anxious workingmen themselves continued to make.[47] No such close association could be plausibly made between pauperism and the rewards earned by American entrepreneurs or lawyers, and these upper-middle elements of the body politic were not, after all, the ones that Tuckerman had primarily in mind when he referred to those most directly susceptible to the corrupting influence of locomotive vagrants.[48] Through his various warnings Tuckerman emerged as one of the important antebellum American voices reinforcing Britain's free-market tough love tradition. Notwithstanding both his equivocations and ambivalence respecting orthodox political economy and his more forgiving attitudes toward the "deserving" working poor, Tuckerman joined Senior and others in constructing able-bodied, "undeserving" paupers as their own kind of slaves, and infectious ones at that. He added the weight of his authority to the transatlantic mythology in which poor laws, by fostering a debilitating and servile pauperism among able-bodied wage earners, effectively poisoned the labor incentives and work habits that existed naturally in a capitalist free market.

William Ellery Channing and
American Antislavery Discourse

During the period when Tuckerman was establishing his reputation as an authority on pauperism, his close friend William Ellery Channing, the foremost Unitarian minister in the United States, published his controversial volume *Slavery* (1835).[49] Where Tuckerman articulated a countermodel of pauperism that significantly figured in representations of free-market, free-labor wage incentives, Channing exemplified northern elite figures who prominently employed the countermodel of chattel slavery to nourish and legitimate the same representations. Consider Channing's enumeration of the evils of southern bondage:

> The motive from which he [the slave] acts debases him. It is the whip. It is corporal punishment. . . . I know it is sometimes said, in reply to these remarks, that all men, as well as slaves, act from necessity; that we have masters in hunger and thirst. . . . Still the two cases are essentially different. The necessity laid on us by natural wants is most kindly in its purpose. It is meant to awaken all our faculties, . . . to give us a new consciousness of the powers derived to us from God. . . . We are further told, that the slave is freed from all care, that he is sure of future support. . . . This is true; but it is also true that nothing can be gained by violating the great laws and essential rights of our nature. . . . God created him to provide for the future, . . . and he cannot be freed from this care without injury to his moral and intellectual life. . . . Be it also remembered, that the same provision which relieves the slave from anxiety cuts him off from hope. . . . It is true that the free laborer may become a pauper; and so may the free rich man, both of the North and the South. Still, our capitalists never dream of flying to slavery as a security against the almshouse. Freedom undoubtedly has its perils. It offers nothing to the slothful and dissolute. Among people left to seek their own good in their own way, some of all classes fail from vice, some from incapacity, some from misfortune. All classes will furnish members to the body of the poor. But in this country the number is small, and ought constantly to decrease.[50]

Much can be said about these antislavery, free-labor assertions of Channing's beyond the general sense in which, as an elaboration of the moral superiority of work incentives in a capitalist free market, they dovetailed both with Tuckerman's strictures against Massachusetts pauperism and with the remark from the British commission *Report* that opened this chapter. They suggest, for example, that Thomas Haskell's provocative thesis regarding the relationship between the market economy and the emergence of antislavery sensibility requires, at the least, some filling out. Haskell posits that in the late eighteenth and early nineteenth centuries, the market placed a premium on such bourgeois virtues as forethought and calculation, that it led to a "widening of causal horizons," and that it habituated British and American reformers to a greater sense of empowerment. They developed a new consciousness of their capacity—and of their moral obligation—to relieve forms of suffering that societies' privileged classes had hitherto accepted as inevitable.[51] Even if one grants Haskell's questionable claim that his thesis effectively precludes class interest as a driving force of the new antislavery humanitarian sensibility, Channing's remarks illustrate the presence of a crucial mediating variable. The privileged classes' market-derived consciousness of cause and effect and of their power to alter existing social conditions was, in the case of antislavery preeminently, attended by an equally essential consciousness that the group that was to be acted on, the individuals whose suffering was to be relieved, in fact possessed a higher nature. They possessed God-given moral and intellectual sensitivities and capabilities that were worthy of recognition and development. Quite striking here, too, is Channing's relative color blindness—the environmentalist conviction which he shared with immediate abolitionists that the institution of chattel slavery had an absolutely unique capacity to stunt and destroy individual agency, irrespective of the race to which slaves happened to belong.[52]

In the manner that Channing's remarks damn chattel slavery for its irremediable hostility to the unfolding of the bondsman's "nobler" faculties, they also champion an ethic of beneficent and "honorable" sternness, even harshness— the term *tough love* again seems appropriate. Humanitarian compassion for Channing, as for Malthus, Senior, and the Anglo-American free-market tradition generally, entailed a withdrawal of crippling paternalist restraints and protections that prevented individuals, and most clearly adults, from becoming self-directing and developing their higher faculties through confrontation with a "stern nature."[53] For all the economic support southern slaves ostensibly enjoyed in old age, they, like Tuckerman's able-bodied paupers, would be better off—spiritually and intellectually, if not necessarily materially—without a guaranteed subsistence. And this is in great measure due to something else in which Channing devoutly believed: the salutary impact on personal character that is generated by anxiety over the need to earn one's own livelihood. This belief, a cultural underpinning of nineteenth-century economic orthodoxy, has not received nearly the attention it deserves from historians.[54] Our own culture is acutely alert to the ways in which personal stress can create health and productivity problems inside and outside the workplace. Dozens of adult education programs today offer management and other self-improvement courses on how to rechannel such stress into productive and constructive avenues. Certainly there were contemporaries of Channing—including some of the labor-radical and proslavery critics of wage slavery to whom he was in part responding—who recognized that stress emanating from the fear of poverty and starvation might prove similarly negative; they perceived that it might, later if not sooner, paralyze and crush the capitalist wage laborer rather than prod him in a "positive" direction.[55] Channing himself might have given greater recognition to this possibility in other contexts. But instead he was intent here, in rebutting the wage-slavery defenses of chattel slavery, to counterpose the "necessity laid down by our natural wants" with the uncivilized, and unnatural, character of the slaveholder's lash. Channing, accordingly, was indisposed to draw a further distinction: he was unwilling to recognize the necessities driving waged laborers as any less ennobling than the disparate work motivations impelling all formally free and autonomous individuals, whatever their social position.

Recent scholarship has increasingly revealed complex Anglo-American cultural currents, including the redefinition of pain and suffering and the growing animus to corporal punishment, that Channing's perspective almost certainly drew upon and reflected.[56] His selective underscoring of the bodily dimension of the chattel slave's oppression—of the slave's dehumanizing relegation to the domain of domestic animals—was in absolute accord here with that of the radical abolitionists with whom he sharply disagreed on tactical and other matters. Like the thrust of abolitionist propaganda, Channing stressed those physical abuses—whippings, rape, the exposure and probing of the slaves' body at auctions—that, from his fundamentally religious perspective, were part and parcel of the slave's spiritual and moral debasement. If nothing else, those physical abuses constituted a systematic assault on the sacrosanct familial bonds and home life that Channing associated with humankind's development of its higher faculties.[57]

On the other hand, Channing was no more inclined than many leading abolitionists were to accentuate the slave's poor diet and other commonly minimal creature comforts, however much such criticism seemed implicit in the recurring antislavery theme that slaves, owing to their lack of formal autonomy and contractual rights, were not compensated for their labor.[58] Such lack of comforts, Channing and these abolitionists believed, did not scar the slave's soul and psyche in the way that daily exposure to repressive physical coercion did.

During this same period Channing was developing his differences from northern labor-movement activists and radicals such as Orestes Brownson. One might be tempted to conclude that Channing, along with like-minded abolitionists, was induced by primarily strategic considerations to highlight those aspects of the slave's physical abuse and suffering that seemed unique to his condition. After all, Brownson and other proponents of the wage-slavery argument had little difficulty establishing that living standards and working conditions for many free laborers in western Europe, and even for some laborers and their families in the northern states, were no better than those for southern slaves. They had more difficulty in demonstrating that the prostitution and other degradations eventuating from free-market coercions and the material impoverishment of free laboring populations were the absolute equivalent of the invasions of the chattel slave's body.[59]

But to impute deliberate strategy to Channing's selective emphasis among slavery's corporal evils is to be overly cynical. In private correspondence he criticized the class-exploitation doctrines of Brownson and other reformers on the ground that "the matter of complaint is, not that the laboring class wants physical comforts, — though I wish these to be earned by fewer hours of labor, — but that they live only for their physical natures."[60] Channing's relative disregard for the material deprivations of southern slaves and his accompanying abolitionist-like contempt for the argument that the existence of materially compensated and satisfied bondsmen vindicated slavery were symptomatic of a mentality that recoiled at the physical sensuality of northern free laborers.[61] To this extent Channing remained unusually ambivalent and cautionary regarding the ideal of a high-wage economy. He was among those public moralists who most resisted the increasing consumer orientation of American society that contributed to the rhetorical emphasis upon manual labor's strictly instrumental value. Paradoxically, Channing's very spiritual, nonmaterialist preoccupations brought him even closer than most abolitionists to "articulating a full-blown market ideology."[62] Channing outdid even many of the abolitionists in the degree to which he targeted as most ethically objectionable not the insufficiency of the bondsmen's recompense but rather its guaranteed, antimarket nature; not the degree to which slavery economically exploited human chattels but rather the degree to which it enforced their intellectual and moral dependence and otherwise debased and "humiliated" them.[63] In his indictment of slavery, Channing provided an eloquent and lofty analogue to the cruder attempts by northern employers themselves, when confronted by labor combinations demanding higher wages, to defuse such agitation by investing the developing urban wage-labor market with "supernatural sanction."[64] Channing's arguments, like similar specimens of elite commentary, dramatize one of the central ironies of the period: the tendency of social values that exalted the cognitive potential and "nobler faculties" of laboring populations to sustain an economic competition that frequently exploited wage laborers in particular.

Channing was not, to say the least, some kind of socialist (unlike his nephew, William Henry Channing), despite his undeniable revulsion both for the general pecuniary orientation of nineteenth-century capitalist societies and for such specific economic developments as factory division of labor.[65] But can one go further to conclude that such commentary as Channing's actually reflected capitalist class apologetics and interests in the manner that it legitimated legally free labor? Arthur M. Schlesinger Jr.'s bludgeoning of Channing years ago on these general grounds retains, for all its facile character, a strong element of plausibility. This is particularly so when one considers Channing's other dismissals of working-class economic deprivation, as in his insistence on the "struggles" and anxieties suffered by hardworking "professional and mercantile men."[66] Channing's response had one obvious context in the political climate of Boston and the larger society. Following the lead of the labor movement that emerged in the 1820s, the second American party system had embraced poverty, inequality, and working-class victimization as major issues of discursive contention. Yet in offering his own Whiggish refutation of such victimization, Channing was not entirely given over to self-deception. American capitalists and professionals did work long hours under competitive pressures, just as the lash of hunger, along with ambition, did generate at least modest movement up the American economic ladder by many working-class and lower-middle-class families. Still, there remains that element of plausibility in Schlesinger's hostile interpretation, one which is largely missing in Haskell's more subtle and brilliantly argued thesis that exemplars of the new Anglo-American humanitarian sensibility, among whom one would certainly include Channing, shared an "elective affinity" for highlighting the evils of formal slavery that in no significant degree incorporated the intention (at any level of consciousness) of advancing capitalist class interests and hegemony.[67]

Channing, it is also true, was like Tuckerman a sometime critic of British political economy, and particularly of the notoriously "unfeeling" Malthusianism that decreed poverty's inevitability, reproved the Christian "duty" of charity, and disclaimed responsibility for the "starvation" of the laboring poor.[68] But this does not in itself compellingly speak against his commentary as a form of capitalist apologetics. Along with other antebellum middle-class and upper-middle-class Americans, Channing was quite instinctively drawn to perpetuating and attacking the conventional demonic portrait of British political economy for purposes of promoting his own more humane, socially interventionist version of the free-market ethos.[69]

Yet Channing's own insistence on the ethical superiority to bondage of individual failure on the free market — through indolence, vice, or even "incapacity" and "misfortune" — remained sufficiently severe. And despite his suggestion that the number of poor should be especially minimal in the United States, the substance of Channing's idealization of the free laborer's formal autonomy hardly rested on the mythology of American economic exceptionalism; it did not rest on an invocation of the uniquely favorable life chances and positive labor incentives that ostensibly attended formal autonomy in the free states. Channing was rather reflecting in his thinking what C. B. Macpherson has characterized as "the political theory of possessive individualism." This was a set of "social assumptions" that, extending back to seventeenth-century English thought, consisted centrally of the notion that "man is free and human" — and unlike the chattel slave enjoyed autonomy in the marketplace — "by virtue of his sole proprietorship of his own person." In his own reliance on such non-American exceptionalist, more universal possessive individualist assumptions, in his emphasis on the value for laboring populations everywhere of bare legal self-ownership, Channing was closer, again, to many of his radical abolitionist contemporaries than to later antislavery Republican politicians who trumpeted northern economic opportunity, including the ability to rise out of waged labor.[70]

Indeed, there is also a close affinity in this regard between Channing's perspective and that of Josiah Conder, whose pamphlet attacking slavery in the British West Indies was cited repeatedly in the parliamentary debates on emancipation, and conceivably influenced Channing as well.[71] In its conflation of economic and moral considerations, Conder's *Wages or the Whip* (1833) was one of the quintessential specimens of early nineteenth-century British antislavery ideology, even as that ideology itself incorporated older Enlightenment notions that morality and wealth develop together.[72] Justice, Conder argued, always accords with what is gainful: "Doing right is, in the long run, cheaper than doing wrong"; slave labor was both immoral and a "blunder in arithmetic." So just as it had demonstrated already on the British mainland, free wage labor, as performed by emancipated West Indies blacks, would prove more profitable than the economically backward institution of chattel slavery, which Conder conventionally characterized as a coercive system that supplied no effective motives for labor and precluded "the stimulus of competition, the sense of gratitude, or the immediate prospect of advantage."[73]

Channing, it is also true, indicated that he, along with William Lloyd Garrison and other radical abolitionists, could never so completely or so comfortably as Conder reduce the case for emancipation to dollars-and-cents terms.[74] This was perhaps particularly so during the period when it became as apparent to Channing as to other observers that ex-slaves in the British West Indies were not maintaining the islands' previous levels of sugar production. Channing's *Emancipation* (1840) is an eloquent declaration, in light of the post-1834 economic patterns, that moral considerations might indeed conflict with pecuniary ones, and that the former by themselves justified Britain's eradication of the domestic and other abominations he believed inherent in chattel slavery.[75] Anticipating the argument of John Stuart Mill, among others, Channing also insisted: "Allow that the freed slaves work less. Has man nothing to do but work? Are not too many here overworked? If a people can live with comfort on less toil, are they not to be envied rather than condemned?"[76]

Yet Channing could never relinquish his faith in the work ethic and the salutary character of free-market labor incentives. Accordingly, he also insisted that the slacking off by the freed slaves was both predictable and short-term: "How natural" it was "to anticipate that men who had worked under the lash, and had looked on exemption from toil as the happiness of paradise, should surrender themselves more or less to sloth, on becoming their own masters! It is the curse of a bad system to unfit men, at first, for a better."[77] And by 1842, the year of his death, he was adding of the West Indies ex-slaves that "in general, they resumed their work after a short burst of joy. The desire of property, of bettering their lot, at once sprang up within them in sufficient strength to counterbalance the love of ease. Some of them have become proprietors of the soil."[78]

Channing's intellectual flexibility, as reflected in his shifting defenses of the British Emancipation Act of 1834, was largely his own.[79] Nonetheless, Channing still shared something basic with Conder, and indeed with many of his British and American middle-class and upper-middle-class contemporaries: a simultaneous receptivity to what Stanley L. Engerman and David Eltis term the "two related strands of the 'free labor' ideology."[80] Both of these strands affirmed the legally free wage earner's inducements for superior industry and productivity. The first strand was the celebration of the "prospect of advantage," the self-interest and the positive opportunity for the worker that resided in his formal autonomy. That opportunity included the free laborer's capability of escaping altogether from wage labor and capitalist authority into independent proprietorship. This was a condition to which Channing referred in the above remarks, and which, most recent historians have argued, was in fact the only sense in which ex-slaves and many white wage earners alike in this period thought of labor as being truly free.[81] But there was also the "more negative" strand of the free-labor ideology, one which at the least implied that the superior productivity of the legally free wage earner and the material needs that drove his industry might admittedly redound less to his benefit than to that of his capitalist employer. This implication, and the related appeal to the hirers of labor, that free wage labor's profitability derived from its cost-cutting cheapness, was more pronounced in antislavery pamphlets such as Conder's than in anything Channing ever wrote.[82] Yet this negative strand of the free-labor ideology retained a presence in Channing's own exaltation of the stimulating "natural" economic necessities to which the wage laborer is exposed by his formal freedom. Channing genuinely sought to elevate the laboring classes and in the process to change the world for the better, but these aims carried endorsement of the therapeutic utility of even the most negative work incentives in a capitalist labor market.

One could attempt to pursue this analysis yet further: one could inquire whether the critics of wage slavery merely exposed Channing's true "capitalist" colors and commitments, or whether they instead, in a kind of validation of Clifford Geertz's emphasis on the role of psychological and cultural "strain" in ideology formation, pushed Channing into mounting an exaggerated, distorted defense of his true commitments.[83] Such a question, however, remains unanswerable, if only because it at least partially would turn on the unconscious and therefore especially elusive and unverifiable motives that drove Channing's defense of free waged labor. But taking the commentary as it stands, one can certainly go beyond the conclusion that he had little or no quarrel with the wage system per se: even low or ungenerous wages retained value for Channing insofar as they stimulated the worker to develop all his faculties through confrontation with "hunger and thirst"—with the most basic coercions of competitive markets.[84]

However, one also should note another basic fact that has been rather neglected in recent scholarly debates.[85] Pronounced moral enmity to chattel slavery only lent reinforcement to a more widespread ideological tendency to sanction emerging relationships between northern capitalists and workers. Glossing over class inequalities in the free states was hardly the exclusive province of Channing and like-minded abolitionists. From the 1830s well into the 1850s—before, at least, a significant number joined the new Republican free-soil coalition—there were innumerable privileged and wealthy middle-class northerners who, because of their economic and political ties to the South or for a variety of other reasons, remained strongly hostile to antislavery activities.[86] Throughout the antebellum period these same individuals also happened to share the faith of Channing and many of the abolitionists in a competitive economic order, especially as it operated in the free states. The social attitudes of these "gentlemen of property and standing" stand as a reminder that there were always counter-tendencies that muddied and circumscribed the distinctive role played by intense moral antipathy to slavery in legitimating northern wage labor and capitalist hegemony.

Resistance to Free-Market, Free-Labor Ideology: Wage-Slavery Discourse

And what of the critics of wage slavery? In striking contrast to the North's "gentlemen of property and standing," this diverse group bitterly contested the favorable terms in which Channing constructed free-market labor incentives in the antebellum free states, objecting on this grounds to the rhetorical assault that Channing and the abolitionists made against chattel slavery. Historians who minimize ideological differences in antebellum America often maintain that even many of these critics of wage slavery, such as northern trade-union activists, remained part of a broad "bourgeois" or "liberal" consensus and sought only to make the market fairer, by rendering its distribution of rewards less skewed in favor of capitalist entrepreneurs and professionals.[87] True enough, what seemed to arouse the most intense outrage among many antebellum labor activists and trade unions was not the unfettered operation of market processes but rather particular forms of government intervention, such as the chartering of corporations and the creation of state workshops in prison labor. In their view such interventions rigged and distorted market processes to benefit capital and undermine free labor, thereby increasing the latter's vulnerability to the spur of poverty.

But this does not mean that historians should discount the hostility that even these labor activists, not to speak of the utopian socialists, commonly manifested for the basic market mechanisms that were commodifying labor, even as they typically retained a simultaneous attachment to private property itself. That the early Working Men's parties, for example, favored equality of opportunity over a strict socialist-like equality of condition does not mean that their thought is reducible to the objective of seeking "meritocracy within capitalism," as one of the most recent examples of the entrepreneurial perspective claims.[88] In part, much of the labor literature was anticapitalist — was antagonistic to the whole drift of American social and economic development — precisely because it rejected the notion that elite occupational groups performed legitimate and valuable functions; certainly they did not perform ones entitling them to greater material and status rewards than the nation's true producers.[89] But the Working Men's Parties and other labor activists also developed some aversion to capitalism itself owing to their inclination to conflate capitalist market mechanisms with the lash of poverty and its perceived ascendance. Between William Ellery Channing and such critics of wage slavery there existed a truly significant philosophical gap. These commentators might agree with Channing that the spur to fulfill one's basic material needs nagged at all human beings at some level. But with respect to wage laborers particularly, they considered Channing's basic distinction between the slaveholder's lash and the lash imposed by men's "natural wants" to be hopelessly arbitrary and specious.[90] To the critics of wage slavery, Channing's "masters in hunger and thirst" took on an exponentially more oppressive dimension when conjoined with the hireling laborer's condition of pronounced economic dependence and vulnerability to exploitation.

Representative of this commentary, already several decades old, is an 1847 editorial in Massachusetts's *Northampton Democrat,* one of the voices for the period's land and labor reform movements:

> There are many among us who talk loud and long of the "unrequited toil" of the black slave . . . but they have nothing to say in behalf of those whose toil brings them a much smaller recompense in proportion to the labor, when it is done from fear of starvation and other evils more serious than the drivers' whip, as though it were more sinful for others to live on the "unrequited toil" of the black slave than it is for us on that of our white brother. The black female is sometimes obliged to yield to the licentious desires of their owners . . . and we are told it is our duty to step in between them and take the part of the defenseless; but when our own white sisters and daughters are obliged to submit to the same evil in order to procure a comfortable living, we must point the finger of scorn at them and bestow our sympathies farther from home. . . . How benevolent and how much better it would be to change the system and compel the poor black . . . to labor for one-fourth less than he now does? . . . Why not emancipate white slaves and allow them to become their own masters [by giving them the means of subsistence — a portion of the soil], and *then* talk about black slavery?[91]

The *Northampton Democrat*'s "charity at home" first theme was typical of the wage-slavery position. In their crusade against southern black slavery, the argument went, northern abolitionists were guilty of practicing a distant and unjustified selective compassion. Abolitionists should redirect their energies to alleviating the more pressing plight of white wage laborers (the *Northern Democrat*'s "brothers" and "sisters") in their own backyard.[92] One might be tempted to characterize this argument as the antebellum version of "angry white males" lashing out against affirmative action for minorities. It is certainly possible that racially based animus and a sense of racial superiority (as embodied in the ambiguous reference to "poor black") fundamentally drove the *Northampton Democrat*'s remarks; possibly it really pinned the misguided nature of the abolitionist crusade on blacks' incapabilities for freedom. It is even more certainly true, as historians now routinely emphasize, that race and class (along with gender, ethnicity, and for that matter an individual's simultaneous membership in geographic, age, educational, and other groups) do not operate as discrete, competing categories or identities.[93] They necessarily interact and operate together, and for this reason alone one cannot truly divest the *Northampton Democrat*'s own perspective of "whiteness" from its comparison of northern and southern labor systems.

But different hierarchies of values and objectives still develop in different historical situations; and one could plausibly argue that the *Northampton Democrat*'s avowed doctrinal objection to the abolitionist crusade remained oriented toward class rather than race in one important sense: it was predicated on the essential similarities between the southern black bondsman and the northern white hireling. They were both eminently exploitable beings. It was precisely, indeed, the southern chattel slaves' relatively good fortune to be victimized by a slightly less exploitative system.[94]

Like many other examples of the counterdiscourse of wage slavery, the *Northampton Democrat* engaged in its own kinds of appropriation and exploitation—hostile borrowings, so to speak, from the rival contemporary discourses that added up to a "discursive transformation."[95] The paper appropriated the language of religious abolitionism when it repudiated as "sinful" the economic exploitation of free wage laborers and the wage earner's fear of starvation—an integral labor incentive of the capitalist free market. And it utilized the cost-cutting superior-cheapness arguments favored by such free-labor advocates as Josiah Conder by turning them directly against the antislavery cause: without the containment and extirpation of the capitalist-employee wage relationship as it currently existed, emancipating the black slaves would merely introduce them into this yet more predatory arrangement. The *Northampton Democrat*'s focus upon the theme of economic exploitation did not directly confront the more basic argument of Channing and other antislavery voices of the 1830s and 1840s. Those proclaimed the ultimate irrelevance of the possibility that chattel slaves retained a higher proportion of the fruits of their labor than northern wage earners did. It was the guaranteed and fixed character of the bondsmen's remuneration, together with the physical force inducing their labor, that was above all objectionable for its devastating effect on their moral and intellectual development.[96] But the substance of fundamental disagreement between the *Northampton Democrat* and such antislavery voices should nonetheless be apparent. The *Northampton Democrat* editorial typified much of the discourse of wage slavery by suggesting, contrary to Channing, that formal autonomy required a bedrock of economic independence and security for it to prove morally and intellectually elevating for the laborer. It further insisted that the hunger and the fear of starvation that intervened and drove many northern wage earners in the absence of such economic independence and security were at least as degrading and as morally illegitimate as the slaveholder's whip.

In many cases a similar insistence did expose unambiguously proslavery, racist propensities. Solon Robinson, the Connecticut-born agricultural writer from Indiana, followed numerous southern apologists in claiming that the greater wretchedness experienced by white wage slaves (and the justification for ten-hour factory legislation) reflected the fact that whites alone possessed the temperamental capacity to be overworked—to be fully responsive to want and the fear of want. Southern slavery, he argued, was a uniquely beneficent institution partially because the black race lacked such a capacity; blacks needed the force of the slaveholder's lash if they were to work at all, but they would not, for "any continued length of time," overdo their exertions at the behest of "avaricious masters."[97] But a good number of northern labor reformers did not hang their invidious comparison of free-market wage slavery to southern bondage on such conspicuously racist assertions. Still more explicitly than did the *Northampton Democrat,* a fellow land-reform voice, George Henry Evans, made the case against prevailing waged-labor incentives on race-neutral grounds. In contrast to Robinson, Evans expressed no doubt that were the slaves of the South freed "tomorrow," they would do exactly as the "poor seamstress" and other "white laborers of the north" were already doing. They would drive themselves ever harder to maximize their "cash" earnings—which in Evans's land-monopoly, exploitation scenario also meant that the primary beneficiaries would be their ex-slaveholder employers, who "would get as much labor performed by two-thirds or three-fourths of the number of their laborers as they now do by the whole."[98]

While attempting to justify his greater hostility to wage slavery, Evans nonetheless claimed to consider southern bondage and the "brute force" of the slaveholder's whip morally objectionable.[99] Did the *Northampton Democrat* as well? A May 1847 editorial attacked southern slavery as an "outrageous . . . violation of natural law," affirmed its opposition to slavery's extension, and offered implicit support for the Wilmot Proviso, which would exclude slavery from the territories acquired as a result of the Mexican War. Consistent with the paper's priorities, however, the editorial tempered this antislavery message with the declaration that the *Northampton Democrat* equally opposed the extension of white slavery within the existing states and territories as the result of speculation in and monopoly of the soil.[100]

The *Northampton Democrat*'s antagonism to chattel slavery may well have been genuine. But as with Evans, its priorities still invite, at the least, questions about the intensity of that antagonism, just as its editorials raise the same basic related questions about the motivation and function of commentary as do Channing's writings. For if Channing's exaltation of free wage-labor incentives advanced the cause of northern capitalist hegemony (whatever his conscious or unconscious intentions may have been), it was also possible that southern chattel slavery's legitimation remained a wholly unintended by-product of the *Northampton Democrat*'s targeting of northern wage slavery. Alternatively, one could, in the case of the wage-slavery critiques made by the *Northampton Democrat* and likeminded northern labor-reform voices, simply be exaggerating the ideological distance between such critiques and the blatantly proslavery uses that were made of them in this period.[101] Perhaps the legitimation of southern chattel slavery was indeed among the subliminal motives driving the *Northampton Democrat*'s brand of labor reformism, even if slavery's legitimation remained overtly peripheral to this brand of labor reformism.

The paper's perspective raises a different question as well: why do individuals of similar backgrounds and class locations often embrace widely divergent attitudes and ideologies? The *Northampton Democrat* was one of a host of northern voices in this period that, through the discourse of wage slavery, manifested a republican commitment to landed and other forms of economic independence, or even to various socialist blueprints, and in so doing contested the justice and legitimacy of ascendant market capitalism and competition. Yet a substantial number of these labor reformers and radicals were at the least small proprietors and in many cases (e.g., some of the leading Brook Farmers) enjoyed even more privileged middle-class and professional status. With the possible exception of religious affiliation, the latter group differed unappreciably in background and status from the mercantile and industrial elites supportive of the status quo.[102]

Why some privileged elements and not others in the antebellum free states developed a marked animus to capitalist market mechanisms remains unclear. What might seem more certain is that the labor reformers' vociferous insistence upon the limited options and opportunities available to northern hirelings — their insistence upon extensive economic coercion and wage slavery as matters of fact — reflected a minority viewpoint. Some historians have indeed underscored that not merely other elite Americans but an indeterminate number of "ordinary" young white males of working-class and lower-middle-class background continued to equate northern market-capitalist arrangements with economic opportunity rather than impoverishment.[103]

But I would emphasize in turn that historians cannot really be much more precise and definitive than this.[104] The apparent absence, outside antebellum labor-reform circles, of pervasive, acute disaffection for northern market-capitalist work compulsions and arrangements doesn't necessarily translate into a commensurately widespread, normative endorsement of those compulsions and arrangements. Nor does it invariably translate into uncritical acceptance of the more roseate American exceptionalist perspectives extolling the salience of positive work incentives.[105] If most early nineteenth-century Americans did not manifest the pronounced dissatisfactions and disagreements that were explicitly voiced by northern labor reformers, they may nonetheless have experienced their own milder, more implicit disaffection; they may have been no more than acquiescent to existing labor incentives and economic arrangements.

Whether it reflected a minority viewpoint or not, the exploitation-immiserization scenario offered by the *Northampton Democrat* and other labor-reform sheets was expressing particular sensitivity to the so-called crisis of skilled labor — to the early nineteenth-century "decline" of the artisan and the craft-apprenticeship structure.[106] In some ways labor reformers exaggerated this decline and its dire consequences for the working class as a whole. Small master artisans and journeymen in luxury trades and some other trades, for example, largely escaped skill dilution and emerged as market "winners" during this period. They appear to have kept up, at least in relative terms, with the gains in wealth and status enjoyed by craft entrepreneurs and other members of the business and professional classes.[107] There also occurred in the early nineteenth century an expansion of the capital equipment and other sectors of the economy in which skilled labor and autonomy persisted even as they were commonly narrowed through manufacturing division of labor.[108] As part of this general development, some specialized workers, such as the head cutters employed in New York's most "respectable" clothing establishments, also secured lucrative subcontracting niches.[109] Finally, "high craftsmanship" in the United States, sustained by "an effective system of long apprenticeships," simply had never enjoyed the strength of tradition that it possessed in Europe.[110] In some measure, labor-reform sheets like the *Northampton Democrat* were bemoaning the decline of a tradition that had never existed.

But there remains the other side of the picture. The wage-slavery complaints of the *Northampton Democrat* and others were addressing a series of unhappy and no less consequential developments that comprise the model of artisan declension and labor hardship still favored by many historians of the period. Technological advances, subdivision of labor, the growth of mass markets, and other features of American metropolitan industrialization did trivialize skills in the printing, tailoring, and other key trades and rendered truly skilled craftwork an increasingly small segment of the total manufacturing picture.[111] The journeymen members of such trades were among the biggest market losers: subdivision of labor and skill dilution in their own enterprises both reduced their bargaining power for better wages and eroded their chances of attaining prized self-employed status in an "honorable" trade.

Modern libertarian and other strong free-market advocates are particularly disposed to accept such developments as unavoidable consequences of changing demand and technology. As one of their number has remarked, "Blacksmiths as a group are not entitled, after the rise of the automobile, to the same income they had fifty years before."[112] Not surprisingly, the changes eroding the craft structure were viewed with less equanimity by early nineteenth-century trade-union movements, not merely in New York and Philadelphia but in Paris and London as well. Thus these movements charged, among other things, that the "property" of journeymen artisans—their labor expertise and their legitimate recompense—was being violated by the parasitic entrepreneurs who employed them.[113] But it wasn't only a question of journeymen's own deskilling; perhaps even less frequently was it a matter of their direct displacement in their own workshops by cheaper human labor tied to a machine or some other implement.[114] The additional threat for skilled journeymen, as well as for master craftsmen and other small employers who clung to honorable practices, lay in those enterprises more exclusively reliant on the cheap, and putatively dishonorable, labor of unskilled women, children, and immigrants. Some of these enterprises were outwork manufactories established by the same opportunity-seeking craft entrepreneurs who employed many of the embittered journeymen. Others were garret shops and other units that had independently sprouted up to form another portion of the bastardized sections of the trades. The larger point is that in an indirect if not direct sense, the female and child sweated labor used in all such enterprises, in American as well as European urban centers, constituted part of the same competitive labor market to which skilled men belonged.[115]

The concerns of such journeymen over their personal well-being were in some measure a function of growing relative inequalities with respect to those above them in the social scale. Their resentments were fueled less by any absolute decline in wages and living standards than by their failure to keep up in wealth and status with the craft entrepreneurs and others (some themselves former artisans) who had most successfully manipulated and monopolized the ways of mass production and other new economic opportunities. In abhorring the "fear of want" as a waged-labor incentive, the *Northampton Democrat* was likely referring, at least in part, to this phenomenon of increasing relative poverty. Many of the journeymen resentments over the same phenomenon were shared by the more economically insecure and marginal of their employers: the small masters who failed to join the ranks of the entrepreneurs while still managing to avoid falling altogether into the wage-earning class.[116]

The northern antebellum occupational structure was a relatively open and flexible one for white males, and possibly any dislocation and erosion in living standards experienced by even some of the most malcontented skilled artisans were short-term. Some journeymen, for example, no doubt did migrate to areas where they could satisfactorily practice their crafts, while others managed in time to enter other trades, including semiskilled factory work in newer and expanding industries, which in fact paid better than their previous craftwork.[117] The experience of all such artisans would support, in a sense, the long-term, aggregate, and rising per capita wage findings of many economic historians.[118] But as David R. Green remarks with respect to London's artisans over the same period, this rising "trend in real wages sits uneasily with the collective experiences" of American craftsmen, which were more immediately reflective of the increasing competition and other forces that were restructuring the labor process in many trades.[119] Much of the discourse of wage slavery, including that contributed by the period's trade-union movements, accordingly was addressing the here and now. And like other protest discourses and movements in American history, it was a discourse of anxiety and disappointed expectations, centering on the perceived immediate and accelerating crisis of urban skilled labor. Furthermore, the position of some of the commentators who developed the most sophisticated models of labor exploitation—Marx again comes to mind—was that even journeymen craftsmen who, along with factory workers and other wage earners, did manage to make real wage gains under early industrial capitalism remained economically servile wage slaves: they were simply better-paid slaves.[120]

In addition, a significant thrust of wage-slavery commentary also perceived a more thorough Europeanizing of labor incentives in the free states—what the *Northampton Democrat* and other labor-reform sheets quite unambiguously referred to as the "fear of starvation." In warning of the ascendance, even in the United States, of absolute poverty as a labor-market incentive, such commentary again included among the vulnerable those artisans whose skills were being undermined and devalued in the marketplace. And here we come to one sense in which the more nonelite, labor-generated contributions to the discourse of wage slavery, for all their own criticisms of recent capitalist developments, actually shared with mainstream views like Channing's at least a limited acceptance of free-market labor incentives.

Some Nonelite Voices on Free-Market Labor Incentives and the Unskilled Other

Consider the following attack on Philadelphia's newly established House of Refuge, or juvenile reformatory, that one Simon made in the *Mechanics' Free Press,* the official organ of Philadelphia's trade-union movement and Working Men's Party of the late 1820s and early 1830s.[121] "An institution having for its object the protection of vagrants and the *offals* of society, from whose gratuitous labour they enrich the institution, and deprive the *honest, moral,* and *virtuous* mechanic of his hard earned labour, must be viewed in a serious and apprehensive light," Simon wrote. He warned that the House of Refuge's vagrants "promise to perform at one half of the present given price," and in so doing these "idle, lazy, indolent, house-breaking scoundrels" would labor to profit not themselves but the directors of the institution, who will thereby "monopolize all description of work, and deprive the regular taught hatter, brush-maker, shoe-maker, tailor, &c. &c. of his living, aye his very existence, to establish their *aims,* and pocket the crumbs that ought to fall to the poor—and all for what—to support vagabonds!! . . . 'the very *refuse* of society.'"[122]

Simon's harshly worded attack on the inmates of the Refuge, which accommodated around 150 youth in its early years, drew on his coexisting animus toward the officials who ostensibly would share in the exploitation of the inmates' labor by indenturing them out to local entrepreneurs.[123] Institutional records reveal that the reformatory children whom Simon characterized as "vagrants" and "offals" were predominantly of poor and indigent working-class families; their fathers tended to be day laborers, sailors, tailors, or other unskilled and semiskilled workers. Most of the children, furthermore, had committed only minor crimes.[124] Of Simon's own identity and background one is likely to remain far more ignorant, a standard problem for historians who seek to extract meaning from the writings of such anonymous contributors to journals like the *Mechanics' Free Press*.

Yet Simon's bitter complaints regarding the competition and underbidding that was likely to result from this new source of cheap labor suggests that he belonged to the ranks of small master mechanics and journeymen for whom the *Mechanics' Free Press* spoke. His complaints were thoroughly of a piece with the protests that the male craft-labor organizations of the antebellum decades lodged against a whole series of cheap and "dishonorable" sources of manufacturing labor: female and immigrant sweatshop, or slop, workers; boy apprentices and helpers in various trades; and adult convict and almshouse laborers, to name but a few.[125] Each of these conflicts has its own distinctive history and features, shaped in part by the different traditions and conditions of different crafts.[126] For example, the vociferous protests that journeymen tailors and members of certain other trades lodged against the participation of working-class women in the competitive marketplace commonly encompassed protective, patriarchal considerations, as well as the more narrowly economic, self-serving ones that figured more prominently in the discrimination that white native-born workingmen supported against immigrants and free blacks.[127] Historians also have claimed that the complaining skilled artisans, in some cases at least, were exaggerating the seriousness of the competitive threat or were even scapegoating the more disadvantaged unskilled workers in confronting their own possible economic and status decline.[128] But the primary concern here is with a somewhat different issue: the implications for capitalist ideology and its diffusion carried by skilled laborers' antagonism toward a wide variety of unskilled laborers and by their attendant frequent indifference regarding the plight of the unskilled, both impulses suggested so clearly in the diatribe by Simon.[129]

Various manifestations of this sometime antagonism and contempt, sometime mere obliviousness, have not gone unnoticed by labor historians. These included the pains that masters and journeymen proudly took to differentiate their own skilled and manly competence from more subsistent, unskilled drudge labor, including the latter's supposed servile and unrepublican readiness to be exploited by capitalists. They also included the irrelevance of the "equal education" and other humanitarian reforms of the early Working Men's Party platforms to the immediate needs and condition of unskilled, largely immigrant labor. Still another manifestation of the disdain, or indifference, was the general failure of the leaders of these Working Men's parties, and of the craft-labor movement as a whole, to extend more radical anticapitalist versions of the labor theory of value to justify greater earnings for the unskilled segments of the workforce, even as they commonly invoked that creed in their own behalf when contesting the superior material rewards and status enjoyed by the so-called mental labor of employers and professional men.[130] In noting such manifestations of the division between skilled and unskilled, labor historians have pointed out some important institutional implications, primarily the absence of a more broadly based, sweeping, and effective challenge by organized labor to developing capitalist structures and prerogatives in the antebellum years, as well as in later periods.[131]

But one might draw attention here to a different, and rather neglected, ideological underpinning—or what was at least an ideological manifestation—of the ascendant power and authority of the capitalist order in this period, a phenomenon suggested in the remark of the French scholar Jacques Rancière that scholars commonly "look too much at worker culture and not enough at its encounters with other cultures."[132] Simon's criticism of the laziness and the moral turpitude of the Philadelphia House of Refuge inmates, included, as noted, an attack on the officials and other privileged elements that would profit from their labor. Nonetheless, that attack simultaneously contained an implicit acceptance of the value of putting the unskilled's feet to the fire—of rendering them more industrious, self-supporting, and "respectable"—although, of course, in constructive ways that somehow would not bring them into competition with the skilled and other laboring people who were already virtuous and independent.[133] One has here a partial, and in all likelihood an unwitting, endorsement of the fundamental bourgeois perspective of a Tuckerman or Channing. It is not that perspective's open endorsement of labor-market competition and of want and the fear of want as essential and salutary components of that competition; such an endorsement, and the dominated consciousness it would imply, was antithetical to the wage-slavery critique explicitly embraced by Simon and his cohorts. But one does have, in the besieged labor elitism of these spokesmen for skilled workers, the elements of a more amorphous, inchoate intersection with, and accommodation to, bourgeois individualist competitive

values. That intersection reinforced market capitalism through its significa-
tion that there were, indeed, morally and culturally inferior, even contemptible
elements of the laboring population, consisting overwhelmingly of the unskilled
and dependent poor, who needed to be driven. In terms of effort and related
personal virtues, as well as in terms of the value of their actual contribution to
the social product—two of the criteria commonly invoked in conceptualizations of distributive justice—skilled artisans were more likely than not to regard the unskilled wage earners and poor as inferior to themselves, just as they
adjudged similarly deficient the greater part of the capitalist and professional
elite.[134]

To suggest that Simon's harsh attitudes were common among members of
the labor stratum to which he likely belonged is not to claim that they were universally or even consistently held within that stratum. Antipathy for developing market arrangements and a related communitarian-republican inclination to
prioritize basic subsistence needs over the property rights of the wealthy could
and did lead some prominent labor activists to take a relatively tolerant view of
the poor relief extended to the most disadvantaged elements of society.[135] In
1844 printer and land-reform leader George Henry Evans characterized public
charity as "public partial retributive justice," and around the same time Democratic Party populist Mike Walsh added that "crime and pauperism are the legitimate and ever-existing progeny of a corrupt and blasphemous state of society
where honest labor is *legally* robbed, by various indirect means, out of more than
two-thirds of its just and hard earned reward."[136]

Significantly, however, Walsh also was following in the tradition of Simon.
His characterization of crime and pauperism appeared in the context of an attack on the proposal of the New York City almshouse commissioners to increase state revenue by contracting prisoners and paupers at a few cents a day
to private manufacturing enterprises. This process would bring these institutionalized populations into competition with self-supporting laboring men. "So
long," Walsh insisted, "as any portion of the working classes are unable to
obtain employment, every shilling earned by a prisoner or a pauper, for the
County or the State, is more than a shilling stolen from the famishing families
of the unemployed laborer." The "public authorities" should have a higher pri-
ority in finding "remunerated employment" for all such honest and independent, if unemployed, laborers.[137]

The Irish-born Walsh spoke, or so he claimed, for the unwashed, mostly
unskilled newly arrived immigrant Irish laborers, as well as for other segments
of the New York working classes.[138] Still, he was among those who, along with

Simon, captured the antagonism that skilled craftsmen harbored for the employment of House of Refuge inmates, adult paupers and convicts, and other pools of cheap labor in ways that would take the bread out of their own mouths. Largely owing to that antagonism and to the extent that they accordingly excluded the unskilled as beneficiaries of their demands, activist skilled artisans and their spokesmen in fact proved less radical than many upper-middle-class proponents of communitarian socialism. The last were the clerics, writers, and other intellectuals who could indulge more generous attitudes toward the unskilled segments of the laboring population, and who tended more readily to include them along with skilled labor in their blueprints for reform, precisely because they did not live under the shadow of economic competition from these unskilled segments.[139]

Historians have long argued over whether skilled craftworkers and other members of the upper echelon of labor—the so-called labor aristocracy in nineteenth-century Britain particularly—significantly strengthened capitalist hegemony by embracing and internalizing the putatively middle-class values of industriousness, temperance, individual self-improvement, and respectability and by generally identifying more with groups above them than with ones below them in the social and occupational scale. The focus here on perceptions of labor-market incentives sheds a bit more light on this long-standing issue. The "encounter" between craftworker and mainstream capitalist middle-class culture and the limited intersection of perceptions with respect to the unskilled and their moral and economic deficiencies did not constitute a case of clear-cut or definitive bourgeois ideological hegemony. Both inside and outside their literature of discontent, early nineteenth-century skilled-labor activists evidenced too much overt resistance to the notion that the market was achieving, or quite possibly could ever achieve, true distributive justice. This last would require at the least what to many artisans seemed problematic: that capitalist employers (along with the professional elite that was no more deserving of its wealth and status) would refrain from pursuing avenues of profit and power that undermined the basis of artisan mutualism. Nor could these same activists accept the fatalistic, though somewhat less complacent bourgeois argument, advanced by Joseph Tuckerman among others, that market forces and their existing distributional results were more or less inevitable, even oftentimes a necessary evil, with which members of civilized nineteenth-century societies had to reach an accommodation and at best could modulate through a more generous Christian spirit. On the contrary, along with communitarian socialists and participants in the land-reform and cooperative movements (and with some of their Chartist and other counterparts in Britain), activists in the craft trade-union movements shared the counterhegemonic belief that market-driven industrial changes were still reversible. The United States in particular seemed to them, in part because of its quantity of unsettled territory, a relative tabula rasa where undesirable institutions were not yet so entrenched that they could not be replaced with radically different social arrangements.[140]

Nor, in seeking to account for the limited intersection of perceptions between craftworker and mainstream capitalist middle-class culture with respect to the unskilled, can one for many of the same reasons regard as more satisfactory a common alternative interpretation to the top-down hegemonic thesis. This holds that the objective existence of abundant economic opportunity throughout the early nineteenth-century United States rendered skilled workers along with other Americans instinctive Lockeans — as naturally individualistic, acquisitive, and liberal as the entrepreneurial and professional middle-class elements above them in the social scale.[141] The mythology of American economic exceptionalism did, it is true, help shape in this regard artisans' very expectations and sense of entitlement. But it also stimulated artisan fears that their work incentives were being Europeanized. Against the Lockean explanation, it was artisans' perception of declining economic opportunity for themselves and their attendant alarm over the decreasing economic and social distance between them and unskilled labor that led these more advantaged segments of the workforce to more readily share bourgeois criticism of the character of the unskilled. Pressures and perceived needs that were sharply distinctive to the urban craftsmen of this period induced them to embrace, in effect, bits and pieces of the ascendant middle-class market ideology.

The possibility remains that this limited embrace of, or intersection with, mainstream middle-class capitalist values was more "spontaneous" than otherwise; genuinely "pluralistic societies," as Thomas Haskell has suggested, may be "almost impossible to tell apart" from hegemonic ones.[142] Some historians have argued, in this connection, that the skilled-artisan criticisms of the unskilled and the regard for industriousness and other character virtues that sustained the criticisms had roots within strictly indigenous working-class traditions, both in England and the United States. But those traditions themselves, it is also worth pointing out, did not develop altogether independently of the economic needs and pressures acting within the more skilled and respectable segments of the working classes. Their development does not speak against the possibility that the intersection of artisan values with mainstream middle-class culture was still in important senses both reflective of capitalist imperatives and hegemony and detrimental to craftsmen's best interests (even, one might add, if individual craftsmen and other workingmen indeed advanced themselves by observing the new norms of sobriety, industry, and economy).[143] Competitive capitalism helped structure urban craftsmen's needs and their very understanding of those needs. Although their consequent efforts to discredit House of Refuge inmates and other cheap and unskilled labor aimed to shore up their own market position and may have thus suited their short-term interest, such attacks on the character deficiencies of the unskilled also fostered labor disunity, thereby advancing the antagonistic interests of capitalist employers, and tended to valorize bourgeois competitive morality.[144] To borrow the terminology of Raymond Williams, skilled artisans' initiatives against competitive capitalism remained "in practice tied to the hegemonic," as evidenced by the very nature of their criticisms of the unskilled.[145] It should be possible to acknowledge this tendency while also recognizing that the criticisms of a Simon or a Walsh, like other attempts to discourage or exclude cheap labor, still remained a strategy to "strengthen labor and weaken capital" by removing "one weapon that capital may use against labor."[146]

A growing number of cultural studies exploring the nature of identity construction in the United States have emphasized how white working-class racism and whiteness itself have historically been "relational" phenomena. Irish and other European immigrant laborers, most notably, defined themselves in relation to blacks.[147] Along similar lines, and drawing on the work of the political anthropologist James C. Scott, some of these studies have furthermore claimed that white working class racism and racist language functioned as a kind of "public transcript" for underlying class grievances. It was safer and more expedient for relatively powerless and low-status white laborers, immigrant and otherwise, to employ violence and act out their frustrations and hostilities against still more impotent and low-status African Americans, as well as against marginalized white abolitionist elements, than it was for them to directly challenge the classes that monopolized economic and state power.[148] By defining their own class interests in racial terms, subordinate whites could more openly and acceptably articulate their opposition to domination and injustice. Some of these cultural studies, deviating from Scott's hidden-transcript concept, also suggest the unwitting nature of this process — the degree to which white workers embraced racism to conceal even from themselves their growing subordination to capital.[149]

Situated well down in the American social order, with only free and enslaved African Americans decisively below them, quite possibly the working-class unskilled immigrant Irish did develop a more univocal sense of self, one rooted in their compensating, superior whiteness, although one may suspect that even in their case identity construction was a far more complex business.[150] But with respect to the antebellum skilled master craftsmen and journeymen, it could hardly be said that they expressed their class interests primarily in racial terms, or that their expression of anticapitalist class hostilities remained part of a hidden transcript. Indeed, rather than stifling or concealing such hostilities from the more economically and politically powerful, and certainly rather than concealing their subordination to capital from themselves, these workers decisively incorporated anticapitalist, class-exploitation themes into their public language of protest. Moreover, the responses these same skilled workers gave to the evolving market economy suggest that their self-definition involved a good deal more than issues of whiteness — that in their case the relational thesis needs expansion beyond any narrow racial base. On the one hand, the artisans clearly and continually defined themselves in relation to the capitalists and professional men above them in the social scale — the individuals who appeared through artifice, cunning, and exploitative practices to be increasing still further their social and economic distance from "honest" laboring men. It must also be said that although race-based cultural studies downplay this particular relational phenomenon, they do not exactly overlook it. It is implicit in their model, according to which white working-class racism in the North was, after all, largely a form of psychological compensation that white wage earners in general developed in tandem with, and in response to, the economic vulnerabilities and indignities imposed on them by competitive capitalism and capitalist discipline.

The more unsatisfying feature of the race-based cultural studies is their general failure as yet to sufficiently consider other relational phenomena centering on the various groups of low-status others, in addition to free and enslaved African Americans, whom many skilled male artisans, at least, viewed as threats to their own social and economic well-being.[151] Such perceptions were shaped by a multitude of factors, including the demographics of a city or region, the economic health of its established and skilled trades, and the inclination of newly arrived groups actually to attempt intrusions into these trades. In Baltimore, Norfolk, or other southern cities, it was the sizable black populations, enslaved or free, whom native-born white artisans strove above all to exclude from their trades and to restrict to menial or domestic work.

In antebellum northern cities and towns, however, the black presence was more negligible, and employers generally lacked, in any case, the willingness of southern slaveholding interests to challenge white labor's racial antipathies (assuming that they did not share such antipathies) and force the issue of blacks' employment in trades. Of course, the very thoroughness of antiblack discriminatory workshop practices and race-based occupational segregation in the early nineteenth-century North might itself be taken as indication of the power of whiteness there—as illustration, indeed, of two sociologists' insistence that "the they-ness imputed to racial minorities by the dominant American society has been qualitatively different from the they-ness imputed to white ethnic minorities."[152] At the unconscious level particularly, whiteness has quite conceivably been more basic than other axes of American self-identification: by the antebellum period "more than two hundred years of slavery and discrimination had planted the notion of black 'otherness' and inferiority . . . deeply into the white psyche."[153]

But much of the scholarship of race-based labor history remains less persuasive in its suggestions that whiteness dominated more conscious, day-to-day anxieties and affirmations of antebellum identity.[154] During the 1840s and 1850s, for example, the very neutering of free blacks as a competitive threat in the northern states helped economic nativism attain greater salience there. Numerous American-born workers may well have retained, together with their nativist attitudes, virulent antiblack prejudices, ones that they shared with their immigrant competitors as well as with individuals outside of the working classes (such as George M. Weston). More specific fears of black economic competition likely also persisted among native-born workers.[155] Nonetheless, whatever their antiblack prejudices and apprehensions, native-born skilled artisans—or in other instances their sons who had been reduced to semiskilled occupations—quite understandably remained more preoccupied with, and often more overtly hostile to, the hordes of immigrant Irish, either for directly invading or for otherwise "degrading" or threatening to degrade traditional crafts.[156]

Native-born workers' perceptions of their immigrant Irish competitors, to address one final related issue, may have themselves incorporated conceptualizations of whiteness: those perceptions may have drawn on Anglo-Saxon cultural strains, common enough among elite Americans, that regarded individuals of "Celtic blood" as marginally white, as constituting the most inferior of the several white "races."[157] Yet it is not at all clear how prominently such conceptualizations figured in working-class nativist antagonisms.[158] The possible existence of a racialized component within artisan anti-Irish nativism would itself seem, moreover, to reinforce one's sense of identity formation as a many-sided, often dynamic, and elusive phenomenon. It strengthens, rather than weakens, the general argument here: that the self-definition undergone by northern white male craftsmen during the antebellum decades of incipient industrialization—during the so-called crisis of skilled labor—was shaped not merely or even primarily by skin color per se; it was shaped at least as much by confrontation with an assortment of negative reference groups of varying ethnicity, gender, and age.[159] These latter groups were broadly linked together by their ostensible lack of a respectable economic expertise or competence; and needless to say, finally, members of such groups were likely to view their own cheapness in very different terms than the comparatively advantaged artisans who disdained and feared it.[160]

Distinctive concerns and anxieties over declining economic opportunity impelled early nineteenth-century skilled laborers to share with elite commentators certain perceptions of the unskilled, dependent, and "undeserving" poor. Even as they feared and resisted competition from the unskilled, craftworkers affirmed, if less consistently than a Tuckerman or Channing, the value of the motivational spur of economic compulsion for those they deemed to be of an undisciplined and economically dependent character. To the extent that they did so, craftworkers lent support to the period's formative free-labor, free-market ideology.

This support carried negative implications for the solidarity and effectiveness of labor movements, but its dimensions should also not be exaggerated. The anticapitalist resentments simultaneously held by many of the same craftworkers limited their embrace of basic market mechanisms. The limited and problematic nature of such an embrace has already been touched on in another sense, and with respect to a wider swath of wage-earning and other "ordinary" antebellum Americans. It was suggested there that the apparent absence of widespread, sharp disaffection for northern market-capitalist arrangements outside of antebellum labor reform circles didn't necessarily denote pervasive, normative endorsement of those arrangements. This issue, the nature of antebellum compliance with competitive capitalism, is one of several explored in the next two chapters.

3

"Buy Cheap, Sell Dear"

In *Hints toward Reform* (1850), Horace Greeley, the Whig editor of the *New-York Tribune,* reflected on "the recent Strikes in different parts of the country, but especially those of the Iron-Puddlers of Pittsburgh":

> An observer's attention will be arrested by their emphatic though uncon-
> scious condemnation of our entire Social framework as defective and
> unjust. Probably half of these men never harbored the idea of a Social
> reconstruction—never even heard of it. Ask them one by one if such an
> idea could be made to work, and they would shake their heads and say,
> "It is all well in theory, but it will never do in practice." But when they
> come to differ with their employers, they at once assume the defectiveness
> of our present Social polity, and argue from it as a point by nobody dis-
> puted: "We *ought* to be paid so much (thus runs their logic) because we *need*
> and they can *afford* it." "*Ought,*" do you say, friends? Don't you realize that
> the whole world around is based upon *must* instead of *ought?*

And then, to demonstrate the truth of his last point, Greeley directed this question at the striking workers, invoking their behavior as consumers rather than wage-earning producers:

> Which one of you, though earning fifteen dollars per week, ever paid five
> cents more than the market price for a bushel of potatoes, or a basket of
> eggs, or a quarter of mutton, because the seller *ought* to be fairly paid for
> his labor, and couldn't really *afford* to sell at the market rate? Nay, which
> of you well-paid puddlers ever gave a poor widow a dollar a piece for mak-
> ing your shirts when you could get them made as well for half a dollar.
> . . . Step forward from the ranks, you gentlemen that have conducted *your
> own* buying and hiring through life on the principle of "*ought,*" and let me
> make my obeisance to each of you! I shall do it right heartily, and with no
> fear of being rendered neck-weary by the operation.

"Heaven speed the day," Greeley added, "when, not only in Iron but in all branches of Industry, the reward of Labor shall be regulated not by 'must,' but by 'ought.'" Therein lay the true and definitive remedy for strikes and, indeed, "the seeds of a revolution more gigantic and pervasive than any Vergniaud or Kossuth ever devised."[1]

Hints toward Reform has an overtly didactic orientation; it consists primarily of lectures to "Popular Lyceums and Young Men's Associations, generally those of the humbler class, existing in country villages and rural townships." As one who had himself risen out of such a class into the journalistic and political elite, Greeley believed himself well qualified to dispense advice. And he had a multiple agenda in *Hints:* that of promoting both land reform and an American Fourierist-style, or Associationist, reorganization of labor and industry; exposing the folly of strikes and other forms of "Jacobinic clamor"; and serving generally as "a reconciler between Conservatism and Radicalism."[2] Greeley's determination to use *Hints* for these ends could only have been increased by the workplace developments and class antagonisms of the late 1840s and early 1850s. This was a period marked by hundreds of bitter strikes such as those conducted by Pittsburgh's skilled iron puddlers, and one in which unions virtually abandoned their earlier practice of allowing employers into their folds as members.[3]

Greeley was a pedagogue and a moralist whose perception of the strikes around him was colored by his Whiggish yearnings for class harmony. Yet the progressive social vision of which those yearnings formed a part—a vision in which "abstract Justice" would replace "Necessity" as the basis of "mankind's dealings with each other"—could entail considerable evenhandedness.[4] Greeley was just as inclined to censure employers' invocation of the "principle of competition"—the supposedly natural ruling force of supply and demand in the marketplace—as a pretext masking their personal greed as he was disposed to dismiss labor unions' "tyranny of capital" rhetoric as self-serving "Locofoco" demagogy.[5] Precisely, moreover, because of his desire to steer a middle course between conservatism and radicalism and between capital and labor, Greeley refrained from conceptualizing the market mechanism and the antagonisms it generated as a function of unequal exchanges that invariably benefited one set of class interests at the expense of another. Unlike John Bray and other contributors to radical political economy, Greeley would not reduce "Buy cheap, sell dear" to a set of structural arrangements by which, inevitably, "capitalists shall continue to be capitalists and working men be working men . . . that enables one class to live in luxury and idleness, and dooms another to incessant toil."[6]

Still, like Bray, and indeed like Karl Marx, though with a far less metaphysical and elaborate theoretical model, Greeley did insist that the ascendance of monetary motivations and exchange value over moral imperatives and use value, together with capital-labor antagonisms, was systemic: "Buy as cheap as possible and sell for the most you can get. That is the actual law." Whatever their greed, "the merchants or employers" did not "make" the law. They too were driven by it, "though they probably admire it more than we do." In any case, Greeley informed wage earners, "be sure that it can never be changed on one side only."[7] Basic economic and social changes were possible, indeed necessary, but they entailed committed, responsible action by all parties. To this considerable extent Greeley resisted the notion that the market mechanism of "Buy cheap, sell dear," along with other principles that he identified with orthodox political economy, were inexorable economic laws, destined to operate without reference to human will or preference. Like other reform-minded Americans of this period, Greeley groped for a formula that somehow would supplant the market mechanism—the source of economic "anarchy" as well as class antagonisms—while preserving other attributes of American capitalism that he deemed truly valuable. These attributes included private property itself together with a differential-reward system that recognized the genuine contributions to society made by various skilled and "mental labor" employments.[8]

I am not insisting that Greeley's rhetoric can by itself bear the full weight of the analysis that follows. Nor am I suggesting that he accurately read the minds of all American wage-earning workers at midcentury. Undoubtedly, for example, there remained many small-producer and other ordinary Americans, industrial wage earners included, who were enthralled by the consumer goods–making and other capabilities of market capitalism, and whose quite unequivocally positive attitudes toward existing economic arrangements reflected the genuine benefits they derived from these.[9]

My position is rather that Greeley's remarks, whatever his objectives and biases, do credibly describe the attitudes of some wage earners, likely many of them, and that they offer a useful springboard into consideration of several major issues. By ascribing a kind of divided mentality to the iron puddlers and other workers—a mentality in which resignation and resistance alternate and mix—those remarks invite, first, another look at the "ambiguities of consent . . . the complexity of popular consciousness under capitalism," as T. Jackson Lears characterizes Antonio Gramsci's particularly seminal contributions in this area of inquiry.[10] Greeley, moreover, linked the workers' divided mentality, along with the pervasive opportunistic, antisocial behavior that he found in all quarters of antebellum society, to the society's putatively dominant "Buy cheap, sell dear" market imperative. That imperative, or ethos, also merits attention, if only because recent scholars continue to question its actual prominence. In this and the next chapter, I advance several principal arguments. Although hardly endorsing, to begin with, a standard neoclassical economic view that "the history of all hitherto existing society is the history of interactions among selfish individuals," I do find that the antebellum spectacle of proprietary capitalist and professional success generated undeniable pressures, both practical and ideological, for acceptance of the work motivations, character traits, and behavior most conducive to individual economic self-aggrandizement, even as the same spectacle also occasioned persisting resistance to these.[11] Examination of this spectacle extends the previous chapter's discussion of skilled craftsmen's limited reinforcement of capitalist ideological hegemony. By taking as one of its subjects the performance of occupational groups above free workers in the social hierarchy, the discussion here is also intended as a counterpart to the earlier chapter's focus on the representations of waged-labor incentives contributed by the base countermodels of paupers and chattel slaves.

Reinforcing the pressures for ideological compliance with the occupational hierarchy, I furthermore find, were two other interrelated developments that have been neglected by historians. These were the increasing complexity and muddiness of the landscape of "true" producers and the additional encouragement to an ecumenical definition of *producer* offered by the growing prominence of diverse consumer appetites. These developments, together with the spectacle of upward economic and social mobility, generated a certain intellectual uncertainty and befuddlement in militant labor and other radical circles. Although they did not lead to a normative endorsement within those circles of the emergent capitalist and professional hierarchy and its legitimacy, they did encourage, during the last decades of the antebellum period, some retreat from the most anticapitalist formulations of the labor theory of value and the radical conceptions of distributional justice that those formulations entailed.

Divided Mentality

Consider the first dichotomy to which Greeley's remarks point. On the one hand, possibly a majority of the wage-earning classes either had remained at the most conscious level altogether oblivious to proposals for a wholesale revamping of competitive capitalist arrangements, or they had rejected these as practical possibilities.[12] Nevertheless, Greeley insisted, the very nature of these workers' agitation, their willingness to conduct prolonged strikes over wages, embodied an unequivocal "condemnation" of the current "Buy cheap, sell dear" economic system as "defective and unjust."

One could advance alternative constructions to Greeley's. Historians have commonly argued, for example, that nineteenth-century workers' willingness to use trade unions and strikes to extract a better wage in fact signified their acceptance of the capitalist "rules of the game," which treated their labor as just another marketable commodity.[13] A few historians, notably John P. Diggins, go further along these lines and completely reverse Greeley's interpretation. They argue that strikes and other actions designed to promote the economic self-interest of workers exposed the hollowness, the hypocrisy, of labor's community-oriented, "republican" language of protest. The language itself may well have been anticapitalist insofar as it repudiated as unprincipled and selfishly anticommunity that which was favored by employers: "the unregulated, unlimited operation of the vaunted 'law of supply and demand.'"[14] But for Diggins, in particular, there was no truly divided mentality among such antebellum workers precisely because their competitive capitalist actions with respect to their employers, as he interprets these, spoke immeasurably louder than their words; those actions were a far more authoritative indicator of their genuine beliefs and values.

Greeley, the Whig visionary, may have been engaging in some wishful thinking: possibly he exaggerated the degree to which the strikes around him constituted unspoken recognition by their participants of the unjust and deficient character of prevailing economic arrangements. Yet identifying the agenda behind Greeley's characterization does not itself invalidate the characterization. It does not require us, first of all, to accept Diggins's contrary argument that strikes and other labor actions in this period constituted a clear-cut abandonment of labor leaders' community-oriented and anticapitalist "Fourth of July" rhetoric. This is too simple an interpretation; it would be equally facile to interpret Marx's willingness to subsidize his work with money he took from Engels, the son of a wealthy capitalist, as an expression of complicity in capitalism that betrayed his socialist principles.[15]

One might also note the fundamental discrepancies between Greeley's representation of workers' divided mentality and James C. Scott's influential "hidden transcript" thesis respecting the values and behavior of subordinate social groups. Greeley's striking workers, of course, enjoyed free speech and other basic constitutional and democratic rights that obviated their need to censor themselves as a matter of practical survival. They remained far less impotent and oppressed, and had less need of a hidden transcript, than the southeast Asian peasants that are the principal subjects of Scott's analysis. It is at the relatively private level, at least in Greeley's account, that American wage earners were in fact at their most quiescent and accepting of capitalist arrangements and the material rewards they received under these. In contrast to Scott's hidden transcript model, these workers' critique of prevailing class relations and their sense of economic injustice acquired a meaningful level of development only through their public struggle and their need to articulate their critique for a public audience. It is their public behavior, or transcript, which gave fullest expression to their anticapitalist class hostilities.[16]

Notwithstanding his focus upon pronouncedly subaltern social elements—the peasants for whom "power relations virtually preclude open forms of resistance and protest"—Scott indicates that it is also with respect to the "working class under capitalism" that he objects to Gramscian notions of "dominated consciousness." Scott suggests that, Gramsci to the contrary, for the second as well as the first group it is "more accurate to consider subordinate classes *less* constrained at the level of thought and ideology, since they can in secluded settings speak with comparative safety, and *more* constrained at the level of political actions and struggle, where the daily exercise of power sharply limits the options available to them."[17] Scott's criticisms of Gramsci would seem to apply similarly to Greeley's description of privately quiescent and publicly confrontational American wage earners.

On the other hand, the hope that Greeley invested in strikes as incipient signs of an ethically based, revolutionary repudiation of the ruling societal dictum of "Buy cheap, sell dear" does dovetail with one of Scott's further observations: "The fact that social criticism remains ideologically limited can never . . . justify the conclusion that the group which makes that criticism is prevented by a hegemonic ideology from consciously formulating a more far-reaching critique."[18]

Did the private quiescence and fatalism—the grudging acquiescence, as it were—that Greeley characterized as part of the divided mentality of antebellum wage earners derive from a top-down "hegemonic ideology"? Did it reflect the extent to which the market-capitalist norms and values of more dominant classes had successfully infiltrated American workers' consciousness? Greeley himself refrained from asserting such hegemonic influence in the sense that he explicitly minimized the agency of the more powerful classes—recall his claim that although employers used the "law" of "Buy cheap, sell dear" to further their interests, they did not "make" that law.

Gramsci himself might well have argued otherwise. But along with some of his followers, he might still have found Greeley's description of fatalistic workers highly congenial to his own concept of subordinate groups' hegemonically generated "contradictory consciousness."[19] Even the most passive forms of consent, not to speak of more enthusiastic agreement and conforming behavior, remain for many neo-Gramscians a manifestation of the degree to which dominant norms and ideologies fix the framework of analysis of the existing system, rendering other possibilities unviable in the minds of consenting groups ("It is all well in theory, but it will never do in practice"). In the wake of Gramsci's contributions, ideological hegemony remains the overriding Marxist explanation of why so few subordinate and oppressed elements, inside and perhaps outside of capitalist societies as well, have developed a revolutionary, egalitarian consciousness: "Suffering is not necessarily cognitively illuminating."[20]

Yet such issues remain highly contestable, in some measure because Gramsci himself "paid scant attention" to the "material conditions of hegemony." While thus noting the degree to which dominant ideologies structure workers' and other exploited groups' sense of their social possibilities, some neo-Gramscians also emphasize that "the ideology that expresses this hegemony must correspond to real interests and aspirations"—must dovetail with at least the minimal needs of the exploited—if it is to maintain their consent and acquiescence.[21] Other scholars on the left, while agreeing with Gramsci's followers on the salience of modern working-class apathy and resignation to capitalist forces, proceed to deny that such attitudes need at all reflect the worker's internalization of dominant values and beliefs. As Terry Eagleton notes, such scholars are more impressed with the role played by putatively nonideological factors—political and legal repressions and above all Marx's "dull compulsion of the economic"—in keeping people in their places.[22] Symptomatic of the related debates over the meaning of Gramsci's concepts, some scholars characterize "the dull compulsion of the economic" as itself falling within the rubric of ideological hegemony.[23]

What useful conclusions from such disagreements can one draw for the discussion at hand? The previous chapter suggested that among early nineteenth-century American skilled artisans specifically, bourgeois capitalist hegemony played some role in fostering critical attitudes toward the character of the unskilled. The concluding part of chapter 4 suggests the workings of top-down ideological hegemony in a further, comparably limited respect: it points to the battery of "commonsense" elite arguments that, apart from the sheer economic exigencies and political-legal constraints inducing compliance with market-capitalist arrangements and the hierarchy those arrangements generated, could only have discouraged consenting workers' sense of viable alternatives to those arrangements.

This is hardly an argument for the significance of a more full-blown ideological incorporation, one in which dominant groups successfully indoctrinate or infuse exploited workers with their own strongly normative attachment to market capitalism. By the same token, the emphasis in this and the next chapter upon ambivalent and merely acquiescent working-class attitudes—upon the absence of pervasive, genuine value harmony—stands apart from the recent liberal-consensus interpretations of Diggins, Joyce Appleby, and other scholars. Like anticapitalist Gramscian perspectives that highlight full-blown ideological incorporation, such interpretations assert the centrality of working-class normative attachment to market-capitalist arrangements. Where they crucially differ is in their tendency to attribute such attachment to workers' more or less autonomous appreciation that America's liberal capitalist conditions might in fact satisfy their economic and other interests hardly less genuinely and fully than they satisfied the interests of more elite groups.[24]

Again, I don't doubt that such liberal-consensus interpretations accurately characterize the perceptions and values (as well as the actual experiences) of a good number of wage-earning and other plebeian Americans, in the antebellum as in other periods.[25] By the mid-nineteenth century if not earlier, immigration and other factors had rendered American working-class cultures too diverse to permit easy generalizations respecting their responses to early industrial and market capitalism. Nonetheless, and in some measure precisely because of that diversity, one should remain wary of interpreting the overriding absence among most antebellum wage earners of overt resistance to capitalist work incentives and arrangements as proof of their enthusiasm, of their affective and strongly normative endorsement of those incentives and arrangements. The absence of discernible objections on the part of the many to the market-capitalist economic race is not, that is to say, ipso facto proof that they viewed that race as either particularly desirable or inherently "fair," meriting at most minor "adjustments" in the existing arrangements.[26] Apropos here are the observations of the economist Lester Thurow that individuals—specifically but by no means exclusively modern-day Americans—have

> different levels of preferences. They have preferences about the rules of the economic game and the distribution of prizes that it should generate; but they also have preferences about maximizing their own position in the current economic game, no matter how much they like or

dislike the economic game they are forced to play. . . . there is nothing self-contradictory in seeking to become extremely wealthy and powerful in our current economic game yet believing that in a better economic game there would be no "extremely wealthy" economic prizes to be had. . . . There is nothing logically self-contradictory in these two preferences, since they simply do not exist in the same domain.[27]

Thurow perhaps overstates the disjunction between his two levels of preferences. Conceivably, some reformers and others—those for whom an alternative, ethically superior set of social arrangements holds particularly compelling importance—are unusually inhibited in engaging in the existing self-maximizing economic game. But the more important point here is Thurow's own: participation in the game does not necessarily imply normative assent. Participants do not invariably perceive the market-capitalist race as even remotely equitable or otherwise desirable. Some may accord it no real legitimacy at all. And just as the two levels of preferences Thurow describes are not "logically self-contradictory," so they suggest (contrary to Diggins) that the propensity of nineteenth-century wage earners to speak a public language of anticapitalist republican ethics while engaging in economically self-interested behavior is not so easily reducible to hypocrisy. Like Greeley's (and Gramsci's) observations, those of Thurow point to a divided mentality, one in which a predominant attitude respecting the existing economic game among Americans who earn wages (as well as among any number of others who are not working-class wage earners) inclines toward a not particularly self-conscious acquiescence.[28] And at least in the mid-nineteenth century, Greeley further suggested, such an attitude was especially marked in the laborer's private arena of day-to-day struggle with adversity. Accumulating grievances and hostilities that erupted into periodic confrontations with employers, the laborer relinquished this acquiescence most of all in the public arena. Here the otherwise latent and even unconscious desire for Thurow's "better economic game" became more sharply manifest.

One can overstate the magnitude of this cognitive development or, even more particularly, its practical implications. One can acknowledge with Greeley that strikes and other confrontations with employers both manifested and stimulated nineteenth-century workers' sense of "the defectiveness" of their "Social polity." But generally speaking, this did not lead them to aggressively seek, through their strike activity, clear-cut alternatives to the capitalist rules of the game. More often workers reached for something less ambitious, more immediately realizable: higher wages (or better working conditions) under a somewhat less inequitable application of those capitalist rules. One cannot disregard all indications that the latter, more modest impulse — unionism "pure and simple" — came to be more rather than less embodied in the "trade union ideology" that developed in the 1850s.[29] As suggested, Greeley was engaging in some wishful thinking in anticipating that a more exalted "revolutionary" alternative to "Buy cheap, sell dear" imperatives sooner or later would emerge triumphant from the social ferment around him.[30]

The Salience of the Market Ethos?

In the second part of his remarks quoted above, Greeley illuminated still more the constraints under which wage earners acted and which impeded their general capacity to formulate and press for a better economic game. Here Greeley accused the Pittsburgh iron puddlers and other striking workers of practicing a double standard. Even as they cried foul against employers who could "afford" to pay better wages, they routinely subordinated considerations of a needs-based ethics to ones of economic self-interest in their own day-to-day dealings as consumers with various sellers of goods and services.[31] Far from practicing what scholars have characterized in other contexts as communal, "neighborly exchanges," the striking workers even sought the most advantageous terms with individuals, such as poor widowed seamstresses, who still more than themselves had to resort out of extreme economic need and vulnerability to repeated "desperate exchanges" in the labor market.[32]

Again, one should duly note Greeley's Whiggish hostility to class antagonisms, which extended to his efforts to circumscribe the legitimacy of strikes and partially drove his representation here of striking workers as something less than paragons of virtue and benevolence. Yet in this instance too Greeley offered some genuine insights into the pressures on the striking wage earners to compromise their more principled impulses, to "buy cheap and sell dear," and generally to behave as self-interested actors in their everyday commercial transactions. The more economic of these pressures, oftentimes driven by declining real wages, are more or less obvious. Less so are the ideological pressures that induced workers, along with other Americans, to behave in economically self-interested maximizing ways.

A number of recent scholars, it should be acknowledged, have thrown into question the distinctive prominence during the antebellum period of a "noncommunal," economically self-maximizing "Buy cheap, sell dear" market ethos. If they have not altogether denied the occurrence of so abrupt or significant a series of events as an early nineteenth-century market "revolution," economic and other historians have nonetheless claimed, for example, to find incremental, quantitative evidence of the preexisting importance of market-oriented acquisitive behavior among eighteenth-century freehold farmers, as well as among other social groups.[33]

While raising questions about the distinctive salience of commodity relations and commercial morality in the antebellum period, this scholarship poses less of a challenge to Greeley's views than do historians who deny that salience altogether—who minimize for this period the economic and cultural force of an acquisitive "Buy cheap, sell dear" imperative. In fact, this challenge is Anglo-American in background, and it is also characteristically associated with an insistence on the significant scope and socially responsible nature of state intervention in the early nineteenth-century economies of England and the United States. Some elaboration of these points is merited here.

In 1905 the historian A. V. Dicey popularized the view that social reform in England had been obstructed until the late nineteenth century by laissez-faire governmental practices and the ideological doctrines that sustained these. He was subsequently joined by J. L. and Barbara Hammond and other left-leaning, in some cases Marxist, historians who were highly critical of the Industrial Revolution's impact on the working and living conditions of the British laboring classes earlier in the nineteenth century. E. J. Hobsbawm typified the view of this "pessimistic" school of interpretation when he wrote with respect to both ideas and social policies, "Few countries have ever been more totally dominated by an *a priori* doctrine than Britain was by *laissez-faire* economics."[34]

Dicey, Hammond, and like-minded scholars were taking their cue partially from some of Greeley's prominent British contemporaries. There was, for example, Thomas Carlyle, with his attacks on the "do-nothingism" of laissez-faire government, the "pig philosophy" of the political economists, and the tyranny of the "cash nexus"—the single-minded concentration on pecuniary gain—that was dehumanizing and corrupting English social relations. The poet and Tory Robert Southey similarly bemoaned the dominance of laissez-faire practices and the underlying commercial morality, and in much the same terms as Greeley: "Throughout the trading part of the community everyone endeavours to purchase at the lowest price and sell at the highest, regardless of equity in either case."[35] There were dozens of others, including John Ruskin, Karl Marx, and Charles Dickens, who sounded the same basic criticisms, albeit from a diversity of political and ideological perspectives (e.g., romantic, Tory, Christian socialist, utopian and "scientific" socialist, Chartist, and that of artisans wedded to the "customs" of their trades). Such a convergence of disenchantment illustrated, as no society had previously, the truth of the remark that "most utopias envision perfectibility as the reverse image of a pecuniary culture."[36]

But to take up the thread of the opposition to Greeley's critical perspective, these disparate voices of Victorian protest hardly went unchallenged even in their own lifetimes. There was, notably, Thomas Babbington Macaulay, who did not deny the unprecedented penetration of market-economic relationships, undergirded by wondrous mechanical power, in early nineteenth-century England. Macaulay, however, insisted on favorably comparing these to the barbarous tenor of earlier social networks (which Greeley himself did not deny despite his criticisms of the market ethos) and on acclaiming the material benefits and elevating implications that these newer relationships held for the laboring as well as the trading classes of Britain.[37] The scholarly nemeses of Hobsbawm and the pessimistic school, such "optimistic" interpreters of the Industrial Revolution as R. M. Hartwell and Thomas Ashton borrowed many of Macaulay's arguments. But with the benefits of perspective, and together with other students of the evolution of the British welfare state, they placed still more stress on another point as well. They insisted that, excepting perhaps for the briefest of intervals in the early nineteenth century—far briefer than Dicey claimed—laissez-faire government in Britain was something of a fiction. Most members of Britain's commercial and industrial middle classes may never have come to share Ruskin's or Dickens's intense revulsion for the crass and inhumanitarian features of "Buy cheap, sell dear."[38] But as Hartwell and like-minded historians suggested, leading early nineteenth-century statesmen and public servants (whether Tory, Whig, or Benthamite radical) were persuaded that an individualistic free-market morality had to be reined in and constrained in important ways, if not for wholly beneficent reasons, then for purposes of responding to popular agitation and averting social disorder.[39] The early Victorian state remained laissez-faire insofar as it lacked the developed administrative structure needed to follow through effectively on interventionist legislation and to truly control "the forces let loose by industrialization."[40] Nonetheless, it enacted a battery of pioneering statutes that were not wholly unsuccessful in such matters as regulating slums and sanitary conditions, limiting the employment of children and women in factories and coal mines, and contributing to the growth of charitable relief agencies at both the central and the local government level.

Numbers of the period's upholders of capitalist free-market morality exceeded Macaulay in their disapprobation of many of such state interventions. These interferences, they held, would do more through their paternalism to psychologically enfeeble and otherwise damage the English laboring classes than would an unrestrained, and supposedly dehumanizing, capitalist cash nexus.

One commentator thus indicted factory hours and other "short-sighted" if "well-meaning" legislation in 1846 as a "partial return to the principle of slavery" and as a "protection of the working classes against the consequences of that competition which is the result of their freedom"; he declared that "it is impossible to have all the good of slavery without some of its evil."[41] Another was similarly appalled by the profusion of public statutory assistance as well as private, voluntary aid and by all the "mischiefs wrought by this ill-regulated tenderness." He further lamented in 1853 that "there is scarcely a conceivable form of human want or wretchedness for which a special and appropriate provision has not been made. . . . From the cradle to the grave, they [England's poor and suffering] are surrounded with importunate benevolence."[42]

Nevertheless, the expansion of the British regulatory state that was condemned by some of the more unbending early Victorian economic individualists was interpreted more favorably by many later scholars, and it was in light of this expansion that the legal historian P. S. Atiyah thus concurred with the optimistic interpreters of the Industrial Revolution: "The influence as well as the unattractiveness of the philosophy of *laissez-faire* were exaggerated at the point of caricature by its contemporaries."[43] Gertrude Himmelfarb refers to many of the same acts of socially responsible legislation in likewise arguing that laissez-faire "was less rigorous, both in theory and practice, than was once supposed." Himmelfarb invokes the Victorian record of private philanthropy to further explode the myth that Victorianism was "ruthlessly materialistic, acquisitive, and self-centered." The "industrial-capitalist-bourgeois revolution" hardly acted to "reduce everything to 'cash payment,'" Marx and other misguided critics to the contrary.[44]

Greeley was one of these Anglo-American critics of the cash nexus, and the remarks he directed at the iron puddlers and other striking workers in 1850 — including his claims that they based their own everyday transactions on relentless "market values" rather than on considerations of "abstract justice" and the "intrinsic value" of the goods being exchanged — are fully comprehensible only within the context of Anglo-American mid-Victorian sensibilities. Historians from Louis Hartz through Dror Wahrman have commented on the distinctive absence of a middle-class "language" in early nineteenth-century American discourse; to the significant extent that preexisting political circumstance, if not necessarily underlying social realities, already rendered American society a more thoroughly "middle-class world," it had, presumably, less need of a middle-class idiom or discursive construction.[45] Yet this particular linguistic absence, whatever its dimensions, should not obscure what was no less significant at the time: the profoundly transatlantic, Anglo-American character of the early nineteenth-century criticisms of commercialism and the market mechanism.

Greeley wore the hat of Whig partisan as well as transatlantic social reformer and visionary: he was simultaneously operating within the context of his own nation's political-ideological controversies. This meant that like Carlyle and other of his British contemporaries, Greeley closely identified the ascendance of an antisocial, individualistic cash nexus with laissez-faire government. Specifically, he held accountable a generation of "sham" Democratic "let alone" policies and rhetoric that, ostensibly supporting the rights of America's "common man," had only served to encourage the self-aggrandizing, socially anarchic commercial morality of "Buy cheap, sell dear." Greeley retained an American liberal thinker's characteristic faith in the benefits of a progressive, free-labor market society. Thus he was both appreciably less feudal and retrograde in his yearnings than a Carlyle or Ruskin and less radically progressive than Marx. Nonetheless, he shared their overriding sense that a laissez-faire-stimulated, selfishly individualistic market imperative was fundamentally inhospitable to a genuinely good and just society.[46]

But this brings us to those historians who tend to make the same association as Greeley did between laissez-faire government practices and individualist self-aggrandizing values but who then, like Atiyah and Himmelfarb with respect to Britain, proceed to draw the opposite conclusion from Greeley and minimize the existence of both in antebellum America. One of the best recent examples is the legal historian William J. Novak. Contrary to the persisting stereotypes of liberalism in this period, Novak argues, a robust common-law tradition of publicly responsible government intervention—at the state and the local if not the national level—rendered veritable fictions the self-regulating "free market" and the attendant "devotion," within and outside the judiciary, to "private interests." With particular reference to the licensing, inspection, and other statutes that defined the "potent . . . public control over buying and selling in the antebellum public economy," Novak further concludes: "In theory, the nineteenth-century market was 'free.' In practice, it was 'well-ordered' and 'well-regulated,'" contrary to the "resilient national myths" or "shibboleths" of "possessive individualism," "laissez faire economics," and "free enterprise."[47]

The focuses of Novak's book are such matters as public health and safety, and his chapter on "public economy" in the antebellum states is the closest he comes to venturing into the domain of labor markets. For this reason his arguments remain something of an indirect denial of what Greeley was both insisting upon and lamenting: the great degree to which a self-maximizing market imperative had superseded the principle of "ought" in the relations between employers and wage earners. Yet Novak's implications and their conflict with Greeley's perspective seem unmistakable. This is partly because Greeley, in pointing out the double standard practiced by justice-seeking striking operatives, was suggesting the virtual omnipresence in antebellum society of a powerful ethos embodying "devotion to private interests." But the challenge that Novak poses to Greeley's perspective is also inherent in his attacks on a more explicit target: the "legal instrumentalism" that Novak characterizes as one of the reigning paradigms within his own discipline of legal history. It is the "caricature" drawn by Morton J. Horwitz and other legal instrumentalists—that of a relentless "jurisprudential commitment to dynamic individual [particularly entrepreneurial capitalists'] rights over the people's welfare"—that Novak is primarily targeting and seeking to replace with his own paradigm emphasizing the potency of common law–grounded, publicly responsible government intervention in the nineteenth-century market economy.[48]

Horwitz's influential paradigm is clearly more in tune than Novak's own with the market ethos described by Greeley. In describing the birth of modern contract law, Horwitz observes:

> In a market, goods came to be thought of as fungible. . . . in a society in which value came to be regarded as entirely subjective, and in which the only basis for assigning value was the concurrence of arbitrary individual desire, principles of substantive justice were inevitably seen as entailing an "arbitrary and uncertain" standard of value. Substantive justice, according to the earlier view, existed in order to prevent men from using the legal system in order to exploit each other. But where things have no "intrinsic value," there can be no substantive measure of exploitation and the parties are, by definition, equal.[49]

My primary concern here is not with nineteenth-century legal developments. And the criticism of Novak and of critical legal scholars generally, that legal instrumentalism is guilty of "reductionalist materialism," may hold considerable merit.[50] But Horwitz's reference to the demise of "intrinsic value" and the victory of economic subjectivism in modern contract law (whether specifically generated by dynamic capitalist interests or not) remains congruent with the impressionistic descriptions of the market economy made by Greeley and such British commentators as Ruskin and Southey.[51] Of course, the cash nexus they were criticizing, whereby market values pushed out considerations of a thing's "intrinsic value," remains elusive—it is not so readily documentable or quantifiable as the British factory acts noted by Himmelfarb or the New York City inspection statutes emphasized by Novak. But many significant social and cultural phenomena do not lend themselves to easy quantification, and as a kind of intellectual historian, I sense that Novak, for all his impressive documentation of the publicly oriented regulatory acts that applied a brake to the sway of "private interests," has missed something important in the culture. Demonstrating the extent to which concrete, socially responsible state actions may have belied the "myth" of laissez-faire government—of state-sanctioned entrepreneurial "free enterprise"—is not to rule out the force of the self-aggrandizing market imperative noted by Greeley and many of his contemporaries.[52] It is arguable that at least as characteristic and influential as the common-law traditions that Novak cites is the sentiment reputedly expressed by a Fall River, Massachusetts, factory agent in 1855: "I regard my work-people just as I regard my machinery. So long as they can do my work for what I choose to pay them, I keep them, getting out of them all I can. What they do, or how they fare, outside of my walls, I don't know, nor do I consider it my business to know. They must look out for themselves, as I do for myself. When my machines get old and useless, I reject them and get new, and these people are part of my machinery."[53]

Novak's book, like the recent studies that have probed the complexities of Victorian British middle-class ideology, may well constitute valuable correctives to older sweeping paradigms and facile stereotypes. Nonetheless in my view it fails to satisfactorily address the emergence in the early nineteenth century of an Anglo-American free-market capitalist competitive ethos, the importance of which was attested to by the bundle of terms and sayings routinely employed, by its critics especially, to characterize it. Along with "Buy cheap, sell dear," terms like "the cash nexus" and adages such as "The worth of a thing is what it will bring" and (one that the Fall River factory agent would have particularly taken to heart) "Every man for himself and the devil take the hindmost" became fundamental to the lexicon of romantic poets, labor-movement leaders, and utopian and other breeds of socialists (and to proslavery conservatives as well, for that matter). As noted, the phenomena that stimulated the use of these maxims, like the market ethos itself, may well remain mostly qualitative and elusive, although historians like Paul E. Johnson have persuasively described some of these even if they have not quantified them in a way that meets the standards of economic historians.[54]

It furthermore seems probable that if as recent economic and other historians suggest, self-maximizing acquisitive behavior in fact widely preceded the accelerating market revolution of the early nineteenth century, it was the industrial and urban capitalist components of that revolution — the rise of exploitative sweatshops and the spread of more impersonal factory and urban environments — that above all accounted for the unprecedented sensitivity to a competitive free-market ethos, as signified by the new pejorative vocabulary.[55] I am inclined, in any case, to believe that commentators like Greeley had it more right than not: that a self-maximizing, competitive free-market ethos (broadly encompassed within the conventionally noted change from "status to contract") did come to increasingly govern a plethora of social and economic relationships.[56]

That such a development necessarily merited the alarm and censure extended to it by Greeley and others is another matter. The early twentieth-century German sociologist Georg Simmel, to cite one notable example, could find much to commend in the cash nexus, philosophically embracing monetary exchange's depersonalization of human obligations as a source of individual liberation.[57] Yet more to the point are the necessary qualifications that are in order, beyond those already noted. Notwithstanding the remarks of the Fall River factory agent, the cash nexus and its erosion of social ties and responsibilities remained checked and tempered in nineteenth-century American society in any number of ways (and not merely in rural communities most removed from market forces). Apart from the government regulations of the type emphasized by Novak, these constraints included community networks based on race, ethnicity, and gender; charitable, fraternal, and other, often religiously based, voluntary associations; and even the more rarefied utopian ideals articulated by the likes of Greeley.[58]

Recent sociologists have invoked such evidence to challenge Karl Polanyi's influential claims as to the increasing "disembeddedness" of economic behavior under early nineteenth-century capitalist market forces. They maintain, contrary to Polanyi, that modern economic transactions — hardly less than ones in earlier, "nonmarket" societies — have continued to be shaped by and embedded in a panoply of personal relationships, status considerations, and other social expectations and obligations, all of which tend to constrain individual economic actors' narrow and opportunistic pursuit of economic gain.[59] In some ways complementing this sociological position is Thomas Haskell's argument, offered in particular connection to the rise of organized antislavery in the late eighteenth and early nineteenth centuries, that although capitalism and its premium on contractual relations may have weakened responsibility to nonfamilial dependents, they also elevated the importance of keeping commitments and in this and other respects increased responsibility to strangers. Haskell's emphasis is upon how the cognitive, humanitarian propensities for checking some of the extreme forms of suffering induced by individually self-maximizing behavior (above all, the more blatant coercions of chattel servitude and the slave trade) were intrinsic to capitalist market morality itself — to the very evolution of Anglo-American capitalist societies.[60]

I don't completely discount such viewpoints and the evidence upon which they draw. Certainly, if only because of the operation of such constraints as philanthropic enterprise and interpersonal networks upon individual economic opportunism, one might be receptive to the position that early nineteenth-century American society, like its British counterpart, viewed and treated not merely chattel slavery but also poverty and other centuries-old social evils with less callous disregard than its eighteenth-century predecessor. Similarly, one not only might be impressed by the growth in social sensitivity and indignation about misery but also might be inclined to regard that cognitive growth as disproportionate to any actual increase in misery. Such arguments have long been particularly central to the anti-Marxist, optimistic interpretations of the Industrial Revolution's impact on British working-class living standards.[61]

Yet I would still insist, with Greeley and similarly minded commentators, on some considerable space for countervailing viewpoints. Early nineteenth-century capitalism and its unregulated excesses may have quite quickly brought into play a variety of antidotes — the public regulations, private philanthropic efforts, community networks, and the like that ameliorated individual suffering and exploitation. But these remained partial antidotes, and some of the worst excesses, such as the sweatshop, hardly abated and even grew during the course of the nineteenth century. The self-aggrandizing, socially destructive materialist values and behavior of the market referred to by the new pejorative vocabulary were hardly figments of overheated imaginations, the fictitious products of a nineteenth-century "romantic nostalgia for a pre-industrial past."[62] The individualistic and competitive market imperative was indeed underlying and compelling, if also amorphous, within nineteenth-century culture, something with which the aforementioned constraints and checks existed in a characteristically dialectical tension.[63]

4

Further Social Constructions
of the Market Mechanism, Economic Justice,
and Competitive Hierarchy

THE SELF-MAXIMIZING market imperative did not constitute the only ideological and cultural force pressuring Greeley's striking workers, notwithstanding their protests against acquisitive employers, to engage in commercial transactions that similarly subordinated considerations of "ought"—ones that subordinated the yet more desperate needs of widowed seamstresses and others. Additional ideological constraints, endemic to antebellum culture and not unrelated to the competitive market ethos, likely operated upon wage earners in a more indirect and subliminal fashion to help shape the double standard described by Greeley.

Upward Mobility

One of these remained the pull of material and occupational success, embedded in the objective possibility that economically self-maximizing behavior in a socially fluid society might result in the wage earner's upward movement into the class of employers. This is not to slight the ambivalence that many of the period's workingmen and labor movements retained toward the spectacle of capitalist and professional achievement and the success ideology that sanctified such achievement. In fact, the very appeal of upward mobility might foster this ambivalence. Consider an article in the Boston *Pilot* of 1853, one of a series on wage earners in American manufacturing establishments who resorted to strikes for shorter hours or higher wages. The article observed that workers directed most of their jealousy not at wealthy capitalists who had inherited their wealth, as one might expect, but rather at employers who had started life poor like themselves. Certainly it happened that "the laborer of yesterday becomes a master today, while the master sinks into the condition of a laborer." Most working-men, the newspaper insisted, wished to exchange places with employers, yet while a few succeeded, most failed and remained envious and hostile toward those who did rise from their ranks.[1] The attractions of occupational mobility generated their own antagonisms toward such mobility.

Just as Horace Greeley had his progressive Whig-utopian blueprint, so the *Pilot*'s perspective was dominated by a conservative, Catholic agenda. The paper identified America's individualistic and pecuniary Protestant culture, and the Protestant Reformation generally, as the source of exploitative working condi-tions. It maintained that not unions and strikes but only the ascendancy in the United States of the more corporate and paternalistic Catholic religion—"a gen-eral return to the Church"—would constitute an effective remedy for the class enmity and jealousy, as well as the material deprivations, of workers who failed to rise.[2] Although the *Pilot,* moreover, rejected essential features of the mythol-ogy of American economic exceptionalism—of pervasive and substantial movement by the white male poor up the social scale—it embraced other criti-cal components of that mythology in making the case for worker jealousy. Thus did the paper elaborate on the points noted above while adding some more:

> The poor man in American can rise. He *may* become an employer [or a politician or a lawyer]. . . . They who have succeeded, compared with them who have not, are less than ten in a hundred. Yet, every man wished to rise,—tried to rise, and almost all, in the beginning, had nearly the same chance. You will notice that the greater number of those who have risen,—not all, thank God,—lose the old feelings they had for the labor-ing interest, and begin to favor the cause of the middle and upper classes, into which they had entered. . . . What made them rise? Most people will answer—industry, sobriety, economy, a steady determination to improve every opportunity, and—luck. Most workingmen, in speaking of the mat-ter, would attribute their rise to one or more of these causes.[3]

"Almost all, in the beginning, had nearly the same chance" to rise. In pinning equal opportunity for white males on the absence of ascribed advantages and overt discrimination, the *Pilot*'s remarks typified the comparatively unsophisti-cated, formulaic character of the mythology of equal opportunity in the ante-bellum period.[4] But more germane here is the paper's accentuation of the social costs exacted by what remained a relatively (compared to Old World societies) competitive and meritocratic economic and social order. Those costs included but extended beyond the jealousy and hostility of wage earners who were left behind in the competitive race. They also encompassed the predatory mentality

—the loss of all fellow feeling for the laboring "interest"—that came to distinguish the minority of workers who emerged from the crucible of competition with the achievement of capitalist or professional status.[5]

One might argue that such commentary as the *Pilot*'s reveals a good deal more about that paper's attitudes and objectives than it does about the attitudes of real workers. But there are several reasons why the newspaper retains value as a commentary on those attitudes. First, real workers would not necessarily prove more revelatory and credible for a good number would likely be indisposed to acknowledge the jealousy noted by the *Pilot*.[6] Second, the labor press itself, with reference to workers in a variety of contexts, frequently lamented the job competitiveness, avarice, and "petty jealousies" that impeded the development of collective consciousness and solidarity.[7] Third, within the structure of intensely competitive, relatively small-scale proprietary capitalism that generally distinguished early nineteenth-century enterprise, the capacity of the wage-earning population to generate middle-class and upper-middle-class success stories was real and long-standing, yet no more so than the ambivalence that labor movements might themselves express regarding those stories.

Indeed, for the *Voice of Industry,* the primary organ of New England's ten-hour movement, the *Pilot*'s theme of worker jealousy toward those who had risen carried less significance than the issue of why workers might wish to rise in the first place. In 1847 the *Voice* pronounced the pervasive American "dignity of Labor" rhetoric hardly less wearisome and objectionable when it flowed from the lips of one, such as Lowell's Mayor Bancroft, who possessed certifiable wage-earning origins as a former factory operative:

> What a compliment to the dignity of Labor, to hear the Mayor of the city of Lowell citing the fact [in a speech before President James K. Polk] that he had *risen* from away down, down, down in the low obscurity of an operative! . . . If the hard labor of the workingman and woman is thus rewarded, why do we see so many, like Mayor Bancroft, abandoning hard labor "with their own hands" and availing themselves of the "hard labor" of *others'* hands? . . . If labor of the hands is thus honored and rewarded, why such a universal scramble (Mayor Bancroft among the rest,) to forego its honors and rewards, by entering into speculation and trade? . . . He also knows that all this prattle by demagogues, about the honors and rewards of Labor, is for effect—mere gull phrases to cheat and bamboozle the masses. . . . his election to office depended upon his leaving the occupation of operative—"getting above" a workingman and becoming a speculator and non-producer.[8]

One might well consider *ambivalence* too mild a term to capture the distaste, the hostility, that the *Voice of Industry* expressed here for laboring people who managed the "rise" into more lucrative and prestigious nonmanual means of livelihood. Labor-reform voices like the *Voice* insisted that poverty and the fear of poverty were the dominant work incentives driving American operatives and other wage laborers, and they characteristically went beyond the Boston *Pilot* in their claims that substantial social mobility was an unrealistic expectation for the majority of these laborers. But here the *Voice* was repudiating the morality of one particular consequence of such mobility: the paper was lamenting the fact that the American "producing" classes were themselves readily capable of spawning social parasites.[9] On the one hand, the *Voice* and other labor-reform voices maintained that increasingly in the United States, as in the Old World, one could not earn a "just reward" and make a decent living—let alone become "wealthy"—through one's own "useful, productive labor."[10] On the other hand, they were also claiming that the wealthier and more esteemed members of society might be and often were merchants, or manufacturing capitalists, or lawyers and politicians, but they would never be, or remain, manual workers, as the history of Mayor Bancroft attested.

Yet these themes of economic exploitation did not achieve hegemonic authority even within the confines of the defenders of the "producers' republic." Hostility to the spectacle of capitalist and professional achievement, accompanied by ideological resistance to the distorted social arrangements that sustained and sanctified such success, could not completely override the appeal of such success. This was particularly so among more moderate labor-reform voices, those which retained some regard for the acquisitive appetites frequently manifested in their more unadulterated forms in the top rungs of the American economic hierarchy. Such voices reserved their most intense aversion for poverty when it constituted one of market capitalism's basic mechanisms for driving waged labor—when it was intertwined with degrading vulnerability to the power of avaricious employers.[11] Yet reformers rarely idealized conditions of poverty and economic subsistence under other circumstances, even if they remained more accepting of these conditions. As Paul K. Conkin notes of George Henry Evans and the National Reform Association of the 1840s, "The popular NRA pamphlet, 'Vote Yourself a Farm,' appealed to acquisitive desires. In it Evans stressed citizens' joint ownership of the public domain and everyone's right to have his own home and till the earth for a profit."[12]

Who Are Society's Producers? Conundrums Faced by
Radical Versions of the Labor Theory of Value

That ambivalence which Evans and other labor reformers retained toward the spectacle of capitalist and professional success was also fueled by persisting confusion or doubt over a fundamental question: which occupations made genuinely productive contributions to society? Who were society's "true" workers, and who were merely its parasites. There was, undeniably, the more radical and confrontational tendency within the nineteenth-century labor-reform tradition, exemplified by the remarks of the *Voice of Industry,* that seemed to betray little such confusion as it quite unequivocally challenged the legitimacy of upper-middle-class "mental labor" employments. One can also discern how the sarcastic and hostile remarks of the *Voice* respecting Mayor Bancroft, like the different observations of Horace Greeley and the Boston *Pilot,* may have been stimulated partially by key late antebellum developments, including the manifestly hardening class divisions under an increasingly large-scale and corporate industrial-capitalist structure and, with this, the declining capacity of individuals to make their fortune without substantial initial capital.[13]

The thrust of late nineteenth-century mainstream trade-union ideology suggests that over time these economic developments came to occasion as much acquiescence and resignation as they did overt bitterness and hostility to the prevailing social hierarchy. But during the first part of the nineteenth century, a different set of circumstances, precisely by fostering doubts over the identity of the true laborer, acted in its own way to blunt the more unequivocal antagonism illustrated in the *Voice.*

One of these circumstances, and among the distinguishing features of mercantile and early industrial capitalism, was the emergence of numerous master artisans or mechanics as full-time craft entrepreneurs, individuals who no longer performed significant manual labor themselves. Recalling the Boston *Pilot*'s central point, one should acknowledge that this kind of upward mobility into the more prosperous ranks of the middle class could generate antagonism and jealousy among other artisans, both masters and wage-earning journeymen—among those who could not emulate with the same results this aggressive and competitive behavior. Nor need one believe that the justifications offered by emergent craft entrepreneurs for their roles—including their defense of a new model of individual success that prioritized "unchecked capital accumulation" over mastery of a craft and mere economic independence—did much to assuage the antagonism and jealousy of the artisans left behind.[14] But the point meriting greater emphasis here is that this phenomenon of the early nineteenth-century economic landscape, prosperous master artisans operating their own businesses, while characteristically maintaining some presence in their work-shops, did muddy the ideological and attitudinal waters. As one scholar notes, the labor-reform, or "rebel artisan," distinction between "the producers and the non-producers"—its attempts to identify the true worker—was "a clumsy weapon" when it confronted this entrepreneurial phenomenon: "To justify an attack against the aristocrats they had to be identified as wealthy non-producers, living off the labor of others; but all the rich were not [or at least, some much less obviously so than others] 'idle parasites.'"[15] Only gradually, intermittently, and in some localities not at all, would manual laborers left behind in the economic race come to publicly denounce, in the manner of the *Voice of Industry,* the worker-turned "entrepreneurial ideal" as unambiguously parasitic and illegitimate.[16]

In addition to the masters-cum-full-time-businessmen, another basic feature of early nineteenth-century commercial and industrial capitalist development, the sheer plethora of new kinds of employments, did its part to generate uncertainty over the nature of true work and the identity of those who performed it. With particular reference to the labor "dogma" opposing state charters for corporations, Louis Hartz observed that "the laborers identified themselves with the only legitimate members of the community. . . . As markets expanded and the factory system appeared, workers failed persistently to grasp the legitimacy of the functions that the new merchant, banking and entrepreneurial groups were performing. Their thinking was wedded to an older period governed by a simple master-workman relation in which both employer and employee performed pretty much the same type of labor."[17] To be sure, George Henry Evans, Theophilus Fisk, and other leaders or supporters of the labor movement of the 1820s and 1830s appear to have reached consensus that some occupational types—bankers, "speculators," real estate moguls and other "landlords," many "professional men"—were "idle," fraudulent, or otherwise "useless to the community at large."[18] These were clearly undeserving of the overwhelming portion—and, indeed, perhaps all—of their material rewards. Lamenting that the United States was all too quickly following in the footsteps of England, one labor sheet estimated in this vein that but one-third of the people of the United States were true "producers"—two-thirds were the "non-producers" who received more than four-fifths of the national product.[19]

Nonetheless, Hartz slighted the indecision that arose within such labor circles over many new occupations. One former "Mechanic" inquired of Evans (who would answer affirmatively) whether general shipping merchants, retail dry goods dealers, grocers, or hardware dealers were pursuers of "useful," legitimate callings, individuals who should accordingly be permitted into the ranks of mechanic organizations.[20] What of these and other of the newer occupational types that were at least semiautonomous or "petty-bourgeois" rather than either wage-earning employees or unambiguous capitalist "exploiters"— ones often tending to occupy, in the view of Marxist scholars particularly, "contradictory class locations"?[21] The same correspondent further pressed the editor of the New York *Working Man's Advocate* in 1830: "Now as there may be, and no doubt is, a diversity of opinion, as to what are useful or useless occupations, I should be pleased if you would make out a list of both, so that the public might see what your views are on this subject."[22]

One significant source of workers' hesitation in condemning many of the newer, and morally questionable, employments was the emergence into these positions of some undoubtedly industrious and otherwise virtuous mechanics. As the same ex-"Mechanic" queried Evans on the relevance of occupational origins: Would "you make any difference between two men similarly situated at present, and who are both alike friendly to the mechanics and their interest; and who are neither at present mechanics, but one of them was formerly a mechanic, the other never was a mechanic?"[23] For this correspondent, as well as for others including Evans himself, former artisans now drawing their livelihood from nonmanual activities, or ones who had accumulated enough of a "sufficiency" to live without need of any active employment at all, might understandably provoke jealousy among their "less fortunate" fellows. But they might still seem to occupy a more ethically elevated social category and appear more deserving of both their present rewards and the "confidence" of existing mechanics than individuals who had never been mechanics.[24]

But remaining no less important was the somewhat distinct source of worker ambivalence toward economic success: the uncertainty over the productive contributions of many of the newer employments, whatever the social origins of those who filled them. Issues of distributive justice were invariably muddied as networks and activities in exchange and distribution, as well as in the direct production of goods, expanded in tandem with growing mass markets. A moderating political expediency, the desire to avoid an exclusivism that would narrow the constituency and the appeal of the Working Men's Party, explains in part why Evans agreed to the period's characteristically broad definition of "a Working Man" as "one who followed any *useful* occupation, mental or physical, for a livelihood."[25] Part of that expediency, too, was Evans's desire to effectively defuse the charges, made by such hostile commentators as the South Carolina political economist Thomas Cooper, that the workingmen were outright level-ers, beyond the ken of political acceptability.[26] But adherence to a broad defi-nition of "Working Man" also reflected Evans's genuine perception, articulated in 1830, that there were in fact ever-increasing numbers of Americans, includ-ing "many who are not *mechanics*," who were engaged in occupations that in one way or another "add to the necessaries, comforts, or conveniences of life."[27] Evans never appears to have abandoned this perception, just as he continued to resist the position, increasingly favored by radicalized journeymen unionists dur-ing the strike years of the mid-1830s, that even friendly small masters like him-self were at least potentially these journeymen's class enemies, warranting exclusion from their unions.[28]

Most of the newer employments that Evans and other labor reformers were unwilling to denounce categorically were white collar and lower middle class. In their petty-bourgeois character, they indeed resembled the more traditional class of master mechanics to which Evans himself belonged as a printer. But there was also a more strictly doctrinal manifestation of the uncertainty and ambiva-lence regarding economic success and emergent occupations that were displayed by Evans and other labor reformers of the period. This consisted of the stum-bling blocks encountered by the more radical anticapitalist versions of the labor theory of value. This issue requires some elaboration.

Whether one views it as a virtual "cliché" or as an "axiom" of American thought, the most general and agreed-upon version of the labor theory of value already enjoyed a long and prominent history by the 1820s.[29] That version broadly asserted that all property and wealth derived from labor inputs, and that an "equitable and natural distribution of wealth was created when each laborer received the fruits of his or her labor."[30] As the recent comprehensive treatment by James L. Huston further indicates, the Founding Fathers and other Ameri-cans of the Revolutionary era widely embraced this general form of the labor theory of value as a conceptual device for distancing the new republic and its social and economic arrangements from the more blatantly ascriptive and exploitative "political economy of aristocracy" that distinguished Old World arrangements. When considered apart from this Old World standard, this general version of the labor theory of value was quite unthreatening and innocuous. Because *labor* retained a variable and elastic meaning, America's elite merchants, lawyers, and even slaveowning planters could justify their wealth and position by reference to their "labor."[31] That many late eighteenth-century American farmers, artisans, and common laborers (free and slave) may have similarly subscribed to the labor theory of value is no more important than the fact that they almost certainly found deficient so supple a definition of *labor*.[32]

Such objections only intensified and grew more overt during the early nineteenth century. Revolution-generated antideferential egalitarianism fed the growing consciousness attending early industrial capitalism that free wage earners, in particular, were being systematically exploited and "robbed" of their rightful earnings by "the Capitalists"—by the monopolistic holders of "past" labor—"by the whole vampire brood of non-producers."[33] In an outpouring of socialist, trade-union, and other oppositional literature were spawned on both sides of the Atlantic more visible and pointed anticapitalist producerist versions of the labor theory of value. Those versions varied widely in intellectual development and depth—in the rigor with which they attacked the various orthodox economic justifications for capitalist profit and in the consistency and precision with which they sought to explain how, exactly, employers stole the fruits of labor from their workers.[34] How uncompromising or radical a given formulation of the theory was also depended on how it addressed a series of related questions: whether, for example, it included even the smaller master employers among the exploiters, and whether it limited true, productive labor to people who worked only with their hands. The most uncompromising versions furthermore concluded that members of the working classes, as the creators of all wealth, had the natural right to the entire product of their labor, and with this the moral right, even the obligation, to resist capital's role in fixing the value of that labor.[35] Unlike Horace Greeley's more philosophical and class-neutral criticisms of the cash-nexus imperative and its commodification of the wage earner's labor, American journeymen artisan and other labor organizations in the Jacksonian period were increasingly disposed, in their own criticisms of the market mechanism, to situate the blame in workshop inequalities, the labor process, and employer agency.[36] They accordingly embraced some of the emergent, more anticapitalist versions of the labor theory of value as a natural ideological tool.

Sean Wilentz provides some of the more prominent examples of how the turn to such anticapitalist versions was stimulated by journeymen skilled artisans' sense that market commodification was invading their personal estate and serving as the prime medium of expropriation by capitalist employers. New York City sailmakers noted in 1835 that "our labor is our property, and we have the inherent right to dispose of it in such parcels as any other species of property." Journeymen cordwainers added that any attempts by employers "to say how much . . . journeymen shall receive for their labor" amounts to a "usurpation of authority."[37] Conflicts over the measurement of labor were both cause and symptom of the growing antagonism. Since the late eighteenth century, the complexity of the measuring system used by master employers had obscured for journeymen the piece-rate value of their labor, but mystification hardened into growing consciousness of exploitation under a panoply of early nineteenth-century developments. These included the failure of the old books of prices to keep up with journeymen's rising cost of living and the relentless division of labor within cabinetmaking and other trades, which created tasks for skilled journeymen that the old books had never enumerated and also enabled masters-cum-capitalists to employ less skilled, sweated labor under the outdated prices.[38]

The movement for the year-round ten-hour day—the organized demand that they be paid by units of time—became, as David Brody notes, one response of disgruntled antebellum journeymen to the "master's monopoly on the measurement of their work," including the related advantage that masters in the building and other trades had been deriving from seasonably variable workdays.[39] Another response, not incompatible with the ten-hour movement because it remained so largely rhetorical, was journeymen's embrace of anticapitalist versions of the labor theory of value. That embrace encompassed, in turn, two rather distinct notions of wage slavery. The first, as many historians have noted, consisted of the journeymen's and other labor activists' producerist aversion, as manly republican citizens, to the "humiliating, servile dependency" on capitalist authority and acquisitiveness that the commodification of their labor signified.[40]

The second notion of wage slavery entailed a consumerist sense of laborers' unfilled needs and wants; it therefore signified not merely the denial to them of their "fair and full equivalent" but the advent of subsistence or "starvation" wages as well.[41] James L. Huston deservedly highlights the importance that this second notion of wage slavery had in the early part of the nineteenth century, as well as later on, although he perhaps too sharply disassociates it from the aversion to economic dependence and labor's commodification that powered the first notion.[42] In the context of the labor activism of the 1830s, the second as well as the first critique of wage slavery warned of the consequences of ceding to capitalists the power to fix the worth of the journeyman's labor. Starvation wages followed all too easily from economic dependence—from vulnerability to and compliance with capitalist invasions and machinations.[43] (Subsistence wages, it was just as commonly held, then proceeded to intensify and clinch the wage earner's economic desperation and dependence.) The labor voices of this period were invoking both senses of wage slavery when they took note of such singular phenomena as that in which competition among predatory and unscrupulous capitalists—their impulse to undersell one another—acted to reduce wage earners' recompense almost as assuredly as did competition among laborers for employment. Here, too, however, these labor voices remained neither altogether clear nor unified on the precise extent of employer agency: trade unionists who retained a producerist bond with "honorable" masters saw these as reluctant, even helpless parties in the wage-lowering process, compelled to emulate the "bad" masters and "avaricious" capitalists who had initiated the process.[44]

Encapsulating many of these themes was one of the more notable formulations of the radical anticapitalist labor theory of value: the 1844 *Address* of the New England Workingmen's Association, which at its organizing convention in Boston that year brought together some two hundred delegates from workers' organizations, land-reform groups, and Associationist and other social-reform movements. The *Address* proclaimed that "labor is the only creator of value," the "actual producers of wealth." But under "our false system" whereby labor "becomes a commodity," the "natural order of things is entirely reversed": reduced to economic dependence, laborers were now systematically deprived of the fruits of their toil by the "non-producing" class of capitalists. How did the *Address* define *labor* and *nonproducers?*: "If there are those in the community who are not actually engaged in manual labor, or in other words who are not producers, who nevertheless receive value, it must follow that by some means they obtain possession of that which is produced by others." Although, the *Address* proceeded, "our condition as workingmen" was not yet "reduced to that extreme of wretchedness to which the laborers of Europe have long since arrived," it warned of the ominous tendencies of a system that was "unjust and oppressive to ourselves, and injurious to the community." It accordingly welcomed "associations" of workingmen and other modes of enlightened corrective action.[45]

One among many of the period's "labor jeremiads," this *Address* contained references to most of the major intellectual influences that shaped American anticapitalist versions of the labor theory of value: republican veneration of landed freehold independence and the heritage of equal rights bequeathed by the Revolution and the Declaration of Independence; the biblical decree that only through "the sweat of thy face thou shall eat bread"; the mythology of American exceptionalism that fastened on social arrangements in the Old World, with their gross political oppressions and economic disparities, as countermodels to be avoided.[46] And although it is not obvious from the particular example of this *Address,* radical versions of the labor theory of value were also a prominent part of the Anglo-American Ricardian socialist tradition (or Smithian socialist, as some scholars prefer), which encompassed the often varying yet consistently anticapitalist doctrines of English writers like John Gray, William Thompson, and Thomas Hodgskin and American ones like Stephen Simpson, Langton Byllesby, Cornelius Blatchly, and William Heighton.[47]

Such conceptions of a nonexploitative producer's republic were also, generally, heavily gendered.[48] In one sense, it is not surprising that the 1844 *Address* made virtually no reference to specific occupational groups; it was not, after all, a craft-specific union manifesto. Still, there is something emblematic in the failure of the *Address,* which issued from the stronghold of the Boston Associates, to apply its anticapitalist version of the labor theory of value explicitly to the situation of the largely female, semiskilled labor force employed in the factories of Lowell and other of the region's mill towns. Symbolically, at least, these factories had come to dominate New England enterprise. There is no question, given the reform groups behind the *Address,* that it was hostile to such establishments, that the *Address* belonged to a narrative tradition which ranked the prisonlike, "despotic" factory system of the Old World as among the most notorious of the countermodels to be avoided. And the *Address* made at least one veiled reference to the creations of Samuel Slater and the Boston Associates when it charged that "through the introduction of labor saving machinery, it [the present system of labor] is constantly supplanting the labor of the male adult, introducing instead of that the helpless female, or the still weaker child."

This remark is itself revelatory. If, in the tradition of such New England labor reformers as Seth Luther and Charles Douglass, the *Address* perceived Lowell and other factory towns as epitomizing the pernicious reversal of the "natural order of things," this was not primarily because Nathan Appleton and Abbott Lawrence had grown rich and powerful by stealing the fruits of factory women's toil. Most labor reformers of the time, and possibly even a majority of the Lowell "girls," accepted that their wages would be, and should be, insufficient for their complete social independence and equality. To this extent reformers and operatives alike supported, together with the Boston Associates, a part of the "hegemonic discourse": that such "woman's wage work did not need to meet the costs of social reproduction [i.e., family maintenance], and therefore was not exploitative when it did not."[49]

For many of the labor reformers of the 1840s, what the Boston Associates were instead primarily guilty of was undermining, through their economic initiatives and technological ingenuity, the economic and moral authority to which male laborer heads of households, like other husbands and fathers, were "naturally" entitled. The farm girls who caught "factory fever," according to this reform narrative, had been enticed out of their more unequivocally supportive and dependent roles within the domestic sphere by the prospect of paid wages and a greater measure of autonomy than they had heretofore possessed. More important yet in this narrative, what these enticements in fact led to, in conjunction with the unsuitably long hours of unhealthy toil inflicted on them by greedy "mill-lords," was the operatives' moral degradation and physical breakdown.[50] Only a limited portion of the factory women themselves came to express objections of this nature. In some measure because they looked upon their mill tenure as limited, as a prelude to marriage and motherhood, quite a few, in fact, appear to have willingly accepted long hours for the greater cumulative wages these brought. Even factory women who grew highly critical of the "speed-ups" and other working conditions of the 1840s thought more in terms of these conditions' effects on the instrumental value of their labor than did most of the male reformers who participated in the Convention of 1844. Exceptions notwithstanding, those reformers remained more interested in protecting "helpless" factory women and other working women than in including them among the direct beneficiaries of the anticapitalist labor theory of value.[51]

Relevant here was another of the *Address*'s claims: "Our present system of labor is false in principle" partly because the laborer "can no longer at will create value which, when created, is to be his own; but he must sell his commodity — his labor — his manhood — to another, to receive therefore [his] miserable pittance." The gendered nature of this formulation was especially consistent with the skilled male artisan exclusivism that marked most antebellum applications of the anticapitalist labor theory of value. It was congruent with the general tendency of the period's craft unionists to self-referentially invoke that theory without extending it to the exploitation experienced by servants, outworkers, casual laborers, and other unskilled and semiskilled workers, of either sex, outside their orbit.[52]

The gender biases of the 1844 *Address* ultimately remain less central to this discussion than one other note of moderation evidenced in its reform vision. The document's avowed wish to restore the "natural order of things" included a subsequent disavowal of leveling: "We should ever distinctly remember our object: not to elevate ourselves by depressing others . . . but to elevate ourselves — to strengthen the bonds of our brotherhood." This note of restraint does not easily jibe with the *Address*'s larger pointed attack on capitalist interests. On one level, it reflected the ideals of Christian fellowship that suffused New England reformism: the religiously inspired exaltation of social harmony and mutuality of interests that prevailed in some labor-activist discourses over the inclination toward class confrontation, social retribution, and vengeance.[53] The

Address's expression of restraint also likely marks it as a product of compromise among multiple reform voices from both working-class and middle-class backgrounds bearing diverse perspectives and agendas.[54] But in this single note of moderation, the *Address* more specifically connected with the sensibility of George Henry Evans (one of the convention's participants), for as earlier suggested, Evans typified, in his newspaper exchanges and elsewhere, the common tendency of the more moderate of the labor-reform activists to pull back from the most radical and confrontational anticapitalist versions of the labor theory of value.

Evans implicitly recognized, on the basis of his own experience, the contributions to productivity emanating from nonmanual inputs: above all the workshop resources and the mental labor supplied by the established and experienced master artisan.[55] Herein lay part of the explanation for his failure to invoke the radical labor theory of value to challenge the legitimacy of many of the newer employments developing around him in New York City. But here, too, lay the nub of the problem. The purer forms of capitalist enterprise — in retailing, financing, and real estate as well as in industrial production — that labor reformers and activists did unsparingly denounce along with elite professional activities posed the same general intellectual hurdles for the radical labor theory of value. Indeed, these enterprises posed stumbling blocks for any doctrine that sought to jettison market-determined rewards for the respective contributions of capital and labor.

How can one bypass a market-determined basis to measure the usefulness, or value, of all of a society's goods and services? Consider, first, the difficulties facing an answer to so basic a question that arise merely from the process of capitalist industrial production itself: How can one bypass the market to achieve a true and just measurement of the value of individual contributions to a jointly made product? The welfare economist Amartya Sen is one among many who have suggested the difficulties here: "If production is an interdependent process, involving the joint use of different resources, it is not generally possible to separate out which resource has produced how much of the total output." Now in this particular instance, Sen in fact is falling back on complexity not for purposes of challenging the radical labor theory of value or any other doctrine that demands increased recognition of the laborer's contribution to the social product.[56] To the contrary, he is here challenging those at the other end of the ideological spectrum who are not satisfied with a value-neutral defense of economic inequalities under market capitalism, but who rather insist that market mechanisms are morally reliable, even morally infallible, determinants of rewards to capital and labor. Sen is challenging, that is, those present-day thinkers who make one or both of two of the basic market-from-desert defenses: the defense that the market in fact distributes wealth in proportion to each individual's industriousness, discipline, and other meritorious character traits and behavior and the argument that the market does distribute wealth according to the individual's contribution to society.[57]

Such arguments were hardly absent from early nineteenth-century political-economic discourse. Indeed, they formed a central part of mainstream and conservative American Whig Party ideology and were a standard rejoinder to the critics' perennial refrain of moral bankruptcy under market-capitalist commodification: "The worth of a thing [labor and everything else] is what it will bring."[58] From Sen's standpoint the moralistically oriented defenses of market capitalism may be no more susceptible to empirical validation than the socialist and other anticapitalist versions of the labor theory of value. In some respects, he suggests, they in fact may hold less intellectual weight than the moral arguments from the left.[59] But it nonetheless remains true that in their own insistence on the importance of distributing material rewards in accordance with moral criteria, the Whiggish arguments faced a fundamentally different task, and a far less daunting one, than did those of antebellum labor radicals. Their task was one of merely rationalizing, rather than turning back, the market-capitalist competitive hierarchy and the formidable economic forces that were establishing it as the status quo.

With the status quo running against them, labor reformers, and most of all proponents of the most uncompromising versions of the labor theory of value, had the greater onus: proving, as the *Address* of the New England Workingmen's Convention insisted, that under emergent processes of production, market outcomes were unjust, wholly out of whack with "real" contributions to the production of goods and services. And largely for the reason described by Sen, trade unionists and other labor reformers could not make this proof to the satisfaction of significant numbers outside their circles — their appeals, at least, were not effective enough to draw these others into active support for their cause. Perhaps unsurprisingly, labor reformers' recourse to traditional language — their frequent, often hazy invocation of the "monopoly" powers possessed by capitalist employers — proved unequal to the task of demonstrating the existence of intolerable distributive injustice.[60]

Radical versions of the labor theory of value faced great intellectual difficulties in disentangling the contributions to social value and productive output made by various inputs. Nor could they make a convincing case that capitalists deserved no rewards. This was because of both the material resources that capitalists contributed to the production process and the entrepreneurial "alertness and discovery," technological inventiveness and general head labor, and other qualities that many displayed in directing those resources along with their waged employees.[61] The intellectual difficulties faced by the most anticapitalist versions of the labor theory of value were compounded and highlighted by the competing Whiggish arguments, which likely did make inroads among many antebellum Americans, plebeian elements included. These were the arguments that under market capitalism and the material and status incentives it provided society's most enterprising and talented members, economic growth and increased productivity would ensure that any increase in relative inequalities would be attended by a yet greater elevation of absolute living and consumption standards. The converse of such capitalist defenses, with their roots in the eighteenth century, was that interference with "natural" market processes — attempts to force, by governmental means or otherwise, an artificial redistribution and equalization of resources — would undermine the incentives of society's most enterprising and productive members, thereby impede if not destroy economic growth, and ultimately impoverish everyone.[62] An expanding pot with unequal spoons was preferable to a declining pot with equal spoons.[63] And the magnitude of the expansion — the size of society's total output — such defenses suggested, was always sensitive to the existing pattern of distribution.[64]

To the difficulties that lay in disentangling the contributions to social value and productive output made by various inputs, the burgeoning state of antebellum consumer preferences added obstacles of their own to radical doctrines aspiring to bypass a market-determined basis in order to measure the usefulness or value of society's goods and services.[65] Decades before John Bates Clark and other American economists developed marginal utility and productivity doctrines as antisocialist weapons, moderate labor reformers like Evans exhibited an incipient awareness of both the reality of expanding individual consumer appetites and their tendency, contrary to the absolutist tenor of the labor theory of value, to bestow a subjective, relativistic dimension to value that could only broaden society's definitions of legitimate producers.[66] Recall here Evans's admission that there were ever-growing numbers of Americans, including "many who are not *mechanics*," who were engaged in occupations that in one way or another "add to the necessaries, comforts, or conveniences of life."[67]

Evans almost certainly harbored contempt for some of the luxuries and putative needs the appetite for which had been stimulated by the market revolution. These were luxuries and tastes that were above all manifest in the urban centers for which Evans expressed a pronounced agrarian republican distaste.[68] But if Evans did not regard all consumer appetites and the production and distribution enterprises that satisfied them with equal approval, he nonetheless recognized the intellectual stumbling blocks that these growing phenomena posed for anticapitalist labor theories of value. That recognition may help explain his evolving reform priorities. One historian has recently noted that the "depression-linked financial difficulties" of the 1830s "cooled the ardor" of many labor activists and trade unionists of the period, and that these difficulties gave Evans specifically the leisure time to read up on the agrarian doctrines of Thomas Paine and Thomas Spence. He consequently reemerged on the labor-reform scene in the early 1840s with a new "one-track mind"—focused on land reform and men's "natural right" to a portion of the soil.[69]

But this narrative of Evans's embrace of land reform may understate his pre-depression intellectual development and political experiences. There was, first, his own claim that it was the proposals of fellow workingman Thomas Skidmore in the late 1820s that made him initially reflect on the problems of land ownership. As Joseph Dorfman writes, Evans subsequently came to preach "a 'new agrarianism' that looked toward Skidmore's ends. Since capital is the result of labor, he argued, there can be no equal right to capital, and it must be left alone. But the soil is the gift of nature, and everyone has a natural right to the soil as well as to the product of his labor."[70]

It also followed, so Evans claimed during the 1840s, that free access to land would rectify the injustice and exploitation inhering in existing wage labor because the laborer would no longer be "*dependant* on the employer": the hireling "would receive the full value of his labor, because he would have the ready alternative of laboring for himself." As Evans recognized, there was a certain segment of eastern wage earners who had no wish to be tillers of the soil, nor did they necessarily aspire to become the employers of others or to assume the risks and responsibilities of owning and operating small enterprises of any kind.[71] Perhaps it was his desire to appeal to such workingmen—those who were not conspicuously unhappy with their status as wage earners—that led Evans to pitch land reform in a way which moderated other associations of wage labor with inevitable servility. With corrective government action the commodification of labor—market determination of wages within capitalism—need not be completely arrested, for now it would proceed under supply-and-demand terms that were far less invasive and disadvantageous to the sellers of that labor. The laborer "would consequently rise to his proper rank in society, instead of being debased in proportion to his usefulness." Such should at least hold true in a country that was so far from being "overpopulated"—one in which there was no compelling reason for "want of employment."[72]

The presence of a large public domain in the United States also meant that man's natural right to land could be realized with singular ease here—there was no need to resort to Skidmore's anti-inheritance agrarianism and disturb present titles to property. But this, in turn, finally, is to suggest that Evans was acting out of some sense of relief when he embarked on his single-minded crusade against land speculation and monopoly and their "idle" beneficiaries in the 1840s. In contrast to his predepression experiences, he had found what seemed to him a fatter, more attractive target. Whatever the real extent and evils of land monopoly and speculation, he had embraced an issue, that of agrarian egalitarianism, in which the lines of responsibility for unjust economic inequality and exploitation seemed more easily identifiable.[73] Land was a form of property that was not the creation of anyone's labor and in which the normal justifications for exclusive individual ownership less clearly applied. In pressing for the equalization of this single primary resource, Evans therefore had found a means of retreat from the producer- and consumer-generated occupational complexities that from the outset of his reform career in the 1820s had only obscured for him, as it had for others, the bases of economic injustice. And these were the very complexities that constituted formidable intellectual obstacles to the anticapitalist versions of the labor theory of value.[74]

Recognizing such obstacles is hardly to deny the great intuitive appeal that radical versions of the labor theory of value, especially the more diluted, labor-oriented ones, retained throughout the early nineteenth century and beyond. The paradox remained compelling even to many who resisted or rejected the most radical versions: in the United States as in the Old World, individuals who performed society's most patently indispensable and onerous types of labor were those who just as clearly enjoyed the fewest material and status rewards, even if they could not be credited with creating all of society's wealth.

Mainstream Jacksonian Democrat ideology exhibited notable blinders with respect to the racial and gendered dimensions of this paradox, just as it rejected the paradox's most radical leveling implications. Still, the intuitive injustice that the paradox embodied—the inverse relationship between the indispensability of labor and its recompense—registered strongly in Jacksonian ideology. In their cries to create a more level playing field for the (white male) "bone and sinew" of "true" producers and to restore the country to them, Jacksonians were both acknowledging the force of this paradox and displaying an even stronger faith than did the Whigs in free-market processes.[75] Because they tended to believe that differences in natural endowments among white males were smaller than Whigs typically claimed, Jacksonians held that a more open economic competition, one unimpeded by corporate "monopolies" and other "artificial privileges," would generate a society marked by fewer and relatively negligible economic and social disparities.[76] Many of today's academic philosophers, with their pervasive beliefs that individuals' natural endowments vary considerably and that the state must address the many unfair disparities that arise from this circumstance, would regard such Jacksonian egalitarianism as naive.[77] Hindsight certainly suggests that by trumpeting limited government and free competition, Jacksonians were taking their own easy way out of the intractable problems posed by poverty and economic inequality: theirs was the analogue to the Whig panacea of painless economic growth.

Radical anticapitalist versions of the labor theory of value, in any case, faced numerous difficulties in broadening their appeal. Even within their own narrow circles, a host of labor reformers, bowing to social and economic pressures, followed Evans and adapted more diluted versions, though some of these may have always been capable of simultaneously expressing thoroughly radical and more compromising versions.[78] It sufficed, in accordance with the latter formulations, to lament that the rewards bestowed by existing social arrangements were in "inverse proportion" to the "usefulness" of individuals, or that under those arrangements the contributions of capitalists or lawyers to the social good were "overvalued."[79] But if some measure of capitalist desert was acknowledged — if capitalists, too, were entitled to a fair share of the fruits — then the issue became how large that share should be. The most notable labor-reform compromise of the period was epitomized in the common blueprint of Association, as laid out by its major theoretician, Albert Brisbane. Three-twelfths of the net returns on the phalansteries' joint-stock private property should properly go to "the Capitalist" as a "fair dividend" for his distinctive contribution to the communities, as against the seven-twelfths representing the "fair reward" of "the Laborer's" efforts (the remaining two-twelfths going to "special talent"). Thus did one general formula attempt to embody the intuitive appeal of the notion that society's most necessary and "repugnant" employments deserved better compensation while simultaneously acknowledging the realities, and even the value and the limited justice, of the capitalist presence.[80]

The antebellum period offers still other doctrinal manifestations, even within the confines of labor reformers and activists, of what were at once the intellectual shortcomings of the radical labor theory of value and the formidable obstacles within mainstream culture to its general acceptance.[81] Recall Greeley's characterization of the position of Pittsburgh's striking iron puddlers in relation to that of their employers: "We *ought* to be paid so much because we *need* and they can *afford* it." Such a needs-based argument appeared to bypass a worker's actual productive contribution as the appropriate basis of his reward. When developed to its ultimate limits, the same argument might in fact emerge as more radically egalitarian than anticapitalist versions of the labor theory of value, just as Marx's "higher phase" of communist society (a society freed of all capitalist vestiges, including conditions of economic scarcity) was more radically egalitarian than its first phase.[82] Yet in antebellum America the needs-based argument remained less radical, or at least less confrontational, to the extent that it downplayed capitalist appropriation and exploitation as the root of social injustice. Statements similar to that described by Greeley can be found in some of the strike manifestos and other labor proceedings of the early 1850s, and what they suggest is a retreat from the most aggressive claims of the radical labor theory of value.[83] Not labor's entitlement to the entire product but rather considerations of relative need here constitute the basis for distributive-justice arguments; the alleviation of economic inequality is promoted without principal reference to desert.

None of this is to claim that by the early 1850s labor activists had entirely abandoned the radical labor theory of value, with its insistence that "a few law-lords, land-lords, and labor-lords" were despoiling and degrading "the mass who create all the wealth."[84] It was precisely such persisting militant rhetoric, during the intense labor unrest of the early 1850s, which Greeley found even more distasteful, as counterproductive demagoguery, than the deficient needs-based argument that he attributed to the iron puddlers.[85] Yet one can discern a variety of attitudinal configurations in the trade-union manifestos of the late antebellum period, and in what was one of the most interesting of these, bitter anticapitalist language in fact coexisted with a rejection of the most radical and uncompromising versions of the labor theory of value. Throughout most of a labor manifesto that he wrote on the eve of the Civil War, H. B. Mullins, a New York tailor, evidenced a desire to have nothing whatever to do with those "white slave-drivers," the capitalists of the free states, to whose tyrannies, he furthermore fumed, such "African negro"–loving "abolitionists" as Charles Sumner had turned a blind eye. Proclaiming the need to rescue the "toiling millions" from their employers' "deathly grasp," Mullins promoted the formation in 1860 of a tailors' cooperative that would contain none but "practical journeymen and cutters" as shareholders. Tailoring, he claimed, was among those trades that "cannot be improved by strikes." Employers in these trades had too many weapons at their disposal, such as the availability of cheap "female labor," to be forced into making "reasonable concessions" to their workmen.[86]

Here one might stop to note the double bind, the vicious circle, that Mullins and other male tradesmen associated with women's waged manufacturing employment particularly. Capitalist market arrangements had, in their view, so undermined their own capacity to meet their family's subsistence needs as to oblige many of their wives, as well as their children, to labor like themselves for "very long hours" in order to eke out a "miserable existence." Yet this commodification of the labor of dependents, much as it served the immediate needs of the individual family units to which they belonged, might also represent a collective intrusion into male workers' own labor markets. This was above all true when it took the form of manufacturing piecework (either home- or workshop-based). Such commodification exacerbated competition and added to the downward spiral of the wages of male workers generally, as in the case of Mullins's own trade. And this tendency, in turn, served only to increase the urgency of the supplementary household income provided by wives and children. Its aggregate impact in depressing male wages, together with the capitalist opportunism he identified with it, probably was enough to convince Mullins that the commodification of female and child labor was as unfortunate as it was necessary under existing social arrangements, although he likely ascribed to it additionally destructive effects on the family life of poor working men.[87]

Yet to take up the original point, much of Mullins's bitterness toward his capitalist adversaries turned on their refusal to make "reasonable concessions" (as well as on their very ability to avoid the need to make these). Such terminology is telling and suggests that Mullins's manifesto remains something other than an expression of extreme republican producerist or socialist notions that waged employment must mean wage slavery. As with Evans's expectation that effective land reform would produce a seller's market in labor, so Mullins pulled back from the position that labor could be separated from one's self with only the most disastrous of consequences. Mullins's major complaint came down to the fact that "the price paid for our labor, and the time employed by us in that labor, are regulated absolutely and entirely by capitalists," language which seems to imply that capitalists, after all, might have some legitimate voice in regulating wages and hours and that such a circumscribed voice was not inconsistent with wage-earner dignity.[88]

Mullins's diatribe teetered on the brink of repudiating the capitalist economic system as intrinsically and fatally flawed because of the power abuses it permitted individual employers. Yet in answer to the question of whether the "tide of capital" can "be arrested in its destructive march," he affirmatively insisted that the working classes of New York and elsewhere, if "united," possessed by way of the suffrage the ability to reform the system, and in fact to redress all their grievances. Mullins also recognized the continued existence of "merchants and other gentlemen who act fairly toward their workmen." Was such fairness dictated by the possibility that these particular employers did not yet possess the means, the temptations, or—perhaps most importantly of all—the coercive pressures inclining them to act otherwise? Mullins did not state his views on this question, although he did tap into one of the period's labor-reform refrains when he hinted that good employers might be obliged to follow bad ones: "Honorable gentlemen of this class are themselves injured by their less honorable neighbors, and moreover, have to contend against the false and unjust axioms that govern society in general."[89] Still, Mullins concurrently personalized capitalist exploitation, identifying adverse relations between capital and labor with the greedy behavior of a select group of individual employers and at least suggesting that their opportunistic stratagems were not absolutely endogenous to the economic order. These moderating tendencies were of a piece with Mullins's aforementioned failure to unequivocally close the door on capitalist desert.

That failure, in turn, highlighted the still greater indecision of others, including those in the labor press: "Profit is a very indefinite thing; its legitimate extent is what no two persons are agreed upon."[90] If other of these labor activists shared Mullins's conviction that particular capitalists exhibited a relentless, positively insatiable greed and thirst for power, some nonetheless remained more reluctant than he to represent this propensity as an overriding characteristic of prevailing arrangements. They were, correspondingly, even clearer than Mullins was in their rejection of the most radical anticapitalist versions of the labor theory of value. In the same year as Mullins's writing, Isaac J. Neal, president of the Moulder's Union, told a group of workingmen in Pittsburgh that unions were necessary "not to invade the rights of capital, but to protect those of the laborer."[91] In still other cases less accommodating, more militant rhetoric than Neal's may have been part of a trade union's negotiating ploy, an effort to make that union a more effective instrument of redistributive justice. And militant rhetoric might also represent something of a cathartic exercise, undertaken by unionists to prepare themselves psychologically to acknowledge their adversaries' productive function and, accordingly, to accede in the bargaining process a legitimate voice to employers in the determination of their waged recompense.

Reinforcing Ideological Pressures

That late antebellum retreat from the radical labor theory of value which did occur dramatized the intellectual stumbling blocks that had always confronted it. By the same token, that retreat also signified more than a settling in of the more limited and pragmatic orientation of trade-union ideology and of craft-workers' attendant acceptance of their labor's subordinate, commodified status within the capitalist market's rules of the game. To return to an earlier point, the rocky trajectory of tenuous and limited acceptance experienced from the first by the radical labor theory of value, above all its central idea that wage-earning manual workers were entitled to the entire product of their labor, also reveals something of workers' underlying ambivalence about economic success and the evolving occupational structure.

One might briefly refer here to the battery of arguments with which American workers had been bombarded for decades: arguments that in one respect or another (and for white males most exclusively) legitimated the individualistic pursuit of economic success, increasingly defined that success in terms of movement into the occupational top ranks, and represented American society's market-capitalist occupational structure as fully compatible with distributive justice. There was the old argument of Alexander Hamilton and some of his disciples that a market-driven capitalist and professional hierarchy generated industrial and other jobs at the other end of the social scale, and that it would be in the interests of the most economically dependent and desperate elements of the population to embrace the entire process of economic development even if they retained only limited expectations respecting their own upward mobility.[92]

There were also the various rights-based "procedural" defenses of the market, anticipating those of Robert Nozick and others today.[93] Presuming the justice of initial acquisitions of private property, these defenses morally prioritized the preservation of antecedent individual property rights and the voluntary character of market interactions. To these they subordinated any challenges to fairness that were raised by the ensuing unequal starting-gate opportunity for individuals and the resulting skewed outcomes of the market interactions. In challenging such venerable procedural defenses by demanding the abolition of property inheritance, in his insistence that meritocratic ideals and true social justice required at the very least an initial and equal distribution of economic resources among individuals by the state, Thomas Skidmore remained an isolated voice even within his own radical circles.[94]

Such procedural defenses of individual property rights were reinforced by the no less venerable arguments that the state's attempts to redistribute resources in the direction of greater equality of condition would be rendered nugatory by ongoing market processes, which would inexorably reproduce the same or similar inequalities. In increasingly complex and civilized societies, these market processes expressed and ratified individuals' naturally different talents and tastes for different employments, their unequal propensities for accumulating property, and their varying capacities for rising in the social scale. The American Whig fondness for such arguments has already been touched on. But as a general category of discourse that warned of either the "futility" or the counterproductive "perversity" of attempts by the state to equalize life chances, such free-market-elitist arguments enjoyed a considerably older history.[95] They were among the favorite weapons of Thomas Malthus in his 1798 attack upon the socially convulsive, "perfectionist" doctrines of William Godwin and the marquis de Condorcet, and they were continuously revived in the United States as well as the Old World to beat back challenges to existing social discrepancies.[96] Thus did Thomas Cooper of South Carolina respond to the "proposals" that were being "insinuated" in the New York Working Men's Party press, specifically by "such men as Skidmore & Co.," to "educate the poor at the expense of the rich; . . . tax the rich for the benefit of the poor; . . . diminish by law the profits of the capitalist; raise the wages of the poor by law," etc. On the one hand, this "proposed insurrection against wealth and capital, and frugality and industry," must prove futile:

> Inequality of bodily strength; inequality of mental energy and capacity; inequality of industry; inequality of frugality and saving: inequality arising from marriage and celibacy — from having a young family and having none; inequality arising from accidents and disease — from temperance and intemperance. Suppose these all to be, as they are and always have been, in incessant operation, will there not be, at the end of the short period of twenty-five years, great inequality of condition? Carelessness, idleness, ignorance, extravagance, intemperance among some — the opposite qualities among others? By this time, will there not be the poor and the rich? Are not all these sources of inequality independent of the system of law, and arising from the nature of man? . . . Let the laws of the land be ever so objectionable, you cannot alter the laws of nature. You may complain of the existence of moral evil and physical evil, but you cannot annihilate them by law.[97]

From the argument against mandated wealth redistribution based on its "futility," Cooper moved to the argument that through its incentives-destroying effect it would, in fact, backfire. More rather than less poverty would eventuate from "the mechanics getting possession of the legislature" of New York, because

> if there can be devised any more efficient scheme to drive capital, industry, honesty, and talent out of the country, I should be glad to see it. . . . What is it that produces demand for labour, that furnishes employment to workmen, that finds the wages to pay them, that keeps up the population of the country? Capital: Capital seeking for profitable employment. Banish this only source of national prosperity by legislative restrictions and taxations—compel people to abide by bargains made by them by law, against their will, and capital will assuredly become emigrant, it will march off to some region, where folly and robbery do not usurp the seat of legislation.[98]

One might respond to Cooper that some wealth redistribution in accordance with the "reforming" proposals to which he objected, or even a less ambitious abolition of banking and other unequal privileges, would at least generate a fairer hierarchy without hopelessly compromising the objectives of economic efficiency and growth. In that hierarchy places of high and low wealth and status would be more perfectly occupied by those who "deserved" them.[99] This became, to a considerable degree, the standard Jacksonian argument, but men of the Whiggish persuasion—politicians, entrepreneurs, clerics—offered an equally standard response. They invoked a strong version of the mythology of American exceptionalism, confirming the peculiar openness and fairness of the pursuit—or nonpursuit—of economic success in the United States. In so doing they offered their most distinctive contribution to the Anglo-American discourse of free-market elitism. There were in the United States no truly Old World–style artificial and ascriptive barriers preventing the natural movement either up or down the social scale. The indolent and dissolute sons of wealthy self-made men would inexorably dissipate their wealth and fall out of the elite, just as the industrious poor would demonstrate the benefits of their character-strengthening indigence by rising from rags to riches and taking their places among the elite.[100] This Whig social-fluidity argument quintessentially exemplified what Stuart M. Blumin characterizes as the particular tendency of the "middle class . . . to express awareness of its common attitudes and beliefs as a denial of the significance of class."[101]

The same social-fluidity argument was mercilessly satirized by Orestes Brownson who, like other labor radicals and left Jacksonians of the time, regarded the American social order as increasingly closed as well as unequal and exploitative.[102] As Brownson's attack on those (e.g., "the Boston clergy and aristocracy") who advanced the class-fluidity argument suggests, none of these or other defenses of a market-capitalist competitive hierarchy enjoyed close to undisputed authority in the early nineteenth century. All encountered ambivalence if not outright resistance, some more strongly than others, both inside and outside the major political parties. Until recently, in this connection, historians have placed most of their emphasis on the role played by evangelical Christianity and religion generally in legitimating capitalist authority and discipline. They have stressed the propensity of employers, for example, to invest the labor market with "supernatural sanction" or to insist that economic inequality reflected some combination of providential design and weak individual moral character whereas the market itself treated all identically.[103] But to this emphasis historians have added a more recent one on the oppositional function of Christianity—the religious sources that partially inspired the labor-oriented labor theory of value and its use by disaffected artisans and other labor reformers to resist the market-capitalist hierarchy.[104] One might similarly note the inclination in this critical discourse, expressive of the most populist, anticapitalist dimension of "evangelical producerism," to negatively transmute the time-honored Protestant character virtues when identifying the qualities needed for success in the new market game: industry, frugality, and economy are supplanted in this oppositional discourse by cunning, greed, and an instinct for the predatory.[105]

Nonetheless, the same scholarship on evangelical producerism has not ignored those variants and countertendencies within it that tempered hostility to capitalist change. Indeed, despite all the varied sources of antebellum resistance to competitive capitalism and the hierarchy it generated, it still seems likely that a significant (if unquantifiable) effect of the different elite arguments made in market capitalism's defense over several decades was to generate doubt, hesitation, and ambivalence in the minds of many, wage-earning workers included, who might have otherwise more forcefully and continuously sought out an alternative to the "Buy cheap, sell dear" economic game.[106] Cumulatively and in the aggregate, such arguments fed that grudging acquiescence and pragmatic acceptance that may have centrally defined the attitudes of many antebellum wage earners.[107] Radical anticapitalist versions of the labor theory of value confronted difficult enough obstacles to their intellectual acceptance in the early nineteenth-century United States. The various labor-reform efforts and experiments to practically implement such versions encountered still more formidable obstacles. Retreat by labor activists from the most radical anticapitalist doctrines was more generally paralleled in nonelite quarters by an unspoken acquiescence to "Buy cheap, sell dear" and other market-capitalist arrangements. The great majority of antebellum Americans, in any case, simply failed to visibly contest that to which the more intellectual and political elite of their number gave vigorous and continuous endorsement. This was the major doctrinal analogue of all the arguments in defense of a market-capitalist competitive hierarchy: the "broad" labor theory of value proclaiming the nation's capitalists and professionals to be, in one sense or another, contributors to the creation of wealth and genuinely productive "workers" in their own right.[108]

Who can say how many antebellum Americans, approximating H. B. Mullins, Greeley's iron puddlers, or in yet some other fashion, conferred only the most tepid and problematic legitimacy (i.e., normative assent) to market-capitalist arrangements? Who can say how many were partially led to do so by the venerable top-down arguments defending those arrangements? What number of destitute, wage-earning, and other nonelite Americans failed to be drawn to alternative plans inspired by the questionable anticapitalist labor theory of value not because they truly endorsed the "established order," but rather because they were persuaded (rightly or wrongly) of the superior wisdom of merely making "the best of a bad lot"? Such imponderables define much of what T. Jackson Lears characterizes as the "ambiguity" of silence.[109]

There remained, to be sure, those whose silence must have entailed less resignation and a fuller, more wholehearted normative endorsement of market-capitalist rules and the existing occupational hierarchy. These included, most obviously, the wage earners and others who, long before the late antebellum pronouncements of an Abraham Lincoln, were tacitly interpreting their own gains and successes (however modest these may have been by comparison) as a legitimation of the northern capitalist ideology of individual opportunity and mobility.[110] But there were also the untold numbers whose very setbacks and disappointments did not prevent them from conferring a comparable legitimacy to prevailing arrangements—those who, in contrast to H. B. Mullins, perceived their failures not in terms of social unfairness but rather in terms of their own personal inadequacies (as, indeed, the capitalist ideology prescribed).[111]

Other phenomena, emphasized by recent historians, no doubt solidified and expanded the normative approval of northern competitive capitalist arrangements, even as they, too, fostered more equivocal, merely consenting attitudes with respect to some of those arrangements in particular (e.g., the large rewards enjoyed at the topmost rungs of the occupational hierarchy). These phenomena included the compensating sense of empowerment and superiority that relatively powerless, if generally enfranchised, wage-earning white males derived from the society's subordination of blacks.[112] There was also the particular "abundance consciousness" with which some of these same workers, Irish immigrants and other impoverished refugees from the Old World, viewed the New, and which acted to solidify their attachment to the capitalist wage-labor system and to the American economic order generally.[113]

Northern nationalism, the free-labor states' ideological preparation for the Civil War, was the last major ingredient to be added to the mix that in the antebellum period blunted, constrained, and forestalled a more critical stance toward the existing economic game — a mix which reinforced beliefs upholding the legitimacy of "the emerging capitalist order of the North."[114] Northern nationalism and the antislavery movement had this effect during the 1850s, however, not merely because they "glorified northern society" and "isolated" slavery as the one "unacceptable form of labor exploitation," although these were certainly important.[115] Lack of confidence and even pessimism regarding the economic order of the free states played their own legitimating role, and these too were part of a northern nationalist, antislavery mentality whose self-confident, optimistic side has been more apparent to historians. The unprecedented degree to which the sectional challenge from the slave South forcefully brought decades-old republican anxieties into the economic realm is one of the principal subjects of the next chapter. But in connection with this chapter's own themes, one might at least note the irony of George M. Weston and other northern antislavery commentators of the 1850s warning that free labor's economic and moral superiority was the very basis of its vulnerability and fragility. Here were Republican proponents of the free-labor market-capitalist structure, which for years had derived cultural reinforcement from its competitive, putatively masculine ethos, proclaiming that structure's need of protection from competitive market forces, albeit ones generated by slave labor. Several generations of northern labor reformers had not appreciably differed in their own appeals for buffers and restraints on the competitive pressures of "Buy cheap, sell dear."

5

George M. Weston and Slave Labor: Free Labor, Gresham's Law, and Antebellum Cultural Anxieties

URING THE heated congressional debates over the Kansas-Nebraska bill in 1854, William S. Barry, representative from Mississippi, criticized the free-soil opposition to the bill for being, among other things, contradictory: "The gentleman from Illinois [Mr. Yates] says, that 'the effect of slave labor is to cheapen, degrade, and exclude free labor.' A while since the charge was, that slave labor was the most expensive, and that free labor was cheaper. Now the reverse is asserted."[1] Barry did not dwell on this alleged contradiction in the free-soil position, moving on to embrace other standard arguments in defense of the slaveholder's constitutional and moral right to bring his slave property into Kansas and Nebraska. But the Republican economic indictments of slavery and its projected territorial expansion were not altogether insensitive to such claims as Barry's, and some of the most prominent of these indictments confronted the proslavery accusation that they rested on contradictory arguments regarding the relative "cheapness" of free and slave labor.

A case in point was *Southern Slavery Reduces Northern Wages,* an address that George M. Weston, the former Democrat and prominent antislavery writer and newspaper editor from Maine, delivered in Washington, D.C., in March 1856.[2] An expression of free-soil, "free labor" outrage over the Kansas-Nebraska Act's repeal of the Missouri Compromise, Weston's address constitutes a notable if brief contribution to late antebellum antislavery Republican political economy, and in this chapter it is considered in this sense. But for purposes of underscoring the unprecedented seriousness of slavery's economic threat to free labor, Weston also made reference to two other sources of cheap labor competition: convict labor in the various states and "pauper labor" in the Old World. Although he did not primarily intend it as such, Weston's jeremiad against chattel slavery also emerges, then, as a window into more long-standing and more pervasive American cultural anxieties regarding the deleterious impact upon American labor conditions and standards of Gresham's law, broadly defined: the principle that nominally cheaper, inferior products or practices tend to drive out superior ones.[3] Using Weston's own ancillary examples of servile and inferior, yet threatening, labor as the subjects of the two chapters following this one, I examine how early- to mid-nineteenth-century Americans had a vigorous conception of Gresham's law and applied it to explain a range of market phenomena, even though an overwhelming proportion of them were assuredly unfamiliar with the term or its most precise monetary meaning. In fact, the antebellum Gresham's law–like anxieties represented a yet darker, more apocalyptic dimension of the self-maximizing "Buy cheap, sell dear" representations of the market mechanism examined in the previous two chapters. Acquisitiveness had been a primary underpinning of Sir Thomas Gresham's sixteenth-century formulation of the principle that was later named after him: Gresham's law posited that the currency driven out of circulation by its depreciated or debased inferior alternate would be either hoarded or exported by individuals owing to its greater intrinsic value. But a variety of early nineteenth-century American constituencies warned of rather more calamitous market outcomes for the particular free labor that they deemed intrinsically superior and whose greater costliness, they insisted, was but an accurate measure of this intrinsic superiority.

Antislavery Political Economy

"Wages are a better stimulus to industry than the lash," Weston affirmed in his address. The notion that slave labor is inefficient because physically coerced and grudgingly offered had centuries-old roots in Western thought. Beyond this, Weston was paying obeisance to what since the middle of the eighteenth century, with the unprecedented growth of antislavery sentiment, had developed into one of the central staples of a more coherent antislavery political-economic orthodoxy. As one of Weston's like-minded contemporaries explained, "The hope of gain and the fear of want are both extinguished by the deprivation of freedom," and the "dread of the lash" that instead actuated the slave "is an extremely feeble" alternative to these "two most powerful" motives prompting the "industrial efforts of freemen."[4] Unlike slave laborers, who (ordinarily) had no contractual voice in determining the "fruits" of their labor, and who had neither opportunity nor incentive to develop their "human capital," free waged workers possessed a tangible vested interest in improving themselves and their work performance. They were better motivated than southern bondsmen and consequently more efficient and productive (in terms of output per worker). In this last sense, indeed, free waged laborers were also cheaper than slaves, belying the illusion created by the higher labor costs that they commonly imposed on employers.[5] And like his fellow Republican proponents of antisouthern free-labor ideology, and as he himself did yet more extensively elsewhere, Weston further noted in his address the additional dire implications for regional economic development carried by a labor system whose individual members were inefficient, unskilled, and materially and culturally deprived. "It is certainly true that wealth is more rapidly augmented under free, than under slave systems, and that, in a large sense, free labor is cheaper than slave labor. . . . Exhausting and impoverishing in all its results and all its influences, . . . slave labor, like many other cheap things, is dear in the end." From this long-term developmental perspective especially, the "cheapness of slave labor" was "a delusion and a snare."[6]

These antislavery political-economic principles did not command universal or unequivocal assent among early nineteenth-century Anglo-American commentators who were markedly hostile to slavery. In particular, some of these commentators, including Weston himself, felt compelled to go beyond, and even contradict in places, the brief but influential discussion by one of the architects of antislavery political-economic orthodoxy, Adam Smith. Smith had suggested that slave labor was uncategorically "dearer" than free labor. But under certain circumstances, the post-Smithian revision ran, slave labor's lower costs in fact could offset its inferior physical performance and productive inefficiency, enabling it to remain absolutely cheaper than free labor and for this reason alone capable of generating generous profits for individual slaveowners.[7] Weston embraced this particular qualification of Smithian orthodoxy as an important part of his own late antebellum antislavery arsenal—of his efforts to underscore the economic menace posed to free labor by an expansionist-minded, economically self-interested slave power. There remained that "aspect of slave labor" which rendered it "temporarily and apparently cheap."[8] And although Weston was not prominent among these, some antislavery commentators throughout the early nineteenth century also were induced to temper or otherwise reformulate claims of free labor's superior cheapness and profitability in response to the ideological and political capital that their adversaries commonly made from Smith's thesis. For in the hands of both southern proslavery writers and northern labor radicals, the notion of free waged labor's superior cheapness and profitability for capitalist employers became something other than an argument for the productivity-inducing stimulus of good wages and abundant economic opportunity. In such hands it became an argument for the northern waged laborer's greater exploitability and more oppressive wage slavery, his (or her) superior output and cheapness proving merely that subsistent wages and the fear of starvation were harsher, more relentless, and more effective labor incentives, and made for greater work intensity, than the slaveholder's lash.[9]

Quite apart from the degree to which early nineteenth-century commentators assented to and qualified the major principles of antislavery political economy, such principles have undergone substantial critical review by scholars in recent years. Contrary to at least much of the original antislavery commentary, historians have confirmed slave labor's overall, vigorous profitability in the antebellum South, although some of the most convincing of these arguments have not claimed from this a superior efficiency in slaves' productive performance that virtually all earlier antislavery writers had denied. Rather, such scholars have attributed the greater part of slavery's profitability to the worldwide consumer demand for cotton textiles that drove southern cotton prices up.[10] Furthermore, close students of slavery's operation in a variety of southern enterprises and communities have uncovered a complexity and diversity of conditions, bearing on slave economic opportunities, incentives, and productivity, that muddy the severe and rigid dichotomy which antebellum commentators like Weston established between a dynamic and progressive northern social and economic order and a hopelessly repressive and backward southern one.[11] As it hardened into an ideology of northern nationalism, pre–Civil War "free laborism" grew correspondingly less inclined to discern and acknowledge the empirical shadings and ambiguities that complicated and weakened its contrast between northern wage labor and southern slave labor. Such shadings and ambiguities, to borrow a phrase from O. Nigel Bolland's study of slave societies in the Americas, should "encourage us to reject the simplistic antimony of 'slavery' and 'freedom.'"[12]

But the yet more relevant point here is that the very insistence of late antebellum free-labor ideology on the severity of this contrast — its trumpeting of the total moral and economic superiority of northern free labor to southern slave labor — carried its own set of tensions, even equivocations, at which Congressman Barry's remarks hinted. Consider, again, Weston's address, where he explains why slavery's exclusion from Kansas and Nebraska remained absolutely imperative, why slavery could not be permitted to establish a foothold in these areas and compete head to head with the more efficient and progressive system of northern free labor. Slave labor

> is irresistibly and unmistakably cheaper [than] any species of free labor . . . when applied to the ruder processes of agriculture . . . in any latitude in which the black race will thrive. . . . Conceding the full force of the fact,

that wages are a better stimulus to industry than the lash, it is still impossible for the free laborer to maintain the contest with a race, so hardy in their own proper climate, so docile, and so cheaply supported. . . . In contrasting free labor with slave labor, and claiming superiority for the former over the latter, we naturally think of free labor as it actually exists at the North and West, where it is educated and intelligent. But free labor is not necessarily either, nor is it in fact either, except under the condition of being fairly paid. When its remuneration is lowered by successive gradations, as it must be when exposed to the competition of slave labor, the freeman ceases to be educated, or intelligent, or to have any superiority to the negro except that of race. . . . It is of no avail, therefore, that educated and intelligent free labor may be an overmatch for slave labor, because in truth, educated and intelligent free labor cannot coexist with slavery. Slave labor wins the victory, not merely by its own strength, but by weakening and deteriorating free labor.[13]

Here, too, Weston's remarks had roots in a decades-old European heritage of antislavery political economy. In his widely read *Treatise on Political Economy,* Jean-Baptiste Say had notably argued, partially on the basis of what he had been told by travelers to slave communities throughout the Americas, that "the industry of the free man, who has no slaves at his command," was unavoidably debased by the "contagion" generated by its clear economic inferior: that of the "degraded beings" of the slave and his master who are "incapable of approximating to the perfection of industry."[14]

The Mythology of American Exceptionalism and Republican Anxieties

Added, however, to such antislavery political-economic orthodoxy was a specifically American exceptionalist mythology that gave Weston's and other expressions of antebellum Republican free-labor ideology much of their distinctive character. It was not wage laborers everywhere, Weston's remarks indicate, but rather the exceptionally well paid and "intelligent" wage laborers of the northern states who were a superior and truly free productive body. Long-standing republican traditions in America, historians commonly hold, had tended to stigmatize the wage-earning condition for its lack of economic independence. Weston was not here unequivocally departing from those traditions. Possibly, along with both other Republican leaders and many wage earners themselves, he above all valued good wages for the saving and investment opportunities they provided; they were the hireling's escape route out of his employment status. Yet the insistence with which Weston counterpoised just wages with poverty suggests that discretionary income and consumerism—the capacity of civilized men to develop and satisfy their refined wants—ranked high in his scheme of values quite apart from economic independence, and that his formulation of American exceptionalist, free-labor ideology did in this sense deviate from a more traditional republicanism. There is the suggestion in his address, in other words, that Weston regarded the generously paid wage earners of the North and West as no less free than their many fellow residents who already enjoyed economic independence as freehold farmers or self-employed artisans or businessmen.

Weston's commitment to the mythology of American, and specifically northern, economic exceptionalism helps explain, furthermore, his aversion to reducing the conflict between slave and free labor to a contest over absolute cheapness, wherein the goal was to depress free wage-labor costs to the "standard of the cost of raising and subsisting" black slaves. It would be a hollow victory, indeed, for the northern system of free labor if it came to exclude and supplant slave labor "only when a certain density of population," and consequently declining wages, "shall bring with it a free labor still cheaper." "In that case," Weston wrote elsewhere, "one species of slavery will only have been substituted for another."[15]

But there is a related, and still more noteworthy, conviction embodied in Weston's address: the economic and moral superiority and the respectability that above all distinguished well-paid northern wage labor were the very basis of its vulnerability and fragility. This conviction reflected one sense in which Weston's ideology did incorporate republicanism with a vengeance and in fact exemplified a significant penetration of venerable republican anxieties into the economic realm.[16] John Adams, James Madison, and other late eighteenth-century leaders had cast doubt on the ability of republics—the best of all polities—to withstand assault from luxury, corruption, and stagnation indefinitely.[17] With other Republican Party ideologues, Weston was now insisting, in the face of the sectional challenge from the slave South, that the survival of the best labor system was likewise particularly dependent on constant vigilance and safeguarding.

Racism, Population Theory, and Slave-Labor Competition

Anti-black racism, his conviction that whites are "a superior race," was also deeply embedded in Weston's political economy. As George M. Fredrickson observes, Weston's writings exemplified a late antebellum proto-Darwinian intellectual tendency in the North that was both negrophobic and antislavery. One of his principal themes was that the condition of chattel servitude thwarted the natural outcome of the economic struggle among races.[18] Weston accordingly dismissed postemancipation racial problems in the South with the insistence that "so far as it is desirable to get rid of the negroes, their very inferiority as a race will accomplish that; nothing being more clear, than that an inferior race, except in the condition of domestication, or slavery, will not multiply in the presence of a superior race."[19] By the same token Weston was prominent among those agreeing that free blacks in the northern states, because they were exposed to competitive labor-market forces, were already proving themselves an inferior and a dying breed. The economic discrimination and legal and educational disabilities imposed on northern blacks — the overt absence of a level playing field — did not, according to this perspective, truly compromise the integrity of the competitive struggle in the free states.[20] Rather, such disabilities were mere certification of innate black inferiority, ones whose removal would in no significant measure alter the outcome of the competitive struggle between the races in the North. Thus did the conservative Philadelphia lawyer and former Whig Sidney George Fisher follow Weston and minimize the import of such discrimination and disabilities: economic opportunities existed in the antebellum North for the black man, but these were "beyond his talents."[21]

In appealing to formally race-neutral competitive market forces as the true arbiter of economic and social position and in ultimately attributing the disadvantages of blacks in the free states to the supposed attributes of blacks themselves, the perspective of Weston, Fisher, and like-minded thinkers foreshadowed what some scholars of late twentieth-century America have described as the ascendant "new racial ideology" of "laissez-faire racism." But the significant differences remain. Unlike Weston and Fisher, proponents of modern "laissez-faire racism" do not — at least explicitly — deduce from inferior black economic performance a biologically based cultural inferiority. Nor do they endorse ascriptive principles of racial discrimination and segregation as ratifications of black difference and inferiority. By virtue of its contrasting insistence upon the existence of a natural and inexorable racial hierarchy, the Weston perspective was accordingly even closer in substance, as well as in time, to another dominant racial ideology. This is what Carol Horton characterizes as the antislavery "phylogenetic liberalism" of Reconstruction-era conservative Republicans and moderate Democrats. That position recognized "no contradiction between the maintenance of certain basic, minimal rights" (life, liberty, and property) for the nation's putatively inferior blacks and continued "systematic practices of racial discrimination against them."[22]

Throughout the antebellum period itself there remained numerous commentators who shared Weston's negrophobic prejudices but not his particular conclusion that blacks removed from bondage posed no serious dangers to American whites. Perhaps at other times and in other contexts Weston would have manifested greater sympathy for such alternative assessments. But in 1856 he was marshaling his arguments against the extension of slavery into new territories. Thus he persisted in one of his central themes: the happy extinction of the black population in the more northern latitudes in fact would be reversed by repealing the Missouri Compromise and opening up Kansas and Nebraska to slaveholders and their bondsmen. Here Weston found it necessary to seriously qualify the argument, common to both northern and southern racist commentary, that black slaves flourished best in tropical regions.[23] He pointed, on the one hand, to the example of the West Indies, where slave populations had not been self-sustaining; tropical diseases had helped check their numbers. Weston underscored the desirability for this very reason of limiting slaves to such latitudes. So too, the "natural increase of the blacks," Weston maintained, had actually been much less rapid in the "extreme" South than it was in the temperate northern slave states (e.g., Maryland, Virginia, and Kentucky), with which Kansas and Nebraska enjoyed a comparable latitude.

Here, then, lay much of the demonical character of the repeal of the Missouri Compromise. Subverting the designs of nature, as well as the intentions of the Founding Fathers, that repeal promised, through the artificial, protective mantle of slavery, to give a more "northerly direction to the development of the negro race." It would thereby arrest that race's ultimate disappearance from the United States. The Kansas-Nebraska Act would appropriate "the finest regions and the most salubrious climates to the growth and expansion of a race, which is the shame and scandal and weakness of our country."[24] Thus did Weston, in his attack on the Kansas-Nebraska Act, bring an antislavery and a negrophobic perspective to the premise that he in fact shared with various proslavery southerners: that "blacks required special protection if they were to function as productive workers."[25].

Weston's claims respecting nineteenth-century population tendencies might well be problematic in their factual basis.[26] Those claims would seem — on the surface at least — to be particularly contravened by recent studies underscoring the increasingly tenuous position of slavery in the more northern nontropical slave states, although Weston himself noted this tenuous position elsewhere in his writings.[27] But there remains no question that Weston, driven partly by his distaste for blacks, would have had no use for a generation of scholarly arguments (forming part of the revisionist "needless war" school of Civil War historiography) which stressed the "natural limits" to slavery's expansion and dismissed the repeal of the Missouri Compromise as a mere abstract victory for the forces of proslavery.[28] Such scholarly arguments, as Harry V. Jaffa notes, commonly reflected racist proclivities of their own. They assumed that blacks were inherently incapable of being efficiently employed in the production of anything other than the handful of plantation staples for which they had been mobilized in the Deep South and the West Indies.[29] Weston, for his part, insisted that few such constraints in fact limited the deployment of black bondsmen. If they remained unsuited for the most highly skilled and intellectually demanding trades, they nonetheless could be cheaply and profitably utilized as manual laborers in a wide variety of enterprises.[30] Even now "in the Northern slave states," he warned, slavery "is directed to the same agricultural productions as in the free States. The white free man in Pennsylvania, who raises wheat, works against the black slave in Maryland and Virginia who does the same thing. The producers of pork and corn at the West, encounter a similar competition in Kentucky and Missouri." Northern industrial enterprises and factory workers might similarly expect increasing competition from firms utilizing slaves whom they either owned or hired. "The time . . . when the Southwest will '*monopolize*' the cotton manufacture of the United States may never come; but it is no idle speculation to suppose, that in this branch of industry, the free laborer may soon begin sensibly to feel the competing pressure of the slave owner."[31]

From Weston's free-soil perspective the profane potential of the market was less a matter of American chattel slavery in and of itself. It was less a matter of the buying and selling and the exploitation and abuse of members of a race that he deemed innately inferior. Rather, that profane potential was primarily defined by the competition, at once formidable and degrading, generated by the inanimate commodities produced by these black human commodities. Weston also perceived, however, that his ominous future scenario of greatly intensifying and cheapening slave-labor competition, with its underselling of free-labor agricultural and manufacturing products in expanding open markets, was contingent on several developments. Prominent among these was a decline in the market price of slaves from the high level they had maintained throughout the 1850s. Weston regarded such a decline as likely if not inevitable. To begin with, the very "philosophy" driving the institution of slavery was one of "reducing the laborer to a bare subsistence." Weston illustrated this point by itemizing the meager amounts expended to feed, clothe, and otherwise sustain slaves on a number of large and medium-sized plantations.[32]

Weston, however, looked to another circumstance to explain how the basic impulse toward minimizing slave-labor costs would actually come to manifest itself in declining market prices for slaves. He pointed to the absence "of prudential checks operating to restrain that species of the population."[33] Weston may partly have been referring here to a built-in tendency of the institution of slavery to stimulate slave reproduction and population growth, independent of the demand for slave labor, through the guaranteed subsistence it provided slaves. But there was also likely some Malthusian racism in Weston's prognosis. Weston was no more inclined than past antislavery commentators to minimize slaveowners' responsibility for breeding bondsmen for an expanding southwestern slave-labor market. But he was nonetheless suggesting that black slaves above all lacked the internalized prudential restraint that might effectively control their sexual appetite and their numbers.

Weston predicted, in any case, that an expanding supply of southern slaves would eventuate in declining market prices. Indeed, "in the end, their [the slaves'] labor must . . . be obtainable at the cost, or possibly a little more than the cost of supporting and governing them." At this juncture free laborers engaged in the production of similar goods would feel the most intense competitive pressures, especially, perhaps, from enterprises utilizing slave hirelings: "At a period of high prices, under which the owner of the slave receives a large hire for him, and under which the free laborer receives large wages, this competition is not felt, and perhaps not thought of. But the Virginia, Kentucky and Missouri owners of slaves must work them when prices fall, and the free laborers of the adjoining States will then realize the full severity of slave competition."[34]

Perhaps because it might undercut his incisive portrait of the "full severity of slave competition," Weston did not in his address pursue one possible further implication of a steadily expanding slave supply. This was the possibility that the maintenance burdens and other economic disadvantages of slave labor might mount at some future date to the point where masters were actually induced to terminate the system of slavery, replacing their bondsmen with less costly free waged laborers of either race. For years some antislavery as well as proslavery commentators had treated this scenario as plausible. But Weston himself would not go so far, and in other writings he in fact dismissed it as a serious possibility by falling back on the ultimate ability of slaveowners to control the numbers of their human property.[35]

Weston did recognize in his address that the sharp decline in slave market prices, which he predicted would maximize the downward pressure on the wages of free laborers outside the slave states, could be arrested for the foreseeable future by increasing the demand for slave labor. This increase might be accomplished either by diverting "a more considerable proportion" of slaves to "mining and manufacturing" or by enlarging still further "the agricultural area upon which they are worked."[36] But if expanding the domain of slave-labor enterprise in either of these ways in fact delayed a substantial decline in slave prices, didn't it then follow, from Weston's own argument, that the depressing impact of slave-labor competition upon free workers would also be averted? The imperatives of his free-soil manifesto hardly disposed Weston to admit to such a possible contradiction in his argument, and it was possibly to lessen the appearance of contradiction that Weston introduced another theme: the mere presence of slaves in the territories, whatever their market value and whatever their initial number, must at the least have a depressing effect on the free laborers within those territories.[37] Here Weston was adding his voice to the chorus of antislavery voices that for decades had denounced the so-called diffusion defense of slavery's expansion, which generally held that spreading a small number of slaves over a large territorial expanse would dilute and thereby weaken the peculiar institution, while having minimally injurious effects upon the white inhabitants of the territorial communities. Many of the diffusion arguments had also invoked, via Malthusian reasoning, putative humanitarian considerations: penning up a geometrically increasing population of slaves, rather than diffusing them, would eventuate in their mass suffering and extermination, either through race war or the slaves' starvation after abandonment by their masters.[38]

As earlier noted, Weston rejected this last, extreme "surplus slave" population scenario as implausible. But beyond this, he dismissed the humanitarian considerations behind diffusion proposals on the grounds that diffusion would reverse "the order of Providence" by "sacrificing the superior to the inferior race." Even if extending the area of slavery did add to the "personal comfort of the slaves, . . . our first and highest duty is to our own race."[39] And make no mistake, Weston insisted, even an initially negligible population of slave laborers in Kansas and Nebraska would, contrary to the diffusion theory, grow in size and come to wield a baleful influence on the region's white inhabitants. The South truly "needs outlets" for its slave population but "not outlets which will increase the volume of the mischief; not outlets which will establish new sources and springs of the fatal stream; not outlets which will carry the disease to new regions while it is left unmitigated in its old seats. Some things may be diluted by being diffused, but slavery, however scattered, retains everywhere all the strength of its original malignity. Virginia had such an outlet in Kentucky, but the temporary relief has long since become only a duplication of the mischief."[40]

The South's Poor Whites and Cultural Osmosis

In these as in other remarks, Weston was thinking of more or less long-term developments. For this reason, and also because he recognized that numerous economic and political contingencies, either favorable or unfavorable to slavery, could come into play at any time, he was often vague or circumspect as to the time frame within which various economic and labor-efficiency measures might complete their proper antislavery course.[41] In his address's short though intricate analysis, however, Weston was more precise and unequivocal in arriving at the standard free-soil conclusion: that of "the inevitable and eternal antagonism" between free and slave labor. The impoverished and demoralized condition of "the great mass of the whites at the South" was the existing proof of the pudding, the harbinger of what must befall free laborers in the North and West were they too "brought within the range of that fatal influence" of competition with the system of slave labor.[42] Indeed, Weston maintained, the southern states needed outlets primarily to benefit their own poor whites. Politically suppressed, this population constituted a greater "enemy" to slaveholders than the slaves themselves, who were naturally docile and had "rarely" revolted.[43] It was in the interests of the South, too, Weston accordingly reasoned, to preserve Kansas and Nebraska territories as free, as a "refuge" for its poor whites, thereby lending what security it could to the "peculiar social organization" within its borders.[44]

Interestingly, in this connection Weston attached no comparable emphasis to another common free-soil theme: the importance of preserving the territories as outlets, or safety valves, for the "surplus" laboring population of the northern free states. Eric Foner, among others, has suggested that an indeterminate number of eastern workingmen were indeed attracted to free-soilism for this reason.[45] But in their cases, at least, such an animating reason implied a critical view of eastern labor conditions — that owing to depressed wage levels and other circumstances, the valued goal of economic independence was moving beyond the workingman's reach. Weston, in contrast, quite lacked this critical perspective. He resisted any close connection between increasing population density, on the one hand, and declining demand for labor and falling wages, on the other. In his full-length book, he accordingly rejected a projected labor surplus as a serious prospect in the North or anywhere else in the United States, for that matter: "It certainly may and does happen, in some cases, that while laborers increase, the call for them increases still faster," and he furthermore insisted that "it is certainly not true that wages are reduced uniformly as population becomes dense. That an operation precisely the reverse of this has been going on in this country within the last thirty years, is a matter of common knowledge."[46]

Rising wages, however, was hardly a matter of "common knowledge" to the eastern workingmen who were drawn to the safety-valve, free-soil theme. The larger point is that Weston, unlike these others, was a vigorous northern exceptionalist. As with many other Republican Party ideologues, all of his anxieties over the threat of slave-labor competition to American wage levels coexisted with his confidence—indeed, his complacency—that were it exclusively left up to forces operating within the free states themselves, these would long remain a region of expansive and widely accessible economic opportunity.

In effect, Weston's free-soil address of 1856 coupled an acceptance of antislavery political-economic orthodoxy with an elaboration of the circumstances in Kansas and Nebraska which would render that orthodoxy nugatory, negating the greater efficiency and productivity and (in these two senses) the superior cheapness of "respectable" free labor. But regardless of what Congressman Barry and other proslavery commentators might have thought, Weston was engaging here less in outright contradiction than in paradox. This was primarily so because of the broadly cultural, rather than the narrowly economic, nature of his analysis. Weston made no mention in this connection of the economies of scale and other technical features that may or may not have given plantation slavery a competitive advantage over small-farm, free-labor enterprises in the North and West, as well as in the South. He stopped at noting the despotic power of slaveholders to unilaterally extend working hours, as well as to screw food and other slave-labor costs down to the minimum.[47]

Excluding slave labor from Kansas and Nebraska was instead absolutely imperative for Weston, as it was for other free-soil ideologues, because of the sorry record of cultural osmosis left by slave enterprise elsewhere. Those industrious and respectable free laborers who were not either repelled and driven out by slavery or discouraged at the outset from settling in a given area were almost inexorably demoralized and gradually transformed through such cultural osmosis. Better-paid and educated free workers were more highly motivated and productive than slaves, but these initial advantages could not long survive competition with slaves. Free laborers were debased as working beings—contaminated or "polluted"—to the level of the slaves themselves.[48] For Weston this process of contagion and degradation required a certain market proximity between slave and free labor, if not absolute spatial proximity, but it also went beyond slavery's assault on the market position of free-labor enterprises.[49] While necessarily entailing the undercutting of the superior economic rewards enjoyed by respectable free workers, it eventually came to encompass the wholesale corruption of their values, their character, and with these, their productive capabilities. In consequence, slavery's economic dominance in the southern states proved only one thing conclusively about slave labor: that "it is cheaper than that sort of free white labor which has been enfeebled and demoralized by the influences of slavery."[50]

In significant senses Republican free-soilism embodied the "pollution ideas" examined by the cultural anthropologist Mary Douglas. It was, among other things, a political agenda that encompassed certain moral and "good citizenship" values that were upheld by "beliefs in dangerous contagion."[51] As a prime illustration of these ideological tendencies within Republican free-soilism, Weston's thesis of cultural osmosis and degradation also bore some strong similarities to the argument that Frederick Law Olmsted developed in his much more extensive and ultimately far better known antislavery writings.

In part, however, because Olmsted was even more committed than Weston to exposing the disincentives and the consequent slothfulness and inefficiency characterizing slave labor, he attached less importance than Weston did to competitive market pressures generated by slave labor as a source of the southern white laborer's degradation.[52] Olmsted, to be sure, did credit the monopolistic power that slave enterprises enjoyed in various communities as one reason why "white labour cannot live in competition with slave-labour. . . . The holder of slave-labour controls the local market for labour, and the cost of slave-labour fixes the cost of everything which is produced by slave-labour."[53] Nonetheless, Olmsted's overall emphasis was upon how "it is not the mere competition of slaves in the market which throws white men out of it."[54] Olmsted proceeded from the axiom that he shared with Weston and all other antislavery commentators: that of "the popular degradation of labor arising from its association with the idea of subjection and submission to the will of a master."[55] Olmsted was even more taken than Weston was with the slave system's consequent cultural tendency to barbarize or "decivilize" southern society and inexorably to imbue the region's laboring whites with the same low standards of work and consumption that characterized slaves themselves.

Olmsted, in other words, penetrated further beyond the indictment that southern white labor's ability to compete with slave labor obliged its acceptance of a comparably low, indeed servile level of remuneration. His distinctive emphasis was upon how most southern white laborers — independent farmers and craftsmen as well as wage earners — eventually failed to desire enough goods and services, particularly those that that were the lifeblood of a complex structure of skilled occupational differentiation, to bestir themselves to compete with slave-based enterprises at all.[56] Conceding even less to any inherent economic advantages possessed by slavery, Olmsted's explanation for the failure of free white labor to drive it from the South was an elaborate confirmation of primarily the second half of Weston's thesis: "Slave labor wins the victory, not merely by its own strength, but by weakening and deteriorating free labor."[57]

Still, Weston and Olmsted remained agreed in their broad representations of nonslaveholding southern whites (and of slaveholding "gentlemen," too, for that matter) as indolent, barbaric, and degraded. Such representations, along with other antislavery themes, were not entirely lacking in validity. But historians are perhaps more inclined now than ever to recognize their biased and hyperbolic qualities and, with these qualities, the complexity of the bourgeois Protestant and other intellectual baggage that observers like Olmsted brought to their representations.[58] Traditional—and by this time rather shopworn—republican-agrarian themes were themselves never far from such renderings. Thus the Pennsylvania Whig Thaddeus Stevens identified in 1850 the most grievous failing of a slave society. It "never can have a body of small proprietors who own the soil and till it with their own hands, and sit down in conscious independence under their own vine and fig-tree. . . . That republic must be feeble, both in peace and war, that has not [such] an intelligent and industrious yeomanry, equally removed from luxury and from poverty" and comprising "the main support of every free government."[59] Stevens's own state was increasingly more notable for its dependent manufacturing wage earners than for its independent yeomanry. But for the Pennsylvania Whig, as for Weston, a pervasive middle-class prosperity—one in which the state's enterprising wage earners shared in varying degree—in fact counted for as much as freehold independence, and on the former score alone, Pennsylvania enjoyed a pronounced superiority over Virginia or Mississippi. In its conflation of newer with residual social strengths, Stevens's indictment of the failings of the slave South was hardly atypical. Eliding from that entire region an industrious, republican yeomanry, one that was both virtuously independent and comfortably middle-class, constituted the most blatant sense in which Stevens, along with Olmsted, Weston, and other prominent free-labor ideologues, saw what they wanted to see in the social order of the South.

Of course, proslavery polemicists were no freer of their own ideological, often republican-inspired exaggerations. Thus they conveniently conceptualized the free states in terms of the contrasts of wealth and the slavery of wages and poverty that were most striking in a handful of northern urban and industrial centers. And just as clearly, the worst-case scenarios painted by the respective antagonists did not go unchallenged by the other. Slavery's defenders, for example, commonly rejected as absurdly simplistic and specious one of the fundamental axioms of an Olmsted, Weston, or Stevens: that slavery was "an enervating pestilence," that it fostered among virtually all southern nonslaveholding white farmers, artisans, and laborers a debilitating contempt for enterprise and manual work—for their own employments.[60] Slavery's defenders did not reject the pestilence axiom merely with respect to nonslaveholding whites who were most physically distant and economically removed from slavery. Indeed, partly because they extolled slavery's civilizing influences upon all who fell within its reach, many proslavery commentators concentrated their fire on the Weston-Olmsted subaxiom: they vigorously denied that nonslaveholding whites who did toil in physical proximity to slave labor were demoralized, debased, and enfeebled.[61]

Confidence and Its Absence in Free-Labor Ideology

Whatever its ideological biases, Weston's address represents an able polemical brief for the process of demoralizing cultural osmosis worked by slavery. But if his analysis of the comparative cheapness of free and slave labor does stand free of outright damaging contradiction, there still remains something deeply curious about the lack of confidence it displayed in well-paid free labor's ability to withstand a direct competitive challenge from slavery. The form of labor that was better motivated, more efficient, more progressive, and altogether superior could hardly avoid, it would seem, being economically and culturally enfeebled by its clear inferior. It could scarcely resist being "overpowered" by a system of production whose only signal advantage was the lower labor costs it exacted, one that depended, moreover, on a putatively inferior race of human beings.[62]

The lack of confidence that Weston displayed in free labor's resilience and competitive strength has been slighted by historians to whom the optimistic side of northern antislavery mentality—its faith in the expansive and dynamic character of free-labor enterprise (above all, that enterprise comprised exclusively of whites)—has been far more apparent.[63] That same lack of confidence, existing in ambiguous tension with free-soil triumphalism, did not escape the attention of antebellum southern and northern Democrats, who attempted to exploit it out of their shared hostility to the Republican agenda. Connecticut senator

Isaac Toucey promoted the Kansas-Nebraska bill and its principle of congressional nonintervention by insisting that at least in the territories in question, if not in more tropical regions, the natural laws of climate and soil would inevitably give free labor the victory in any competitive struggle with slavery. Toucey needled the free-soil sensibilities of Weston and his congressional counterparts and their platform of blocking slavery's expansion through federal action with a pointed remark respecting Kansas and Nebraska: "It is a grain country, a country of wheat and corn; and it is a very poor compliment to the power and efficiency of the free labor of the North to believe that, in its own proper home, it could be supplanted and driven out by that which is comparatively feeble and inefficient."[64]

Northern Democrats like Toucey, one might plausibly conclude, at times were capable of expressing greater confidence in northern free labor's superior energies and competitive strength than did the Republicans themselves — the standard-bearers of the party of free-labor ideology. Nor should one dismiss such expressions as mere political opportunism or rationalization. The northern Democratic opposition to Republican free-soilism no doubt reflected many considerations, including ones of political strategy reflecting pressures from the party's southern wing. But prominent among these considerations as well was a genuine faith in: (1) the capacity of free labor to exclude and otherwise competitively prevail over slave labor in the existing territories without the assistance of a congressional ban; and (2) the capacity of free farmers and wage-earners to coexist in any case in proximity to slaveowners and their bondsmen without being corrupted and enfeebled.[65] Northern Democrats might well differ among themselves in the degree to which they embraced one or both of these two tenets. But Republicans, nonetheless, were as a group perceptibly more equivocal about the first tenet and unmistakably dismissive of the second.

This is not to deny that Republicans, following some abolitionists, manifested their own particular faith in the strength of free labor, most of all when it was employed in more complex and intellectually demanding kinds of industry and enterprise. Weston himself was among the many Republicans who at times did illustrate the more optimistic, triumphal dimension of free-labor ideology. This was the other side of the coin, the one that underscored free labor's inherent virtues and, especially, its initial superiority over slave labor. He could even insist that at such places as New Orleans, "under an almost tropical sun, white men, brought up to habits of steady and continuous industry" — which reflect "the training of free communities" — "are able to supplant slaves in the rudest and severest employments."[66] Along with William H. Seward and other Republicans and not wholly unlike some of the northern Democrats, Weston could express, accordingly, his confidence in the tendency of "gradual and peaceful processes," most particularly of all in the higher stages of a nation's progress, to supplant populations of "African" slaves with those of "white artisans and farmers." Actual expectation, not merely hope, fueled Weston's proclamation that "an inferior civilization must give room to that which is superior."[67] Nor, as Eric Foner has argued, were optimism and confidence absent from the ideological support that Weston, among others, lent to the various free-labor emigration schemes afoot in the 1850s. The organized infusion of antislavery migrants into the border slave states, as well as into Kansas and Nebraska, Weston and others claimed, could effectively undermine slavery, partly by arousing the latent antislavery feelings of southern poor whites.[68]

Still, attention must be paid to that other, coexisting dimension of free-soil, free-labor polemics that figured particularly prominently in Weston's address. This was the dimension that doubted the resilience and competitive strength of respectable, intelligent free labor, that questioned free labor's capacity, for all its initial superiority, to withstand for long the economic challenge and cultural pressures emanating from slave labor. On some occasions, to be sure, and as suggested earlier in the case of Olmsted, antislavery spokesmen did not intend their analysis as an admission of any inherent vulnerabilities on free labor's part. They offered it, rather, as a commentary on the power of "monopoly" enjoyed in southern communities by the privileged, slaveholding "oligarchy" — that "colossal aggregation of wealth," in the derisive words of the Jacksonian Democrat turned Republican Francis P. Blair Jr. On such occasions, that is to say, the antislavery emphasis was upon the uneven and unfair, as well as upon the polluting and degrading, nature of the competition between free and slave labor enterprises. This competition was unfair, as well as harmful, free-soilers further indicated, even if some of the slavocracy had managed to establish their monopoly more or less spontaneously — even, that is, if they had amassed their human property without the benefit of state-chartered privileges or other acts of direct governmental complicity.[69] The same antislavery sense of slave labor as oppressively monopolistic contributed to the Republican theme of slave labor as both a sectional and an intrasouthern threat, that labor constituting the foundation of a politically and economically formidable slave-power elite. "This slaveholding aristocracy is banded together to crush the free labor interests North and South. Its feelings and purposes are even more opposed to the free labor interests of all races South, than to the same interests North."[70]

Precisely because they so often spoke in terms of the "aristocratic" slave power, free-soilers remained generally ambiguous as to whether they also viewed as monopolists the many small southern farmers and craftsmen who were dependent on only one or a few chattel slaves and whose production for the market was negligible.[71] Unlike the elite who employed, either through ownership or rent, the largest numbers of slaves, such small slaveholders exerted less obvious power over the prices of commodities and the remuneration of free waged laborers. But when antislavery commentators did recognize their existence at all, they likely viewed even these smaller slaveholders as monopolists in a broader sense — that they too appropriated the fruits of slave labor and dictated the rewards of labor to their bondsmen.[72]

More importantly, free-soilers did not limit the threat, the cancer, of slavery to the large, "oligarchic" planters and entrepreneurs whom they characterized as the most blatant monopolists. In free-soil eyes even the smallest, nonelite slave-involved operations might pose competitive dangers for free labor merely by virtue of slavery's morally degrading, enfeebling, and polluting influence. For this reason the lack of confidence in free labor's resilience and competitive strength conveyed by Weston and other Republican voices went deeper and drew on notions of cultural contagion and economic debasement that transcended the specific specter of "slavocratic" monopoly.[73]

Similarly the Republican anxieties over free labor's vulnerabilities and fragility extended beyond what economists might categorize as market "externalities": the violence and the political fraud in which proslavery forces were willing to engage in order to secure slavery in Bleeding Kansas.[74] Such proslavery activities were among a number of late antebellum developments — which also included the taunting challenges George Fitzhugh, James H. Hammond, and other aggressive proslavery ideologues directed at northern economic arrangements and social conditions — to which antislavery, free-labor ideology evolved in specific response.[75] Still, these developments of the 1850s confirmed, rather than fundamentally drove, the most central of free-soil, Republican presumptions: that free labor in fact needed the assistance of legal supports to prevail over slave enterprise in the territories.[76]

This presumption was driven by the deeper uncertainties as to free labor's competitive strength and resilience, and if these uncertainties are particularly conspicuous in George M. Weston's political economy, they are nonetheless also manifest in the free-soil, free-labor commentary of Frederick Law Olmsted and other Republicans. By the same token, the Republicans' collective fears as to the fragility of superior free labor possessed an older lineage and represented more than just another expression of late antebellum antislavery responsiveness.[77] They merit greater attention not merely because they are curious, or because they have been slighted by scholars, but precisely because they do exemplify broad and long-standing Gresham's law–like tensions and anxieties in nineteenth-century American society and carry added cultural significance for this reason.

6

Convict Labor, Free Labor, and Gresham's Law

REFERENCE HAS already been made to the republican themes that provided an intellectual underpinning to George M. Weston's attack on the repeal of the Missouri Compromise—to his characterization of the best labor system as the most fragile one, the one most vulnerable to decay. And as also suggested, the free-soilism of Weston and his cohorts represented an intersection of these indigenous American republican concerns with the transcultural fears of contagion examined by Mary Douglas and other scholars. But there is more to be said about the antebellum economic context within which Weston reformulated venerable republican anxieties. Weston provided guidance here. In addressing the "controversy" over the relative cheapness of free and slave labor and in underscoring the threat of slave-labor competition, Weston drew in his lecture on several parallel controversies. Thus at one point he noted that

> it is not inappropriate to observe that in many of the States in which the system of penitentiaries exists, very considerable objection has been made to the employment of their inmates in trades and handicrafts, in which they would compete with honest citizens. In some of the States, if parties have not been formed upon this question, certainly candidates for office have been interrogated in reference to it, and it has entered as an active element into the popular elections. If this jealousy on the part of workingmen of the competition of a few hundred persons condemned to penal servitude, was natural and justifiable, an occasion for it immeasurably greater exists in the competition of the three millions of persons condemned to perpetual servitude in the Southern States.[1]

No doubt Weston is opportunistically invoking here the prison-labor controversy; he is appropriating it for the cause that he really cares about. Such appropriation was hardly unusual in the early nineteenth century. Indeed, in tending to focus attention on a few particularly prominent linguistic borrowings — above all labor reformers' milking of such terms as *wage slavery* and *white slavery* — historians have slighted the variety and the magnitude of discursive and ideological appropriation engaged in by the period's social and political activists.[2] And in this particular instance Weston's utilization of the threat of convict-labor competition for strictly free-soil purposes — which led him to downplay that threat's relative seriousness — was to prove prescient in one important sense.[3] As ideological contributions to the outbreak of the Civil War, the free-soil, free-labor principles typified by his address did represent an undeniable culminating point. They did become the most fateful and politically significant manifestations yet of a pervasive cultural inclination: that of dramatizing, castigating, and at times invariably exaggerating the operation of Gresham's law–like processes in the labor markets of the period. Nonetheless, the prison-labor controversy to which Weston pointed merits discussion for its own genuine role in both signifying and fostering this underlying inclination.

The nub of the controversy was the practice of many state prisons, above all in the northern states, of exacting labor from their inmates by hiring them out to private contractors in the building, shoemaking, and other trades. David J. Rothman suggests that such contracting out of convict labor by prison officials became increasingly popular after 1850. He takes the rise of this expedient, revenue-maximizing practice as one further indication of the pervasive decline of a more idealistic reformatory zeal that had distinguished a previous generation of prison, poorhouse, and asylum officials.[4] Still, Massachusetts and other states had begun contracting out their prison labor as early as the first decade of the nineteenth century, and by the late 1820s and early 1830s, the practice was provoking considerable controversy and opposition among the groups of workingmen referred to by Weston. In New York State alone, petitions of protest gathered over 200,000 signatures in 1834.[5] Demands to curtail or abolish convict-labor competition were standard features of the platforms of the Jacksonian era's trade unions and Working Men's parties, and they expressed, in particular, the sentiments of members of traditional crafts that were experiencing discernible skill dilution.[6]

The contract laborers targeted by these protests never totaled more than a couple of thousand at a time in states that contained many thousands of free manufacturing tradesmen. Even historians most sympathetic to the labor organizations have recognized that in this respect they could be overly alarmist: their tendency was to exaggerate the existing impact of convict-labor contracting on the well-being of "honest" tradesmen in even the more affected trades.[7] The possibility for exaggeration was compounded by the difficulty of singling out prison industry from the other circumstances—including industrial deskilling, immigration, and economic recession—that simultaneously acted to depress free wage rates and incomes.[8] As one scholar remarks, "The workers most involved in opposing prison labor were the displaced artisans and mechanics whose skills had already become obsolete due to advancing industrialization" and "mechanized factory labor as a whole."[9] Yet despite the conclusion of this and other historians that the workingmen critics of convict-labor competition found in prison industry a "convenient scapegoat" for their troubles, the workingmen themselves were hardly oblivious to these other unfriendly circumstances.[10] Rather, many of them may have fastened on and magnified the prison-industry evil partly because they perceived it as remediable through political pressure to a degree that economic recession and industrial deskilling were not.

At the same time, and as several examples in this discussion suggest, there remain plausible grounds for pinpointing convict labor as at least a significant contributor to the economic ills of many tradesmen. One is, after all, referring in such cases to limited labor and consumer markets, in which even the seemingly negligible accretions to labor pools and product outputs contributed by the convict contract system likely had some depressing impact on prices and wages. This effect was exacerbated by the contract system's tendency to concentrate prison labor in a relatively small number of crafts.[11] Convict laborers, moreover, might be employed in prison industries year-round, whereas independent workingmen were subject to cyclical and seasonal unemployment. Thus convict labor's impact in terms of contribution to the total craft product might well be disproportionate (above all within the more immediate environs of the prisons) to the numbers of convicts actually employed.

Perhaps even more important, protesting labor organizations and their supporters were clear that they were equally concerned with the damaging "principle" they found to be at work.[12] In claiming that the unchecked application of this principle by state prison officials in time would swell the number of contract laborers, together with the population of trained ex-convicts, to levels that would prove truly disastrous for workingmen, the early labor movement exhibited a fixation on future worst-case scenarios with which Weston, the free-soiler, could well sympathize.[13] This was, in fact, one of only several existing parallels between the opposition to contract convict labor in the states and the opposition to chattel slavery in the federal territories.

In states like New York, where the controversy proved especially intense and protracted, the antebellum critics of convict labor and, above all, of contracting convicts out to private employers identified three general evils: (1) the direct assault that the "detestable competition" of "imperfectly educated" convict labor waged on the livelihood of honest tradesmen; (2) the destructive impact, both economic and moral, that ex-convicts had on the tradesmen and "legitimate" apprentices whose workshops and communities they now joined; (3) the ancillary damage that "making honorable labor a part of the punishment of convicts," together with society's acceptance of the practice, inflicted on the "public reputation" of tradesmen and on the "respectability" of their employments.[14] The first of these imputed evils — the one that was most thoroughly materialist in nature — most directly summons up the specter of Gresham's law–like competitive processes prevailing in the labor markets of the period. But the other two criticisms of convict labor also were grounded in the same broad and underlying cultural anxieties regarding cheap and inferior labor that Weston manifested in his antislavery address of 1856. The objective here is to illustrate these parallels, rather than to provide a detailed history of either contract convict-labor practices or free workers' campaign against convict-labor competition generally, a campaign that extended into the early twentieth century.

Contract Convict Labor: Underbidding and Unfair Competition

As suggested, the hostilities of workingmen and their sympathizers were aroused less by the imposition of a labor regimen on prison inmates than by the nature of the labor competition eventuating from contract convict-labor practices.[15] State prison officials were charged with entering into an unholy partnership with private contractors, enabling the latter both to hire inmates for as little as one-quarter the cost of free labor and to establish and operate factory-like "mammoth workshops" within the prisons themselves. Utilizing the cheap labor of the contract laborers, frequently in conjunction with machinery, these workshops turned out manufacturing goods at prices with which independent enterprises "of small means" could scarcely compete.[16] Typical was the petition that manufacturers of silk hats in New York, a business that employed between thirty and forty journeymen, addressed in 1834 to a state assembly investigating committee. Noting that their journeymen previously could earn $2.50 a day when fully employed, the petition protested that employers currently contracted for eighteen inmates of Sing Sing Prison at only 30 cents a day each to perform the same work and consequently were able to offer an appreciably cheaper product. The petitioners complained that they could only survive such competition by significantly reducing their own prices and with this the wages they paid out, at the cost of great "injury" to themselves and their journeymen.[17]

In fact, some employers of legitimate journeymen, either yielding to economic pressures or out of a less desperate desire to seize the main chance, were among those who turned to the contracting of prison labor.[18] And not surprisingly, when wage-earning journeymen of the period spoke for themselves, they commonly included the opportunistic practices of such employers among the major sources of their economic misfortunes. This was, after all, a time of intense labor unrest, marked by growing estrangement of journeymen from master mechanic–manufacturers in a variety of urban trades especially. The more estranged and militant of journeymen, accordingly, attacked convict labor as a developing "scab"-labor pool — a bargaining weapon — that their own avaricious employers would increasingly hold over their heads were the contract system permitted to expand.[19] Journeymen generally, in any case, were no less hostile than the silk hat makers and other resistant small manufacturers to the competition, existing and imminent, offered by contract convict labor. They were a major component of the delegates to the mechanic conventions that convened in New York and other states during the 1830s and 1840s and issued a stream of resolutions and addresses attacking state prisons for depressing the labor market with their "state slaves." In this literature of protest, journeymen and the employers who joined them could repeatedly agree, the undercutting from prison-labor competition must force unwanted vocational changes upon victimized mechanics, if not outright unemployment and public charity. Particularly victimized were those tradesmen who had families to support on their earnings, in pointed contrast to the predominantly young and single male convicts.[20] Just as frequently, the participants in these convention proceedings insisted that society's "mechanic interests" were not requesting special dispensation and protection. They were asking merely to be "let alone" by the state, which, by their own sense of the legitimate division between public and private, in this instance had extended its authority most inequitably and inappropriately into the domain of economic enterprise.[21]

This last argument raises basic and familiar issues with respect to Jacksonian Americans' attitudes toward capitalist market processes. In pressing for a public policy of noninterference by state prisons in their economic affairs, workingmen at times explicitly disclaimed any hostility to fair competition in the free market; they disclaimed their opposition, that is, to private enterprise that did not expressly enjoy the advantage of state-granted monopoly privileges.[22] On the contrary, workingmen at these times adduced contract convict labor as one of the more blatant instances of government-stimulated manipulation of the labor market. It was conspicuous proof of how an impartial law of supply and demand did not in practice govern journeymen's earnings. On some occasions, too, labor activists and organizations also directed this criticism against certain kinds of relatively private, if still judicially permitted, economic behavior—against, notably, the wage agreements, blacklisting, and other collusive practices engaged in by groups of employers.[23] But with respect, certainly, to more overt acts of government complicity, the free-market, laissez-faire-based objections to contract convict labor as unnatural competition bore strong affinities to the mainstream Jacksonian Democratic attack on state-issued corporate charters and similar "artificial" privileges and monopolies. This was the Jacksonian tradition that feared the state and elite use of the state as the principal threat to individual liberty.[24] The most competitive-market, "entrepreneurial" attacks on the "State Prison Monopoly" even included the claim that the "free mechanic" would cease his complaints if contractors merely refrained from underbidding, if they instead hired their convicts at the "fair market price."[25]

Even such relatively moderate, narrowly based criticisms of contract convict labor clashed with the most uncompromising defenses of the practice. Where the critics insisted that "it is now an established principle in political economy that government ought not to interfere with industry," the forthright defenders appealed to moral and classical economic principles of their own.[26] A New York Senate committee report of 1834 insisted that "the tendency of the [contract labor] system is to command the highest prices which the market will afford" for the "services of the convicts." In other words, these services were already "let out at a fair value." That some contractors at Auburn Prison had been obliged to "abandon" their efforts was itself proof that the contractor of convict labor "cannot afford" "to undersell the market"—to offer lesser prices for the same "mechanical productions obtained from the hands of any other workman." The government contracts did not—perhaps could not—upset self-regulating market forces. Nor was there any true prison-labor "monopoly" in the restrictive sense of that term, not merely because the convicts were "let out to different persons, at different branches of business," but also because the convict's "services are freely offered to all, and are sold, and sold only, to such as will pay the highest price for the same."[27] Against the critics' claim that in fact "none but large capitalists, and those who reside in the near vicinity of the prisons can be parties to such competition," the report of 1834 insisted that a level playing field already existed, with the rewards going to those mechanics with "greater foresight" and "a better knowledge of the business." If some of New York's mechanics were failing, they had only themselves, then, to blame. "Success in life depends not merely on peculiar advantages, or fortunate occurrences, but is invariably commanded by the skilful, the industrious, the enterprizing, and the prudent, and by these alone." Finally, the committee report followed these last Whiggish, American exceptionalist formulations with an invocation of "Say's law of markets" in response to the workingmen petitions. Consumer markets could not be overstocked as a result of convict labor and oppress the state's mechanics in this way because "it is a well established principle in political economy, that extended production introduces extended demand."[28]

Another New York Senate committee report seven years later made, if possible, an even more uncompromising, Whiggish defense of contract convict labor. This was marked by a conservative insistence on the naturalness of class harmony and on, indeed, the absence of true classes in American society. The mechanic critics of convict labor, the report insisted, were seeking "partial legislation"; they were driven by their erroneous assumption that "the community is divided into classes or castes, and what may be beneficial to the whole as a mass, may be, and often is, injurious to some of these classes, individually." Moreover, "the petitioners are mistaken in assuming an identity of interest among themselves as a class; if there be conflicting interest between themselves and other classes, the same theory would cut them up and subdivide them into lesser classes." Here, in attacking the notion that there existed a single, unified mechanic "interest" or "class," one that was injured by convict labor, the report appealed to basic consumer considerations. Suppressing the prison manufacture of shoes might possibly benefit shoemakers as producers. But by rendering the production of shoes more expensive, such action would hardly serve the interests of, say, New York's cabinetmakers or coopers. On the contrary, the report concluded, "it is the interest of the whole, to have all the productions of human labor and skill as good and as cheap as possible."[29] Finally, the same open opportunity structure that discouraged the formation of distinct, conflicting, and dangerous class interests in America permitted a beneficent free competition among individuals to flourish there. Like the earlier senate committee inquiry, the 1841 report here acknowledged the existence of contract convict-labor competition but similarly insisted on its legitimacy and even its value by shifting the spotlight to the performance of free mechanics themselves: "If then the combination of capital, skill and machinery, in the State prisons, with the distribution of labor, has enabled the State or contractors to render, even constrained and enforced labor, more productive than the voluntary and free, stimulated by *every* motive of interest, the true remedy is not the destruction of the State prisons, but the adoption of their improvements by the mechanics themselves."[30]

Generally, however, it was more characteristic of the defenders of convict-labor competition to turn back workingmen criticisms by taking the reverse tact, by altogether minimizing the economic impact of that competition on wage levels and market prices. Illustrative of this tendency was the report of S. C. Dunham, the agent of the Auburn State Prison in 1834. Dunham sought to show both that the competitive evils associated with convict labor had been exaggerated and that owing to the numerous economic disadvantages and risks he encountered, the private contractor "pays as much for the labor of the convicts as he can afford."[31] The number of prisoners employed in both Auburn and Sing-Sing at *"mechanical labor,"* Dunham claimed, was not over 1,100 men, hardly enough to have a substantially depressing effect on the wages of New York journeymen.[32] And while the goods that these contract workers produced might indeed be sold at lower prices, their output was scarcely sufficient to effect appreciable price reductions in the state's manufacturing economy. Moreover, and quite apart from their low numbers, Dunham argued, contract convict laborers could constitute no genuine competitive threat to skilled tradesmen and were inherently incapable of significantly undercutting and driving the latter from the market. This was precisely because of their inferiority as workers, as measured either by their output or by the quality of their product. "There is not that assiduity and dispatch in his work that there is with the journeyman laborer." And this inferiority, Dunham reasoned, was in turn perfectly understandable in view of the fact that the convict "does not labor with a view to the interests of his employer," the contractor.[33] Most other defenses of the state's prison system would follow Dunham in emphasizing the unthreatening, even inferior nature of contract-convict competition, usually by making similar reference to the low numbers of convict laborers and to the trifling value of their gross product. Even the New York Senate committee report of 1841 endorsed this position in the end, despite its earlier embrace of contract prison labor both for lowering the price of consumer goods and for setting a positive example of enterprise for mechanics on the outside.[34]

A logic similar to Dunham's, one recalls, was also at the core of antislavery political-economic orthodoxy. This was the logic that, most notably contributing to the more confident dimension of antebellum free-labor ideology, anticipated the disappearance of a poorly motivated, inefficient, and altogether inferior slave mode of production at the hands of free labor. Yet it was the tradesmen's anxieties and criticisms regarding contract convict labor, not such defenses of the practice as Dunham's, that most strongly foreshadowed Republican free-soilism. It was their objections and protests that anticipated, in particular, the more alarmist, less confident dimension of free-labor ideology through their own bemoaning of the sway of Gresham's law. For Weston and other free-soilers, the superior cheapness of slave labor and slave-based consumer items would hardly constitute a point in slavery's favor, would hardly be something that they could identify with the common good.[35] Nor, in their view, would the morally pernicious, dishonorable features of slave labor preclude its capacity, under a variety of circumstances, to undersell and drive out respectable free labor. So, too, reasoned the critics of convict-labor competition. Contradicting S. C. Dunham's sanguine claims, Austin Baldwin, a manufacturer of carpenter's planes in Albany, New York, in fact appeared to argue in 1842 that at a certain point the inferiority of convicts employed by contractors altogether ceased being a function of the prisoners' physical performance. Instead, that inferiority became exactly and exclusively a matter of the "ruinous consequences" which convict labor held for others. "During the infancy" of the rival production of planes by the inmates of Auburn State Prison, Baldwin noted in his response to a state assembly committee,

> the convict journeymen were but raw hands, and of course the work but a very inferior quality, [and] we did not at once feel any very serious inconvenience from this competition, although they soon began to supply orders for the coarse and leading articles in our line; but, after a few years, when the "felons" had acquired a knowledge of the trade, and the prison factory became better established, we found the heaviest and most profitable portion of our business leaving us, on account of the ability of our customers to furnish themselves at a less rate than we could possibly afford.[36]

Baldwin did remain ambiguous on one point. This was whether the initial "acknowledged superiority" of his firm's products in fact ceased to exist, or whether that superiority came simply to be offset in his customers' minds by the relative inexpensiveness of prison-made planes, achieved through the contractors' introduction of machinery and other cost-efficient measures. Still, Baldwin was more willing than most opponents of prison industry to acknowledge the productivity — and hence the competitive threat — of convict laborers in terms of the quality as well as the sheer quantity of their output. Here, indeed, Baldwin was likely more the exception than the rule among antebellum articulators of Gresham's law–like anxieties. In their attacks on cheap-labor competition, nearly all of these were first and foremost targeting, along with Baldwin, the dishonorable lowering of price and wage scales. But they were also, if commonly by implication only, invoking cheapness in a second sense as well. Their attacks included pejorative suggestions of the inferior work standards, the "cheap" product quality, putatively embodied in this "detestable" and "unfair" competition. In failing to do this in the case of the prison-industry controversies, Baldwin was possibly reflecting his perspective as a small proprietor and employer of skilled artisans. Because of their characteristic pride in craft, journeymen mechanics themselves may have been simply less disposed than Baldwin to include his acknowledgment of comparable quality in their own attacks on convict-labor competition; they were more inclined to repudiate convict labor as cheap in both senses of the term.

In one respect, too, such artisan attacks were broadly congruent with long-standing intellectual currents. Beginning with William Petty in the early modern period, theorists of the detailed social division of labor and manufacturing specialization, of which early nineteenth-century prison industry was one specimen, had tended to associate these processes with the development of mass consumer markets. Like New York's skilled artisans themselves, theorists had associated these processes with greater quantitative output and the lowering of commodity prices, not with any propensity on their part to produce high-quality goods. The difference here was that such commentators generally celebrated these phenomena in very unjourneymen-like terms.[37]

Baldwin's notions of the cheapness of convict labor may not have been completely reflective of the artisan criticisms. Nonetheless, the bitter consequences for his business that he described in his testimony—price and wage reductions, layoffs, and the "downsizing" of operations in an effort to survive the prison-labor competition—remained similar to the scenarios of declining market power outlined by the silk hat manufacturers and dozens of other small manufacturers and journeymen. And merely by denouncing state-supported contract convict labor as subversive of truly open market processes—as powerful, "unfair competition" waged by "a class of grasping, avaricious men"—Baldwin and other critics of the practice also foreshadowed one of the prominent free-soil themes of Weston, Olmsted, and Blair. This was the theme that denounced the "slave oligarchy" as a monopolistic presence which depressed the earnings of free white laborers in the South.[38]

But more was at least implicit in some of the economic critiques of convict-labor competition. Oftentimes, that is, their animosity toward Gresham's law processes was more than merely antimonopolistic in temper. Rather than unequivocally embracing the market as a panacea and opposing contract labor as an unjust intrusion on market relations, that animosity suggested a certain revulsion for unrestricted free-market processes and activities themselves.[39] There was revulsion for an unrestrained, predatory capitalism beyond that sustained by corporate charters and other acts of state intervention. In such criticisms convict-labor competition emerges as one of several manifestations of an abhorrent market-cheapening ethos: state prison officials were exploiting consumer interests and desires to strike a bargain with private contractors at the expense of independent labor's wages and respectability. Small manufacturers and their journeymen, together with other labor-movement activists, might still remain most overtly enraged by what they perceived as the most blatant government policies of "arbitrary interference." Against such prejudicial interference, they might still prefer to take their chances with a relatively unregulated market ethos as the arbiter of their fortunes.[40] But mechanics' sense of besiegement from a variety of forces and events also could lead them to question the ethical right of people with power—be they state legislative and prison officials, merchant capitalists, or master mechanics turned contractors—to avail themselves of any methods and of any dishonorable, albeit competitive, forms of labor that helped dilute and cheapen the skills of respectable artisans. Upon noting that "the mechanics have difficulties and prejudices enough weighing against them, without the government's adding their opposition also," one critic of state-supported convict labor thus proceeded to contextualize his criticisms in terms of the additional sources of labor competition that likewise provoked his animus: the "influx of multitudes every year from the worse than enslaved districts of the Old World; also the emptying of the poor houses, jails, and houses of refuge, in a supply of apprentices, bound out by poor-masters and overseers."[41]

Of course, in varying measure these and other sources of cheap labor also could be construed as an outcome of state policies—e.g., the "class legislation" of Old World nations drove the migration of impoverished immigrants to the United States. Apropos here is the point made elsewhere: private property, like free markets, is the creature of state power. As the historical sociologist William G. Roy further notes, "There is no such thing as a noninterventionist state; property underlies all social and economic relationships and is defined and enforced by the state." The latter creates "the conditions within which economic activities take place."[42] Yet the previous point also remains valid. Antebellum labor-movement activists could follow a James Freeman Clarke or Horace Greeley and extend their abhorrence and criticisms to various labor-commodifying, labor-cheapening practices and activities that they did not primarily attribute to government interference per se.

Meriting emphasis, again, are the parallels with George Weston's free-soil attacks on the deployment of chattel slaves in both agricultural and manufacturing enterprises. That under certain circumstances prison industry could, like black slave labor, be fully competitive with respectable free labor was not an argument which, in the eyes of its most severe critics, disproved its essential inferiority. Rather, economic viability—and the resultant capacity of "bad" laborers to drive out "good" ones even under conditions that were not blatantly monopolistic—merely underscored the fact that the essential core of such inferiority did not reside in the capabilities and performance of the system's unfree participants.[43] It resided, instead, in the system's putative economic and moral consequences for those outside it. Nor did their insistence on the competitive fragility of respectable, truly free labor—their anxieties over free labor's economic debasement to the level of "servile" labor—lead either free-soilers or prison industry's critics in the direction of actually doubting the existence of basic, meaningful distinctions between free and servile labor; they only affirmed those distinctions all the more.[44]

The Pernicious Impact of Ex-Convict Workers

One of the most bitter tradesmen complaints, as Austin Baldwin's testimony suggested, was that convicts—this "refuse of society"—were rewarded for their crimes by acquiring new, valuable mechanic skills during their training and tenure as convict laborers.[45] So equipped with these marketable skills, such complaints noted, the convicts must continue to depress the wages of honest tradesmen even after their release by entering already overstocked labor pools.[46]

That contract labor's critics here found themselves in frequent disagreement with the system's defenders was largely owing to the economic changes that were rendering "trade" and "mechanic" skills dynamic and ambiguous categories in this period. Consensus could not even be reached on the number of inmates who began their sentences possessing no authentic trade whatever. In contrast to prison industry's defenders, the critics who magnified the threat emanating from convict-labor training and competition tended to maximize the number of those initially unskilled.[47] Disagreement then centered on the nature of the skills in which convicts were trained. Prison officials, contractors, and other defenders of convict labor took a common position: inmates characteristically mastered a single specialized, mechanized technique only. They did not acquire the full-blown trade expertise that would make them truly competitive with other mechanics upon their discharge from prison.[48]

Not surprisingly, this response proved least comforting and persuasive to the journeymen members of the building and other trades that had already proved most vulnerable to subdivision of labor, skill dilution, and other aspects of metropolitan industrialization. Armed with a different perspective on the nature of recent economic change, such journeymen and their supporters were particularly receptive to the contrary notion that the specialized expertise of "half-trained," "dishonorable" laborers, whatever their source, age, sex, or ethnicity, did indeed comprise a "power of competition" that seriously threatened the economic position of skilled artisans.[49] It was for these critics most of all that convict-labor training and competition constituted one of a number of unconscionable specimens of Gresham's law.

In New York protesting workingmen and their supporters did achieve a modest victory of sorts, pushing through legislation that restricted the kind of training received by convict laborers. An initial act of 1835 stipulated that in branches of industry supplied chiefly by domestic labor, the number of convicts to be employed should be limited to the number of convicts who had learned a trade before coming to the prison. But as suggested above, a characteristic tendency of the prison wardens and other defenders of existing practices was to exploit, sometimes in different ways, the ambiguities imposed by economic change. On the one hand, as Orlando F. Lewis notes, the defenders evaded this restrictive legislation by representing as real tradesmen "all those who claimed to have followed *any* trade before coming to prison."[50] On the other hand, by apportioning one or two of the fragmented skills required by prison industry among those convicts whom they admitted were "tradeless," administrators and contractors could insist that in this way, too, they were in compliance with the 1835 law.[51] A second, 1842 law, following in the wake of further workingmen petitions, attempted to tighten the restrictions by explicitly prohibiting the employment of convicts in trades that they had not learned before their imprisonment.[52] Free workingmen were soon complaining that this legislation as well was being commonly evaded by prison officials and contractors, although it did eventuate in the canceling of contracts at both Auburn and Sing Sing.[53]

Consistent, too, with their concern over convict labor's wider moral implications, there remained workingmen's additional grievance, one that included but also extended beyond the humiliation of merely "becoming associated with anyone who had been attainted by crime."[54] Discharged convicts, now equipped with some skills, must actually "poison the minds and corrupt the habits of the young men and journeymen" among whom they came to live and work.[55] Workingmen characteristically linked this moral evil with the more strictly economic ones that they ascribed to convict labor. A typical petition complained that honest mechanics must associate with discharged convicts who had learned their trade "not by a respectable and faithful apprenticeship, but during a period of punishment for crime against society and its laws."[56] The insult of a "demoralizing and degrading" presence was thus added to the injury of convict-labor training and underbidding that had already been inflicted on respectable laborers.[57] Through the prison system "the mechanic ranks" became "the sewer into which is poured all the rogues and felons of society."[58]

Perhaps the most basic assumption underlying such complaints was that ex-convicts remained unredeemed by their punishment.[59] Ironically, given their own insistence on the dignity and virtues of manual labor, workingmen thus rejected one of the primary arguments embraced by the defenders of convict labor. This was the argument that through its disciplinary and other features, prison labor served to elevate and reform convicts' moral character.[60] Workingmen's bitter disdain for this defense was evident in their declaration "that we have no confidence in the schemes of theoretical philanthropists, who have fallen in love with out State prison system, nor of the boasted moral reform of the felons confined in these prisons; and we want some better proof than has yet been offered, before we are convinced" that such men have "all at once become honest, upright, and good."[61]

The New York legislative investigations included occasional testimony from employers and other firsthand observers supporting such skepticism. Their testimony claimed that periods of incarceration averaging between two and ten years, during which time "the Thief, Burglar, Rowdy, and Vagabond" had been put to labor, had done nothing to alleviate these individuals' propensities for "immorality and crime."[62] Yet such limited firsthand observation by itself cannot explain the protest literature's insistence upon the contagious character of these propensities. It cannot fully account for this literature's fixation upon the susceptibility of respectable mechanics and apprentices to moral contamination by unredeemed ex-convicts, a fixation that some master mechanics in fact honored by refusing to employ discharged prisoners.[63]

One can point to several influences that likely stimulated these particular mechanic anxieties. In arguing for the silencing, or "isolation," of the prisoner as the only possible basis for his moral reformation, early nineteenth-century penal writers themselves harped on the "monstrous intercourse"—the "corrupting" influence upon one another—of which convicts were capable. The mechanic criticisms explicitly borrowed this point of emphasis from the penal literature.[64] The similarities in theme furthermore suggest the impact on mechanic anxieties of such prominent genres as urban sensationalist and "advice" literature and their own embedded notions of psychological manipulation and influence.[65] These genres permeated American culture with tales—alternately didactic and titillating—of the alcoholic, sexual, and other morally ruinous temptations and seductions that city life and those already corrupted by it held out to hardworking, ambitious, and innocent young people from the countryside.[66]

But also among the relevant and influential components of American mythology were the same republican-based themes that helped shape the free-soilism of George Weston and his fellow Republicans. The most virtuous and respectable communities of free workers rested on fragile foundations not merely because they could be undersold, cheapened, and thereby injured through strictly economic forces operating in the competitive marketplace. Such workers were also uniquely vulnerable to decay through a more amorphous process of cultural osmosis. They might readily degenerate to the same condition as that of the degraded laborers whose contagious vices they imbibed through a demoralizing spatial proximity.

Furthermore, and as in the case of free-soilism, the republican-inspired attacks on the ex-convicts spawned by prison industry assumed, and at times explicitly insisted, that such contagion could only run in the one negative direction with respect to morals and status; the contagion could never be of a positive nature. "When honest men associate with rogues, the very connection reduces the character of the former down to the standard of the latter; it can never have the effect of raising the standard of the rogue to that of the honest man, in the estimation of the world."[67]

A Double Standard

There is no need to belabor the parallels between these particular criticisms of convict labor and some of the major themes in Weston's free-soilism—to wit: the discursive parallels that the contaminating influence of ex-convict laborers upon communities of honest tradesmen held to the enfeebling cultural impact of black slavery upon nonslaveholding white laborers and farmers in the South. Nor would it seem necessary to do more here than suggest the likelihood that the former as well as the second of these representations was exaggerated. Republican free-labor ideology's overzealous portrait of southern poor-white demoralization was anticipated by a comparably overheated sense, running through the protests against convict labor, of the honest mechanic's susceptibility to the poisoning influence of the ex-prisoner in his midst.

But exaggerated fears remained genuine ones; one cannot plausibly reduce to the level of cynical protest strategy the prominence that the critics of convict labor gave to the theme of mechanic degeneracy. At the same time, this remains a theme that subsequent scholarship has generally neglected. Historians, to be sure, have extensively examined artisan republicanism, including that component consisting of the small producer's resentment toward the unskilled for the role they played in the disintegration of the trades. But scholars nonetheless have slighted the considerable extent to which mechanics' very sense of the fragility of the trades was stimulated by republican-inspired anxieties over their own possible moral degeneracy through a process of cultural osmosis.

Because, in expressing such anxieties, skilled mechanics directed some of their resentment against the disproportionately poor and unskilled who were being trained and deployed as convict laborers, what has been noted in chapter 2 regarding Simon's diatribe against the "lazy" inmates of Philadelphia's House of Refuge might also be suggested with respect to the convict-labor controversies. Competitive capitalist market pressures fed skilled mechanics' sense of aggrieved respectability and encouraged their use of the lexicon of upper-middle-class moralism in condemning convict laborers for their character deficiencies. Even apart from the influences likely wielded by penal, urban sensationalist, and advice literature, there are grounds for suspecting that the mechanic protests did reflect some internalization of middle-class values, some bourgeois ideological hegemony at work.[68] But once this tendency is noted, no more than in the case of Simon should its centrality be exaggerated. This is so if only because the workingmen's anxieties did not contradict but rather fed into the class resentments and conviction of social injustice that attended all of their complaints regarding convict labor. The pronounced lack of sympathy that antebellum workingmen and their supporters manifested for convicts in this period—either for the circumstances leading to the convicts' incarceration, or for the convicts' own economic exploitation under the contract system, or for the difficulties attending the convicts' reentry into society after discharge from prison—should be placed in the context of this same overriding sense of unfairness.[69] Why was the mechanic class above all exposed to the pernicious influence of the prison-trained ex-convict? Why were mechanics singled out "as the only class who are sufficiently degraded to be the companions and fellow-laborers of all the thieves and felons who have been detected in their villainies"?[70] And why were mechanics alone obliged to bear the freight of a state prison system that seemed faulty in its basic premises? As some New York mechanics put these points in 1842, for more than ten years "the friends of the mechanical interest have [sought] to convince the people of the folly of that false sympathy that holds out inducements for the commission of crime, by placing the convict felon on a better footing in society at the expiration of his imprisonment than before his confinement, whilst the interests of the honest mechanic are entirely neglected, his character degraded, his business ruined."[71]

Meetings like this one regularly complained of how the prison labor system, in multiple economic and moral ways, imposed an "odium" upon the "fair name" of mechanics.[72] Such a characterization indicates considerable defensiveness. And as suggested, that defensiveness was itself stimulated by the perception of skilled tradesmen that both their livelihood and their status—the integrity of the "mechanical arts"—were under assault from a confluence of social and economic circumstances that included but extended beyond the convict-labor system. Yet the attitude of defensiveness does not diminish the force of some of the criticisms directed against prison industry. Elaborating, for example, on their general insistence that the "mechanic interest" was bearing an unjust burden, New York workingmen critics pointedly asked why no convicts were ever trained to enter any of the "liberal professions": "How long, think you, would lawyers, theologians, physicians and teachers, patiently endure to have their numbers increased by the addition of felon graduates from the prisons of our State? But is it less unjust to fill our ranks?"[73]

That these workingmen almost invariably framed this argument in the form of a rhetorical question may suggest that few of them actually sought or hoped to open the professions to convict labor.[74] Whatever their commitments to an artisan republican, equal-rights creed, they had too keen a sense of the resistant social and political forces that, quite beyond the disabling backgrounds and limited capabilities of many of the convicts, precluded such a development as a serious possibility.[75] Raising the issue was instead an appeal for empathy from legislators and others; it was a rhetorical stratagem for winning support for changes that would alleviate in other ways the inequitable burden on the "mechanic interest."[76] Interestingly, New York's mechanics failed to press with equal frequency and animation the question of why the state did not ease their burden by rechanneling prison inmates into unskilled physical-labor employments—canal digging and the like. Recognition of the various practical difficulties facing such an undertaking no doubt partially explained mechanics' relatively muted response on this issue.[77] But their greater fixation on the immunity of the liberal professions from convict-labor competition also indicates, again, how the mechanic protests combined festering class defensiveness and frustrations with a more calculated intent of testing the empathetic capabilities of those New Yorkers who practiced elite occupations and occupied policy-making positions. And, too, if "earning" had indeed emerged by the Jacksonian era as a principal "ethical basis of democratic citizenship"—a point of commonality between the upper middle classes and more recently enfranchised mechanics and other male workers—this was all the more reason why mechanics could not passively accept the blow to their earning capacity represented by convict-labor competition.[78]

The elected officials, prison administrators, and private contractors who comprised the core of convict labor's antebellum defenders did not speak with one voice in response to such pressures of protest. Hardly unsurprisingly, they did not, over several decades and across many states, take a uniformly uncompromising position with respect to recruitment, training, and other contract convict-labor practices. Yet virtually all of them highly prioritized the system's revenue-generating, tax-alleviating advantages for state governments and citizens.[79] They also, in the uplifting tradition of the early nineteenth-century Benevolent Empire, defended its economic, moral, and psychological benefits for convicts and ex-convicts, even as many of the workingmen critics' concern for their own respectability may have likewise drawn on the moral force of the Second Great Awakening.[80]

In addition, the defenders of the prison contract system persisted in their claims that the most severe critics exaggerated the damage it inflicted on free mechanics, while also failing to offer any substantial alternative plans.[81] To this last claim the labor press offered one particular response in behalf of the aggrieved party: "As a body, the mechanics do not consider themselves called upon to answer the question put to them so often, when speaking on this subject, 'what will you do with them (the convicts)?' They do not consider themselves bound to propose a remedy. They themselves are the sufferers. It is the duty of the state, which imposed the unjust burthen, to take it off."[82]

Even some of the more sympathetic appraisers of the mechanics' grievances have found this rather huffy and belligerent response less than satisfactory.[83] In fact, the mechanic and other critics of New York's contract system did not disclaim all responsibility; for example, they did on occasion suggest alternative trades that might be introduced into the state prisons to employ the inmates.[84] But the political system, in New York State at least, did not in any case prove wholly unresponsive to the mechanic complaints, whatever the generally negative tenor of these. Convict-labor competition would remain a thorn in the side of labor organizations throughout the nineteenth century. But the later ante-bellum period itself was marked by a decline of protests from their peak inten-sity. And although this decline partially reflected the collapse of the Jacksonian era Working Men's parties that had been a primary vehicle of the protests, it was also in some measure attributable to the ameliorative measures taken by the state in the 1840s. These included the act of 1842 that tightened up the previous one of 1835, together with the canceling of some contracts found in violation of this restrictive legislation. Also taking the edge off the most vociferous trades-men complaints was the construction of a third state prison in the mid-1840s that did not engage in private contracting at all, and that employed its inmates in iron production rather than in work that competed with any of the estab-lished crafts.[85]

Yet such ameliorative measures only began to address the more basic under-lying issues raised by the workingmen's protests. Not much more, really, than the forthright defenses of state prison industry did the enacted reforms include a satisfactory answer to the charge that contract convict labor constituted a form of unjust discrimination against mechanics, and that nothing better revealed this prejudice—the double standard embodied in those practices—than the system's failure to expose professionals to even minimal competition from "convict slaves."[86] Whatever the practical obstacles to such a development, one might also reasonably infer from the general silence on this issue on the part of prison industry's defenders their endorsement of basic structures of differential social power and prestige. Explicitly they typically insisted that only the mechanic arts and trades could practically be taught and executed within the confines of a prison.[87] For the most part implicitly—and, one can plausibly assume, to a much greater degree than the workingmen petitioners—they dismissed as simply bizarre the notion that if convicts could be made morally and intellectually suit-able for the mechanic trades, then they could be similarly trained and equipped to enter one of the liberal professions.[88]

And this particular characteristic of the convict-labor debates—the over-whelming extent to which the Gresham's law concerns over underselling, cheap-ening, and degradation were played out with exclusive reference to manual-labor employments—constituted a final sense in which those debates anticipated and paralleled the slavery debates of the late antebellum years. Francis P. Blair Jr. would pick up the line of argument used by the mechanic critics of the prison labor system. He would contend in 1858 that the slaveholding "oligarchs" in fact "have no more right to inflict this degradation on mechanics, by placing slave labor in competition with their free labor," than they had to educate their slaves "and put them into the learned professions." But of course, Blair noted, the slaveholding oligarchs never contemplated exercising their formal "constitutional right" to utilize slave labor in this last way, if only because they themselves were commonly engaged in these very "learned professions . . . here the shoe pinches."[89] As with the workingmen critics of convict-labor practices, so for Blair and a few of his free-soil colleagues, fundamental patterns of social stratification could become debate fodder: the pervasively unequal impact of unfree labor practices upon different occupational groups could and did become one more issue with which to hammer a system of social injustice.

But such efforts notwithstanding, the emphasis still ultimately belongs on the delimiting effects of social-stratification patterns and assumptions. The emphasis belongs on the institutional and ideological protection that these provided professional and other elite groups, both North and South, against competition from degrading, unfree labor. Property and power differentials and prevailing social values imposed boundaries in the convict-labor controversies analogous to the boundaries that they imposed in the debates over poor relief and the social classes that were supposedly corrupted by such relief. These differentials and values assured that the Gresham's law–inspired anxieties remained to an overwhelming degree matters of competition between "respectable" and "servile" forms of manual labor exclusively.

7

The "Pauper Labor" of the Old World,
Free Labor, and Gresham's Law

THE EARLY NINETEENTH-CENTURY controversies over "converting our State prisons into manufacturing establishments" and thereby bringing the labor of our "honest" workingmen "to a level with that of the very refuse of society" were replicated with respect to dozens of smaller county and municipal correctional institutions, all similarly seeking to exact productive labor from their charges.[1] These controversies raise further questions worthy of exploration, not the least of these being the apparent general absence of an overt racialist dimension from the mechanic complaints. Hostile racial epithets were notably absent from the mechanic campaigns waged against contract labor at Sing Sing and Auburn. The absence seems curious in part because the African-American component of the antebellum state prison population was not insignificant, averaging perhaps 10 percent at Auburn and over twice that at Sing Sing (the latter's larger African-American proportion was hardly surprising given its location near New York City). In addition, the African-American prison component was, in general, greatly disproportionate (commonly by at least eight times) to that of the black component of the total population in New York and other northern states. The absence of an overt racialist dimension from the mechanic protests seems curious for still another reason: these protests peaked during the same period whose defining feature, in many historians' view, was the emergence "among the vast majority of whites in the North" of a highly sensitized consciousness of "white supremacy," together with an unprecedented hostility (as exemplified in the antiabolition, anti-"amalgamationist" mob) to perceived threats to that supremacy.[2]

One might plausibly have expected, for all these reasons, that the "respectable" white journeyman mechanics who (along with employers like Austin Baldwin) denounced convict laborers as the "refuse of society" would have expressed particular displeasure at the indignity of being in competition with black convict "refuse"; it seems unlikely that they would have simply effaced black convict competitors from their consciousness.[3] Conceivably, the absence of such expressed displeasure reflects the possibility that African-Americans prisoners (along with female convicts of any race) ordinarily comprised an insignificant fraction of the inmates who were contracted out in ways that white male mechanics perceived as threatening to their livelihood or status.[4] Then, too, because of prevailing racial discriminatory practices in the antebellum North, including the complicity of employers in these practices, white journeymen may have never even seriously entertained the notion that black ex-convicts could be among the discharged prisoners who joined their workshops and degraded them by this means. Yet another possibility: tradesmen perceptions may have been influenced by the fact that blacks in many eastern prisons were increasingly dwarfed in absolute numbers by the foreign-born, especially Irish immigrant, inmate population. By 1860 the foreign-born made up over 52 percent of Sing Sing's prison population and nearly 30 percent of Auburn's.[5]

These explanations for the invisibility of the African-American presence in the antebellum protests over convict contract labor remain conjectural. But at least with respect to the protests over New York State prison industry, the invisibility itself seems unquestionable. It also seems consistent with a view expressed earlier: that the early Industrial Revolution, together with the emergence of various kinds of cheap and servile labor, stimulated many apprehensions among relatively skilled tradesmen as to their possible economic and social degradation, and that any particular anxieties they had relating to their racial self-definition, or whiteness, were only one part of these total anxieties.[6]

The parameters of this chapter's subject discourage further speculation along these lines. They also preclude further consideration of the various reform measures that were proposed and in some cases implemented during the antebellum debates over convict contract labor. One of these reform measures, though, does provide a convenient segue into further examination of the subject of free labor, Gresham's law, and antebellum cultural anxieties. New York's statutory restrictions on the training of inmates, the legislation of 1835 and 1842, exempted from their purview the employment of convicts in the manufacture of the kind of articles that were principally imported from abroad. This exemption emerged from an ideological context that was far broader than the legislation's objective, which was to encourage prison industry to concentrate on manufactures that competed only with European imports. The ideological context had everything to do with the putative nature of the laboring population that manufactured these imported items: the subsistent, degraded, so-called pauper labor of England and other Old World nations. New York's prison-contract statutes embodied the ideal, indifferently pursued as it was by the defenders of existing practices, of pushing one kind of unfree, servile labor in directions that would throw it up exclusively against Old World laboring populations. These populations were mythologized as likewise degraded and cheap and just as economically and morally dangerous to bodies of respectable free workers.

It remained, however, a matter of disagreement as to whether American convict labor and European pauper labor wielded malignant competitive powers that were in fact comparable in magnitude to one other. Buffalo's mechanics and manufacturers petitioned in 1834 that convict-labor competition was "more ruinous and destructive of all mechanical skill and enterprize" than the pauper labor of foreign countries, against which American tariffs provided protection.[7] Not surprisingly, a contributor to the *National Magazine and Industrial Record* disagreed, though he was not necessarily unsympathetic to the workingmen protests: "May not Europe be considered in the light of a great state prison, and a protective tariff as a law to abolish State Prison Monopoly?" All those who opposed competition from "degraded labour at home" should support a protective tariff against competition from degraded labor abroad.[8] A voice that clearly was unsympathetic to the workingmen petitioners against prison contract labor, the Whiggish New York Senate committee report of 1841 discussed earlier, prioritized even more uncompromisingly the cause of tariff protection: "Why complain of the competition of even two thousand domestic paupers and convicts, when they are obliged to compete with more than twenty millions of foreign ones; many millions of whom are compelled to labor for much less than *thirty-four cents per day,* to enable their masters to undersell our own citizen mechanics in our own market."[9]

Such disagreements recall an earlier point: that the social discourse of the antebellum period, like that of other periods, was marked by continuous parallelings and thematic appropriations, driven by different and oftentimes conflicting agendas and ideological objectives. Debates over which form of unfree labor, domestic convict labor or European pauper labor, posed the greater competitive threat to America's respectable workingmen contributed only a fragment of the sum total of these parallelings and thematic appropriations. To serve his own purpose of underscoring the primacy of the free-soil cause, George M. Weston found it no less useful than the New York Senate committee of 1841 to minimize the relative seriousness of convict-labor competition.[10] But toward those same free-soil ends, Weston also turned in his address of 1856 to the ongoing parallel controversy over the competitive threat posed by European pauper labor: "New England cannot view, and has not viewed, with equal complacency, that social organization out of which arises what is called the '*pauper labor*' of Europe. She feels the pressure of it, in the competition of commerce and manufactures, and has insisted upon protection against it by tariffs. The cheapness of slave labor engaged in raising sugar, enures to her benefit; the cheapness of English labor, engaged in manufacturing cotton, interferes in the markets of the world with her own productions."[11]

Weston here was issuing a wake-up call. He acknowledged that in its past concentration on the production of cotton, tobacco, rice, and sugar, the cheap slave labor of the South, like that of more tropical regions, had redounded in basic ways to the benefit of the free states, as Democrats particularly had long claimed. Weston admitted that "it is not easy to perceive, that the northern laborer has been otherwise than benefited by" this slave labor "in the cheapening of those important and essential articles of universal consumption." But all this, he went on, must increasingly change if black slavery was permitted to expand in "northerly" directions. Slave labor and new slave-grown products would then come to occupy the same position of competitive antagonism with respect to the laboring and other interests of the free states that European pauper labor had occupied for decades. With its economic interests now adversely affected, New England would no longer be able to turn a blind eye, as it had in the past, to "an organization of labor" so "wasteful of life" and so "stained with cruelty."[12]

Thus did Weston invoke European pauper labor to underscore the threat posed by slavery's geographic and market expansion. But more than was the case in his treatment of workingmen complaints over prison industry, he here dramatized slavery's menace less by minimizing the relative magnitude of the European pauper-labor threat than by taking the latter seriously as an antecedent model. In fact, Weston's commentary on overseas labor competition could be mistaken for some of the modern-day warnings regarding the economic implications of free-market capitalism's "globalization": "So intimate, indeed, are the relations of even distant nations in these latter days, and so wide-reaching are the influences of modern commerce, that the serf system of eastern Europe is felt on the shores of Lake Michigan. The grains of Podolia and the Ukraine, are produced at prices, and brought to Odessa by methods of transportation, impossible if labor was paid, and sold there at rates which affect the markets and profits of the farmers of Wisconsin."[13]

Weston invoked the pauper labor of the Old World to score points against domestic slavery. But the American representations of foreign pauper labor remained, more than anything else, an inextricable part of the early nineteenth-century debates over trade policy. On the one hand, therefore, those representations were an outgrowth of an already formidable body of formal and technical transatlantic political-economic literature debating the relative merits of protection and free trade. This literature was, at this time at least, considerably larger and richer than that addressing the economics of either slave or convict labor. On the other hand, the American pauper-labor imagery was also a function of the political opportunism, impact of special-interest groups, compromises, and bargains that contributed, beyond theory, to the formation and enactment of trade policies during the second and third American party systems. This is not to deny that the formal trade doctrines advanced by even the greatest and most foundational political economists for this period, beginning with Adam Smith, were themselves value-laden, ideological, and even shallowly opportunistic in places, just as were their other theoretical contributions.[14] Nor is it to overlook the fact that in the antebellum United States certainly, the distinction between the writing of political economy and partisan activity could be nebulous, as the example of a Calvin Colton or George Weston illustrates. American representations of foreign pauper labor in the public language of the period were part and parcel of an ongoing political party exchange whose participants selectively, and with varying degrees of crudeness and sophistication, drew on abstract transatlantic doctrines of international trade while simultaneously grafting onto them their own indigenous partisan objectives and ideological impulses.[15]

So long as the putatively servile pauper laborers of the Old World remained geographically distant, they never generated among most of these participants any particular concerns that they might infect and debase respectable, truly free American labor in some of the ways that more physically proximate slaves or discharged convicts could. They did not, that is to say, provoke from the assorted guardians of American free labor the same dire warnings that they constituted a source of demoralizing and corrupting cultural contagion. This absence of physical proximity was especially underscored in another of the period's discursive permutations on the theme of cheap labor, that embedded in the literature of economic nativism. The *Champion of American Labor*, published in New York by An Association of Mechanics, insisted that so long as European "pauper laborers" were confined to Europe, the damage they inflicted on "American" workers, through the lower-cost goods that they produced, was limited. Indeed, high tariffs alone would benefit only the capitalists that promoted them through the Whig Party. True protection for native-born workers, the *Champion* proceeded, consisted of ending or at least significantly curtailing immigration itself, including capitalist agents' recruitment of cheap labor from abroad for work on canals and other enterprises.[16]

For such economic nativists, as for cultural and religious ones, physical proximity was everything. The *Champion of American Labor* dwelt on the direct job competition, the unemployment through more indirect means, and the depressed wage levels that the transplantation of Irish and other Old World pauper labor ostensibly inflicted on native-born workers.[17] Cultural and religious nativists, commonly of more elite backgrounds than the artisan *Champion,* were more preoccupied with other social costs wrought by this same physical proximity. Those included the immigrants' pervasive corruption and debasement of American Protestant values, institutions, and standards; their character and behavior were represented as a source of contagion in the broader cultural sense of the term. The social costs also included the literal life-threatening contagion that impoverished, vice-prone, and germ-carrying Irish Catholic immigrants were charged with bringing to New York and other population centers periodically ravaged by epidemic disease.[18]

Yet these various nativist obsessions, centering on the influx of the famine Irish, by no means obviated antebellum perceptions that Old World pauper laborers, as the tools of European capital, threatened American conditions even when they remained in the Old World. The prevailing depictions of these geographically removed laboring populations as politically oppressed and economically subsistent were embedded in long-standing, potent, and in many cases ideologically self-serving representations of the Old World generally. And the fact that owing to their physical distance, the "unfree" laboring populations of the Ukraine, Ireland, or even Manchester, England, remained abstractions for at least the nonimmigrant components of American audiences did not necessarily diminish the credibility and power of the stereotypes fostered by party politicians, newspaper editors, and others.[19] Indeed, the physical nonpresence of these Old World populations likely encouraged antebellum Americans' intellectual tendency to disregard any countervailing evidence that might challenge and undermine the dominant portrayals of these groups as ground-down, degraded, and economically desperate and driven. For such reasons as these, and as Weston's example itself suggests, European pauper labor might easily appear a formidable market threat regardless of its physical remoteness, and even as that same remoteness encouraged a concurrent American disposition to view these particular others in a relatively sympathetic light. To the extent, moreover, that it was indeed perceived as exerting a depressing influence on the wages and material well-being of American workers, Old World pauper labor was likewise seen as an assault on their moral well-being. In the pervasive antebellum anxieties stimulated by the competitive challenges arising from ostensibly cheap and inferior bodies of labor, the specter of European pauper labor accordingly figured significantly.

Consistent with European pauper labor's character as a mythologized entity in mid-nineteenth-century American discourse, the term itself had problematic features. Some of those who used it expressed a quite explicit belief in its technical accuracy. The Home League for the Protection of American Labor and the Promotion of Reciprocal Commerce noted in 1842 that "it is for the interest of the Capitalist to pay a higher rate of wages to the free American who supports himself independently rather than to give lower rates to such degraded and pauper dependents as are maintained by poor laws in foreign countries."[20] This characterization of the Old World laborers with whom American workers competed reflected nothing so much as the powerful legacy left by pre-1834 poor-relief practices in England, whereby the inadequate wages earned by intermittently employed, able-bodied laborers were indeed made up by parish allowances from the poor rates. Yet it remains questionable how widespread such aid-in-wage relief practices in fact ever were. In addition, these practices became less widespread (above all for able-bodied males and their dependents) under the New Poor Law enacted expressly to curtail them. Nor did the Home League and like-minded American commentators offer much evidence to support their generalizing beyond England to the complex and varied circumstances of other European countries. How many members of the laboring populations of these other countries were in the early nineteenth century the recipients of poor relief (either state or private) that acted to simultaneously supplement and cap market wage levels?[21]

By its nature sloganeering elides complexity and contradictory evidence. That the menacing catchwords "the pauper labor of the Old World" constituted at least a quasi misnomer in the strict and technical sense was, moreover, less important than the fact that most Americans were employing and debating those words in their broader, more metaphorical sense. By pauper labor they above all meant labor driven by starvation wages. The specter of European pauper labor emerged, in this connection, as the special handmaiden of the wage-differential issue, which in the third decade of the nineteenth century established itself as a staple of political-economic and Whig Party justifications for a protective tariff in defense of American manufacturing enterprise specifically.[22]

Most American invocations of European pauper labor, accordingly, boiled down to references to the so-called pauper labor employed in England's manufactories. In view of the concurrent American focus on the wage-differential issue, this was not without irony, for England's manufacturing workers, as informed Americans and Europeans recognized, in fact earned substantially higher wages than laboring populations on the Continent and by this standard might be construed as anything but pauper laborers. Yet it remained competition from England's workers, those belonging to the premier commercial and industrial power in the world, about which Americans were, with some reason, above all concerned.[23] Historians have often singled out the intense antipathy that Henry C. Carey and other leading Whig protectionists bore for England, or at least for its policy-setting elites. They have underscored Whig efforts to expose the vampirish tendencies of British "free trade" policy as the international embodiment of the monopolistic and predatory proclivities within class-ridden English society itself.[24] Yet the "free trade" Democrats on the other side of the tariff issue hardly embraced English society either. Just as routinely as their adversaries, and frequently with the same self-congratulatory American air, they castigated England for the taxation, landed inheritance, and other oppressive laws and institutions that skewed its distribution of wealth and kept the general recompense of its laboring population appreciably below that in the United States. Indeed, it was the Democrats, following Andrew Jackson's lead, who had conspicuously emerged on most fronts as the party of Anglophobic sentiment. The vigorous protectionism of Whig politicians was at least partly driven by the desire to keep pace with the Democrats, to prevent them from wholly cornering the market on a valuable political commodity.

But where many of the free-trade Democrats parted company from the Whigs was in questioning whether the appellation "pauper labor," even in its broader sense, was an accurate characterization of England's manufacturing workers. They questioned, that is, the magnitude, and even the existence, of an actual wage gap between those English and those American laborers employed in their nations' industrial sectors. Other of the Whigs' Democratic opponents acknowledged a significant wage differential. Yet they minimized on other grounds the effective capacity of England's industrial pauper laborers, under a liberalized trade policy, to depress the wages, reduce the employment, and otherwise damage the life chances of American workers. The positions staked out by antebellum Democrats in the trade debates revealed that they were as wedded in their own way to ideals of American economic exceptionalism as were protectionist Whigs. By the same token the Democrats stand in marked contrast to modern-day proponents of free trade who insist that American workers have to lower their expectations in order to compete with Third World wage earners. Still, in merely contesting such questions, in debating the actual nature of the competitive threat issuing from English and European pauper labor, Whig and

Democratic politicians were raising basic issues of international trade policy that remain with us today.

Because, too, these antebellum trade debates engaged a geographically external competitive threat, they generated somewhat more straightforward assertions of national integrity and American nationalism than did the controversies over slave and convict labor. These debates, in fact, well illustrate the tendency of ideologies of national identity to incorporate coexisting beliefs — in this instance ones regarding social class especially.[25] But whatever their distinctive features, the debates about foreign pauper labor and trade policy exposed the same basic Gresham's law–like tensions that the antebellum controversies over slave and convict labor did.

Foreign Pauper Labor and Whig Protectionism

Consider one of Horace Greeley's many statements in defense of a protective tariff, specifically the tariff that Congress had enacted two years earlier, in 1842. In what had become by this time a "pauper labor" mantra, the Whig journalist first rhetorically inquired whether "any man can seriously doubt" that "the overthrow" of the "policy of Protection . . . would subject the Laborers of our country to a depressing and ruinous competition with the beggared Labour of Europe, Asia, or wherever Labor is ground down to the lowest apology for subsistence?" More interesting is what Greeley followed this with: "I am quite aware that ill-paid, untaught, half-famished Labor is far less efficient than that of energetic, intelligent Freemen, and that the price of a day's work may be considerably less in other countries than here, and yet production be as cheap here as there. But to this there is obviously a limit; and if the tailor, the boot-maker, the weaver of Britain and Germany is paid but twenty-five cents a day, it will be idle to expect our employers to maintain an unchecked rivalry with their foreign competition and pay their workmen a dollar a day."[26]

In part of this statement, Greeley distanced himself from cruder versions of the pauper-labor argument, those favored by such fellow Whig polemicists as Calvin Colton. As Michael Hudson observes, these cruder versions portrayed international prices as "a direct function of wage differentials *unadjusted* for differences in labor productivity."[27] Greeley, in contrast, appears relatively sensitive to the argument that American wage laborers' greater intelligence, energy, and productivity, all in part the products of superior wages and living standards, enabled American employers to partially offset the competitive price advantage possessed by foreign rivals who relied on lower-cost pauper labor. Nonetheless,

Greeley insisted in the end on the "limit" as to what these American strengths could accomplish, and he reverted to the standard Whig protectionist warnings as to the compelling Gresham's law–like effects of foreign pauper-labor competition. He held to the position that without duties which sufficiently raised the price of rival foreign goods so as to discourage their purchase in domestic markets, American "mechanics and manufacturers" must, in Henry Clay's words, "sink in an unequal contest with the pauper labor of Europe."[28]

Unless checked in some way, Greeley insisted in the end, bad labor drives out, or destroys, good labor. Like George Weston's affirmations of this tendency in the late antebellum free-soil controversies, Greeley's contribution of 1844 to the ongoing trade-policy debates is noteworthy for its ambivalent attitude regarding the competitive strength of well-paid, "intelligent" free labor. True enough, it remains possible that Greeley actually was not troubled by any real ambivalence or conflict. Possibly his expressed recognition of the superior energy and productiveness of well-paid American manufacturing labor amounted to little more than Whig partisan strategy. By paying lip service, and thereby demonstrating his attentiveness, to antiprotectionist considerations that altogether denied foreign pauper labor's insuperable advantages, Greeley may have believed that his ultimate insistence on those advantages would appear more convincing to his readers. But it seems more likely that Greeley was not simply playing partisan rhetorical games, and that while he did attach decisive weight in the end to the Gresham's law forces embodied in "cheap" foreign-labor competition, he nonetheless took seriously the considerations that undermined the cruder versions of the pauper-labor protectionist argument. These considerations merit closer examination, particularly because they often assumed still greater prominence within the American antiprotectionist, free-trade camp.

Uppermost was the notion, popularized if not originated by Adam Smith in his attack on eighteenth-century mercantilism, that just as wages offered a superior labor incentive to the slaveholder's lash, so generous wages constituted a more effective incentive yet.[29] British mercantilist writers had commonly argued that natural indolence was particularly pronounced among laboring people, and that above-subsistence wages merely permitted them to indulge their preference for leisure over work.[30] Following a smaller number of other commentators, Smith claimed, to the contrary, that laborers shared the innate acquisitiveness, the passion for continually expanding wants, of more privileged individuals. Employers could turn this acquisitiveness to their own advantage and improve the motivation, industriousness, and efficiency of their workers by paying them above-subsistence wages.[31] Since Smith's time, classical and then neoclassical economic models tended generally—if not without significant ambiguities and contradictory tendencies—to attach greater emphasis to the converse relationship. This was the extent to which, at least in competitive labor markets, higher wages followed on the wage earner's increased productivity.[32] Nonetheless, the relationship that Smith identified established its own place in the structure of thought attending the emergence of the first industrializing, free wage-labor capitalist societies. Even Thomas Malthus and David Ricardo incorporated Smith's high-wage scenario into some of their writings, despite their seminal contributions to the "dismal science" of political economy. Against their grimmer contributions featuring the human proclivity toward overpopulation, the "stationary state," and the "wages-fund," they too gave limited recognition to Smith's suggestion that rising real wages were a stimulus to improved worker habits and increased industriousness and productivity.

Why should American Whigs like Greeley have embraced this same theme, a component of British political economy, which adduced a positive relationship between high wages and worker productivity? Most important, that theme supported the major Whig doctrine that American society realized as no other the naturally harmonious, mutually beneficial relationship between capitalists and wage earners.[33] Conservative and moderate Whigs especially celebrated American society—at least for its legally free white male population—as an equitable and "open" hierarchy, one in which industrious and productive workingmen, no less than their employers, invariably reaped ample material and social rewards from an expanding economic pie.[34] At the same time, their devotion to American exceptionalism and their aversion to class conflict also encouraged Whig politicians, together with Henry C. Carey and other members of the "American school" of political economy, to repudiate the "English school" of Malthus and Ricardo for what they not without grounds took to be the latter's dominant theme. This consisted of distribution principles that stressed, contrary to the Whigs, the near inevitability of subsistence wage levels and the inverse relationship between wages and capitalist profits. In attacking these distribution principles for legitimating the unjustly ascriptive, class-privileged nature of English society, American Whigs thereby tended to ignore the degree to which their own convictions of class harmony had some intellectual basis in British political economy. This was the strand of thought, dating from Smith, that adduced a positive relationship between generous wages, worker industriousness, and capitalist profits.

British political economists generally, and Smith and Ricardo most prominently, were also avid proponents of international free trade, and this provided yet more reason for the Whig condemnations of English political economy.[35] Pennsylvania's Thaddeus Stevens insisted in 1852 that reciprocal trade laws were just "only when nations are equally advanced in skill, in capital, and in the powers of production."[36] He was joined by other Whigs in noting that England had entered on a free-trade course only after years of building up its commercial and industrial supremacy through protective policies of its own: "Free Trade all over the world is British monopoly of trade all over the world."[37] Such arguments anticipated something of the more academic challenges to free trade's theoretical and "idealistic" appeal that persist to this day. This is the insistence that what might well be the most beneficial policy for the world as a whole may ill serve the best interests of individual countries.[38]

There were, in addition, certain "internal" ideological considerations that explain why Whigs made the original pauper-labor argument in the 1830s a centerpiece of their protectionist platform. Much of the impetus came from the rise of trade unionism at this time. By demonstrating their concern, through the pauper-labor argument, for the continued economic elevation and well-being of American labor, Whigs aimed to defuse the threat of trade-union militancy; they would also win labor votes away from the Democrats in a period of greatly expanded male suffrage.[39] Whigs thereby departed from Federalist and earlier Whig arguments in support of protection for American manufacturing. Those older arguments, as John R. Commons indicated long ago, had been more strongly "capitalistic" in their orientation, although they did include common references to the increased security of employment that protective tariffs achieved. Building on the conventional wisdom that low-cost labor was a requisite for extensive manufacturing enterprise, protectionists from Alexander Hamilton through those of the mid-1820s had openly regarded high American wage rates as, if anything, an unfortunate liability.[40] In fact they had commonly insisted, when making the case for the goal of national industrial self-sufficiency, that opponents and skeptics exaggerated the superiority of American to English wage rates. Such self-sufficiency might be partially realized by tapping into the cheap labor pool of women and children. Many of the same protectionists before the 1830s had also defended high tariffs as merely temporary expedients to foster the growth of "infant industries"; these expedients would no longer be necessary once American wage levels still more closely and uniformly approximated European levels.[41]

The pauper-labor arguments of the 1830s and later that followed these high tariff themes thus signaled both a more prolabor orientation within American protectionism and a measured abandonment, or tempering, of the position that high duties would suffice as short-lived expedients. Extolled as never before within the protectionist camp, America's high wage levels, Whigs indicated, would need protection from foreign competition for a period of indefinitely long duration—past, very conceivably, the infant-industries stage.[42] That assumption itself reflected one of the fundamental Gresham's law–related threads that ran through the antebellum championing of various forms of respectable labor. Free-soilers like Weston, as well as the mechanic opponents of contract convict labor, argued that the better-paid, more honorable body of labor was also the more fragile body; the economic relationship obtaining between it and cheap labor was necessarily a one-way street, inexorably leading to the degradation of the first rather than the elevation of the second. So, too, insisted such leading Whig protectionists as Andrew Stewart of Pennsylvania. In his attack on the Democratic "revenue-only" tariff of 1846, Stewart observed: "Low labor wants no protection against high labor, but the high must be protected against the low, or by free competition be brought down to its level. This follows just as certainly as the removal of a wall which separated two unequal bodies of water, would bring the one down to the level of the other."[43]

The rise of trade unionism and the spread of male suffrage encouraged the initial protectionist turnabout and celebration of high American wages in the form of the pauper-labor argument. It remained for the subsequent protectionist refinements in that argument to more fully embody the classical economic theme that higher wages improved labor's motivation and productivity. Horace Greeley was here hardly the most original antebellum voice. That distinction belonged to an associate of Henry C. Carey, the political economist E. Peshine Smith. Drawing especially on Baron Justus von Liebig's investigations in agricultural chemistry and physiology, Smith argued in several writings in the 1850s that although well-paid laborers might cost more to their employer on a daily basis, their increased energy and work capacity proved more than offsetting. High per diem wage rates meant low unit-labor costs.[44] No less than Carey, Smith exemplified the Whig, and indeed the general American, tendency to stereotype English classical economy as profoundly antagonistic to the notion that "high profits and high wages can coexist." He dismissed not merely Malthus and Ricardo but such of their successors as John Stuart Mill for perpetuating an economic model that, hardly less than British mercantilism, was rooted in the reactionary and untenable conviction that "the labouring population" consisted of "so many animals, with definite, never-increasing wants."[45]

Smith proceeded to contrast English classical economic thought with the more enlightened American system of political economy. The latter, he wrote, "rests upon the belief, that in order to make labor cheap, the laborer must be well-fed, well-clothed, well-lodged, well-instructed, not only in the details of his handicraft, but in all general knowledge that can in any way be made subsidiary to it. All these cost money to the employer and repay it with interest. . . . High proportional wages are the index of cheap production."[46] With other Whigs like Calvin Colton and Andrew Stewart, and with many Democrats as well, Smith appears to have shared the view that the subsistence recompense paid foreign pauper laborers was a function of long-standing market failure. A confluence of such entrenched Old World circumstances as onerous taxes, land monopoly, and the laboring classes' lack of political representation eventuated in wages lower than those which would prevail in more fully competitive markets. Yet because such wage distortions acted as well to rob its pauper-labor victims of energy and incentive, the wage differential between Europe and America also became a measure of Old World labor's inferior productivity.[47]

Peshine Smith's work is among the important precursors of twentieth-century human-capital theory and related inquiries into how nutritional and social deprivation and unhealthy living and working conditions act to sap the productivity and shorten the lives of the working poor in modern industrialized countries.[48] He offered possibly the most fully developed argument in the antebellum period that well-fed and well-educated American wage labor outperformed European pauper labor. At the same time, Smith remained, like Greeley, a strong proponent of protective tariffs. In Smith's case, however, protectionism was more a reflection of the special importance that he attached to a nation's technological development than to any particular anxiety he harbored over competition from foreign pauper labor.[49] Here Smith built upon Henry Carey's extended criticisms of Ricardo's doctrine of diminishing returns in agriculture. Reversing Ricardo's formula, Carey claimed that man progressed from the worst to the best soils, but that it was partly to prevent these soils from being exhausted through extensive use that man needed to develop a localized economic balance between agriculture and industry. To Carey's analysis Smith, here too reflecting the influence of the work of Baron von Liebig and others in the fields of organic chemistry and physical science, added an emphasis on technology's potential ability to sustain and improve soil fertility. Smith was convinced that in the case of the United States, fulfillment of that technological potential was obstructed by trade with England. Because of the reliance on England's manufacturing goods that it encouraged, this trade impeded America from accumulating industrial capital, blocked the development of adequate domestic manufacturing bases, and led to soil-depleting modes of farm cultivation. In making the case that trade with England thereby prevented the United States from realizing its full productive powers, Smith "afforded a new and much more scientific defense of protectionism than had hitherto been enunciated."[50]

Foreign Pauper Labor and Democrat Free-Tradeism

Peshine Smith's sophisticated protectionism did not display the lack of confidence that standard pauper-labor arguments exhibited regarding well-paid American wage labor's ability to withstand competition from the degraded, inferior pauper labor of the Old World. Smith's protectionism also distinguished itself from Greeley's refinement of the cruder pauper-labor argument, a refinement that also recognized, but to a lesser degree, the competitive advantage deriving from the superior recompense, intelligence, and productivity of American wage earners. Still, any recognition of a positive relationship between high wages and worker productivity did tend to throw into question the competitive threat posed by poorly paid foreign labor. Although, then, this positive relationship came to be expressed in its most advanced form by a protectionist, Peshine Smith, it was free-trade Democrats who most insistently invoked and popularized it as part of their partisan opposition to Whig policies. It was such Democratic arguments that Greeley was, above all, directly acknowledging when he agreed that "ill-paid, untaught, half-famished Labor is far less efficient than that of energetic, intelligent Freemen, and that the price of a day's work may be considerably less in other countries than here, and yet production be as cheap here as there."[51]

It would shortly become Robert J. Walker, the Polk administration's secretary of the treasury, whom Greeley was acknowledging most of all by such statements. Walker was the instrumental shaper of the 1846 tariff that was vilified by Whigs for its appreciable lowering of duties. He was also one of a number of antiprotectionist Democrats who used the same argument articulated by Greeley to go beyond the Whig editor and deny altogether the existence of a foreign pauper-labor threat.[52] Without Greeley's subsequent qualification, Walker insisted in one of his Treasury Reports that "the energetic American freeman can and does perform far more effective labor in a day, than what is called by the restrictionists the pauper labor of Europe; and, therefore, the employer here can pay more for a day's toil to our workingmen. Measured by the day, the wages here may be higher than in Europe; but measured by the work done on that day, there is but little difference."[53]

Walker issued his reports during a period marked by frequent cooperative movements, utopian communal experiments in capital-labor relations, and a persisting tendency, exhibited by mainstream Democrats and Whigs alike, to associate wage labor with an unrepublican dependency, however satisfactory that labor's recompense might be at particular moments. Not surprisingly, Walker proceeded to add to his remarks the hopeful prediction that "our capitalists (as some already have) shall find it to be their true interest" to allow their employees to become shareholders and profit sharers in their enterprises. "The intelligent workingmen of our country are far better prepared for the adoption of this truly republican system than those of any other nation." Such an elevation in position would increase still more the motivation, energy, and competitive ability of American workers while, not incidentally, increasing capitalist profits: "What is called the pauper labor of Europe is already inferior to our labor, but would be rendered still more powerless to compete with us when labor here participated with capital in the profits."[54]

Similar in thrust to that of the protectionist Peshine Smith was Walker's wholesale discounting of the foreign pauper-labor threat, along with his related suggestions that greater economic incentives and higher material-living standards in America made for superior labor energy and productivity. The latter, in turn, could eventuate in the capitalist employer routinely paying out still higher wages. In contrast to Smith, however, Walker also remained wedded to the dimension of Ricardian economics that highlighted the inverse relationship between profits and wages under prevailing capitalist-hireling arrangements. At times it suited Walker's antiprotectionist purposes to follow the classical economists and more neutrally describe relationships between capital and labor as matters of hard, inexorable economic law. "No legislation of man," he wrote, can change the fact that profits and wages can only rise together if total capital, "the source from which wages are paid," is augmented, and no tariff (or, for that matter, "any organization of labor") can effect such an increase.[55]

But on other occasions the populist perspective that Walker shared with other Jacksonian Democrats was more in evidence: the inverse relationship between profits and wages he then presented more as a function of sheer capitalist power and greed—a perspective hardly shared by either Ricardo himself or by such followers as James Mill.[56] A populist reading of political-economic doctrine rendered Democrats like Walker even more antagonistic than all but the most reform-minded Whigs (such as Greeley) to the dependency of the wage-labor condition. Possibly even more important, the Democratic distaste for this condition was distinguished by a specifically anti-industrial-capitalist edge. Walker manifested all of these propensities in his objections to tariff protection. "A protective tariff," he noted in his Treasury Report of 1845, "is a question regarding the enhancement of the profits of capital. That is its object, and not to augment the wages of labor, which would reduce those profits. . . . When the number of manufactories is not great, the power of the system to regulate the wages of labor is inconsiderable; but as the profit of capital, invested in manufactures, is augmented by the protective tariff, there is a corresponding increase of power, until the control of such capital over the wages of labor becomes irresistible."[57] In addition to such provocative, distinctly non-Whig claims that protective duties acted to benefit northern manufacturing capitalists far more than they did their wage-earning employees, Walker advanced in his Treasury Reports of this period other free-trade arguments also at variance with Peshine Smith's views. He set forth these claims despite their agreement as to the productivity and competitive benefits distinguishing a high-wage economy.[58]

Some of the Democrats who sprang to the defense of Walker and his tariff added to their own dismissals of the foreign pauper-labor threat a yet stronger animus to American industrial-capitalist development. Illinois congressman O. B. Ficklin acknowledged that he represented the interests of western corn-growing farmers who favored reciprocity of trade with Britain to facilitate the marketing of their surplus product. He sought to partly privilege these interests by describing his constituents as people who "bow not to the behests and commands of superintendents either in factories or furnaces." Ficklin proceeded to mock the protectionists' "catch-phrase of the day, the 'pauper labor of Europe,'" by endorsing the position that "there is but very little difference in the wages paid to the British operative and those paid to the American. They differ but little in nominal amount; and when we take into consideration the fact that the American operative toils more hours, and produces more cloth, yarn, or whatever it may be, than the British, the balance will incline in favor of the British operative and against the American—against the British manufacturer, and in favor of the American."[59]

Ficklin's way of dismissing the British pauper-labor threat, thereby discrediting the protectionist position, was to remove the positive connotations that others, including even his fellow Democrat Walker, had attached to the greater efficiency and productivity of American manufacturing operatives. More decisively yet than the treasury secretary, and in keeping with Jacksonian Democrat agrarian and plebeian rhetorical traditions, Ficklin characterized capital-labor relations as a zero-sum game. Cotton goods could be made more cheaply in New England than in Britain, but the competitive advantages that industrial capitalists at Lowell and elsewhere enjoyed over their British rivals came completely at the expense of their operatives. By this time, Ficklin claimed, Lowell's operatives worked longer hours at a more intense pace than their Old World counterparts and were hardly less exploited. The pauper labor of England amounted to little more than an illusion perpetrated by vested American political and economic interests to conceal these very developments.[60]

Ficklin and those Democrats who seconded him were not completely off the mark, particularly in their claims that at Lowell and other New England factory towns during the late 1840s, piece wage rates were declining and workloads increasing. Historians generally agree that Lowell's female weavers, for example, were able to raise their absolute wages only because they were pressured to increase their output by taking on more looms at increased speeds.[61] Scholarly findings, on the other hand, do not reach the heights of Ficklin's rhetorical antipathy: "What could be more manifestly contrary to the designs of Providence, or to the true interests of our wide-spread country, than to have a large proportion of the females of this land confined through life to shops and factories? — doomed to be old maids, and to live without an object or aim beyond their mere animal wants."[62]

Democratic barbs against the increasing "wickedness" of the American factory system, including the operatives' unwholesome dependence on the "accumulated wealth and power" of the Appletons, the Lawrences, and other Whig millowners, had for years been integral to their antiprotectionism.[63] Ficklin was only continuing a tradition by making political capital of the more frenetic work pace and the general deterioration of labor conditions at Lowell and other of the highly visible "Waltham system" mills. Such developments followed the so-called golden age during which Whig industrialists and politicians had no less opportunistically celebrated the same mills as New World industrial showcases. This is not to claim that Democratic opportunism, any more than the Whig, precluded ideological substance. Democrats, like Whigs, harbored genuine anxiety over the Europeanization of American social and economic arrangements — over the descent of those arrangements toward a more closed and ascriptive hierarchy. In their defense of Walker's tariff, in any case, Democrats carried forward the party's traditional warnings: these baleful Europeanizing tendencies would be stimulated, not averted, by Whig protectionism and the industrial-capitalist enterprises that Whig public policies in general fostered. In the words of New Hampshire Democrat Moses Norris, a kindred spirit of Ficklin, developments at Lowell and other factory centers proved that in the United States no less than in the "monarchies of the Old World," a nation's commercial restrictions "tend to aggregate wealth in the hands of a few, to the impoverishment of the masses."[64]

The logic of his free-trade position, Norris evidently concluded, compelled him to press still further and to maintain, with Ficklin, that English pauper labor was itself a myth, a fiction. After all, had not England successfully freed itself of the corn laws and other commercial restrictions that continued to make degraded and oppressed pauper laborers of the Continental masses? "Had the highly prohibitory system of France, Spain, and Russia," Norris rhetorically inquired, shown "a tendency to raise the moral, intellectual, or physical condition of the operative and the laboring masses of these countries?" Of course not. But "the commercial system of England was remarkably free, when compared with those of the other Powers he had named." In England, consequently, "the wages of labor were higher, the human intellect more untrammeled, and human rights better appreciated and more firmly guarded."[65]

Ficklin argued that American manufacturing laborers could compete with English ones because they were no less underpaid, overworked, and driven. Norris argued similarly but also put a somewhat more positive twist on the American-English comparison by emphasizing the degree to which England's recent enactment of free-trade policies had already tended to liberate and elevate its manufacturing workers. But both Ficklin and Norris were claiming that the existing condition of American and English operatives was now more or less the same. Other Democratic voices endorsed this view, motivated in some cases by such additional objectives as vindicating southern chattel slavery through reference to labor exploitation in the free states. Under such circumstances, in fact, the choice of language suggests that defending a particular foreign-trade policy may have been quite secondary. The *Ohio Statesman,* for example, took away from the debates over the Walker tariff the conclusion that "the pauper labor of England is better paid than the free labor of the northern slave factories at Lowell."[66]

Some Whigs feared that such Democratic claims, minimizing the disparity in the conditions of American and English operatives or even contending that the latter were now earning higher real wages, would do "considerable injury" to their own "very effective" pauper-labor argument.[67] Yet such antiprotectionist claims remained ones that many of Ficklin's and Norris's Democratic colleagues downpedaled or even avoided. This was perhaps not surprising. It was in keeping with Democratic Party traditions to claim that protectionist-generated industrial conditions in the United States were gradually deteriorating to Old World standards. But it may still have seemed unacceptably extreme, and even subversive, to many Democrats to also conclude with Ficklin and Norris that English pauper labor was now merely a rhetorical construction, wholly the product of Whig claptrap. Consistent with their celebration of agrarianism and freehold independence, Democrats for years had been no less inclined than Whigs to demonize ascriptively based land monopoly and other entrenched social arrangements in England and continental Europe. Denying the existence of pauper labor there would not do. Drawing too tightly the parallel between English and American factory labor, and between Old World and American working conditions generally, was best left to the unacceptably radical and alarmist labor and utopian socialist movements that had been on the scene since the 1820s. For this reason, too, the particular line of argument advanced by Ficklin and Norris remained one that other mainstream Democrats likely felt uncomfortable with and which they in any case failed to pursue. Walker himself would go no further than his equivocal references to "what is called the pauper labor of Europe."

Democrats more typically confined themselves to conventional, populist denunciations of protectionism as embodying the Whig penchant for hypocrisy and policies of special privilege. New York's *Daily Plebeian* editorialized of "these Whig lovers of the laboring classes": "Why cannot they be honest, and say they want high taxes on imports because they are paid by the laboring millions, and not by the rich few, and to give them command of the market, that they can keep down the price of labor by importing foreign laborers. . . . We warn the American mechanics, farmers, and other working men that high protecting duties have pauperized the laborers of the old world, and that, if submitted to here, they will reduce the laborers of the United States to the miserable condition of the operative classes in the British Kingdom."[68]

Land monopoly, the *Plebeian* noted elsewhere, persisted in Britain whatever its recent reforms in trade policy. In rather sharp contradiction to the portrayals by Ficklin and Norris, the paper elaborated on how such monopoly deprived Britain's factory laborers of any alternative "but to submit to the exactions of the capitalist." This sad fact itself became, in the hands of the *Plebeian,* yet further ammunition in its partisan exposure of the dangers that protective trade barriers posed for America's still respectable freeholders: "In the United States, our laborers can choose their occupation, if they are oppressed in one branch of business, they can change for another. The great body of our people are tillers of the soil, and so long as they can have the markets of the world to sell their surplus labor they are independent of associated wealth."[69]

Despite sharing with the Whigs the orthodoxy that England's operatives remained subsistent and degraded pauper laborers, the majority of Democratic voices, including the *Plebeian,* were in complete sync with Ficklin and Norris on the more essential Democratic Party line. This was the general position that under conditions of free trade, English manufacturing labor did not constitute a competitive threat to American workers in ways that would inflict significant and long-lasting damage on them. Already described has been the first of the major Democratic antiprotectionist arguments, advanced by Walker and others. This was the argument that dismissed the significance of any nominal wage differentials: because of the superior intelligence and productivity of better-paid American manufacturing workers, the enterprises that employed them could and would withstand the market competition offered by British and other foreign rivals utilizing lower-cost labor.[70] But the Democrats also offered a second major labor-based free-trade argument. This one did not so directly challenge the Whigs' Gresham's law–like insistence that in the absence of protective trade barriers, foreign manufacturing enterprises would employ their cheaper, degraded workers to successfully undersell American firms. Rather than denying that British manufacturing labor, in particular, constituted a serious competitive threat, this second Democratic argument invoked notions of national "comparative advantage" to minimize on other grounds the ill consequences of foreign pauper-labor competition.

Already by the early nineteenth century, as Douglas A. Irwin observes, "the burden of proof" in trade theory and debate had shifted to where it remains to this day: requiring "those advocating restrictions on trade to demonstrate how such policies would contribute to a nation's economic wealth."[71] Free-trade doctrine gained ascendancy owing primarily to Adam Smith and the classical economists who consolidated his position. This is not to deny the intuitive appeal that the pauper-labor protectionist argument, the most readily comprehensible of notions, also acquired and in fact has continued to hold among various economists, intellectuals, politicians, and constituencies in the United States.[72] Still, liberal free-trade doctrine established its own, even more compelling force as a complex and intriguing blend of economic self-interest and humanitarian idealism. In response to seventeenth- and eighteenth-century mercantilist arguments against free trade, classical free-tradeism developed the comparative-costs argument. Countries naturally differed in their ability to produce different products cheaply, and gains in the aggregate wealth of each would be maximized by a free exchange of goods that recognized and encouraged this natural propensity for specialization. Attempts to cultivate through protective trade barriers and other forms of governmental interference particular industries where they would not naturally arise or were not well suited would only detract from more profitable employments and would reduce a nation's wealth and trade leverage.

To the pure economics of this comparative-advantage argument—Smith's notion of the invisible, self-interested hand writ on an international scale—early nineteenth-century liberal thought added an idealistic, even utopian dimension, a reaction to centuries of European warfare. International cooperation and world peace could only be achieved by trade policies that broke down national barriers and encouraged countries to intimately complement one another's economies through the allocation of resources in ways that reflected each nation's individual, specialized strengths and factor endowments (in land, labor, and capital).[73]

One of the many American statements of these transatlantic comparative-advantage doctrines was offered in the February 1846 issue of the *United States Magazine and Democratic Review,* the leading organ of the Democratic Party. In defending Robert J. Walker's most recent Treasury Report, "Some Reflections of a Free Trader" noted, first, the pacific implications of "mutual free trade" and the ethical superiority of these to protectionism's "principles of exclusiveness, local selfishness, and national jealousy." Unlike some other Democrat free-trade voices, "Reflections" did not doubt that "our laboring classes," northern operatives included, "enjoyed a far better remuneration for their toil than their rivals beyond the Atlantic." But consistent with free trade's ideal of international cooperation, "Reflections" proceeded to contest a central claim made by Andrew Stewart and other protectionist Whigs. In so doing, it was also raising at least a limited challenge to the themes of republican economic fragility and negative contagion that were so pervasive in early nineteenth-century American culture. "Reflections" insisted that the removal of trade barriers would act to reduce wage differentials less by lowering American wage levels than by raising foreign ones: "It is *not* true, that under a system of free trade, the rate of wages here would fall to their present standard in Europe. They would, indeed, approach nearer to an equality than they now sustain; but it would be an approximation of which foreign labor would more feel the benefit than ours the burthen."[74]

Moving to related economic considerations, "Reflections" caught some of the standard pauper-labor protectionist arguments in a contradiction. Not so differently from such Democratic voices as the *Plebeian,* Calvin Colton and other leading Whig protectionists had made much of the relative labor scarcity, economic options, and consequent independence from which America's manufacturing wage earners happily profited. In fact, Colton attributed high industrial wages in the United States primarily to these factors, rather than to any superior productive powers possessed by either the nation's operatives or the industrial capital that they operated.[75] Yet as the *Democratic Review's* "Reflections" pointed out, American labor hardly needed tariff protection if it was as independent as protectionists like Colton claimed. By such protectionists' own admission, access to cheap land and occupational flexibility, not governmental protection from foreign pauper labor, were the bulwark against the depression of American wages. "In this view of the case," "Reflections" noted, the "fallacy, that [without protection] wages here will fall to the standard of wages abroad, disappears; such a result can only happen when the country is as densely filled, and land as dear. That day, is as yet, far remote; and, probably, the genius of civilization may find means hereafter to avert the calamities of repletion ere they arrive."[76]

"Reflections" then directed a nontechnical formulation of the comparative-advantages argument not only against protectionists' apocalyptic pauper-labor warnings but also against their major accompanying "sophistry." This was the protectionists' insistence on the importance of government-stimulated, manufacturing-based "home markets" for the agricultural surplus produced by America's farmers. American enterprise and the nation's laborers, "Reflections" insisted to the contrary, did not need government's protective devices and its other "artificial" regulations to find their most profitable avenues:

If the people of this country can, in general, better invest their labor in tillage than in manufactures; and, by artificial legislation, a considerable portion of industry is diverted to the latter, the consequence will indeed be an appearance of local thrift in the manufacturing districts, while, in point of fact, the prosperity of the whole country is diminished. . . . if we, as a people, are better adapted, under all circumstances, to engage in manufactures rather than agriculture, it is fair to presume that the private sagacity of freemen will find it out, without the hints and helps of government.[77]

Whatever its intellectual validity as a formal doctrine in the free-trade arsenal, the comparative-advantage argument performed a number of ideological functions for antebellum Democrats. Henry Carey and other members of the Whiggish, "American" school of political economy persistently sought to link Democratic laissez-faire ideology with the most pessimistic arguments of British political economy. The comparative-advantage argument enabled free-trade Democrats to partially undercut these darker associations and to play up instead their ties to the liberal idealism of Richard Cobden and his Manchester school.[78]

Second, the comparative-advantages argument afforded Democrats a means of rhetorically minimizing the damage inflicted by competition from foreign, especially British industrial, pauper labor in a way that did not oblige them to commit the quasi heresy of denying the existence of such pauper labor. Robert Walker's words illustrated in this regard the value of the classical economic model, particularly Ricardo's contributions: "If labor is dear here and low abroad, in the exchange of products we get more of theirs for a smaller amount of ours, and gain by the exchange. The cheapness of foreign labor is an argument in favor of exchange with them." Walker appears not to have consciously intended it as such, but modern proponents of "unequal exchange" and "dependency" critiques of free trade might well read this statement as an American brief for exploiting nations reliant on pauper labor, rather than developing a mutually beneficial relationship with them.[79] More certain is that Walker, in thereby converting the existence of cheap foreign labor into an argument against protection, saw himself as both the Democratic partisan rebutting Whig alarmist accusations and the principled advocate of the position, shared by "Reflections" and others, that "the natural laws which control trade between nations" are "perfect and harmonious."[80]

These benefits for individual nations and the international order might very well come, Walker indicated on occasion, at the expense of the artificially high wages, and even the jobs themselves, of some American operatives. If British industrial capital, through the use of lower-cost labor, remained better suited to produce manufacturing goods for the world and the American markets, and if they were able to push their unprotected American rivals out of these markets, so be it. "The argument," Walker noted, "that we must encourage our infant manufactures was always fallacious, for they would encourage themselves as soon as the country was adapted to them." Not merely, then, did protective tariffs inflict higher prices on American consumers. Through their creation of an artificial home market, they also flew in the face of the "natural laws of trade" by forcing the country's industry into "less productive pursuits," thereby keeping workers employed unproductively and unprofitably. So Walker summarized protection's efficiency-dampening effect: "Wages throughout the whole country become lower than they were before, because the aggregate profits of the capital of the nation engaged in all its industry is diminished. . . . While wages may be temporarily augmented in some pursuits favored by law, they are diminished in all others. . . . The effect of a protective tariff in truth is, not to enhance wages, but to depress them."[81]

"In the absence of tariffs, the division of labor would be according to the laws of nature of each nation."[82] Drawing from the comparative-advantages doctrine, Walker suggested that a substantial segment of America's industrial firms and operatives offered inefficient, weak competition to Britain's. But this suggestion struck a discordant note with his expressed confidence that better-paid, more energetic and productive American operatives would nicely survive such competition. Frequently, to be sure, Walker insisted that the economic initiatives of the Polk administration—those inclined toward hard money as well as free trade—served the country's "manufacturing classes" as well as they did its other interests.[83] Nonetheless, Walker seemed willing to accept the lowered wages, and even the unemployment, of American operatives as the inevitable costs of "weaning" the nation's manufactures from legislative protection.

This willingness exposed a Democratic political vulnerability that Whigs sought to exploit. Democrats might try to minimize these costs and the individual suffering that they entailed by insisting upon their short-term nature: at worst, cheap manufacturing imports from England would force the nation's industrial wage earners to abandon their present occupations for agricultural ones. Horace Greeley, among other Whigs, would have none of this particular Democratic free-trade argument. He seized upon it as emblematic of the insensitivity to the needs of laboring people that distinguished the argument's classical economic architects. In response to remarks made by John Ramsay McCulloch, Ricardo's disciple and "one of the most renowned doctors of the Free Trade school," Greeley remarked that

a man has daily wants, needs, that cannot be postponed nor ignored; he is deteriorated by idleness, as a mere machine is not; he often has a wife and children to be subsisted, and a home to be broken up and abandoned when the failure of employment compels a change of vocation. The coolness with which McCulloch and his school speak of depriving a man of the work which he has devoted years to mastering and has now at his fingers' ends, and setting him adrift, to pick up something else whereof he knows nothing, and in which he must naturally prove clumsy and inefficient, proves them singularly ill-informed in the premises, or callous to the moans of wide-spread human misery.[84]

Democratic politicians commonly refuted such charges of callousness by insisting that America's manufacturing wage earners in many cases would be better off in the agricultural and other nonindustrial employments for which their nation remained more naturally suited. Here, too, the comparative-advantages argument, as formal economic doctrine, dovetailed with the strictly indigenous ideological biases and objectives shared by many antebellum Democrats. Walker was not "anti-development"—at least not in any unambiguous sense. But even his free-tradeism, for all its relative economic sophistication and disclaimers of hostility to manufacturing interests, evidenced a certain anti-industrial—if not wholly agrarian—primitivism. Not without a celebratory tone was his remark that "a vast majority of the labor of this country is employed in agriculture, commerce, navigation, and the nonprotected pursuits."[85]

Such a bias was inextricably bound up with the previously noted distributional justice theme to which Walker, Norris, Ficklin, and a generation of other Democrats gave routine voice: it was industrial capitalists rather than their wage-earning employees who reaped the lion's share of the unjustified gains accruing from tariff protection.[86] Mainstream Democrats shared with more certifiable labor radicals the conviction that the disparities of power between capital and wage labor were especially striking and unhealthy in New England's pioneer textile corporations. This conviction bore a symbiotic relationship with their increasingly wishful insistence that for a period of indefinitely long duration America's natural destiny was to remain a geographically expanding, predominantly agricultural republic. As Walker, the *Plebeian,* and others expressed this connection, the lowering of trade barriers, in conjunction with cheap prices for western lands, would enable America's existing and aspiring freehold farmers to market their surpluses abroad, sustain a comfortable living from the land, and avoid falling under the thumb of northeastern industrial capital.

This more exclusively agrarian, American exceptionalist vision was for free-trade Democrats intellectually consistent with the world order of complementary national economies. It indulged, in addition, their genuine biases against extensive domestic industrialization. Finally, on the more crudely opportunistic level of political appeal, it simply helped Democrats keep pace with the Whigs' alternative American exceptionalist formulations.[87]

Economic Discourse

Long ago F. W. Taussig remarked on the near impossibility of testing the accuracy of the arguments, including those directly reliant on the representations of foreign pauper labor, that Whigs and Democrats threw at one another in the antebellum trade debates. This was so in spite of the various claims that the rival party members made respecting the impact upon American economic growth and wage levels of such "watershed" tariff legislation as the acts of 1828 and 1842. Taussig explained that "it is almost impossible to trace the economic effect of any legislative measure that remains in force no more than four years," and "in the years between 1832 and 1860 there was great vacillation in the tariff policy of the United States." Walker's 1846 tariff did remain in force for an unequaled period of eleven years, and it was for this reason exempt from Taussig's explanation. Yet the 1846 legislation also "effected no more than a moderation in the application of protection."[88] Moreover, the 1846 tariff's period of operation, like that of other trade legislation, coincided with currency and credit fluctuations, growth in transportation networks, technological advances, and other major domestic economic developments that were only tangentially or ambiguously related to its provisions.[89] All of these circumstances suggest again the soundness of Taussig's generalization as to the "exaggeration of the effect of protective duties which is as common among their opponents as among their advocates."[90]

The exaggerated character of both Whig and Democratic claims regarding the influence of trade legislation upon profits and wages and upon prosperity and recession was of a piece with the partisan bickering and sloganeering over foreign pauper labor specifically. Certainly the representations appearing in the antebellum debates offer little contradiction to Alfred E. Eckes Jr.'s recent observation that "simplistic image, slogans, and myths" have always shaped American attitudes toward trade policy.[91] Eckes's remark is consistent with this discussion's emphasis upon how rival party ideologies and agendas, not to speak of the sheer careerism of individual political actors, played instrumental roles in generating and manipulating the representations of pauper labor. Even Democrats' injection of countervailing evidence to challenge the stereotype of debased British pauper labor — and to underscore the claptrap nature of the term itself — was in considerable measure a function of political opportunism.

However, another point should also be raised here: the fact that self-serving objectives played key roles in driving the pauper-labor representations does not in itself invalidate the representations. In his classic history of economic thought, Joseph A. Schumpeter remarked that "the scientific character of a given piece of analysis is independent of the motive for the sake of which it is undertaken. . . . It may be an interesting question to ask *why* a man says what he says; but whatever the answer, it does not tell us anything about whether what he says is true or false. . . . The most stubborn class interest may induce true and valuable analysis, the most disinterested motive may lead to nothing but error and triviality."[92]

Schumpeter was speaking here of a more formal and analytical economic literature than that comprising the Whig-Democratic exchanges over trade policy and European pauper labor. But his remarks are still relevant. The posturing and sloganeering typified by Whigs like Andrew Stewart and Democrats like Moses Norris did capture different facets of the complex and dynamic social and economic landscape, on both sides of the Atlantic, that shaped international market competition. Such sources as the British Parliament's factory commission reports did contain a mass of data—on wages and profits, industrial outputs, imports and exports, etc.—that supported, albeit in far more limited degree than either of the antagonists were disposed to admit, each of their representations of the nature and magnitude of the foreign pauper-labor threat.

One can put this point differently, and tie it in with the larger discussion here. Central to the partisan debates over foreign pauper labor, as to the debates over slave-labor and convict-labor competition, was whether or not better-recompensed, "intelligent," and "respectable" "free" labor—usually though not invariably recognized as correspondingly superior in efficiency and productivity—could offset the competitive advantages residing in lower-cost "servile" labor.[93] All of these broad labor contests turned on an array of complex variables, which might have both short-term and long-term effects, and many of which signaled conflicting tendencies. The distinct likelihood accordingly emerges that there was no uniform outcome: whether free or servile labor enjoyed the decisive advantage in each of these general contests was in fact only resolvable on a less abstract and more microeconomic, case-by-case basis. Yet the same absence of empirical clarity and certitude also confirms the relevance of Schumpeter's point. There remains the theoretical possibility that the most opportunistic of the participants in the antebellum debates were among those who held the more ultimately accurate position. This is possible whatever the degree to which all of the participants found support for their opposing arguments in discrete economic phenomena and bodies of statistical evidence, and whatever the extent to which they all overgeneralized from their data.

Some Elaborations and Conclusions

THE POSTMODERN linguistic turn can only extend and deepen one's sense that individual Whig and Democratic partisan extrapolations from various facts, events, and data are highly incomplete, if not altogether improbable, sources of objective truth. By characterizing these, along with all other historical documents, as mediating "texts" capable of only producing images of the past, rather than recovering the past itself, the linguistic turn profoundly complicates but also generally reinforces older scholarly traditions. These traditions grounded the empirical limitations of such partisan contributions in their ideological and other biases and in the commensurate selectivity with which they chose, arranged, and interpreted hard data.

My interest, however, remains less in what postmodern perspectives have rendered still more problematic: the recovery of objective truth, or in this case the validity of the economic knowledge generated by participants in the antebellum trade-policy debates. It rather lies in the pervasive Gresham's law–like cultural anxieties common to all the different exchanges over the competitive threat posed by cheap labor.[1] Although the antebellum trade debates had their own independent identity as an outgrowth of formal economic literature, they were simultaneously part of a larger and more informal social discourse distinguished by its ideologically driven paralleling and thematic appropriations. In this context the penchant for exaggeration and overgeneralizing, along with the related paralleling and appropriations, takes on cultural meaning beyond matters of empirical truth. Meriting final comment are some of the further commonalties that linked the antebellum perceptions of different sources of cheap labor competition—perceptions into which George M. Weston's free-soil address of 1856 provided an earlier segue.

One can, first, identify in the political ideology of antebellum Democrats a certain continuity of confidence in the capacity of American free labor to withstand, without the aid of government supports and without significant material or status injury to itself, competition from cheap labor. Historians have long noted leading Democrats' rhetorical commitment to laissez-faire ideals. But the discussion here highlights a significant underpinning of that commitment. This was an invisible-hand mentality that, transcending the morass of moment-to-moment partisan agendas and individual political objectives, linked the Democrat's free-trade construction of the foreign pauper-labor threat to the late antebellum northern Democratic doctrine of popular sovereignty in the federal territories. Walker and his colleagues partly dismissed the pauper-labor threat by invoking "natural laws of trade." Rooted in the distinctive economic strengths and inclinations of individual nations, these would determine the optimum directions for American free labor and enterprise. So, too, Stephen A. Douglas and his following rejected the heavy hand of distant (as well as sectionally divisive) government intervention. They invested their confidence in an abstract formula of local majority will that embodied the same elemental economic forces determinative of the relative viability and appeal of different forms of labor and enterprise. Those forces also strongly suggested, to their minds, that free-labor enterprises either would altogether exclude or might at least tolerably coexist with slaveowners and their labor in the federal territories. Numerous historians have characterized early nineteenth-century Democrats as more backward-looking and more anxiety-ridden about economic change than their major party rivals.[2] True enough, Democrats were generally more hostile to business and professional elites, tending to envision an inevitable conflict between these and the nation's virtuous "bone and sinew." But it was protectionist Whigs and free-soil Republicans who were most antagonistic to other kinds of economic developments and relationships. It was they who were more given to the Gresham's law–like anxieties that conceptualized a deleterious competition between American free labor and various forms of cheap servile labor.

This is not to deny the permutations and amalgams that coexisted with the positions broadly distinguishing the major political parties. As much as any Jacksonian Democratic organ, the abolitionist *National Era,* for example, expressed during the 1850s a confidence in "Free Labor" that fueled its own criticisms of "the interposition of Government" in the form of protective tariffs: "Free Labor, we reply, takes care of itself. When it finds one channel of enterprise closed, it seeks another. . . . give it the benefit of a common school education, and the only protection it will need will be found in its own energy, versatility, intelligence, and instincts."[3] Yet the confidence in free labor that stimulated the *Era*'s free-tradeism was, after all, crucially qualified. The paper counted itself among a legion of free-soil voices which insisted that free labor, for all its versatility and intelligence, was unlikely to find adequate channels of enterprise in territory permitting slave labor's intrusion: free labor could not "mingle with slave labor without degradation."[4]

The *National Era* was hardly the only free-trade voice contributing to Gresham's law apprehensions of a fundamental antagonism between free and slave labor. Still, protectionist Whiggery's linkage with free-soil Republicanism proved more politically significant, if only because there developed from it a plebeian appeal rivaling in potency that of the Jacksonian Democrats. This circumstance has been recognized by historians who underscore the Whigs' first development of the pauper-labor protectionist argument. It has been noted by other scholars who admire the Republicans for their ability to improve upon the Whigs' persisting elitist orientation and to surpass their predecessors in northern political appeal by democratizing the Whigs' moralistic concerns with the infusion of a white egalitarian slavery restrictionism.[5]

Of course, ex-Democrats themselves, free traders or otherwise, made a central contribution to this democratizing process — this being the antimonopoly theme that Francis Blair Jr., James Doolittle, and others brought with them into the Republican Party. The theme that poor whites of the South bore the burden of slaveholding practices — that they were demoralized and enfeebled by a slave power that impeded economic competition, blocked occupational opportunity, and severely skewed the distribution of wealth — represented a powerful transmutation of the Jacksonian mind-set. That mind-set had similarly condemned protective tariffs and other Whig measures as the privileged classes' use of the state to distort market processes and to consolidate their wealth and power at the expense of the common people. The antimonopoly strand in Republican free-soilism had comparable affinities with the mechanic criticisms that government-supported contract convict labor was generative of economic debasement, moral contagion, and an inequitable and elitist double standard.[6] And if, too, Republican free-soilism successfully appropriated and absorbed the "radical egalitarian" themes of both Jacksonian Democracy and the Working Men's Party platforms of the 1820s and 1830s, it was also owing to the pronounced strand of racism that it carried over. Wedding the long-standing appeal of free or inexpensive homesteads in the public domain to a "Jacksonian racial ideology" that would reserve these homesteads for free white citizens, Republicans like Blair and George M. Weston forged a formidable weapon against "the slave plantation system."[7]

Such ideological affinities notwithstanding, actual membership rolls remain a more undocumented, problematic link between the antislaveryism of the

Republican coalition and the mechanic opposition to prison industry to which Weston referred in his address of 1856. Republican rank-and-file support undoubtedly did include by the late 1850s some of the earlier workingmen activists against contract convict labor, individuals who may have been particularly receptive to Weston's antislavery themes because they were already sensitized to warnings about cheap labor competition. Quite possibly, some of these workingmen activists, or at least those who were native-born and Protestant, came to the Republican free-soil coalition via the Know-Nothing movement. For such individuals post-1845 economic nativism — their animus to the presence of famine Irish immigrant laborers in their own neighborhoods — was a natural way station between the opposition to state convict "refuse" and absorption of the message that slave labor on the remote Kansas plains constituted a competitive threat of comparable proportions.[8]

Yet there is no empirical study (or at least none of which I am aware) that has quantified such a progression of protest, or that has even taken the first step: that of attempting to identify the thousands of individuals who during the Jacksonian and antebellum periods petitioned and otherwise protested against prison industry in New York and elsewhere. Many of these individuals, furthermore, may have never bought the Republican message of an aggressive and menacing slavocracy. Notwithstanding the attempts of a Blair to invest that slavocracy in the hated garbs of monopoly, some prominent northern labor-movement activists, at least, continued through the 1850s to spurn Republican free-labor themes as a dodge; they saw these as an attempt to distract workingmen in the free states from the various ills that more immediately and genuinely oppressed them.[9] This is to suggest again that during the early nineteenth century the pervasive fears and complaints over cheap labor and Gresham's law–like processes generated as much political discord and fragmentation among interest and social groups as they produced common agreement and unified action.

But if there are reasons to question how many of the surviving opponents of prison industry supported the free-soil crusade championed by Weston, there remained basic thematic commonalties in the two movements. Those commonalties also linked them with the recurrent antebellum anxieties regarding foreign pauper labor, as well as with anxieties over other sources of cheap labor not considered here.[10] The most important of these commonalties remained the underlying inclination to believe that Gresham's law–like processes tended to determine the outcome of economic competition. This was the sense that unless obstructed, cheap and "inferior" labor would invariably set the standard and reduce that respectable free labor which it did not altogether drive out to its own debased economic and moral level. Such a cultural inclination, or way of thinking, was not unique to the early nineteenth century. It may have subsequently become even more pervasive, just as anxieties over cheap labor competition had been voiced for centuries by skilled journeymen and small masters in Europe.

Gresham's law themes nonetheless attained unprecedented force in the early nineteenth-century United States, and the broad economic context that permitted republican-inspired anxieties over fragile, truly free labor to crystallize and flourish as never before had much to do with the market revolution. In particular, the widespread inclination to dramatize the power of Gresham's law–like processes in the period's labor markets was closely related to perceptions (which included acquiescent attitudes as well as notably critical and oppositional ones) that a general market ethos of "Buy cheap and sell dear" drove behavior as never before.[11]

The boundaries between the social and the intellectual history of an era are continuously permeable, and there existed plausible structural bases for these perceptions of an ascendant market ethos. Among these were the broadest of the antebellum period's social changes. These included the indeterminate increase in the proportion of American farmers who became semisubsistent or even more fully reliant on commodity production and trade (domestic or international) for their livelihoods and the concurrent rise in the proportion of the American labor force employed for wages: from approximately 12 percent in 1800 to 40 percent in 1860, according to one estimate.[12] The new economic dependencies for working people generated by the growth of an increasingly market-oriented economy, in tandem with the commodification of the labor power of many of their numbers, did not preclude their attainment of unprecedented material comforts. But their vulnerability to economic downturns, unemployment, and immiserization increased as well. The frequent antebellum complaints regarding commercial and other economic practices, encapsulated in the pejorative references to the cash nexus, as well as to "Buy cheap, sell dear," had numerous transatlantic intellectual sources, middle- and upper-class as well as authentically working-class. But many of the more elite intellectual currents were themselves measures of psychological resistance or discomfort over the vulnerabilities specific to laboring populations — and the attendant labor militancy and social unrest — that were generated by the period's most sweeping social and economic changes.[13]

Within these general market-economy and labor-force developments, there developed more particular and more extreme structural bases stimulating the perceptions of an ascendant market ethos. Contract convict labor and the threat of underselling it posed for artisanal enterprises were among these. But even more notable, and meriting some extended comment here, were other phenomena. These were the notorious sweatshops and related manufacturing out-work that during the first half of the nineteenth century spread on both sides of the Atlantic, primarily in urban centers but also in the rural hinterlands, to accommodate the needs of mushrooming mass consumer markets.[14]

In England such social critics and investigators as Henry Mayhew and Charles Kingsley thus identified the so-called dishonorable sectors of the trades: the slopwork and other enterprises that recruited many of the most unskilled and vulnerable of society's laborers and utilized subcontracting and other work-organizing mechanisms to turn out such items as "cheap clothes and nasty."[15] Mayhew, Kingsley, and other British commentators, along with such American ones as Philadelphia's Mathew Carey, identified Gresham's law processes as an integral characteristic of the sweated industries. Slopbranch competition exhibi-ted a seemingly natural tendency to exert continued downward pressure on the wages of the sweated workers themselves, while simultaneously threatening to depress wage standards and conditions within the more traditional and respectable sections of the trades. The chronic abundance of sweated workers did not by itself explain the pitifully low wages, as Mayhew took particular pains to demonstrate.[16] The thin profit margins and otherwise intensely competitive conditions for many small masters and capitalists, the dilution and obfuscation of employer responsibility for working conditions that the use of subcontract-ing facilitated, the piecework wage system and the entire atmosphere of the bur-geoning sweated industries, together encouraged employers to maximize and enlarge the advantage created by the surplus of unskilled laboring people des-perate for work. This was a surplus that, as James Freeman Clarke, Henry Ward Beecher, and a host of other antebellum commentators agreed, consisted dis-proportionately of females whose economic options had been markedly restricted by gender-based labor-market segmentation and its embeddedness in the "tyranny of custom."[17] Given the difficulty of "exit" to other opportunities that confronted many of these working people, one of the central economic paradoxes of the period came, accordingly, to be highlighted by the sweated industries. This was the paradox that competition among the buyers of labor— commonly the subcontracting employers seeking to sustain their marginal profits—could have the same general effect of depressing wage rates as did the very competition among laborers for work.[18]

This and other features of the sweated industries embodied and accentuated the most predatory, unscrupulous, and labor-cheapening tendencies of early industrial capitalism. Indeed, sweated manufacturing labor offered dark, ironic confirmation of a political-economic staple that dated from the eighteenth century. This was the dictum that because free workers paid by the piece had a "more immediate interest in the quantity of work performed," they were generally more highly motivated and industrious than were laborers paid by the day, just as the latter enjoyed a like superiority over chattel slaves.[19] Grasping for an explanation for early industrial capitalism's predatory labor-cheapening tendencies, the Boston minister-to-the-poor Joseph Tuckerman was among many who nonetheless sought solace in the ostensibly inexorable "laws" of supply and demand. These forces, Tuckerman wrote in 1830, imposed practical limits on the degree to which the most predatory employers—those who had not imbibed Christian love—could "grind" their piece wage workers and other of the laboring poor. Fortunately, Tuckerman insisted, the "rate of wages does not depend on this class of employers" but rather "principally, upon the want of the products of the labour of the poor, and upon the proportion of the supply of labour to the demand for it." Mathew Carey, however, was among those who remained yet more impressed by the Gresham's law tendencies within the sweated industries of the free states, and he indicated that Tuckerman's analysis of market forces was too simple and roseate: "When the number of workpeople greatly exceeds the demand for their labour, the persons to whom allusion is made . . . have unfortunately great influence in lowering the rate of wages. Those who seek for employment and find great difficulty in procuring it, very frequently underbid each other. The persons alluded to avail themselves of this disposition, and reduce the rates below the usual standard. The example is followed by others, who would never have originally made any reduction. . . . To reduce prices in such cases, is easy—to raise them extremely difficult."[20]

Carey was an unusually informed observer, and his concerns over sweated labor were indeed rather anomalous for his time. Even in 1860, thirty years after Carey's writing, sweated industries and those they employed likely still represented a relatively small blip on the American economic landscape, mostly prominent in that handful of urban centers where the influx of poor immigrants was reconstituting the working class.[21] Historians, to be sure, also increasingly recognize that the blip was not so small as once thought: many of the participants, above all sweated outworkers in rural as well as urban areas, were in fact ignored and underenumerated by the various antebellum censuses. But this is itself to suggest some of the reasons why Carey's dismay was atypical. Much seamstressing and other sweated outwork were embedded in household economies, and when its existence was not altogether invisible to others, its oppressive character might nonetheless be readily naturalized as family labor. This was partly so if only because a good portion of it in fact remained kin-related—a case of masters or journeyman tailors taking out work for their wives and daughters at home.

As the magnitude of sweated work grew to meet mass consumer demand, there were ever more outworkers as well as inside workers, including the impoverished widows noted by Carey, who came to be directly employed by non-kin. But coming into play here, as well, was the aforementioned tendency of sub-contracting to diffuse and obfuscate responsibility, or culpability, for exploitation. On the one hand, as Christine Stansell notes, Brooks Brothers and other respectable wholesale and retail concerns that profited most handsomely from rampant price-cutting "kept their hands clean" because they left it to their contractors to set the piece rates for their outside workers.[22] At the same time, it was not lost on some observers that many of the smaller manufacturers and contractors, who drew on the same pool of sweated workers, were themselves hardly thriving in their do-or-die competition with one another. As Horace Greeley's *New-York Tribune* acknowledged of the city's smaller clothing makers, "If they were all the purest of philanthropists, they could not raise the wages of their seamstresses to anything like a living price. Necessity rests as heavily upon them as upon the occupant of the most contracted garret."[23]

Conditions of subcontracting did not, however, altogether blunt the sense that rapacity and exploitation figured in the "miserable pittance" paid sweated workers. As the *Tribune* recognized elsewhere, someone was benefiting disproportionately from that pittance. Of the city's millinery business, it conjectured that "in the keen and bitter competition which pervades every branch of business the price of labor is kept down to the lowest possible point—although one would suppose that the large profits of Millinery [most conspicuous in the 'fashionable' retail establishments] bore so magnificent relations to the cost of labor as to avoid the necessity of such a result."[24] Contractors and others who directly engaged the sweated workers remained the most visible targets of suspicion. Some of these, most notably of all the in-shop piece masters who were employed in the larger New York clothing establishments, in fact lived well above the margins, and while a portion of these might in turn pay the "many hands under them" adequately by the standards of the day, others manifestly did not.[25] One of a series of unsigned articles on "Labor and the Laborers" appearing in the *Tribune* in 1853 targeted clothing firms that withheld and cheated on their payments to their seamstresses, and that, more basically yet, set the "lowest scale" of wages even as they received the "highest prices" for their products. The laws of "trade competition" that the *Tribune* had elsewhere accepted as regrettably true for the hordes of desperate clothing manufacturers—and that rendered the long hours and "miserable pittance" endured by their seamstresses merely oppressive—were denounced in this article as a convenient trope: they were a contemptible pretext for "selfish meanness" and outright, conspicuous labor exploitation. The not inconsiderable number of employers who enjoyed handsome profits—who had in fact become "opulent" through their "murderous" treatment of "defenseless" females—should refrain from compounding their sins. They should desist from "pleading," in a bogus rationalization of their subsistent wage scales, that they were "compelled to act as others do, or retire from the struggle altogether."[26]

In one significant sense this last *Tribune* piece took issue with the Mathew Carey–like position that the *Tribune*'s own millinery article of eight years earlier had also embraced in the form of a rhetorical question: "When or where was the price of labor *not* cut down as low and as far as possible? What branch of employers, as a class, have ever come forward to arrest the downward tendency of wages?"[27] The later article of 1853 begged to differ: its investigations revealed that even within the extreme context of New York metropolitan industrialization, supply-and-demand, labor-cheapening forces were not proving inexorable—not for employers of true character. The article insisted, rather, on what was not "too generally known": "that there are many employers who refuse to take advantage of the low terms at which labor may be had." There remained "honorable" individuals—Tuckerman's true Christians—who declined to follow the "ghouls" and "prey upon the souls and bodies of their work-women." And in this Manichaean portrait of the city's clothing trade, the good employers were all the more honorable because—Adam Smith's high-wage economy scenario to the contrary—they enjoyed no appreciable economic benefits from their refusal to capitulate to the worst Gresham's law impulses. These employers paid their seamstresses "in some instances as much as ten times the price that is allowed at the 'cheap shops,' though the execution of the work is not proportionately superior, and only the same amount of time is expended on it."[28]

The *Tribune* exposé of 1853 offered some concluding insight into how sweated enterprises had penetrated public consciousness up to this point: "The community at large is less deserving of censure than are the [unscrupulous] employers, for the former, with a few exceptions, are ignorant of the starvation wages paid; many may have heard the prices casually mentioned, but have dismissed the subject from their minds under a very natural conviction that the statements have been highly colored." This basis for exonerating the "community" from responsibility for conditions might well invite skepticism: the notion that community inaction could be passed off to a general disbelief regarding sweated conditions suggests an all-too-naive reformist optimism. Still, the article's accompanying suggestion that such disbelief had supplanted complete obliviousness in the public mind did point to a significant truth: that by the 1850s the abhorrence expressed by Carey was no longer so prescient; sweated enterprises had indeed expanded their impact on antebellum consciousness. As with the earlier (and rather sunnier) representations of the showcase mills of Lowell, the symbolic significance and iconographic power of sweated industries — best exemplified by the transatlantic cult of the destitute needlewoman and her descent into prostitution — had by 1860 if anything grown quite disproportionate to those industries' objective scope and economic representativeness in the United States.[29]

In some measure that symbolic significance and iconographic power were mere functions of evolving literary tastes — functions of a growing readership market in subjects sentimental and lurid. But they also owed a good deal to the ominous apprehension, and fact, that sweated industries did represent the most conspicuous example of the intense and savage competition and attendant labor-cheapening contagion that early nineteenth-century free-market processes were capable of generating.[30] Waged craftsmen on both sides of the Atlantic might hold themselves superior in manly skill, strength, and independence to sweated female laborers. But along with other critics of labor conditions, they could and did commonly point to a process in their own trades that was parallel to the one described by Carey. This was a process in which a contingent of opportunistic, "bad" employers possessed agency and "good" master artisans were reluctantly obliged to ensure their own enterprises' economic survival by following the bad ones in screwing down labor costs.

Economic historians have generally held that free-market processes, albeit not without significant state interventions and in tandem with economic growth and market expansion, raised real wages for American manufacturing workers overall during the four decades prior to the Civil War.[31] This paradigm would at least seem deficient with respect to the experiences of the sweated and other of antebellum society's most desperately vulnerable free waged laborers. As the various exposés in the *Tribune* and other venues suggested, female seamstresses in New York or Philadelphia appear as an occupational group to have been virtually as impoverished in 1860 as they had been in 1830, even if some were indeed better off for having escaped famine in Ireland. Yet the economic-history paradigm is not incompatible with the climate of anxiety and accusation on which this discussion has focused. One can hardly discount the American exceptionalist perception that factory workers and other segments of the labor force, encompassing a wide range of expertise and skill levels, did continue to enjoy better wages and living standards than their counterparts in the more labor-abundant and politically inegalitarian Old World. But the concomitant sense that such American workers had a good deal to lose could only stimulate the recurrent antebellum fears that cheap labor competition was a constant threat to destroy the material advantages bestowed by the various New World republican conditions. Just as the market revolution extended older anxieties over republican political fragility more deeply into the economic realm, so the more alarmist perceptions of the market revolution derived some of their strength from the materialist expectations embedded in the American exceptionalist mythology. This is so even as these alarmist perceptions, along with the market and industrial revolutions themselves, were transatlantic in scope.

One can both romanticize and exaggerate the communal, anti-individualistic behavior of the pre-market-revolution era. One can also understate the positive features of the market revolution—the ways in which the expansion of commerce, market relations, and occupational choices proved socially and psychologically liberating as well as materially beneficial for substantial segments of all classes of the population.[32] Virtually by definition, this discussion's focus upon Gresham's law–like phenomena tends toward such understatement. It invariably highlights the more negative and the more anxiety-inducing features of the market revolution, including its tendency to render people more rather than less vulnerable to forces beyond their control. Still, what has been accentuated here merits accentuation. As did the exceptionalist mythology, so did more strictly empirical developments such as the rise of the sweated industries and other manifestations of the relatively unregulated character of the early Industrial Revolution stimulate the alarmist perceptions of the market revolution in the United States. In no small measure owing to such developments, Anglo-American culture in general assimilated a sense that a "Buy cheap, sell dear" market ethos —an ethos that many identified as above all destructively labor-cheapening — governed economic relations as never before.[33] Labor reformers, above all, tended to conflate the capitalist market mechanism and its waged-labor incentives with bare necessity—an ascendant, hateful lash of poverty.

This is not to exaggerate the pervasiveness, the depth, or the intractability of the philosophical repudiation of the market ethos in the antebellum United States. Labor-movement complaints about the vulnerability of journeyman and other wage earners to market forces and capitalist greed retained, for example, a certain "whose ox was being gored" mentality. Throughout the early nineteenth century, such movements displayed an intermittent willingness to play by the supply-and-demand rules that treated their labor as a marketable commodity so long as these rules were fairly applied—so long as they were not rigged by judicial decisions and other modes of state interference to privilege the rights of capital to organize.[34] The issue of long-range significance was whether the skill and labor-market advantages enjoyed by large numbers of antebellum American wage earners would survive in the face of the "Buy cheap, sell dear" ethos, and whether they might even (especially with the help of union power) capitalize on it, whatever the designs of the employers with whom they contracted.

The more optimistic vein of British political economy, which early nineteenth-century Americans above all identified with Adam Smith, posited that high wages produced more efficient wage labor—that more highly motivated wage labor would prosper because of its superior ability to turn out more and/or higher-quality goods. The mythology of American economic exceptionalism, trumpeting the positive work motivations embedded in a labor-scarce, socially fluid, and materially abundant environment, fundamentally harmonized with this optimistic vein of political economy.[35] Even the attacks on slavery and "indiscriminate" poor relief, offered by the likes of William Ellery Channing and Joseph Tuckerman, respectively, didn't truly repudiate the ideal of a high-wage economy. It was more a matter of their highlighting, in their own naturalization of free-market labor incentives, the concurrent motivational and ennobling value of the spur of bare economic necessity. Conversely, the same stimulus of poverty—of material adversity and insecurity—was likewise acclaimed as character-strengthening by some of the most fervent American exceptionalists, even as their representations more insistently conjoined this stimulus with the manifold opportunities enjoyed by poor boys and other northern hirelings to distance themselves from poverty through hard and productive labor.

Rather than perceiving it as disciplinary in any therapeutic or ennobling sense, northern labor reformers and activists, in contrast, generally characterized the spur of poverty as perniciously coercive, degrading, and ultimately demoralizing, at least in the context of northern capital–waged-labor relationships. In so doing, labor reformers were hardly more disposed than others to reject the high-wage economy ideal—regardless of the fact that many of their number, along with exceptionalists, continued to regard movement out of waged dependence as the principal desired result of high wages. But any agreement on reformers' part that generous rewards and the laborer's hope of actually improving his (or her) situation spurred "the greatest amount of industry" was overwhelmed by their sense that northern capitalists were in fact finding "starvation wages" to be sufficiently labor inducing, while at the same time quite optimally profitable.[36] It was the nature of their various exploitation, diminishing-opportunity scenarios to exist in skeptical counterpoint to those of celebratory American exceptionalists and to minimize both the favorable material realities behind the high-wage economy ideal and the likelihood of the ideal's fuller realization in the future. On both these grounds labor reformers questioned the legitimacy of wage labor.

To put these last points somewhat differently, it was antebellum labor reformers, above all, who were haunted by the circumstances under which the greater productivity of well-paid, respectable, "truly free" labor was trumped by the superior cheapness of poorly renumerated, "unintelligent," "servile" labor, even as the same possibility also penetrated the political economy of mainstream antislavery commentators, protective-tariff advocates, and others. Yet to a significant degree such reformers were merely reaffirming what Adam Smith himself had noted: that the overriding inclination of employers, through combinations and other means, was to keep down labor costs.[37] If for no other reason, Smith had offered his high-wage dictums to challenge the blatantly elitist utility-of-poverty, leisure-preference notions of worker psychology that had constituted major eighteenth-century ideological rationales for employers' wage-minimizing efforts.[38] The thrust of the mythology of American economic exceptionalism and the related egalitarian discourse that trumpeted the "dignity" of labor in the new republic was to attenuate and marginalize such utility-of-poverty arguments.[39] But the ineluctable facts of profit-maximizing, competitive capitalism — all of the pressures, inducements, and temptations that conditioned employers to withhold productivity gains and otherwise pay their workers no more than they needed to in order to retain their services — remained hardly less dominant in the early nineteenth-century United States than they had in Smith's Britain.[40] Only now a less elitist argument — one invoking the insuperable market forces of supply and demand — provided the preeminent rationale for such a capitalist propensity.

That same propensity, it also deserves note, drew on a skepticism which was not altogether lacking in foundation. This is first to suggest that the validity of the high-wage argument as a predictor of worker psychology always had its limits — that as an empirical matter dependent on a wide range of work-site, cultural, and environmental conditions, workers' desire for leisure and rest continued after Smith's time to complicate and impede their responsiveness to above-subsistence wages in the manner that he generalized.[41] Even beyond reasons of age and gender differences, employees manifestly varied in their productive inclinations and capacities. Early industrial entrepreneurs were themselves partially acknowledging this fact when they turned to payment by results (piece wages) over time wages, especially where monitoring of individual worker effort and performance was ineffective or prohibitively expensive. By the same token, the turn toward piece wages signaled, at least in certain trades, employers' own limited acknowledgment of the high-wage economy model: the implication that some workers would be seduced by the prospect of greater earnings represented an erosion of the leisure-preference arguments that had homogenized the work propensities of the laboring classes into a desire for a fixed minimum income.[42] Even as they conducted their own efforts to indoctrinate their workforces with habits conducive to industrial work regimens, American employers (again reflecting the more egalitarian, less class-entrenched nature of their culture) may have been as a group that much less encumbered with the elitist presumption that their employees were naturally lazier, less ambitious beings than themselves — individuals less responsive to positive incentives than to various punitive ones. But American like British employers nonetheless faced overriding uncertainties as to what constituted optimal wage rates, ones at which firms would be sure to recover their costs in competitive product markets. Such uncertainties were only compounded by the persisting difficulties in precisely measuring individual worker variations in effort and output.

In retrospect, the mid-nineteenth-century high-wage notions of a Peshine Smith carried particular force for the American and other Western economies of his time, ones in which labor was just emerging from rather minimal standards of living. By helping to raise nutritional, educational, and general social standards above subsistence levels, rising wages could indeed appreciably improve the productive abilities of workers, as well as advance the interests of manufacturing capitalists by expanding workers' consumer capabilities.[43] Nevertheless, for the reasons suggested above, it was not illogical for American employers of the period, like their British counterparts, to retain some of the long-standing elite doubts, or at least to find it virtually inconceivable that more generous monetary incentives (along with shorter hours) might increase labor intensity and efficiency to the point of actually lowering labor costs per unit of output.[44] They had some reason to believe that the productive benefits to be gained thereby remained limited, and that the competitive market, in the United States no less than in England, more certainly rewarded labor contracts and firm policies that minimized aggregate labor costs.

Even among the early nineteenth-century American labor reformers who were most critical of both the resultant propensity and the ascendant supply-and-demand rationales for capitalist wage minimizing, there existed multiple permutations. Horace Greeley and others of a progressive Whig bent were most conflicted of all in their views, largely because the ideal of capitalist-labor harmony remained so firm a fixture in their particular American exceptionalisms. There was, for example, the more obscure yet illuminating case of Philip C. Friese, the author of an 1853 tract, *An Essay on Wages*. Friese sought to distance himself from a generation of radical reformers — the Thomas Skidmores, Orestes Brownsons, and the like — who, by opposing "the honest accumulation of capital" and by attempting "to excite the hostility of workingmen against it," demonstrated that they were "not real friends of the workingmen. There is no necessary antagonism between the interests of employers and those of our workingmen." And what better proof of this identity of interests, Friese noted, than Adam Smith's high-wage dictum: "The greater efficiency of our working-men is greatly due to the higher wages they that they receive. . . . the low wages of Europe are not as profitable to the employer there, as our higher wages are to our employers."

Yet Friese devoted most of his tract to reaffirming the alarmist positions shared by virtually all American radical reformers: he joined in highlighting those tendencies that in fact rendered profit maximizing synonymous with wage minimizing. "In regard to our wages, there is a law as silent and unseen as gravitation, as mighty, too, whose unimpeded action would drag our working population into the bottomless gulf of pauper wages." As Friese explained this "law of unconscious competition among workingmen," circulating capital, out of which wages were paid, was "limited in amount," "concentrated in comparatively few hands," and might be employed "according to the interest or caprice of its owners." Against this circumstance Friese invoked, as had Brownson, James Freeman Clarke, and many others before him, the contrasting "cannot wait" situation of the workingman: the latter's labor was "constantly in the market. It must be exchanged for wages, or the workingman must starve. . . . Capital, as a purchaser of a perishable article, is enabled to hold back, until applicants for employment reduce their demands for wages to an acceptable amount, by underbidding each other. This underbidding of workingmen against each other is a further element of the law. . . . Capital is thus invariably the hirer of labor, not labor the hirer of capital," and it enjoyed a fundamental "position of superiority in fixing the compensation of labor."

From the Whiggish-like insistence that he intended "no disparagement of capital"—from his insistence, indeed, that American capital "was the result of saving" and hence "the fruit of virtue"—Friese thus proceeded to accentuate all of the wage-minimizing temptations and proclivities that nonetheless made it into a force of "tyranny." Nor would Friese completely reduce these to the economic necessities and competitive pressures with which American capitalists were commonly faced. Most, he generalized, could afford to compensate their workers more generously, and while his own high-wage–efficiency arguments might suggest that it was in their interest to do so, the "undue power" that they enjoyed encouraged them to act otherwise. In addition to promoting his own rather idiosyncratic protective-tariff proposals, Friese ended up embracing all the major reform movements of the time—worker cooperatives, trade unions, the ten-hour movement—as ancillary means of counteracting the oversupply of labor, reducing capital's advantage, and, perforce, inducing employers to be more "magnanimous" in their wage policies.[45]

"Let no one suppose," Friese warned with respect to the United States, that the European "curse" of low wages "is impossible, or so improbable, as to afford no ground for reasonable apprehension."[46] The most philosophically extreme of the antebellum doomsayers respecting the high-wage economy ideal —those who amplified this warning—extended beyond Friese and other northern reformers. They included the southern intellectuals and political leaders who made undisguised proslavery use of "Buy cheap, sell dear" anxieties, and who joined in predicting an increasingly catastrophic future for the northern laboring classes as a whole. By way of contrast, such commentators exempted from the pernicious influence of the cash nexus the paternalistic, precapitalist relationship that ostensibly prevailed between southern masters and black chattel slaves.

But proving more momentous, at least in the shorter term, were the specifically antislavery directions that anxieties over—and attempts to restrain—the market ethos and its related Gresham's law tendencies came to assume. Several decades after Mathew Carey, in his response to Joseph Tuckerman, noted the disproportionate control that unscrupulous northern employers exercised over the wages paid the free laboring poor, New England's "learned blacksmith," Elihu Burritt, warned that northern capitalists increasingly believed that southern slavery "must determine the compensation and honor of free labour."[47] He was both anticipated and followed by other antislavery commentators, George M. Weston included, all working from the same premise that the "cheapness of slave labor rules the labor market where it is found"; its effect was such that "wages will run down to the *lowest* level, and the humanity of the worker must run down with them."[48]

From this increasingly prevalent antislavery perspective, southern chattel slavery's own commercial and exploitative (if not exactly market-capitalist) character might well appear more rather than less pronounced and conspicuous. That character was most fundamentally defined by the alienable and fungible status of slave property itself: by the slaveowner's ability to buy or sell bondspeople with complete disregard for their domestic relationships. It was this particular commercial attribute of slavery that continued to most excite the moral outrage of many abolitionists.[49]

But for the increasing numbers of northerners who like Weston were more drawn to white-centered free-labor ideology than to abolitionist evangelical humanitarianism, it was that other commercial dimension of chattel slavery which proved especially unsettling and objectionable. This was the evident capacity of bondmen—these human exchange commodities—to produce other commodities cheaply and to prove fully responsive to the market mechanism. As the most extreme form of labor commodification, the "peculiar institution" was to such antislavery minds peculiar primarily for its destructive potential, relative to other kinds of "servile" labor, to demean more reputable and efficient labor and labor power. It was peculiar for its unequaled power to undersell, exclude, pollute, and demoralize that enterprise, both self-employed and waged, which was commonly extolled as honorable and superior.

Concerns about forms of servile labor and labor-degrading processes that were distinct from the machinations of the southern slavocracy did not disappear from the free states in the late antebellum period.[50] But those concerns, above all the most radical and utopian anticapitalist critiques of northern wage slavery, did tend to be eclipsed, defused, undermined, and more thoroughly marginalized under the force of an ascendant antisouthern, northern nationalism—i.e., Republican free-labor ideology.[51] Where it did not attempt to altogether "southernize" the causes of northern social problems, that ideology remained insistent (and for many persuasively so) that chattel slavery threatened to make a particular shambles of high-wage, American exceptionalist scenarios. Northern voices like Philip Friese, following Carey and Tuckerman, might continue to debate the precise nature of the market forces endogenous to specific labor markets in the free states that regulated, and commonly depressed, wage rates in these markets. Northern commentators would reach easier and fuller agreement on the cheapening and polluting impact wielded by southern slave labor. Such was the signal free-soil theme that George M. Weston and his Republican cohorts derived from the market revolution.

Notes

Introduction

1. By one estimate the proportion of the American labor force employed for wages rose from 12 percent in 1800 to 40 percent in 1860, increasing twenty times over. By 1850 these "hireling" laborers, the great majority of whom performed manual work of one kind or another, outnumbered southern chattel slaves. By 1860 they surpassed the fully self-employed members of the American labor force, although an indeterminate number also continued to engage (along with other family members) in secondary, nonwaged activities to supplement their wage income (Stanley Lebergott, "The Pattern of Employment since 1800," in *American Economic History*, ed. Seymour Harris [New York, 1961], 291–92).

2. Alice Kessler-Harris, *A Woman's Wage: Historical Meanings and Social Consequences* (Lexington, Ky., 1989); Richard Biernacki, *The Fabrication of Labour: Germany and Britain, 1640–1914* (Berkeley, Calif., 1995).

3. Jonathan A. Glickstein, *Concepts of Free Labor in Antebellum America* (New Haven, 1991); "Henry Clay's Sympathy with Labor," *Emancipator,* rept. in *Herald of Freedom* (Concord, N.H.), March 1, 1844.

4. In an important book on subjects close to my own, James L. Huston argues that America's Revolutionary leaders passed on four primary "axioms" that until their breakdown in the late nineteenth century remained largely unchallenged and unrevised and defined a virtual American "consensus." The first of these was the "labor theory of property/value," by which an "equitable and natural distribution of wealth was created when each laborer received the fruits of his or her labor" (Huston, *Securing the Fruits of Labor: The American Concept of Wealth Distribution, 1765–1900* [Baton Rouge, La., 1998], xi). But here (as on matters of labor incentives), there was likely as much substantive disagreement as there was genuine consensus. This is so if only because early nineteenth-century Americans varied in their normative enthusiasm for the claim (advanced most insistently by Whigs like Edward Everett) that capitalists and professionals qualified as workingmen through their exclusively mental activities. Huston's intermittent acknowledgment of the shallowness of the consensus he identifies does not fully meet the persisting question: how meaningful is an axiom like the labor theory of property/value—how genuine is its hold on common beliefs—if the individuals who putatively subscribe to it (quite apart even from the most visible reform movement dissenters) disagree on the definition of the terms that comprise the axiom?

5. Marx to François Lafargue, Nov. 12, 1866, in *Karl Marx on America and the Civil War,* ed. and trans. Saul K. Padover (New York, 1972), 274–75; Herman Schlüter, *Lincoln, Labor, and Slavery* (New York, 1913), 61–62, 81–84; Philip S. Foner, *History of the Labor Movement in the United States,* vol. 1, *From Colonial Times to the Founding of the American Federation of Labor* (New York, 1947), 270–96; Bernard Mandel, *Labor: Free and Slave; Workingmen and the Anti-Slavery Movement in the United States* (New York, 1955), 26–27, 82, 111–69; Herbert Shapiro, "Labor and Antislavery: Reflections on the Literature," *Nature, Society, and Thought* 2:4 (1989): 471–90; "The Advocates of Association and Slavery—Horace Greeley," *Weekly Herald and Philanthropist* (Cincinnati), June 18, 1845; William Lloyd Garrison's reply to Chas F. Hovey, in "English Monopoly and Suffering," *Liberator* (Boston), Jan. 9, 1846.

6. This is not to deny that the South's ideological preparation for the Civil War included a parallel externalizing tendency. The celebratory northern nationalism, or exceptionalism, articulated by ex-Whig-Republicans was an antisouthern formulation of Whigs' decades-old insistence on the openness of the northern social order, the harmony of interests between capital and wage labor there, etc. Because of the tradition of Democratic skepticism regarding such claims, the northern nationalism of Democrats who joined the Republican coalition was often more equivocal.

7. I find merit in the American antislavery-Marxist position even though slave labor's depressing impact on the bargaining power and wages of northern workers would have required for its maximization an integration between northern and southern labor markets that did not exist in the antebellum period.

8. Some of the radical critics, particularly old labor-movement activists and land reformers, bitterly held out against Republican ideology's overriding denial of northern wage and white slavery. Others, such as leading Associationist socialists, abandoned or tempered their anticapitalist radical views and themselves joined the Republican defense of the northern social order against assaults from the South. Including but extending beyond late antebellum northern nationalism were intellectual currents that likewise acted to rein in more radical visions (John Higham, *From Boundlessness to Consolidation* [Ann Arbor, Mich., 1969]). Although I do not agree with its interpretation of antebellum reform activity, Timothy Messer-Kruse, *The Yankee International: Marxism and the American Reform Tradition, 1848–1876* (Chapel Hill, N.C., 1998), valuably documents the emergence of a reinvigorated northern anticapitalist tradition in the postwar period (though one whose radicalism, like that of most early nineteenth-century American labor-reform movements, did not generally extend to opposing private property); compare with Alan Dawley, *Class and Community: The Industrial Revolution in Lynn* (Cambridge, Mass., 1976), 238–40.

9. Christopher Lasch argues that the free-labor ideology of Lincoln, Olmsted, and other Republicans only secondarily valued education for the instrumental value it added to manual labor—for its enhancement of individuals' ability to rise out of manual-labor employments. Rather, Republicans primarily sought to demonstrate the expansive nature of manual labor's intrinsic mental content, in answer to the southern proslavery "mudsill" arguments that cast doubt on the compatibility of manual-labor employments with intellectual and social refinement. I believe that Lasch is less describing Republican free-labor ideology than he is the social attitudes of a William Ellery Channing, who was so insistent on the unbounded intellectual and moral heights that free manual laborers could reach that he disdained (in contrast to the Republicans) liberal capitalist success values that trum-

peted escape from manual-labor occupations through upward mobility (Lasch, *The Revolt of the Elites and the Betrayal of Democracy* [New York, 1995], 66–69; Glickstein, *Concepts of Free Labor,* 88–89). Still, my disagreement with Lasch's interpretation is itself a nice illustration of the ambiguities that may arise from the antebellum tendency to commingle perceptions of work's intrinsic character with those of its instrumental value.

10. S [Sidney George Fisher], "Domestic Servants," *North American and United States Gazette* (Philadelphia), May 23, 1857.

11. Some of the hardest and lowest of this physical labor was in fact unwaged: it was the self-employed casual work of the northern cities—e.g., rag picking and bone gathering ("The Rag-Pickers of New York," *New York Herald,* Oct. 5, 1853). Olmsted might have joined some of his contemporaries and extended his exceptionalist claims to include such employments.

12. Frederick Law Olmsted, *The Cotton Kingdom* (1861), ed. Arthur M. Schlesinger (New York, 1970), 557.

13. Olmsted, *A Journey in the Back Country* (1860; rept. New York, 1970), 301.

14. Olmsted, *Cotton Kingdom,* 489, 493.

15. The origins of the mythology of American economic exceptionalism remain elusive. There were formulations extending back to John Smith of early seventeenth-century Virginia; for emphasis on the early national contributions, see Joyce Appleby, *Inheriting the Revolution: The First Generation of Americans* (Cambridge, Mass., 2000).

16. For ways in which American antebellum economic morality evolved to reflect the risks of proprietorship—the experiences of both those who suffered bankruptcy and those who profited from others' financial misfortunes—see Edward J. Balleisen, *Navigating Failure: Bankruptcy and Commercial Society in Antebellum America* (Chapel Hill, N.C., 2001), 159–62, 213–19.

17. Clayne Pope, "Social Mobility, Free Labor, and the American Dream," in *The Terms of Labor: Slavery, Serfdom, and Free Labor,* ed. Stanley L. Engerman (Stanford, Calif., 1999), 270–71; Stephan Thernstrom, *Poverty and Progress: Social Mobility in a Nineteenth-Century City* (Cambridge, Mass., 1964); Steven Herscovici, "Migration and Economic Mobility: Wealth Accumulation and Occupational Change among Antebellum Migrants and Persisters," *Journal of Economic History* 58 (Dec. 1998): 927–56; Joseph P. Ferrie, *Yankeys Now: Immigrants in the Antebellum United States, 1840–1860* (New York, 1999), 127–29.

18. Olmsted also strove to vanquish such worries (*Cotton Kingdom,* 557 n).

19. If members of the most disadvantaged groups in the antebellum North were unlikely to have accepted Olmsted's celebratory judgment as descriptive of their own labor's instrumental value, it does not necessarily follow that even most were highly dissatisfied with their job segregation and other adverse conditions. Some of the marginalized, for example (in illustration of the phenomenon of adaptation), likely shaped their preferences to accord with "corrupt public opinion" (as characterized by one critic) and their objectively narrow set of opportunities (M. H. Freeman, "The Educational Wants of the Free Colored People," *Anglo-African Magazine* 1 [April 1859]: 117; Sarah M. Grimké, *Letters on the Equality of the Sexes and the Condition of Women* [Boston, 1838], 51).

20. Marx and Engels, *Circular against Kriege,* May 1846, in Padover, *On America,* 5.

21. "Proceedings of the Colored National Convention," Rochester, N.Y., 1853, in *Minutes of the Proceedings of the National Negro Conventions, 1830–1864,* ed. Howard Holman Bell

(New York, 1969), 21–28; Thomas Dublin, *Women at Work: The Transformation of Work and Community in Lowell, Massachusetts, 1826–1860* (New York, 1981), 86–131.

22. Jeffrey G. Williamson and Peter H. Lindert, *American Inequality: A Macroeconomic History* (New York, 1980), 42–63, 103; Diane Lindstrom, "Economic Structure, Demographic Change, and Income Inequality in Antebellum New York," in *Power, Culture, and Place: Essays on New York City*, ed. John Hull Mollenkopf (New York, 1989), 18–20.

23. For American-British wage differentials, see John A. James and Jonathan S. Skinner, "The Resolution of the Labor-Scarcity Paradox," *Journal of Economic History* 45 (Sept. 1985): 537; for a forceful economic history statement that there were few true market losers in this period, see Diane Lindstrom's review of the "Special Issue on Capitalism in the Early Republic," *Journal of the Early Republic* 16 (Summer 1996), March 7, 1997, posting in H-Net of the Society for Historians of the Early American Republic.

24. Thomas Weiss, "U.S. Labor Force Estimates and Economic Growth, 1800–1860," in *American Economic Growth and Standards of Living before the Civil War*, ed. Robert E. Gallman and John Joseph Wallis (Chicago, 1992), 27; Robert A. Margo, *Wages and Labor Markets in the United States, 1820–1860* (Chicago, 2000), 2; quote from Kenneth L. Sokoloff and Georgia C. Villaflor, "The Market for Manufacturing Workers during Early Industrialization: The American Northeast, 1820–1860," in *Strategic Factors in Nineteenth Century American Economic History*, ed. Claudia Goldin and Hugh Rockoff (Chicago, 1992), 31.

25. The "hidden" depression primarily afflicted native-born nonfarm workers in the North (Robert William Fogel, *Without Consent or Contract: The Rise and Fall of American Slavery* [New York, 1989], 355–58). It should also be noted that Sokoloff and Villaflor, "Market for Manufacturing Workers," qualifies its optimistic portrait of the 1820–60 period as a whole by taking cognizance of the real wage stagnation of the 1850s (44); see also Sokoloff, "The Puzzling Record of Real Wage Growth in Early Industrial America: 1820–1860," in *Studies in Labor Markets and Institutions*, ed. Sokoloff (Los Angeles, 1992), 9–47.

26. Fogel, *Toward a New Synthesis on the Role of Economic Issues in the Political Realignment of the 1850s*, National Bureau of Economic Research, Working Paper Series on Historical Factors in Long Run Growth, no. 34 (Cambridge, Mass., 1992): 36; Fogel, "Problems in Measuring the Real Wages of Native Non-Farm Workers in the North, 1846–1855," in *Without Consent or Contract. Evidence and Methods*, ed. Fogel, Ralph A. Galantine, and Richard L. Manning (New York, 1992), 482–83; Claudia Goldin and Robert A. Margo, "Wages, Prices, and Labor Markets before the Civil War," in Goldin and Rockoff, *Strategic Factors*, 92–93.

27. Margo, *Wages and Labor Markets*, 1–4, 144, 148, 155–56, 180. Williamson and Lindert, *American Inequality* (68–75, 281–86), introduced the prevailing view, contested by Margo, that the ratio of skilled workers' pay to common laborers' pay rose during the antebellum period; see also Jeffrey G. Williamson, "Is Inequality Inevitable under Capitalism? The American Case," in *Capitalism and Equality in America: Modern Capitalism*, ed. Peter L. Berger (Lanham, Md., 1987), 58–68. Margo's more pessimistic portrait of the fortunes of traditional artisans also contrasts with the conclusions of Sokoloff and Villafor, "Market for Manufacturing Workers," 61–62.

28. Margo, *Wages and Labor Markets*, 1–2.

29. See note 17 above.

30. Margo, *Wages and Labor Markets*, 1, 4, 143, 153–56.

31. Fogel, *Synthesis*, 26. Such pessimistic claims were a staple of the "new" labor and

social history that emerged in the 1970s and 1980s, but many of them also appear in the earlier labor histories of the antebellum period written by Norman Ware, William Sullivan, and others; on the decades-long "mutual hostility" between labor history and the neoclassical economic mainstream, see Gavin Wright, "Labor History and Labor Economics," in *The Future of Economics,* ed. Alexander J. Field (New Brunswick, N.J., 1995), 318, 341.

32. One should not exaggerate these differences. Some economic historians have themselves examined the marginalization and labor-market segmentation experienced by particular social groups, although they remain inclined to frame these in a more positive light—e.g., Diane Lindstrom's reference to the "unusual opportunities for female employment" that large antebellum cities provided ("Economic Structure," 13). Labor historians, for their part, have commonly emphasized how white skilled sectors of the labor force did enjoy (at least during certain periods) significant economic gains, frequently at the expense of the minorities and women whom they excluded from their organizations. Growing quantitative research on human welfare trends offers its own challenge to the standard optimistic claims of economic historians; it is finding that whatever the increases in per capita income in the United States among other Western nations during early industrialization, average height and other indexes of well-being stagnated (Dora L. Costa and Richard H. Steckel, "Long-Term Trends in Health, Welfare, and Economic Growth in the United States," in *Health and Welfare during Industrialization,* ed. Steckel and Roderick Floud [Chicago, 1997], 73–77).

33. Peter Way, *Common Labour: Workers and the Digging of North American Canals, 1780–1860* (Cambridge, 1993), 109.

34. For example, labor-market segmentation helped undercut the economic opportunities for women created by industrialization. It partially offset what Claudia Goldin emphasizes: the "narrowing of the [gender] earnings gap in manufacturing across the nineteenth century" that arose from the tendency of increasing division of labor and machinery to reduce the need for skill and strength and render male and female labor more interchangeable (Goldin, *Understanding the Gender Gap: An Economic History of American Women* [New York, 1990], 87). In certain industries capital-intensive mechanization itself tended to offset the gender-equalizing effects of deskilling; it conferred on in-place male workers greater power to resist female labor intrusions, thereby reinforcing gender-based labor-market segmentation (Jens Christiansen, Peter Philips, and Mark Prus, "Women, Technology, and Work: The Gender Division of Labor in U.S. Manufacturing, 1850 to 1919," *Research in Economic History* 16 [1996]: 103–26). America's overall labor scarcity notwithstanding, women emerged as a cheap early nineteenth-century industrial workforce as households became proletarianized, or at least increasingly dependent on wage labor (Margaret Coleman, "Low Wages, Labor Shortage, Wage and Labor Structures, and Poverty, 1810–1840, in the Northeastern United States" [Ph.D. diss., New School for Social Research, 1995]). In accounting for the historical segmentation of labor markets on the basis of race, gender, and/or ethnicity, "split labor market" models attach greatest weight to the self-protective instincts of more privileged workers to exclude sources of cheap labor competition. "Segmentation" models proper, particularly Marxist ones, alternatively highlight the role played by capitalist intentions and interests in keeping labor markets and the working class divided, often along the same racial, gender, or ethnic lines. But as the sociologist Michael Buroway has noted, whatever "divide-and-conquer" interests

capitalists share as a class may be frequently overridden by the profit-maximizing interests of individual employers to fully exploit cheap labor and disregard the split labor barriers favored by more advantaged workers. It was in fact largely owing to this last circumstance that the relatively privileged artisans belonging to traditional crafts met with indifferent success in reducing the downward pressure on their wages. Some trades remained resistant to skill dilution, subdivision of labor, and competition from "dishonorable" segments that drew on the expanding pools of cheap juvenile, female, and immigrant labor. But more generally, skilled journeymen could not, in the period of metropolitan industrialization and relatively weak unions, sustain exclusionist shelters that would effectively insulate either their wage standards or their own work processes from such competitive market pressures. At the same time, the female sweatshop laborers and outworkers who were utilized by employers to undermine artisan shelters and job skills characteristically remained confined to their low-paid, dead-end employments, largely owing to the gender norms that restricted their occupational options. Such developments raise much-debated questions of whether and how much capitalist deskilling processes, pronounced as they may be, in fact act to homogenize the labor force and erode (gender-) segmented, stratified labor markets (Howard Botwinick, *Persistent Inequalities: Wage Disparity under Capitalist Competition* [Princeton, N.J., 1993]), 47–48, 104; Marcel van der Linden and Jan Lucassen, "Introduction," in *Racism and the Labour Market: Historical Studies,* ed. Linden and Lucassen [Bern, Germany, 1995], 12–14).

35. For criticisms of the American labor scarcity/labor dearness paradigm (and of E. J. Habakkuk's influential comparative study of Britain and American technology) with respect to factor substitution in American manufacturing, see Peter Temin, "Labor Scarcity and the Problem of American Industrial Efficiency in the 1850s," *Journal of Economic History* 26 (Sept. 1966): 277–98; Temin, "Labor Scarcity in America," *Journal of Interdisciplinary History* 1 (Winter 1971): 251–64; for an extrapolation from the findings of Temin and others, one that offers a "low-cost labor interpretation of the antebellum United States" against the neoclassical economic view that "American workers were equitably rewarded by an economy in which labor was exceedingly scarce — the result of a favorable land-labor ratio," see Carville Earle, *Geographical Inquiry and American Historical Problems* (Stanford, Calif., 1992), 175, 178, 407.

36. Alexis de Tocqueville, *Democracy in America* (1835), ed. J. P. Mayer, trans. George Lawrence (Garden City, N.Y., 1969), 2:535–38.

37. See the speeches in the *Congressional Globe* by such Republicans as Hannibal Hamlin, Zachariah Chandler, and Henry Wilson, made in rebuttal of South Carolina senator James Henry Hammond's proslavery mudsill speech of March 1858.

38. Sean Wilentz, "Against Exceptionalism: Class Consciousness and the American Labor Movement, 1790–1920," *International Labor and Working-Class History* 26 (Fall 1984): 1–24.

39. See the *New-York Daily Tribune*'s Aug. 1845–Jan. 1846 series, "Labor in New-York: Its Circumstances, Conditions, and Rewards," including E's report (Aug. 28) on the wage-reducing "grinding competition" within the bookbinding trade; see also the Nov. 11 profile of "The Cabinet-Makers."

40. This is not to deny that long-standing English artisan traditions themselves contributed to the pride and sense of entitlement felt by American craftsmen (some of whom

were British-born) (Howard B. Rock, "Artisans and Paradigms," *Labor History* 40 [Feb. 1999]: 43). The mythology of American economic exceptionalism also gave impetus to what Judith N. Shklar has emphasized: the facility with which "self-directed 'earning'" became a principal "ethical basis for democratic citizenship" in the early nineteenth-century United States. Yet to recall earlier points, Shklar too easily accepts a series of related clichés: that such ascendant currents as Republican free-labor ideology invested manual labor with an unproblematic dignity, and that "no one doubted the labor theory of value which declared that labor had created all wealth" (as if the definition of true labor went uncontested in the antebellum era) (Shklar, *American Citizenship: The Quest for Inclusion* [Cambridge, Mass., 1991], 67–68).

41. Tocqueville, *Democracy in America,* ed. and abridged by Richard D. Heffner (New York, 1956), 237; see also p. 593 of *Democracy* edition cited in note 36.

42. See here Edward Pessen's exchanges with Robert E. Gallman and Stuart M. Blumin in *Social Science History* 3–6 (Winter 1978–Summer 1982).

43. Because of their more obvious tendency to conceptualize the "degenerate" (those who are contaminated as well as those who do the contaminating) as racially or biologically deficient, the medical and scientific languages of physical and moral degeneration that flourished in late nineteenth-century Europe offer limited parallels to the antebellum American themes of contagion noted here (Daniel Pick, *Faces of Degeneration: A European Disorder, c. 1848–c.1918* [Cambridge, 1989]).

44. But to extend the point raised in the previous note, Tuckerman's fears of pauperism as a contagious disease were not conspicuously racialist. Unlike some late nineteenth-century commentators, he did not conceptualize indiscriminate relief as triggering an innate or biological propensity of poor people to turn from labor to a degenerate mendicancy (John Marriott, "In Darkest England: The Poor, the Crowd, and Race in the Nineteenth-Century Metropolis," in *New Ethnicities, Old Racisms?* ed. Phil Cohen [London, 1999], 82–100).

45. Emancipation helped erode northern blacks' limited positioning within the skilled artisan trades. During the early nineteenth century they came to be yet more generally confined to unskilled labor, low-grade service, and other menial employments, and they were even driven out of many of these by Irish immigrants during the 1840s and 1850s. Insofar as they were shut out of both the burgeoning factory sector and even the most "dishonorable" forms of manufacturing work and therefore offered no competitive threat whatever to skilled or semiskilled white manufacturing workers, the labor-market segmentation experienced by antebellum northern blacks was yet more extreme than that of white women.

46. David W. Stowe, review of books by Jacobson and Lipsitz, *Journal of American History* 86 (Dec. 1999): 1359. While emphasizing the pervasiveness and depth of antiblack racial prejudices, much whiteness scholarship simultaneously posits that the very power of whiteness as an axis of self-identification is attested to by its unconsciousness for white Americans — or at least for the majority who have embraced whiteness as the normative national, nonracial identity. Such arguments as to the homogenizing importance, and invisibility, of white racialness conceivably hold yet more truth for periods following the antebellum decades, as some of this scholarship maintains — see Grace Elizabeth Hale, *Making Whiteness: The Culture of Segregation in the South, 1890–1940* (New York, 1998), xi–xii, 4–8. Yet

the power of whiteness as a concept that subliminally links white people to a position of social dominance, effectively effacing class and other intraracial distinctions in a uniform, unproblematic construction of black otherness, remains questionable even for the modern-day United States; see John Hartigan Jr.'s perceptive study of the heterogeneous racial perceptions of Detroit's white inhabitants, *Racial Situations: Class Predicaments of Whiteness in Detroit* (Princeton, N.J., 1999), 16–17, 82. In de-reifying whiteness, Hartigan's is a case study of the instability of white identity that Matthew Frye Jacobson also underscores (at least for the period extending from the mid-nineteenth to the mid-twentieth century) in *Whiteness of a Different Color: European Immigrants and the Alchemy of Race* (Cambridge, Mass., 1998).

47. Apart from the varied patterns of labor-market segmentation experienced by free black, Irish immigrant, and other certifiably working-class females, the legal and normative impediments to women's equal participation in the competitive race were also synonymous with the channeling of middle-class family resources into a material base that helped launch putatively self-made men in pursuit of commercial and professional attainment (Linda Kerber, "Can a Woman Be an Individual? The Discourse of Self-Reliance," in *American Chameleon: Individualism in Trans-national Context,* ed. Richard O. Curry and Lawrence B. Goodheart [Kent, Ohio, 1991], 159, 166); for another take on antebellum competitive anxieties, see Brian Roberts, *American Alchemy: The California Gold Rush and Middle-Class Culture* (Chapel Hill, N.C., 2000), 45–47, 117.

48. For one of the mid-nineteenth-century criticisms of gender-biased educational norms and training practices that entered into what modern scholars term "discrimination before the market" (as distinct, for example, from pay discrimination for the same work), see the discussion of Henry Ward Beecher.

49. Throughout this study I endorse the view—shared by many antebellum critics—that gender-based occupational segregation, through the overcrowding effect, was a paramount contributing factor to the low wages paid such workers as the seamstresses. I do not mean to imply that the same factors were necessarily responsible, in equal degree, for the inferior wages paid female laborers in other industries throughout the nineteenth century.

50. Achille Murat, *The United States of North America,* 2d ed. (London, 1833), 343.

51. Ibid., 344.

52. For parallel discussions of whether southern proslavery thought's grounding in racist and ascriptive principles did or did not disqualify it for membership in the American liberal tradition, see David F. Ericson and Louisa Bertch Green, eds., *The Liberal Tradition in American Politics: Reassessing the Legacy of American Liberalism* (New York, 1999), particularly the essays by Ericson and Rogers M. Smith.

53. David Brion Davis, *Slavery and Human Progress* (New York, 1984), 113–14.

54. Murat, *United States,* 108–9.

55. Junius Redivivus [William Bridges Adams], "A Note on Negro Slavery," appended to Murat's *United States,* 376–77. Despite his assault on Murat's proslavery justifications, Adams was hardly free of racial prejudice (380–82).

56. For this and his other defenses of southern slavery, see Murat, *United States,* 91–94.

57. Ibid., 342. As Frederick Law Olmsted's above-quoted remarks suggest, defenses of the competitive free market in the North became more characteristically conjoined with attacks on, rather than with defenses of, southern chattel slavery, especially with the escalation of sectional tensions.

58. Clarke was born in Hanover, New Hampshire, in 1810 and graduated from Harvard College and Harvard Divinity School. Before his move to Boston, he ministered Kentucky's first Unitarian church in Louisville between 1833 and 1840, during which time he also established and edited the first Transcendentalist journal, the *Western Messenger.*

59. J. F. C., "Fourierism," *Christian Examiner,* 4th ser., 2 (July 1844): 60.

60. Ibid., 70. In the most incipient sense, Clarke, Orestes Brownson, and others who made the "cannot wait" argument anticipated issues raised by John E. Roemer and other contemporary analytical Marxists. The latter regard Marx's labor theory of value (and its discrepancy between labor power and labor cost) as an intellectually unsalvageable tool for explaining exploitation under capitalism. They emphasize instead differences in property holdings, particularly the initial maldistribution of wealth and its coercive effects, that may exist independent of particular labor processes. Exploitation, Roemer writes, "takes place because of the distribution of the means of production, not at the point of production" ("Property Relations vs. Surplus Value in Marxian Exploitation," *Philosophy and Public Affairs* 11 [Fall 1982]: 184; see also the essays in Andrew Reeve, ed., *Modern Theories of Exploitation* [London, 1987]). Because Clarke conveyed with respect to his worker who "cannot wait" a sense of a slack labor market and meager employment prospects, one might be also tempted to contextualize his remarks in the protracted depression that had ended only one year earlier. Yet as suggested later, Clarke's exploitation scenario was more philosophical and transcendant than this; it seemed equally to refer to periods of economic prosperity and growth during which, under conditions of "free competition," the more cunning, resourceful, and powerful continue to advance at the expense of the weaker and the disadvantaged. In any case, Clarke typified antebellum labor reformers in having a concept of economic exploitation in mind: the bargain that the resource-poor worker is obliged to accept is unfavorable and unfair—lacking in reciprocity—not merely because his wages are low, but because, Clarke assumes, these do not equal the market value of what he produces.

61. For discussions suggesting working-class choice, opportunity, and nonexploitation scenarios, see Pope, "Mobility," 267–68; Herscovici, "Migration"; Wendy Gamber, "A Gendered Enterprise: Placing Nineteenth-Century Businesswomen in History," *Business History Review* 72 (Summer 1998): 192–96.

62. Robert J. Steinfeld and Stanley L. Engerman, "Labor—Free or Coerced? A Historical Reassessment of Differences and Similarities," in *Free and Unfree Labour: The Debate Continues,* ed. Tom Brass and Marcel van der Linden (Bern, Germany, 1997), 121–22.

63. Richard Hofstadter claimed that economic historians had "quite effectively resuscitated" the safety-valve idea. But they have done so primarily by suggesting how the presence of western territory alleviated the downward pressures on the wages of those workers who remained in the East. They have not overturned earlier criticisms that the safety-valve thesis, in its nineteenth-century formulations, understated the costs and other difficulties of removal to the West, most of all for eastern workmen during periods of unemployment. Revisions of the safety-valve thesis, in other words, afford greater basis for questioning the representativeness of Clarke's impoverished (and presumably eastern-based) male breadwinner; they provide less basis for minimizing that breadwinner's particular plight (Hofstadter, *The Progressive Historians: Turner, Beard, Parrington* [New York, 1969], 153–56). A recent quantitative study concludes that although the cost of travel to the nation's interior was "not a tremendous burden" for European immigrant laborers in

New York City, the expense for those who hoped to enter or reenter farming there remained onerous (Ferrie, *Yankeys Now,* 57–58); for a more full-scale assault on the safety-valve thesis and its resuscitations, see Earle, *Geographical Inquiry,* 180–88, 407–8.

64. See also "The Slavery of Poverty with a Plea for Its Abolition," in *New-York Quarterly Pamphleteer,* no. 1 (May 1842): 8.

65. J. F. C., "Fourierism," 70, 75.

66. See, for example, Russell R. Menard, "From Servant to Freeholder: Status Mobility and Property Accumulation in Seventeenth-Century Maryland," *William and Mary Quarterly,* 3d ser., 30 (Jan. 1973): 37–64. In generally defending the reputation of eighteenth-century America as a land of economic opportunity for oppressed Europeans, one recent study, however, tends to minimize the exploitative features of indentured servitude, arguing among other things that many colonial tenants simply chose not to become freeholders (Marilyn C. Baseler, *"Asylum for Mankind": America, 1607–1800* [Ithaca, N.Y., 1998], 88–119); see also, on the effective limits to masters' power, Christine Daniels, "'Liberty to Complaine': Servant Petitions in Maryland, 1652–1797," in *The Many Legalities of Early America,* ed. Christopher L. Tomlins and Bruce H. Mann (Chapel Hill, N.C., 2001), 219–49.

67. Robert J. Steinfeld, *The Invention of Free Labor: The Employment Relation in English and American Law and Culture, 1350–1870* (Chapel Hill, N.C., 1991), 160–75.

68. There were related ironies when early nineteenth-century working-class parents (or poor-relief authorities, in the case of destitute orphans) exercised their liberty of contract with respect to the services of minors and contracted these out to manufacturers and other private employers (Steinfeld, *Invention,* 149–53).

69. See the essays in Brass and Van der Linden, *Free and Unfree Labour.* Marxist scholars agree that limited resources and options force proletarians to sell their labor power, and that capitalism is intrinsically oppressive and unjust for this and other reasons. But even many of these scholars distinguish such a universe of constraints and substantive involuntariness from a more direct coercion—one implying an intentional agent, as in the guise of the slaveholder (R. G. Peffer, *Marxism, Morality, and Social Justice* [Princeton, N.J., 1990], 149–50). For, however, an assessment of physical compulsions, economic pressures, and nonpecuniary legal ones which concludes that the distinction between free and coerced labor is inevitably a conventional and arbitrary one (because in all cases laborers are induced to choose between unpleasant alternatives), see Robert J. Steinfeld, *Coercion, Contract, and Free Labor in the Nineteenth Century* (Cambridge, 2001), 1–26.

70. As Clarke favorably summarized Channing's antiabolitionist position, "Slavery is a wrong and evil; but it does not follow, that immediate Emancipation is right, or that the slaveholder is a sinner." The North should not "endanger the peace and tranquility of the South" (Clarke, "Channing on Slavery," *Western Messenger* [Louisville], 3 [April 1836]: 628).

71. Employees' forfeiture of wages owed them emerged in the early nineteenth-century North as the standard court-approved sanction against wage earners' exercise of their freedom to depart their work before their contracts expired (Steinfeld, *Invention,* 149–51); for the distinctiveness that this pecuniary penalty for contract breach lent to American meanings of free labor prior to its undermining by late nineteenth-century reform legislation, see also Steinfeld, *Coercion, Contract.* But however significantly wage forfeiture or its threat actually figured in the experience of antebellum factory operatives and other northern workers, even labor-reform commentary of the period tended to slight it discur-

sively—to situate contractual pecuniary sanctions anonymously among the general economic pressures that drove wage slaves.

72. "Fourierism and Agrarianism. No. II," *Working Man's Advocate* (New York), Sept. 7, 1844. Defining and measuring absolute want by specifying minimum consumption levels and other criteria continue to generate academic debate. Little of this ambiguity entered the distributional-injustice arguments advanced by George Henry Evans and other antebellum labor reformers. Aside from complaining about unjust relative deprivation, they generally found it sufficient to claim that increasing numbers of America's hardworking mechanics and other true producers could at best "obtain the bare necessities of life" ("'Best Friends,'" ibid., Sept. 20, 1834).

73. Orestes A. Brownson, "The Laboring Classes," *Boston Quarterly Review* 3 (July 1840): 371–72.

74. J. F. C., "Fourierism," 70–71. Thus, in rebuttal of the particular proslavery argument advanced by Murat and others, Clarke observed: "We know that anger and brutish obstinancy are often stronger than interest, and something more is needed to protect the poor beast from ill treatment than the calculating reason of his master. So undoubtedly it is for the interest of the southern planter to treat his slaves well, and not overwork them. But this, we know, does not always protect them from his caprice, violence, and blind love of present gain" (68–69).

75. On cases of "mutually advantageous" as well as "consensual" exploitative transactions—exploitative because the exploiter benefits unfairly or excessively from the outcome, even though the exploited party also derives benefits—see Alan Wertheimer, *Exploitation* (Princeton, N.J., 1996), ix, 23–24. Wertheimer indicates that exploitative relationships that are mutually advantageous in the strictly material sense may yet be harmful to the exploited party in a moral sense, reflecting his utilization as a mere instrument for another's private gain. Clarke's own language suggests that he might have found this notion congenial.

76. J. F. C., "Fourierism," 62–63; see here Steinfeld and Engerman, "Labor," 107–26. The authors credit much of their position to the writings of the progressive Legal Realist thinker Robert Hale, who went far beyond Clarke and other earlier reformers in developing the position that economic laissez-faire (Clarke's let-aloneism) was in fact a structured regime of legal entitlements.

77. To the extent, too, that America's land reformers and other antimonopolist reformers were calling on government primarily to nullify its iniquitous intervention in the market, their stance was different from that of the plebeian perpetuators of the moral economy tradition within England; these looked to state regulations as an important means of sustaining wage rates and securing other entitlements for the laboring population in the face of rapacious capitalist forces (Adrian Randall and Andrew Charlesworth, "The Moral Economy: Riots, Markets, and Social Conflict," in *Moral Economy and Popular Protest: Crowds, Conflict, and Authority,* ed. Randall and Charlesworth [New York, 2000], 23–24).

78. As a vocal critic of southern slavery by the mid-1840s, Clarke may well have subscribed to the standard abolitionist position that the term *wage slavery* reprehensibly slighted the more pernicious coercions of chattel servitude, a point of view that would have put him at odds with a large number of northern labor reformers. But he also may have believed that by this time the term had become highly provocative, divisive, and counter-

productive and was best avoided for merely strategic reasons (Clark, *Antislavery Days* [1883; rept. Westport, Conn., 1970], 130; Clark, *Slavery in the United States* [Boston, 1843]; Clark, *The Annexation of Texas* [Boston, 1844]).

79. J. F. C., "Fourierism," 73–78.

80. Anne C. Rose, *Transcendentalism as a Social Movement, 1830–1850* (New Haven, 1981), 142–43; John L. Thomas, "Romantic Reform in America, 1815–1865," *American Quarterly* 17 (Winter 1965): 656–81. Clarke's basic criticism of Associationism was also leveled by more hostile commentators who unlike him stood outside the period's romantic reform perspectives altogether; these tended to dismiss as naively sentimental and ineffectual all humanitarian attacks on the outward manifestations of human corruption; one of many examples is H. B. [Hosea Ballou 2d], "Fourierism, and Similar Schemes," *Universalist Quarterly and General Review* 2 (Jan. 1845): 52–76.

81. In their celebration of equal opportunity in the United States, moderate and conservative Whigs turned this argument around to insist that privileged backgrounds, above all inherited wealth, were more disabling than birth into poverty: the sons of the rich were least likely to cultivate those talents required for material success and other forms of distinction in the American meritocracy.

82. For an Associationist statement similar to Clarke's, see Parke Godwin, "Political Economy," *Harbinger,* April 1, 1848. None of the above is to suggest that such antebellum criticisms approached modern academics' scrutinizing of notions of equal opportunity and merit; see the essays in Neal Devins and Davison M. Douglas, eds., *Redefining Equality* (New York, 1998), 51–81; on merit and meritocracy as normative concepts (reflecting underlying conceptions of the good and just society), see Amartya Sen, "Merit and Justice," in *Meritocracy and Economic Inequality,* ed. Kenneth Arrow, Samuel Bowles, and Steven Durlauf (Princeton, N.J., 2000), 5–16.

83. Terry Eagleton, *The Illusions of Postmodernism* (Oxford, Eng., 1996), 116–17; Karl Marx, *Critique of the Gotha Program* (1875), in *Marx and Engels,* ed. Lewis Feuer (Garden City, N.Y., 1959), 117–20. Eagleton proceeds, in endorsing Marx's communist vision: "To treat two people [truly] equally must surely mean not giving them exactly the same treatment but attending equally to their different needs"; see also Agnes Heller, *The Theory of Need in Marx* (New York, 1976), 122–23. To the extent that Marx tied principles of justice to equal rights and saw both as indelibly marked by bourgeois limitations, he may in fact have envisaged the "higher phase" of communist society, with its distribution of the social product on the basis of individual need rather than ability or productive contribution, as "a society beyond justice." For one discussion of this possibility and the related debate over whether or not Marx regarded capitalism, and the wage relation specifically, as unjust (rather than merely exploitative), see Norman Geras, "The Controversy about Marx and Justice," *New Left Review,* no. 150 (March–April 1985): 53–54, 47–85; for one attempt to reconstruct (and then critique as unrealizable) Marx's sketchy vision of postcapitalist society, see N. Scott Arnold, *Marx's Radical Critique of Capitalist Society* (New York, 1990), 135–280; for the difficulties involved in defining and identifying needs, see Kate Soper, *On Human Needs: Open and Closed Theories in a Marxist Perspective* (Sussex, Eng., 1981); Robert E. Goodin, "Relative Needs," in *Needs and Welfare,* ed. Alan Ware and Goodin (London, 1991), 12–33; recognition of human beings' widely varying needs for resources has assumed a central role in discussions of people's "capabilities" for attaining an equal level of functioning; see the

essays in Martha Nussbaum and Jonathan Glover, eds., *Women, Culture, and Development: A Study of Human Capabilities* (Oxford, Eng., 1995).

84. That Clarke and Marx shared a vision of a good society that was free of exploitative "free competition" is hardly to claim that they agreed on means, or that their reform sensibilities held much else in common. Clarke would have been horrified by Marx's invocation of class struggle and violent social revolution. There is no less doubt that Marx would have disdained Clarke's call for individual personal redemption, just as he scornfully dismissed the position of the Fourierists and other utopian socialists that the noncompetitive, good society could emerge through ethical argumentation and communal experiment divorced from political and class struggle. Although he may not have shared their attraction to aristocratic social ties and values, Clarke's spiritual remedy for let-aloneism bore particular similarities with the perspective of England's mid-Victorian Christian socialists; his priorities remain open to some of the criticisms that left scholars have made of this group of public moralists; John Saville, "The Christian Socialists of 1848," in *Democracy and the Labour Movement,* ed. Saville (London, 1954), 135–59.

85. J. F. C., "Fourierism," 73–78.

86. "The *Christian Examiner* on the Doctrine of Fourier," *Phalanx* (New York), Aug. 24, 1844.

87. David Friedman, *The Machinery of Freedom: Guide to a Radical Capitalism* (New York, 1973), 184.

88. Adrian Ellis and Krishan Kumar, "Preface," in *Dilemmas of Liberal Democracies: Studies in Fred Hirsch's Social Limits to Growth,* ed. Ellis and Kumar (London, 1983), x.

89. Typical of this prescription literature was *Manual of Self-Education* 1 (Aug. 1842), excerpted in *Antebellum American Culture,* ed. David Brion Davis (University Park, Pa., 1997), 71–72; Henry Ward Beecher, *Lectures to Young Men,* new ed. (Boston, 1867), 26–28, 74–78; Freeman Hunt, *Worth and Wealth* (New York, 1856), 216.

90. In voicing its own concerns over the pecuniary excesses of early nineteenth-century competitive capitalist enterprise, some of the more mainstream commentary itself veered toward the labor-reform view that such excesses were increasingly endemic rather than atypical—see here Freeman Hunt's jeremiads against merchants who failed to "act from Christian motives," having succumbed to the omnipresent temptations of selfishness and deceit in trade. However, Hunt's accompanying insistence that unscrupulous and exploitative practices proved more often than not self-destructive—that they were unlikely to yield lasting economic rewards—remained one that was dubiously received by more radical critics of the American economic order (Hunt, *Worth,* 446–47; "Integrity of Business Men," *Hunt's Merchant's Magazine and Commercial Review* 20 [June 1849]: 682–83).

91. J. F. C., "Fourierism," 63. As part of their retention of the institution of private property, the Associationist communities earmarked within their joint-stock property organization specific rewards for the contributions of capital. But despite the criticisms that they drew from the more radical Owenites, Associationist doctrines and communities were pronouncedly anticapitalist in fundamental ways: they rejected market-determined wages, occupational specialization, competitive individualism, and other basic features of the nation's prevailing social arrangements. Carl J. Guarneri is more inclined than I am to highlight accommodationist, "semi-capitalist," and American nationalist, exceptionalist tendencies within Associationism (Guarneri, "Brook Farm, Fourierism, and the Nationalist

Dilemma in American Utopianism," in *Transient and Permanent: The Transcendentalist Movement and Its Contexts,* ed. Charles Capper and Conrad Edick Wright [Boston, 1999], 456–64).

92. J. F. C. "Fourierism," 68–70. Other commentators similarly critical of gendered labor segmentation and occupational overcrowding emphasized, at the same time, that the majority of poor working-class women of whom Clarke was speaking were simply not qualified at this juncture "to fill any position requiring skill or business faculties of any kind"—hence their need for fair educational opportunity in bookkeeping, arithmetic, and the like ("Employment for Women," *New-York Times,* Nov. 11, 1858).

93. Many students of capitalism across time and space would resist as overly Marxist this singling out of one of capitalism's production-relations attributes; for an overview, see Richard Grassby, *The Idea of Capitalism before the Industrial Revolution* (Lanham, Md., 1999). Of course, too, a variety of safety-net measures, distinguishing the evolution of American and other liberal mixed economies of the twentieth century, have sought to soften the blow of capitalism—to blunt for the worst-off the most extreme effects of poverty. Yet coercion for such individuals remains real enough. As Donald Weiss notes, although those who "'drop out'" as contributors to "social productivity" are ostensibly guaranteed minimum standards of nourishment and health, they must nonetheless "suffer some significant economic hardship, relative to the standards of their time. . . . the specific contents of the economic factors of 'drudgery' and 'coercion' are historically relative" (Weiss, *The Specter of Capitalism and the Promise of a Classless Society* [Atlantic Highlands, N.J., 1993], 38, 91).

94. Patrick Joyce, *Democratic Subjects: Studies in the History of the Self and the Social in Nineteenth-Century England* (Cambridge, 1994), 25. In his paraphrasing here of the arguments of Jacques Rancière regarding artisans in mid-nineteenth-century France, Joyce generally endorses them as congruent with his own embrace of the linguistic turn.

95. For different concepts of "skill," see Craig Littler, *The Development of the Labour Process in Capitalist Societies* (London, 1981), 7–11.

96. James Vernon, "Who's Afraid of the 'Linguistic Turn'? The Politics of Social History and Its Discontents," *Social History* 19 (Jan. 1994): 96; see also Eleni Varikas, "Gender, Experience, and Subjectivity: The Tilly-Scott Disagreement," *New Left Review,* no. 211 (May–June 1995): 99–100.

97. For the substantive nature of London artisan skills and the relentless competitive pressures to which these were subjected in a developing world of "cheap goods" and "equally cheap labor," see David R. Green, *From Artisans to Paupers: Economic Change and Poverty in London, 1790–1870* (Hants, Eng., 1995), 83. That the early nineteenth-century artisan experience, in the United States as well as Europe, is the subject of controversy over poststructuralist approaches stressing labor's "non-material formative contexts" (6) may be seen in the forum on Christopher Tomlins, "Why Wait for Industrialism? Work, Legal Culture, and the Example of Early America—An Historiographical Argument," *Labor History* 40 (Feb. 1999): 5–52.

98. Geoff Eley and Keith Nield, "Starting Over: The Present, the Post-Modern, and the Moment of Social History," *Social History* 20 (Oct. 1995): 359; for the authors' own more limited embrace of poststructural arguments, see also Eley, "Is All the World a Text? From Social History to the History of Society Two Decades Later," in *The Historic Turn in the Human Sciences,* ed. Terrence J. McDonald (Ann Arbor, Mich., 1995), 214–26; Eley and Nield, "Farewell to the Working Class?" *International Labor and Working-Class History* 57 (Spring 2000): 1–30, 76–87.

99. James Epstein, *Radical Expression: Political Language, Ritual, and Symbol in England, 1790–1850* (New York, 1994), 70–71; see also Marc W. Steinberg, *Fighting Words: Working-Class Formation, Collective Action, and Discourse in Early Nineteenth-Century England* (Ithaca, N.Y., 1999), 19, 167. Some Marxist students of Chartism, such as Bryan D. Palmer, John Foster, and Neville Kirk, push this last point more heavily than Epstein does. For Palmer's suggestion that there was "a class struggle within language" in late eighteenth- and early nineteenth-century Britain, see "Response to Joan Scott," *International Labor and Working-Class History*, no. 31 (Spring 1987): 18; see also Kirk, "History, Language, Ideas, and Post-Modernism: A Materialist View," *Social History* 19 (May 1994): 226–28, 235; Ellen Meikins Wood, *The Retreat from Class: A New "True" Socialism* (London, 1986), 102–12; for James Vernon's more catholic interpretation, directed at Epstein and others, see *Politics and the People: A Study in English Political Culture, c. 1815–1867* (Cambridge, 1993), 297–330; Martin Hewitt, *The Emergence of Stability in the Industrial City: Manchester, 1832–67* (Hants, Eng., 1996), 11–19.

100. Richard Price, *British Society, 1680–1880: Dynamism, Containment, and Change* (Cambridge, 1999), 293.

101. See John R. Hall, ed., *Reworking Class* (Ithaca, N.Y., 1997), esp. Hall's introductory essay. Subject to continuing debate is whether due attention to linguistic structures is compatible with a broader, cultural Marxism, and whether the most fervent proponents of the linguistic turn, in rejecting Marxism, have tended to equate it with its most reductive and determinist forms (Eley and Nield, "Starting Over," 357; Kirk, "History Language," 222; Marc W. Steinberg, "Culturally Speaking: Finding a Commons between Post-Structuralism and the Thompsonian Perspective," *Social History* 21 [May 1996]: 193–214); for the contrary, insistent characterization of Marxism as a discredited "foundational materialism," a creed that invariably and wrongfully essentializes the category of class, see Patrick Joyce, "The End of Social History?" ibid., 20 (Jan. 1995): 75; Joyce, "The End of Social History? A Brief Reply to Eley and Nield," ibid., 21 (Jan. 1996): 97–98; see also "Roundtable" on the linguistic turn in *Social Science History* 22 (Spring 1998): 1–45.

102. Adrian Wilson, "A Critical Portrait of Social History," in *Rethinking Social History: English Society, 1570–1920, and Its Interpretation,* ed. Wilson (Manchester, Eng., 1993), 24.

103. Steinberg, *Fighting Words,* 14. Consistent with my recognition of the prescriptive and normative power of representations and social constructions, I employ Foucault's term *discourse* here, even as I resist the most extreme antifoundational poststructural claims (disparagingly characterized by some as "linguistic determinism"); for relationships between discourse, ideology, and language, see Terry Eagleton, *Ideology: An Introduction* (London, 1991), 8–10; Trevor Purvis and Alan Hunt, "Discourse, Ideology, Discourse, Ideology, Discourse, Ideology . . . ," *British Journal of Sociology* 44 (Sept. 1993): 473–99. I also depart from what some scholars regard as Marx's dominant, pejorative concept of ideology insofar as I consider the oppositional and "counterhegemonic" perspectives developed by subordinate groups, including the revolutionary working-class consciousness idealized by Marx, to be ideological—perhaps no less so than the so-called apologias, mystifications, and illusions (e.g., the voluntariness of the capitalist-worker transaction) propagated by more powerful classes to legitimate their position and interests. That Marx himself did more than look at capitalism from the anticapitalist "proletarian point of view"—that he regarded the latter as in its own ways scientifically deficient, biased, and ideological, though still more penetrating than the bourgeois, dominant point of view—is argued in Bhikhu Parekh, *Marx's Theory of Ideology* (London, 1982), 48, 169–85.

104. Wilson, "A Critical Portrait," 9–58; Steinberg, "Post-Structuralism," 209.

105. Nancy Fraser, "From Redistribution to Recognition? Dilemmas of Justice in a 'Post-Socialist' Age," *New Left Review,* no. 212 (July–Aug. 1995): 72.

106. William H. Sewell Jr., "Toward a Post-materialist Rhetoric for Labor History," in *Rethinking Labor History: Essays on Discourse and Class Analysis,* ed. Leonard R. Berlanstein (Urbana, Ill., 1993), 19–24.

107. One of these other targets was the inordinate materialism of a national culture that encouraged male youth to "overcrowd" urban professional and mercantile employments to the neglect of farming (J. F. C., "Fourierism," 68–70).

108. For a quasi-Marxist interpretation that attributes inequality and exploitation to organizational and other structural processes, acting independently of cultural prejudices and other "bad attitudes," see Charles Tilly, *Durable Inequality* (Berkeley, Calif., 1998); see also, for a more specific assertion of the primacy of economic circumstances over cultural practices (with respect to American black-white generational inequality), Dalton Conley, *Being Black, Living in the Red: Race, Wealth, and Social Policy in America* (Berkeley, Calif., 1999).

109. One example would be the largely unconscious ideological functions served by the creed of the self-made man in the antebellum period. The distinctively bourgeois premium that this success creed (and the American exceptionalist mythology to which it was allied) placed upon industriousness, patience, self-reliance, and other character virtues paradoxically intensified as the vicissitudes and vagaries of a developing market economy came to weaken the actual correlation between such virtues and the achievement of property and wealth. Inner worth assumed even greater importance as it became more evident, first, that "the *causes* on which success or failure shall depend" are "numerous" or "hidden," and second, that strictly "material measures of personal worth could be highly deceptive" (R. W. Cushman, *Elements of Success* [Washington, D.C., 1848], 19–20; Gary J. Kornblith, "Becoming Joseph T. Buckingham: The Struggle for Artisanal Independence in Early-Nineteenth-Century Boston," in *American Artisans: Crafting Social Identity, 1750–1850,* ed. Howard B. Rock, Robert Asher, and Paul A. Gilje [Baltimore, 1995], 133–34).

1. The World's Dirty Work and the Wages That Sweeten It

1. Alasdair Clayre, *Work and Play: Ideas and Experience of Work and Leisure* (New York, 1974), 43–44.

2. Krishan Kumar, *The Rise of Modern Society: Aspects of the Social and Political Development of the West* (Oxford, Eng., 1988), 233–34.

3. Ibid., 234.

4. Glickstein, *Concepts of Free Labor;* Mark Y. Hanley, *Beyond a Christian Commonwealth: The Protestant Quarrel with the American Republic, 1830–1860* (Chapel Hill, N.C., 1994), 93–103.

5. On Carlyle, see Glickstein, *Concepts of Free Labor,* 266–69, 447.

6. Dale B. Light Jr., "Class, Ethnicity, and the Urban Ecology in a Nineteenth-Century City: Philadelphia's Irish, 1840–1890" (Ph.D. diss., Univ. of Pennsylvania, 1979), 75–76; Howard Chudacoff, "Success and Security: The Meaning of Social Mobility in America," *Reviews in American History* 10 (Dec. 1982): 106. In part because of such immigrant preferences, I resist the conclusion that a premium on one kind of labor's instrumental value (wage earners' ability to achieve an "American standard of living") only developed as

a way of legitimating the wage system when the United States developed into a more thorough-going consumer society toward the end of the nineteenth century. Within both working-class and non-working-class exceptionalist formulations, such an emphasis upon American labor's consumerist capabilities much earlier coexisted with the (republican) premium on that other kind of extrinsic rewards: upward mobility out of waged economic dependence. By the same token, criticisms of repetitive and unsatisfying work persisted into the late nineteenth and twentieth centuries, and for this reason I would also resist the generalization that over time emphasis upon any and all types of extrinsic rewards has eclipsed concerns about the intrinsic dignity and value of manual labor.

7. Duncan Kennedy, *Sexy Dressing, Etc.* (Cambridge, Mass., 1993), 97. For more extended treatment of how legal frameworks have historically constituted as well as merely regulated labor markets, see Steinfeld, *Coercion, Contract.*

8. Such a question was rarely far beneath the surface of radical agendas; for one example, from a rally of the International Workers of the World in Philadelphia in 1873, see Messer-Kruse, *Yankee International,* 224.

9. For the argument that dominant cultural values have encouraged workers in Western societies generally to embrace a relatively instrumental view of work, see Stephen A. Marglin, "Losing Touch: The Cultural Conditions of Worker Accommodation and Resistance," in *Dominating Knowledge: Development, Culture, and Resistance,* ed. Frederique Apfell Marglin and Stephen A. Marglin (Oxford, Eng., 1990), 217–82.

10. See here, on Francis Wayland, the leading American professor of moral economy, Paul K. Conkin, *Prophets of Prosperity: America's First Political Economists* (Bloomington, Ind., 1981), 119.

11. Alonzo Potter, *Political Economy: Its Objects, Uses, and Principles: Considered with Reference to the Condition of the American People* (New York, 1840), 59, 62.

12. "Correspondents," *Phalanx,* June 29, 1844, 183–84.

13. The debate occurred between November 1846 and May 1847 in Greeley's *Tribune* and the *Morning Courier and New-York Enquirer,* which Raymond helped edit. The pieces were published as *Association Discussed* (New York, 1847).

14. Reply of *Courier and Enquirer,* April 16, *Association Discussed,* 70.

15. Ibid.

16. Raymond was also thinking primarily of the instrumental value inhering in the manual and other labor of legally free males. He certainly did not have in mind married women's unpaid household labor, nor was he even thinking of the wages earned by some American wives in their separate labor outside the household, because the state statutes abrogating husbands' legal title to these earnings were still in the future. Actually, Raymond supported such statutory reforms.

17. Glickstein, *Concepts of Free Labor;* Nicholas K. Bromell, *By the Sweat of the Brow: Literature and Labor in Antebellum America* (Chicago, 1993), 1–58.

18. See Daniel Webster, "Address at Convention of Whigs of Essex County, Massachusetts," Nov. 9, 1843, in Webster, *The Writings and Speeches of Daniel Webster* (Boston, 1903), 3:176–77.

19. Gordon S. Wood, *The Radicalism of the American Revolution* (New York, 1991), 275–86.

20. Lawrence B. Glickman, *A Living Wage: American Workers and the Making of Consumer Society* (Ithaca, N.Y., 1997). Glickman perceptively treats the ways that the late nineteenth-century "living wage" discourse was discriminatory with respect to female and nonwhite

wage earners, although he slights the pre–Civil War ideological antecedents that I refer to in the text.

21. In finding an increased maldistribution of wealth in early- to mid-nineteenth-century America, historians generally agree on the growing share of wealth held by elite occupational and economic groups, and by the highest 10 percent of the population particularly (Williamson and Lindert, *American Inequality;* Edward Pessen, *Riches, Class, and Power: America before the Civil War* [Washington, D.C., 1973]); for some dissenting findings, see Carole Shammas, "A New Look at Long-Term Trends in Wealth Inequality," *American Historical Review* 98 (April 1993): 412–31.

22. Abraham Lincoln, for one, employed the "race of life" phraseology, although there is continuing question as to whether his defenses of the antebellum social order of the free states indeed marked the triumph of an acquisitive capitalist-professional ethos, and the endorsement of an open hierarchy, over a more egalitarian small-producer–labor bias; for a fresh perspective, see Allen C. Guelzo, *Abraham Lincoln: Redeemer President* (Grand Rapids, Mich., 1999), 121–24.

23. See the labor sheet *The Champion of American Labor,* "Published By An Association of Mechanics" (New York).

24. See the reminiscence, Harriet H. Robinson, *Loom and Spindle; or Life among the Earl Mill Girls* (New York, 1898), 69. Still, mill girls writing in the *Lowell Offering* also soft-pedaled their increased autonomy in order to dispel the criticisms made by defenders of traditional values (Thomas Dublin, *Transforming Women's Work: New England Lives in the Industrial Revolution* [Ithaca, N.Y., 1994], 94).

25. "The Philosophy of Labor. No. 2," *Chronotype* (Boston), July 20, 1846. On Wright, the likely author of the column, see Lawrence B. Goodheart, *Abolitionist, Activist, Atheist: Elizur Wright and the Reform Impulse* (Kent, Ohio, 1990), 129–31; and Bruce Laurie, "The 'Fair Field' of the 'Middle Ground': Abolitionism, Labor Reform, and the Making of an Antislavery Bloc in Antebellum Massachusetts," in *Labor Histories: Class, Politics, and the Working-Class Experience,* ed. Eric Arneson, Julie Greene, and Bruce Laurie (Urbana, Ill., 1998), 49–56.

26. "The Abolition of Poverty," *Chronotype,* Dec. 24, 1847.

27. I have in mind here, first, Fred Hirsch's thesis of "positional goods" and the dimension that it has added to concepts of relative poverty (*Social Limits to Growth* [London, 1977]). There are, second, the debates over the unvarying, unambiguous nature of hunger, starvation, physical efficiency, and minimum capabilities—over the basis for sustaining a concept of absolute poverty; see Amartya Sen, "Poor, Relatively Speaking," *Oxford Economic Papers* 35 (July 1983): 153–69; Peter Townsend, "A Sociological Approach to the Measurement of Poverty—A Rejoinder to Professor Amartya Sen," and Sen's rejoinder, ibid., 37 (Dec. 1985): 659–76; on the unreliability of daily caloric intake and other measures of absolute poverty, see Stewart Macpherson and Richard Silburn, "The Meaning and Measurement of Poverty," in *Poverty: A Persistent Global Reality,* ed. John Dixon and David Macarov (London, 1998), 1–19.

28. For example, the recent studies on the "internal economy" maintained by many southern bondsmen have raised new questions about the validity of the assumption, shared by the *Chronotype* and other antebellum antislavery voices, that the fortunes of chattel servitude were overwhelmingly and inevitably tied to the slaveholder's lash and to slavery's capacity overall for imposing an absolute coercion and repression.

29. "Capital and Labor," Philadelphia *Public Ledger,* Oct. 20, 1843, see also "The Social Condition of England," *North American Review* 65 (July–Oct. 1847): 461–504.

30. Noel W. Thompson, *The People's Science: The Popular Political Economy of Exploitation and Crisis, 1816–34* (Cambridge, 1984); Gregory Claeys, *Machinery, Money, and the Millennium: From Moral Economy to Socialism, 1815–60* (Cambridge, 1987); Edward Pessen, *Most Uncommon Jacksonians: The Radical Leaders of the Early Labor Movement* (Albany, 1967); Sean Wilentz, *Chants Democratic: New York City and the Rise of the American Working Class, 1788–1850* (New York, 1984).

31. Sidney Sherwood, *Tendencies in American Economic Thought* (Baltimore, 1897), 26; typifying the *Public Ledger's* mainstream perspective is "The Report of the Late Meeting," March 20, 1838.

32. Adam Smith, *An Inquiry into the Nature and Causes of the Wealth of Nations* (1776; rept. New York, 1937), 81; Edgar S. Furniss, *The Position of the Laborer in a System of Nationalism* (New York, 1957); A. W. Bob Coats, *On the History of Economic Thought* (London, 1992), 63–116; Peter Mathias, *The Transformation of England: Essays in the Economic and Social History of England in the Eighteenth Century* (London, 1979), 148–67; Donna T. Andrew, *Philanthropy and Police: London Charity in the Eighteenth Century* (Princeton, N.J., 1998), 141–43; M. G. Marshall, "Scottish Economic Thought and the High Wage Economy: Hume, Smith, and McCulloch on Wages and Work Motivation," *Scottish Journal of Political Economy* 45 (Aug. 1998): 309–21; Marshall, "Luxury, Economic Development, and Work Motivation: David Hume, Adam Smith, and J. R. McCulloch," *History of Political Economy* 32 (Fall 2000): 632–38. William Grampp, however, challenges the view that British mercantilist writers held a less "enlightened" opinion of the laboring classes than did Smith and later classical economists (*Economic Liberalism* [New York, 1965], 1:69, 2:18–19).

33. Coats, *Economic Thought,* 159–85; Gertrude Himmelfarb, *The Idea of Poverty: England in the Early Industrial Age* (New York, 1984), 23–176.

34. Malthus above all softened his arguments in the revised editions that followed his original essay on population (1798) — see *An Essay on the Principle of Population,* ed. Anthony Flew (Harmondsworth, Eng., 1970). However, even Malthus's original formulation contained an optimistic dimension of sorts in its attempt to reconcile the evils and miseries of population pressure with the notion of a benevolent God. It was in the third (1821) edition of Ricardo's key work, *Principles of Political Economy and Taxation,* that he added to his seemingly gloomy principles (such as those predictive of the "stationary state") his more pessimistic conclusions regarding technological unemployment. Even the most optimistic passages in Malthus and Ricardo convey little expectation that more than a small proportion of British laborers would ever convert the bourgeois tastes and elevated "social" (or "relative") subsistence they managed to acquire into upward mobility out of the working classes (J. M. Pullen, "Malthus' Theological Ideas and Their Influence on His Principle of Population," *History of Political Economy* 13 [Spring 1981]: 51; E. N. Santurri, "Theodicy and Social Policy in Malthus' Thought," in *Thomas Robert Malthus: Critical Assessments,* ed. John Cunningham Wood [London, 1986], 1:402–18; F. R. Kolb, "The Stationary State of Ricardo and Malthus: Neither Pessimistic nor Prophetic," ibid., 3:174–90; Samuel Hollander, "On Malthus's Population Principle and Social Reform," *History of Political Economy* 18 [Summer 1986]: 187–236; Maxine Berg, *The Machinery Question and the Making of Political Economy, 1815–1848* [Cambridge, 1980], 43–74; Donald Winch, *Riches and Poverty: An Intellectual History of Political Economy in Britain, 1750–1834* [Cambridge, 1996], 257–73; Paul

Fabra, *Capitalism versus Anti-Capitalism: The Triumph of Ricardian over Marxist Political Economy* [New Brunswick, N.J., 1993], 40–45).

35. Not all thinkers on even the progressive side of issues took as unmixed blessing the laboring classes' expanding taste for consumer goods and higher living standards. The Leeds surgeon Charles T. Thackrah criticized child factory labor and supported ten-hour legislation, but he attributed the ill health and high mortality of many English craft and factory workers to their own willingness to work inordinately long hours, in pursuit of wages that would enable them to gratify unnecessary "artificial wants" (Thackrah, *The Effects of Arts, Trades, and Professions, and of Civic States and Habits of Living, on Health and Longevity,* 2d enlarged ed. [London, 1832], 203–10).

36. Mark Blaug, *Economic History and the History of Economics* (New York, 1986), 91–114; Ronald L. Meek, *Economics and Ideology and Other Essays* (London, 1967), 51–73; Thompson, *People's Rights;* Claeys, *Machinery;* Ellen Frankel Paul, *Moral Revolution and Economic Science: The Demise of Laissez-Faire in Nineteenth-Century British Political Economy* (Westport, Conn., 1979); Maxine Berg, "Progress and Providence in Early Nineteenth-Century Political Economy," *Social History* 15 (Oct. 1990): 367–75; Herbert Hovenkamp, "The Political Economy of Substantive Due Process," in *Property Rights in the Age of Enterprise,* ed. Richard W. Ely Jr. (New York, 1997), 214–17; Marshall, "Scottish Economic Thought," 321–26; Marshall, "Luxury, Economic Development," 638–47. That British political economy continued to emphasize (for all its own qualifications) the desirability of a high-wage economy that would acknowledge workers' ambitions for improvement, rather than merely their fear of starvation, hardly means that this intellectual tendency was commonly reflected in more generous wage policies voluntarily implemented by British factory and other employers in the period of early industrial capitalism. As McCulloch noted, "few masters willingly consent to raise wages" (quoted in Howard Dickman, *Industrial Democracy in America: Ideological Origins of National Labor Relations Policy* [La Salle, Ill., 1987], 59).

37. For, however, Marx's distinctions between "classical" and "vulgar" bourgeois political economy as rationales for capitalism, see Patrick Murray, "Karl Marx as a Historical Materialist Historian of Political Economy," *History of Political Economy* 20 (Spring 1988): 95–105; Parekh, *Marx's Theory,* 52–72.

38. Hovenkamp, "Political Economy," 219–20.

39. Maurice F. Neufeld, "Realms of Thought and Organized Labor in the Age of Jackson," *Labor History* 10 (Winter 1969): 31–32; Neufeld's reference is to the idea of the centrality of the productive classes, including the labor theory of value.

40. I characterize this slighting and ignoring as a significant tendency, particularly among journalists, politicians, and others within the general and reasonably informed public. But there were exceptions, especially among those who could find some ideological use in the post-Ricardian mellowing itself. See, for example, the speech of Daniel Webster in which he approvingly quotes J. Ramsay McCulloch's defense of high wages in arguing for an American protective tariff ("Address at Convention," 176); see also Louisiana representative Bannon G. Thibodeaux's speech, *Congressional Globe,* 29th Cong., 2d sess., *Appendix,* June 30, 1846, 42–43. Among antebellum American academics and writers of economic treatises—individuals whose business it was to remain most closely informed about the advances made by the British disciples of Malthus and Ricardo—slighting of the mellowing that those advances represented was more deliberate than that displayed by the general public. American political economists commonly interpreted and dismissed

the contributions of a Senior or McCulloch as inappreciable alterations of the original dismal scenarios. McCulloch's particular efforts to rescue political economy from the "pessimism" of Malthus and Ricardo were dismissed as unconvincing by many of his own countrymen (Mary Poovey, *A History of the Modern Fact: Mechanisms of Knowledge in the Sciences of Wealth and Society* [Chicago, 1998], 303–6).

41. The Ricardian-derived moralistic parables written in the 1830s by Harriet Martineau "helped to create that vulgar and already outmoded image of the 'dismal science' which passed for economic thought among the general public up to the 1870s" (Mark Blaug, *Ricardian Economics: A Historical Study* [New Haven, 1958], 129–39).

42. Fred Somkin, *Unquiet Eagle: Memory and Desire in the Idea of American Freedom, 1815–1860* (Ithaca, N.Y., 1967), 30–31; Sherwood, *Tendencies,* 28.

43. Calvin Colton, *The Rights of Labor* (New York, 1846), 3–10.

44. Donald E. Brown, *Hierarchy, History, and Human Nature: The Social Origins of Historical Consciousness* (Tucson, Ariz., 1988), 14.

45. Compare Tony A. Freyer, *Producers versus Capitalists: Constitutional Conflict in Antebellum America* (Charlottesville, Va., 1994), 3, 49, with Andrew Dawson, "Reassessing Henry Carey (1793–1879): The Problems of Writing Political Economy in Nineteenth-Century America," *Journal of American Studies* 34 (Dec. 2000): 482.

46. Simeon Nash, remarks at Ohio's constitutional convention of 1850–51, in Nicole Etcheson, *The Emerging Midwest: Upland Southerners and the Political Culture of the Old Northwest, 1787–1861* (Bloomington, Ind., 1996), 66; Glickstein, *Concepts of Free Labor,* 345; Carl Siracusa, *A Mechanical People: Perceptions of the Industrial Order in Massachusetts, 1815–1880* (Middletown, Conn., 1979), 93–94.

47. O. A. B., "Rich and Poor," *Boston Weekly Reformer,* July 21, 1837.

48. Whiggish commentators like Carey, both entrepreneurial and American exceptionalist in their thinking, often articulated versions of the classical wages-fund principle that little resembled the most rigid, pessimistic versions.

49. In fact, some prominent members of this configuration took exception to Malthus's law of geometrical population growth and its seeming corollary, as expressed in the 1798 edition of the *Essay,* that the laboring poor were virtually ungovernable in their sexual appetites, altogether resistant to the self-discipline counseled by the social ranks above them. The poor-law reformer Joseph Tuckerman believed that Malthus's unduly fatalistic and pessimistic formulations undercut certain of the valuable axioms of middle-class, free-market competitive morality referred to in the text.

50. George Arnold, *Third Semi-Annual Report as Minister-At-Large in New York City, 1833* (New York, 1834), 8–9; "Poor Laws," *American Quarterly Review* 4 (Sept. 1833): 82. For all his moralistic strictures, Arnold was not insensitive to environmental circumstances beyond the poor's control that encouraged their "gross appetites" and lack of intellectual discipline, and which indeed, in contrast to the bane of "indiscriminate alms-giving," called for Christian charity and intervention of a temperate and voluntary nature (*Second Semi-Annual Report, 1832,* 9–21).

51. "Wealth and Want," New York *Journal of Commerce,* quoted in *Tribune,* Oct. 14, 1848; see also the remarks of Robert M. Hartley, the Presbyterian founder of the city's leading private philanthropic agency, the New York Association for Improving the Condition of the Poor (Isaac Smithson Hartley, ed., *Memorial of Robert Milham Hartley* [Utica, N.Y., 1880], 311–41). Hartley's valorization of the fear of want as a natural labor incentive, always a

component of his antebellum attacks on indiscriminate poor relief, is reinforced here by his revulsion against more recent American trade-union demands and the "atrocities" of the Paris Commune — the latest attempts to guarantee a subsistence to individuals in disregard of vital economic laws and property rights.

52. Deborah Stone, *Policy Paradox: The Art of Political Decision-Making* (New York, 1998), 104.

53. Herbert J. Gans, *Making Sense of America: Sociological Analyses and Essays* (Lanham, Md., 1999), 77–81. Gans is primarily addressing the assorted "positive" functions of poverty in more recent American history.

54. Junius H. Hatch, in New York *Assembly Journal,* March 26, 1822, 878.

55. Coats, *Economic Thought,* 167.

56. "Pauperism and Crime," *Evangelist* (New York), March 4, 1858. The gendered nature of these remarks — the reference to that poverty which destructively "unmans" — enjoyed a long tradition in Anglo-American poor-law thought and policy in its implication that the resulting condition of pauper dependency was a particularly unnatural and unfortunate one for males. As Lynn Hollen Lees notes in the case of Britain's Royal Commission *Report* of 1834, the greater abhorrence and the more punitive outlook manifested toward male pauperism were driven by prevailing concepts of masculinity and fatherhood and by no means necessarily worked to the advantage of the female poor. In some instances that outlook rendered invisible the existence of impoverished female laborers and their employment exigencies and problems. At the same time, England's New Poor Law and early nineteenth-century Anglo-American poor-law reformers generally reserved some of their considerable disapprobation for unmarried dependent mothers, singling them out among the various categories of impoverished females (e.g., widows, deserted wives) (Lees, *The Solidarities of Strangers: The English Poor Laws and the People, 1700–1948* [Cambridge, 1998], 139); for further discussion of how Britain's New Poor Law of 1834 embodied the male breadwinner ideal, see Mitchell Dean, *The Constitution of Poverty: Toward a Genealogy of Liberal Governance* (London, 1991), 98; for qualifications, see Anna Clark, "The New Poor Law and the Breadwinner Wage: Contrasting Assumptions," *Journal of Social History* 34 (Winter 2000): 261–77.

57. T. R. Malthus, *An Essay on the Principle of Population,* 5th ed. (London, 1817), 3:42–43; for this same distinction among some late eighteenth-century social theorists, see Andrew, *Philanthropy and Police,* 139–41.

58. Questions of empirical accuracy aside, and notwithstanding the *Chronotype*'s previously discussed muddying of the issue, these critics were as often as not apocalyptically claiming an absolute, rather than a merely relative, immiserization.

59. Review of Colton's *The Rights of Labor,* in *Chronotype,* Oct. 28, 1846. Mention should also be made of those other critics of northern wage slavery, particularly associated with Jacksonian, "Locofoco" Democracy, who identified the root evil as one of insufficient fair competition, rather than that of excessive competition: they targeted the impediments to a level playing field (for white males) created by banking and other monopolies and "unequal privileges." Yet despite its sanctification of free competition in the marketplace, British classical economy after Adam Smith failed to draw a generally enthusiastic response from this Democratic group of wage slavery's critics either. Democratic Party politicians' embrace of Old World, Malthusian-Ricardian doctrines of population, rent, and wages was discernibly less conspicuous than was Whig rejection of these notions.

60. Unlike David R. Roediger, I find no general patterns in the antebellum usage of such seemingly race-neutral expressions as "wage slavery" vis-à-vis the "white slavery" term to which Roediger attaches special significance. My impressionistic sense, moreover, is that the former term was employed as frequently as "white slavery" was in the labor press as well as in other antebellum commentary. It remains questionable, in any case, once all of these terms had entered the American public domain by the early nineteenth century, whether individual usage of one rather than another invariably carried the intricate and heavy social psychology implications (e.g., group distancing and group projection) that Roediger ascribes to them (Roediger, *The Wages of Whiteness: Race and the Making of the American Working Class* [London, 1991], 72–74).

61. Ibid., 106.

62. H. R. S., "Slavery in the U.S.," *Alphadelphia Tocsin,* rept. in *Working Man's Advocate,* June 7, 1845. Rather than unilaterally opposing emancipation, H. R. S. proposed, consistent with the agenda of the paper, that Congress appropriate to black families freeholds of forty acres in territory west of the Mississippi River.

63. "Consistency of Reformers," *Working Man's Advocate,* June 28, 1845; see also Evans's comments in "Slavery and Slave Trading," ibid., June 7, 1845. In his heated exchanges with abolitionists, Evans endorsed the long-standing Democratic charge that they sought to reduce "both Northern and Southern slaves to the lowest level of wages dependence, and to anarchical competition with each other, for the privilege of doing the drudgery of capital" (Evans's *Young America,* quoted in "Land and Liberty," *National Era* [Washington, D.C.], March 2, 1848); for critical assessment of the "implications" of Evans's position for the cause of slave emancipation, see Roediger, *Wages of Whiteness,* 77–80; Roediger, "Race, Labor, and Gender in the Languages of Antebellum Social Protest," in Engerman, *Terms of Labor,* 177. Evans periodically asserted that blacks have "as good a right to be free" as whites, and he claimed as well to be more enlightened than most American whites and to "harbor no prejudice against color." However, in prioritizing land reform over abolition, he advanced not only the slaves-would-be-made-worse-off argument but also more clearly white-centered claims — e.g., "there is more real suffering among the landless whites of the north, than among the blacks of the south." In some measure this claim reflected the standard — and commonly race-neutral — position of labor reformers that the "lash of want" was as oppressive and soul-destroying as the "brute force" of the slaveholder's whip. Yet Evans evidenced some undeniable white myopia by generally (though not always) failing to include among the greatest northern sufferers the population of free blacks, who were, after all, disproportionately exposed to the "lash of want." I nonetheless believe that some recent historians have gone too far in using Evans, among other prominent labor reformers, as an example with which to hammer the so-called white-labor apologists school of Herbert Gutman and his followers. I am referring here not only to Roediger's discussions but to the even more hostile treatment accorded Evans by Theodore W. Allen, who insists that "hateful" white supremacism belied Evans's "pretense of concern for all laborers, slave and waged." Noel Ignatiev also reads beyond the evidence in generalizing that land reformers, along with the Associationists, aimed through the wage-slavery argument "not at broadening the abolitionist vision but at deflecting it." Labor reformers may have wrongly deprioritized emancipation on the ground that southern chattel slavery constituted only one expression of more basic and pervasive disparities in resources and power in American society. But in only some instances was it clear

that white-supremacist values drove such a characterization. Such values were likely particularly negligible in explaining why middle-class Associationists and other utopian socialists embraced their relatively systematic critiques of competitive capitalism and wage slavery. Even more fully than labor leaders like Evans, many of these reformers, to borrow Thomas L. Haskell's terminology, were working from "a more advanced humanitarian perspective that really assigned equal importance to all varieties of exploitation, whether of slave or free labor" (Haskell, "Capitalism and the Origins of the Humanitarian Sensibility," in *The Antislavery Debate: Capitalism and Abolitionism as a Problem in Historical Interpretation,* ed. Thomas Bender [Berkeley, Calif., 1992], 121 n); Allen, *The Invention of the White Race* 1 [London, 1994]: 164; Ignatiev, *How the Irish Became White* [New York, 1995], 80, 213); a more favorable treatment of Evans's views on abolition and race, closer to my own sense, is Paul Goodman, *Of One Blood: Abolitionism and the Origins of Racial Equality* (Berkeley, Calif., 1998), 165–67; Evans's remarks are in "To Gerrit Smith," *People's Rights* (New York), July 24, 1844; see also Evans, "To Gerrit Smith," *Working Man's Advocate,* Aug. 17, 1844.

64. This appears to be Roediger's claim ("Race, Labor," 179).

65. Evans, "To Gerrit Smith," *Working Man's Advocate,* Aug. 17, 1844; "To the Working Man of the United States," *Radical* (Granville, N.J.), Jan. 1841.

66. Hence one of the common labor-reform accusations leveled at conditions in the Lowell mills during the 1840s: too sick and exhausted after a few years to continue at their jobs, the native-born New England female operatives were returning to their homes "to die."

67. For a study that frames the issues somewhat differently, and which holds that Evans's land-reform program typified antebellum "dissenting" perspectives on American economic development in that it was both "radical" in its critique and traditionally (as well as ineffectually) "republican" in its solutions, see Huston, *Securing the Fruits,* 272–73. Such a view does fuller justice to the ideological complexities than do persisting "entrepreneurial" interpretations that blanketly impute to early nineteenth-century artisans "the same mercenary values as the larger capitalists" had (Anthony Gronowicz, *Race and Class Politics in New York City before the Civil War* [Boston, 1998], 49). Recent economic historians have minimized both the actual existence of land monopoly and the negative consequences of land speculation (e.g., its creation of permanent tenant farmers) in nineteenth-century America; for a discussion that finds some validity in the older, more critical view of land policy held by Evans and like-minded historians, see Jon Gjerde, "'Roots of Maladjustment' in the Land: Paul Wallace Gates," *Reviews in American History* 19 (March 1991): 142–53.

68. British Owenite socialists, at least, nonetheless varied significantly in the degree to which they perceived competition — their central explanatory notion for the ills of modern society — as a specific outgrowth of the economic system (Gregory Claeys, "Language, Class, and Historical Consciousness in Nineteenth Century Britain," *Economics and Society* 14 [May 1985]: 247–54).

69. For this as well as other ironies and theoretical drawbacks in southern proslavery Malthusianism, see Eugene D. Genovese and Elizabeth Fox-Genovese, "Slavery, Economic Development, and the Law: The Dilemma of the Southern Political Economists, 1800–1860," *Washington and Lee Law Review* 41 (Winter 1984): 23–30; a more positive assessment is J. J. Spengler, "Malthusianism and the Debate on Slavery," *South Atlantic Quarterly*

34 (April 1935): 178–89; see also Spengler, "Population Theory in the Ante-Bellum South," *Journal of Southern History* 2 (Aug. 1936): 360–89. There were also the different southern apprehensions regarding the continuing natural increase of the slaves themselves and their eventual "death struggle" with the white race (or some similar calamity) should the slaves be penned up in the existing slave states by an increasingly hostile northern majority. Northern Democratic anti-free-soil and proslavery voices expressed sympathy for such apprehensions, as when Stephen A. Douglas accused Lincoln in their 1858 debates of seeking "to put slavery in a course of ultimate extinction by [the slaves'] starvation" (David Zarefsky, *Lincoln, Douglas, and Slavery: In the Crucible of Public Debate* [Chicago, 1990], 189–90). Notwithstanding the political opportunism inhering in many of the proslavery invocations of Malthusian population principles, they could also reflect genuine apprehensions over the implications of healthy, proliferating black bodies. Those anxieties constituted an interesting variant on British Malthusian fears earlier in the century (Catherine Gallagher, "The Body versus the Social Body in the Works of Thomas Malthus and Henry Mayhew," *Representations* 14 [Spring 1986]: 83–106).

70. As Paul Conkin observes of George Tucker, the most distinguished member of this school, "Surely no one ever offered a gloomier reason for eventual emancipation" (Conkin, *Prophets of Prosperity,* 161).

71. Review of H. C. Carey's *Principles of Social Science,* in *North American and United States Gazette* (Philadelphia), March 27, 1858. The immediate proslavery barb for these remarks was South Carolina James H. Hammond's Senate mudsill speech. Deliberately or otherwise, Carlyle's own notorious proslavery sympathies were passed over by the reviewer.

72. Joseph J. Spengler, "Population Doctrines in the United States," *Journal of Political Economy* 41 (Aug. 1933): 433–67, and (Oct. 1933): 639–72; George Johnson Cady, "The Early American Reaction to the Theory of Malthus," ibid., 39 (Oct. 1931): 601–32; Conkin, *Prophets of Prosperity,* 313; Huston, *Securing the Fruits,* 152–83; Sidney Fine, *Laissez Faire and the General-Welfare State: A Study of Conflict in American Thought, 1865–1901* (Ann Arbor, Mich., 1964), 47–52; Dorothy Ross, *The Origins of American Social Science* (Cambridge, 1991), 13–50.

73. The meeting occurred in the church customarily presided over by the Universalist minister Edwin H. Chapin. There are at least two versions, with slightly different wording, of Beecher's address. One, a paraphrase, is in "A Free Library for Women," *Tribune,* Oct. 27, 1858. The other version is in Henry Ward Beecher and James T. Brady, *The Pulpit and Rostrum: Sermons, Orations, Popular Lectures, &c., Addresses on Mental Culture for Women* (New York, 1859), 21–31. That there exist at least two different versions of the same public speech is quite typical for the period, given early nineteenth-century newspaper reporters' variable proficiency in shorthand.

74. Beecher, "Library." In his reference to the virtually primordial character of the seamstresses' "oppression," Mayor Tiemann was engaging in less hyperbole than one might suppose: some historians trace female sweated and slop work generally as far back as the sixteenth century in Europe. However, in the United States the exploitation of the seamstresses—in fact, the very emergence of the seamstress as a category of worker—generally reflected the transformation of much traditional female needlework into market-driven wage labor under early nineteenth-century industrialization and the growth of the ready-made clothing trade (Christine Stansell, *City of Women: Sex and Class in New York, 1789–1860* [Urbana, Ill., 1986], 105–9; Mary Jo Buhle, "Needlewomen and the Vicissitudes of Modern Life: A Study of Middle-Class Construction in the Antebellum Northeast," in

Visible Women: New Essays on American Activism, ed. Nancy A. Hewitt and Suzanne Lebsock [Urbana, Ill., 1992], 149; Egal Feldman, *Fit for Men: A Study of New York's Clothing Trade* [Washington, D.C., 1960], 93–120).

75. Beecher, "Library."

76. See Beecher, "Northern and Southern Theories of Man and Society," *National Anti-Slavery Standard* (New York), Jan. 27, 1855. More directly and self-consciously than a Beecher or a William Ellery Channing, Senior and other British proponents of a free-market morality were also positioning themselves in opposition to a tradition of "just-price" and "fair-wage" moral economy, most recently expressed in a wave of early nineteenth-century English farmworker riots (Roger Wells, "The Moral Economy of the English Countryside," in Randall and Charlesworth, *Moral Economy and Popular Protest,* 251).

77. Beecher, "Library"; Beecher, *Pulpit,* 23–24.

78. Beecher, "Library"; Beecher, *Pulpit,* 24–25.

79. Ellen Carol DuBois, *Feminism and Suffrage: The Emergence of an Independent Women's Movement in America, 1848–1869* (Ithaca, N.Y., 1978), 136–37.

80. See also Clifford E. Clark Jr., *Henry Ward Beecher: Spokesman for a Middle-Class America* (Urbana, Ill., 1978) 107–8. The great majority of the city's single women who worked in manufacturing outside the home were well under thirty and thus still of marrying age. Beecher's apparent assumption that "many" were nonetheless fated for celibacy likely reflected awareness of New York City's long-standing skewed sex ratio; in 1860 there were 125 women of marrying age for every 100 men (Stansell, *City of Women,* 83).

81. In the conflict that Susan L. Porter has identified between the more "strictly economic values of the marketplace" and "hegemonic cultural values" that deplored woman's work outside the home (often to the point of casting aspersions on women who performed such work), Beecher—on this occasion at least—lent his support to the former (Porter, "Victorian Values in the Marketplace: Single Women and Work in Boston, 1800–1850," *Social Science History* 17 (Spring 1993): 128). Amy Dru Stanley, on the other hand, highlights the contributions of antislavery voices, including Beecher's, to separate-spheres ideology—an ideology that, she furthermore argues, generally served to effectively valorize free-market relations and male waged labor specifically by arresting waged labor's traditional republican associations with (feminine) dependency (Stanley, "Home Life and the Morality of the Market," in *The Market Revolution in America: Social, Political, and Religious Expressions, 1800–1880,* ed. Melvyn Stokes and Stephen Conway [Charlottesville, Va., 1996], 74–96).

82. Beecher, "Library." Beecher's relative acceptance here of the naturalness of women's paid work also distinguished him from many Englishmen (both working-class radicals and middle- and upper-class philanthropists) who protested the impoverishment of needle-women in their own country (Helen Rogers, "'The Good Are Not Always Powerful, nor the Powerful Always Good': The Politics of Women's Needlework in Mid-Victorian London," *Victorian Studies* 40 [Summer 1997]: 605–9).

83. Beecher, *Pulpit,* 26. The low wages paid seamstresses had, to be sure, other mutually reinforcing causes as well (Stansell, *City of Women,* 105–21; Ava Baron and Susan E. Klepp, "'If I Didn't Have My Sewing Machine . . .': Women and Sewing-Machine Technology," in *A Needle, a Bobbin, a Strike: Women Needleworkers in America,* ed. Joan Jensen and Sue

Davidson [Philadelphia, 1984], 23–24; Dolores Janiewski, "Making Common Cause: The Needlewomen of New York, 1831–69," *Signs* 1 [Spring 1976]: 777–86). Beecher also blunted his general criticisms of the "oppressive tyrannies of overseers and employers" and simultaneously sought, in another of his retreats from separate-spheres ideology, to collapse home and market into a single category: he praised "some of the largest employers" for beginning to rise above short-term profit considerations "to make their establishments in some sort an artificial family" (*Pulpit,* 30).

84. On the embeddedness of patriarchal subordination in Western liberal cultures, and especially contract theory, see Carole Pateman, *The Sexual Contract* (Stanford, Calif., 1988), 134–36. Pateman's position, that gender inequality derives from a system of patriarchy that is autonomous of capitalist relations and that is in fact the primary form of social inequality, is hardly the only position even among feminist scholars; for the highly contentious issues, see Sylvia Walby, *Patriarchy at Work: Patriarchal and Capitalist Relations in Employment* (Cambridge, 1986), 5–49. In multiple ways state laws upheld the man-made cultural norms that Beecher, along with a host of other antebellum commentators, blamed for labor-market segmentation and other economic ills suffered by wage-earning American females. Nonetheless, those norms do not easily fall under the rubric of a government-generated "political economy of aristocracy" that James L. Huston characterizes as the principal "axiom" shaping early nineteenth-century Americans' understanding of "distortions" in a society's natural distribution of wealth (*Securing the Fruits,* 7).

85. Beecher's remarks, such as those quoted in note 83, suggest that he was primarily speaking to the situation of inside-shop female employees rather than outworkers.

86. Nancy Isenberg, *Sex and Citizenship in Antebellum America* (Chapel Hill, N.C., 1998), 175. For the antebellum tendency to devalue, and render "invisible," both housework and the income-producing activities (e.g., keeping boarders as well as manufacturing home-work) performed by women within the household, see Jeanne Boydston, *Home and Work: Housework, Wages, and the Ideology of Labor in the Early Republic* (New York, 1990); on the nineteenth-century state earnings statutes that validated the invisibility of such labor by granting wives "rights only in income earned *outside the family context that was not used for family support,*" see Reva B. Siegel, "Home as Work: The First Woman's Rights Claims concerning Wives' Household Labor, 1850–1880," *Yale Law Journal* 103 (March 1994): 1084–85; for Caroline Dall and other mid-nineteenth-century women's-rights advocates who were yet harder than Beecher on the mores that limited women's employment opportunities and devalued their labor's worth, see also Amy Dru Stanley, *From Bondage to Contract: Wage Labor, Marriage, and the Market in the Age of Slave Emancipation* (Cambridge, 1998), 231–32; for primary feminist writings, see Ann Russo and Cheris Kramarae, eds., *The Radical Women's Press of the 1850s* (New York, 1991), 95–123.

87. Siegel, "Home as Work," 1128.

88. Beecher, "Library." In lending its support to the woman's library proposal, the *New-York Times* remarked that "intelligent women" who were somehow able to acquire a "fair education and some knowledge of business, can always find employment in this City at wages ranging from $5 to $12 a week"—far above what the overwhelming majority of the manufacturing women earned ("Employment for Women," Nov. 11, 1858).

89. Beecher, *Pulpit,* 30. As implied by his reference to "fallen" women, Beecher did not

view as absolute the entrapment in needlework and other legitimate, if ill-rewarded, employment. James T. Brady was yet more explicit in his address, warning that without the needed reforms, many manufacturing women would continue to be driven by their desperate poverty into the "degradation" and "shame" of prostitution. For the argument that working-class females who turned to prostitution may have perceived it more positively — as not merely an economically rational vocational choice but also as a release from prevailing gender constraints and social conventions — see Marilynn Wood Hill, *Their Sisters' Keepers: Prostitution in New York City, 1830–1870* (Berkeley, Calif., 1993). Consciously or otherwise, Beecher also appears to have thought of the library plan in terms of its benefits for native-born single women particularly. Just as he screened out the significant numbers of seamstresses and other workingwomen who were married, so he was silent about the fact that increasing numbers of the seamstresses were recently arrived Irish and German females, whose deficient education and marketable skills could less easily have been attributable to the northern cultural mores and practices that he was criticizing (Buhle, "Needlewomen," 160–61). Although (as Beecher did suggest) a majority of the seamstresses in late antebellum New York and other large cities were almost certainly born into poverty, there was, too, throughout this period a significant component that had experienced downward social mobility — e.g., the "decayed gentlewomen," married or otherwise, who had suffered financial misfortunes (Kathleen Waters Sander, *The Business of Charity* [Urbana, Ill., 1998], 11; "Labor in New-York. No. I. The Seamstresses," *Tribune,* Aug. 14, 1845).

90. One should not dismiss this assumption as completely implausible; awareness of the famed "Improvement Circles" formed by Lowell's female operatives in the 1830s and 1840s still resonated through American culture.

91. Stansell, *City of Women,* 152–54. Beecher observed that "the enlightened philanthropy" of E. M. Powell, named secretary at the meeting, was "at the root of this movement" to publicize and alleviate the plight of the city's working women; for Powell's earlier advocacy of a library for the seamstresses and others, see "The Workwomen of New-York," letter to *Tribune,* July 9, 1858. In that letter Powell also touched on the general quiescence of the women she was trying to help: "They live silently, they work silently, and a great many of them die silently and sadly." For all her good intentions, Powell could be quite condescending about her subjects — see here also, E. M. P., "Library for Women," letter to the *New-York Times,* Nov. 11, 1858. In noting a comparable absence of collective action among England's distressed needlewomen, Helen Rogers criticizes poststructural approaches that highlight the creation of agency and power through discourse: "There was, after all, more" to the needlewomen's powerlessness than their "words going unheard. If the rhetoric employed by the reformers [and others] disempowered the slopwomen, they were surely more disempowered by starvation wages" (Rogers, "Good," 617–18). Yet poststructural emphases remain congruent with the common theme of Beecher and other nineteenth-century critics: that cultural norms and practices, by delimiting female employment opportunities, helped ensure that needlewomen would be paid starvation wages.

92. Stansell, *City of Women,* 113; Buhle, "Needlewomen," 161.

93. Beecher acknowledged that the sewing machine was causing "much suffering" among seamstresses during this period of "transition." But he insisted that such technological innovation nonetheless was to be welcomed for its promise to eventually eliminate

hand sewing, which had shown itself to be a source of still greater and more durable suffering among seamstresses ("Library"). Although sewing technology did over the next half century eliminate most hand sewing, both in central shops and as a form of homework, Beecher vastly exaggerated the degree to which the machines would actually improve the lot of the seamstress (Baron and Klepp, "Machine," 41–52; Feldman, *Fit for Men,* 105–11).

94. Quote from Alvin Kernan's critical assessment of poststructuralism, *The Death of Literature* (New Haven, 1990), 73, 113. Although Beecher's address features manifold ambiguities, the primary of these are not notably inherent in the language of the text, as poststructuralism, particularly deconstruction theory, tends generally to assert. For example, the *Tribune* version reports that Beecher's oblique but unmistakable attack on the South was followed by "hisses" as well as "cheers" from the audience. How to interpret the hisses: as endorsement of Beecher's criticisms? As, to the contrary, a prosouthern response to those criticisms? As, somewhat differently still, a reproach on Beecher for using this occasion to attack the South? Or as some or all of the above, in view of the likely variegated persuasions of the audience? The unknowability of the answer to this question suggests the relevance of some critical remarks directed at deconstruction by William H. Sewell, in review of Joan Wallach Scott's *Gender and the Politics of History,* in *History and Theory* 29:1 (1990): 81.

95. Daniel T. Rodgers, *The Work Ethic in Industrial America, 1850–1920* (Chicago, 1978), 12–13, 97; William G. McLoughlin, *The Meaning of Henry Ward Beecher* (New York, 1970), 138–44; for characterization of Beecher's antebellum addresses as part of his attempt to "commodify" his own intellect within the context of the newly emergent and lucrative public-lecture system, see Donald M. Scott, "Knowledge and the Marketplace," in James Gilbert et al., *The Mythmaking Frame of Mind: Social Imagination and American Culture* (Belmont, Calif. 1994), 91–112; see also Kenneth Cmiel, *Democratic Eloquence: The Fight over Popular Speech in Nineteenth-Century America* (New York, 1990), 58–59; and Debby Applegate, "Henry Ward Beecher and the 'Great Middle Class': Mass-Marketed Intimacy and Middle-Class Identity," in *The Middling Sorts: Explorations in the History of the American Middle Class,* ed. Burton J. Bledstein and Robert D. Johnston (New York, 2001), 111–24.

96. Deborah Valenze, *The First Industrial Woman* (New York, 1995), 138–39; see also Kathryn Sutherland, "Adam Smith's Master Narrative: Women and the *Wealth of Nations,*" in *Adam Smith's Wealth of Nations,* ed. Stephen Copley and Sutherland (Manchester, Eng., 1995), 97–121.

97. I am indebted here to Marc W. Steinberg, "The Dialogue of Struggle: The Contest over Ideological Boundaries in the Case of London Silk Weavers in the Early Nineteenth Century," *Social Science History* 18 (Winter 1994): 505–41. Whereas Steinberg's focus is upon the contesting done by an assertive subordinate group, my focus is upon Beecher's own negotiations with a set of cultural expectations and pressures—with the internal threats and contradictions to American exceptionalism and free-labor ideology that resided in such stubborn facts as northern metropolitan industrialization and segmented labor markets.

98. For two such typical uses of the principle of supply and demand to discredit trade-union efforts at controlling wage rates, see the letter of 1849 from Boston's master tailors to the city's Mayor Bigelow, quoted in Henry Marcus Schreiber, "The Working People of Boston in the Middle of the Nineteenth Century" (Ph.D. diss., Boston Univ., 1950), 217, and the letter from "An Experienced Mechanic," in "The Labor Question," *Tribune,* April

2, 1851; see also Kim Voss, *The Making of American Exceptionalism: The Knights of Labor and Class Formation in the Nineteenth Century* (Ithaca, N.Y., 1993), 30–31; Mary Blewett, *Constant Turmoil: The Politics of Industrial Life in Nineteenth-Century New England* (Amherst, Mass., 2000), 8, 63.

99. Quote from H. B. Mullins (a New York City tailor and advocate of producers' cooperatives), *A Voice from the Workshop* (New York, 1860), 8.

100. To cite one example, the material suffering of the seamstresses was characterized by many middle-class commentators (though not Beecher) as largely self-imposed, attributable to the "false pride" and "stubbornness" of working-class females who turned down positions in domestic service and voluntarily "chose" to remain in a more precarious, overcrowded, and poorly recompensed employment. The New York *Evening Post*'s proposed solution demonstrated its own fidelity to supply-and-demand principles: "As long as the larger proportion of women are incompetent or unwilling to earn anything except by plain sewing, . . . it would be better for all of them, in the long run, to reduce wages to the famine point, so as to force all who had sufficient strength into other employments. This at least would diminish competition, and give the remaining ones a better chance" (quoted in Henry C. Carey, *Principles of Social Science* [Philadelphia, 1858], 1:240).

101. Hayek himself suggested the limited appeal of his argument in *Law, Legislation, and Liberty* (Chicago, 1976), 2:71–74.

102. "Labor Question," *Tribune*, April 2, 1851. Horace Greeley's editorial here is in fact an attack on land monopoly and other forces, more institutional than individual, that thwarted the "genuine and legitimate action" of supply and demand.

103. T. W. Hutchison, "The 'Marginal Revolution' and the Decline and Fall of English Classical Political Economy," in *The Marginal Revolution in Economics: Interpretation and Evaluation*, ed. R. D. Collison Black, A. W. Coats, and Craufurd D. W. Goodwin (Durham, N.C., 1973), 189–90.

104. Herbert Hovenkamp, *Enterprise and American Law, 1836–1937* (Cambridge, Mass., 1991), 223.

105. See Mill, "Newman's Political Economy" (1851), in Mill, *Essays on Economics and Society*, ed. J. M. Robson (Toronto, 1967), 449; Samuel Hollander, *The Economics of John Stuart Mill* (London, 1985), 1:409–22, 2:950–54.

106. American conditions may still have slowed widespread rejection of the wages-fund notion specifically. Herbert Hovenkamp surmises that this rejection came later in the United States than in Britain because it had less brutal associations in the former: American economists and others could more easily endorse it "without accepting starvation as a corollary." Because, too, of the greater ease with which individuals in the United States (above all, white males) could move into less crowded fields of employment, wage doctrines and more informal beliefs that stressed an individual's productivity and other personal attributes as determinant of his recompense remained in less open conflict with doctrines like the wages-fund that emphasized aggregate behavior and conditions (Hovenkamp, *Enterprise and American Law*, 196).

107. For, however, a recent dissent from more Marxist-oriented legal studies in its insistence on the generally "egalitarian and humanitarian" (rather than the "pro-corporate," "pro-entrepreneurial") character of judicial rulings on the enforcement of labor contracts and other regulatory matters, see Peter Karsten, *Heart versus Head: Judge-Made Law in*

Nineteenth-Century America (Chapel Hill, N.C., 1997); contrast with the revisionist reaffirmation of the fundamentally "bourgeois capitalist" nature of legal constructions of the employment relation in James D. Schmidt, *Free to Work: Labor Law, Emancipation, and Reconstruction, 1815–1880* (Athens, Ga., 1999). Like Karsten, Schmidt distances himself from what Karsten refers to as Morton J. Horwitz's "somewhat conspiratorial, class-oriented version of the 'transformation of American law'"(326–27). But Schmidt remains closer than Karsten does to critical legal-studies scholars like Christopher L. Tomlins who tend to see nineteenth-century labor contracts as a mirror image of emergent liberal capitalist hegemony—as products of a common ideological inclination (rather than of a conscious collusion) among jurists and employers to legitimate power imbalances and disadvantageous conditions for wage-earning laborers. For Adam Smith's particular criticisms of employer combinations to lower wages, see Edd S. Noell, "Adam Smith on Economic Justice in the Labor Market," *Journal of the History of Economic Thought* 17 (Fall 1995): 228–46; see also Emma Rothschild, *Economic Sentiments: Adam Smith, Condorcet, and the Enlightenment* (Cambridge, Mass., 2001), 61–71.

108. Louis Hartz, *Economic Policy and Democratic Thought: Pennsylvania, 1776–1860* (Chicago, 1948); Oscar and Mary Handlin, *Commonwealth, a Study of the Role of Government in the American Economy: Massachusetts, 1774–1861* (New York, 1947); for emphasis on the central regulatory role of state and local governments in this period that distances itself from the "entrepreneurial"-interventionist model of Hartz and the Handlins, see William J. Novak, *The People's Welfare: Law and Regulation in Nineteenth-Century America* (Chapel Hill, N.C., 1996); Karl Polanyi, *The Great Transformation* (Boston, 1944); Dean, *Constitution of Poverty;* Christopher L. Tomlins, *Law, Labor, and Ideology in the New Republic* (Cambridge, 1993); Karen Orren, *Belated Feudalism: Labor, the Law, and Liberal Development in the United States* (Cambridge, 1991); William M. Reddy, *Money and Liberty in Modern Europe: A Critique of Historical Understanding* (Cambridge, 1987); Walter Licht, *Getting Work: Philadelphia, 1840–1950* (Cambridge, Mass., 1992); Kessler-Harris, *Woman's Wage.*

109. Barrington Moore Jr., *Moral Aspects of Economic Growth, and Other Essays* (Ithaca, N.Y., 1998), 42–44; Eric Hobsbawm, *Labouring Men: Studies in the History of Labour* (London, 1964), 352; Immanuel Wallerstein, *Unthinking Social Science: The Limits of Nineteenth-Century Paradigms* (Cambridge, 1991), 207–17; for Marx's own reference to the selective embrace by the "capitalist class" of the "'sacred' law of supply and demand," see *Marx and Engels on the Trade Unions,* ed. Kenneth Lapides (New York, 1981), 97.

110. John Stuart Mill, *Principles of Political Economy,* 7th ed. (1871; rept. New York, 1965), 388.

2. Pressures from Below: Pauperism, Chattel Slavery, and the Ideological Construction of Free-Market Labor Incentives

1. *Report from His Majesty's Commissioners for Inquiring into the Administration and Practical Operation of the Poor Laws* (London, 1834), 87.

2. Polanyi, *Great Transformation;* David Brion Davis, *The Problem of Slavery in the Age of Revolution, 1770–1823* (Ithaca, N.Y., 1975), 356–66, 458–68; see also Patricia Hollis, "Anti-Slavery and British Working-Class Radicalism in the Year of Reform," 303–6, and Stanley L. Engerman and David Eltis, "Economic Aspects of the Abolition Debate," 284–86,

both in *Anti-Slavery, Religion, and Reform: Essays in Memory of Roger Anstey*, ed. Christine Bolt and Seymour Drescher (Kent, Eng., 1980); Lees, *Solidarities of Strangers*, 100. In contrast to the prominent role that their attacks on pauperism played in their valorization of the free-labor market, Senior and other British classical economists made little effort to follow up on Adam Smith and actually detail the putative economic costs and disadvantages of chattel slavery (Seymour Drescher, "Cartwhip and Billy Roller: Antislavery and Reform Symbolism in Industrializing Britain," *Journal of Social History* 15 [Fall 1981]: 4–6; see also Drescher, *Capitalism and Antislavery: British Mobilization in Comparative Perspective* [New York, 1987], 151–52, where Drescher may be overly dismissive of the ideological connections between British antislavery sentiment and the animus for outdoor public relief that was building in the decades prior to the New Poor Law).

3. Joseph Tuckerman, *The Principles and Results of the Ministry at Large, in Boston* (Boston, 1838), 269.

4. In 1827 the American Unitarian Association appointed Tuckerman to its new post of minister at large to the poor of Boston. Tuckerman served for several years, issuing regular published reports. In 1832 he was appointed by the Massachusetts Assembly to a committee of four to review the findings of the 1821 Quincy committee on the state's poor-relief policies. Despite the institutional movement toward "well-regulated" alms-houses, which he endorsed, Tuckerman's objective of a total abolition of poor laws and public outdoor relief was not realized, nor was his general hope that state regulation and involvement in social issues such as poverty would be reduced and replaced by the Christian "voluntarism" of individual citizens (Daniel T. McColgan, *Joseph Tuckerman: Pioneer in American Social Work* [Washington, D.C., 1943], 197–98). The movement to abolish public outdoor relief went further in some states, such as Pennsylvania and Delaware, than in others; for its general persistence, see Benjamin Joseph Klebaner, *Public Poor Relief in America, 1790–1860* (1952; rept. New York, 1976), chap. 3; David J. Rothman, *The Discovery of the Asylum: Social Order and Disorder in the New Republic* (Boston, 1971), 165–205; Michael B. Katz, *In the Shadow of the Poorhouse: A Social History of Welfare in America* (New York, 1986), 10–25.

5. The Harvard-educated Tuckerman (1778–1840), Daniel Walker Howe observes, "was as close as an American of his day could come to being a genuine aristocrat. His family had been prosperous Boston businessmen and Anglicans since the seventeenth century" (Howe, *The Unitarian Conscience: Harvard Moral Philosophy, 1805–1861* [1970; rept. Middletown, Conn., 1988], 313).

6. How widespread the practice of making up wages by "allowances" from the poor rates ever actually became in pre-1834 England remains questionable (Alan Kidd, *State, Society, and the Poor in Nineteenth-Century England* [New York, 1999], 1–45).

7. For the postmodern stress on the primacy of language and its skepticism regarding the objective, foundational nature of experience, see Joan W. Scott, "The Evidence of Experience," in McDonald, *Historic Turn*, 379–406. Yet I would not in this as in other instances push too far such privileging of language over a prediscursive reality. There were also more conventional reasons for Tuckerman's invocation of the views of the commission's *Report*. His publication of *Principles and Results* followed a long visit to England, where he directly observed (and albeit subjectively interpreted) conditions of poverty, as well as encountering firsthand many of that country's prevailing ideas about pauperism

and poor laws (E. E. Hale, "Introduction" to Joseph Tuckerman, *On the Elevation of the Poor* [Boston, 1874], 9–10). Tuckerman's hostility to legally mandated outdoor relief also predated the 1834 commission *Report* and reflected the transatlantic alarm and frustration regarding the "disease" of pauperism of which the British commission *Report* was the most signal product.

8. Commission *Report,* 348; McColgan, *Tuckerman,* 218.

9. "Thornton on Over-Population," *Edinburgh Review* 85 (Jan. 1847): 171–72, rept. in *The Working Classes in the Victorian Age: Debates on the Issue from 19th Century Critical Journals,* vol. 2, *Urban Conditions, 1839–1848* (Hants, Eng., 1973). Scholars have questioned the sincerity, as well as the practical significance, of the rhetoric of empowerment favored by the *Edinburgh Review* and other nineteenth-century critics of "indiscriminate" poor relief (K. D. M. Snell, *Annals of the Labouring Poor: Social Change and Agrarian England, 1660–1900* [Cambridge, 1985], 120–23).

10. H. S. Jones, *Victorian Political Thought* (New York, 2000), 41.

11. [Nassau Senior], "Poor Law Reform," *Edinburgh Review* 74 (Oct. 1841): 32–33.

12. Tuckerman, *Elevation,* 62.

13. Ibid.; Appleby, *Inheriting the Revolution,* 5–6; Appleby, "The Vexed Story of Capitalism Told by American Historians," *Journal of the Early Republic* 21 (Spring 2001): 1–18.

14. Steven Schlossman, "The 'Culture of Poverty' in Ante-Bellum Social Thought," *Science and Society* 38 (Summer 1974): 150–66. Several decades before the arrival of the famine Irish, northern free blacks had also been commonly stigmatized as a culture of poverty, and some poor-relief authorities openly discriminated against them in their allocation of outdoor relief; on Philadelphia's overseers of the poor, see Gary B. Nash, *Forging Freedom: The Formation of Philadelphia's Black Community, 1720–1840* (Cambridge, Mass., 1988), 272. Tuckerman, however, was in fact praised by abolitionist William Lloyd Garrison for his work among Boston's black poor (Howe, *Unitarian Conscience,* 243, 281).

15. Tuckerman quoted in Howard M. Wach, "Unitarian Philanthropy and Cultural Hegemony in Comparative Perspective: Manchester and Boston, 1827–1838," *Journal of Social History* 26 (Spring 1993): 544; Tuckerman, *Elevation,* 56; McColgan, *Tuckerman,* 216–18; Howe, *Unitarian Conscience,* 240–41.

16. For the compatibility of Chalmers's moral paternalism with laissez-faire economic individualism, see Boyd Hilton, *The Age of Atonement: The Influence of Evangelicalism on Social and Economic Thought, 1785–1865* (Oxford, Eng., 1988), 86–88; A. M. C. Waterman, *Revolution, Economics, and Religion: Christian Political Economy, 1798–1833* (Cambridge, 1991), 222; for a contrary, less persuasive interpretation, see Stewart J. Brown, *Thomas Chalmers and the Godly Commonwealth in Scotland* (New York, 1982).

17. Thomas Chalmers, *The Christian and Civic Economy of Large Towns* (Edinburgh, 1826), 3:405–6; Steinberg, *Fighting Words,* 200. For friendlier assessments than mine of Chalmers's social views, see Brown, *Chalmers,* 121; Mary T. Furgol, "Chalmers and Poor Relief: An Incidental Sideline?" in *The Practical and the Pious: Essays on Thomas Chalmers (1788–1847),* ed. A. C. Cheyne (Edinburgh, 1984), 115–29.

18. For Tuckerman's insistence that the lax nature of poor-relief laws and practices in Boston made it a magnet for the undeserving poor, see *Elevation,* 91–92; for his data on those receiving public assistance in Massachusetts in 1833 (some 4.5% of the state population)—a number that he found "astounding" given the nation's "resources of self-

subsistence"—see Tuckerman, *Principles,* 279–80, 306. One can argue, as David J. Rothman does, that the objective magnitude of dependent poverty in this period, both inside and outside Massachusetts, remained limited, and that the apprehensions expressed by elite commentators like Tuckerman strikingly exaggerated the problem (*Discovery of Asylum,* 155–79). Yet Tuckerman also had a prescient sense of structural unemployment as a cause of urban pauperism.

19. Tuckerman, *Principles,* 280; Tuckerman, *Elevation,* 141–49, 159–66, 185; Howe, *Unitarian Conscience,* 251.

20. Precisely where he emphasized that intemperance was only the main proximate, rather than the truly ultimate, cause of pauperism and poverty, Tuckerman's reasoning was more circumstantial and environmentalist than it was moralistic (Tuckerman, *Elevation,* 114–20; Tuckerman, *Principles,* 166; Tuckerman, *An Essay on the Wages Paid to Females for Their Labour; in the Form of a Letter, from a Gentlemen in Boston to His Friend in Philadelphia* [Philadelphia, 1830], rept. in *Low Wages and Great Sins: Two Antebellum American Views on Prostitution and the Working Girl,* ed. David J. Rothman and Sheila M. Rothman [New York, 1987]). In defending the reform vision of Tuckerman and like-minded activists, Joel Schwartz asserts that "drinking actually was responsible for a significantly greater share of social problems" in the earlier part of the nineteenth century. He also quite persuasively argues that even as Tuckerman, Robert Hartley, and Charles Loring Brace recognized the environmental factors contributing to intemperance, poverty, and pauperism, they reasonably encouraged the sobriety, industry, and other character virtues that helped people escape dependency and destitution. Yet Schwartz remains too easily accepting of the political-economic market-capitalist values that circumscribed the vision of Tuckerman and others. In view of the early nineteenth-century maldistribution of wealth, it does not suffice to say (in defense of why Tuckerman and others targeted pauperism more than poverty for reduction) that "there was simply too little wealth to go around in the nineteenth century for poverty to be seen as a soluble problem." Closer to my own perspective is that of Eric C. Schneider, although Schneider also posits what I do not discern: a decisive evolution in Tuckerman's attitudes toward a more pronounced Malthusian moralism (Schwartz, *Fighting Poverty with Virtue: Moral Reform and America's Urban Poor, 1825–2000* [Bloomington, Ind., 2000], 30, 7; Schneider, *In the Web of Class: Delinquents and Reformers in Boston, 1810s–1930s* [New York, 1992], 19–24).

21. Wach, "Philanthropy," 543; Tuckerman, *Elevation,* 104; Tuckerman, *Principles,* 166–68. For the same reason, poor-law officials favored noncash assistance (food, clothing, or wood for fuel) as outdoor relief: it reduced recipients' discretionary power to dissipate their assistance on liquor.

22. Tuckerman, *Elevation,* 54, 177–78. Tuckerman was accompanied by other Euro-American reformers who grappled yet more explicitly than he with the ambiguous relationships between categories and conditions—not merely how intemperance, sexual depravity, and like "moral" phenomena encouraged bodily disease and breakdown, but also how revolting environmental and other "physical" circumstances contributed to, and even determined, moral perversity (Christopher Hamlin, *Public Health and Social Justice in the Age of Chadwick* [Cambridge, 1998]; Andrew R. Aisenberg, *Contagion: Disease, Government, and the "Social Question" in Nineteenth-Century France* [Stanford, Calif., 1999]).

23. Tuckerman, *Elevation,* 182, 168–86; for a slightly different classification, see Tuckerman, *Wages,* 42–52.

24. Tuckerman, *Elevation,* 182, 178.

25. Amy Gutmann, "Introduction," in Robert Solow, *Work and Welfare,* ed. Gutmann (Princeton, N.J., 1998), xv.

26. McColgan, *Tuckerman,* 284–85; Tuckerman, *Elevation,* 93, 153–162; Tuckerman, *Principles,* 278–84. Modern-day defenders of welfare benefits exhibit a much different sensibility from that of Tuckerman, Chalmers, and their like-minded Victorian contemporaries. Robert Solow notes: "I cannot see that taking alms from the well-off is any less damaging to 'independence' than is a wage supplement from the state, or even the dole. If anything, I would guess that the psychological-sociological balance favors the state. Servility and gratitude toward one's 'betters' is not my idea of propriety in a democracy" (Solow, "Response to Comments," in *Work and Welfare,* 88).

27. Tuckerman, *Elevation,* 84–86; Tuckerman, *Principles,* 300; Albert O. Hirschman, *The Rhetoric of Reaction: Perversity, Futility, Jeopardy* (Cambridge, Mass., 1991), 71–75.

28. Tuckerman, *Wages,* 35–38; Tuckerman, *Principles,* 299–300. For an interpretation that slights the more liberal capitalist, free-market, and antistatist dimensions of Tuckerman's thought (which he manifested with respect to both wage earnings and poor relief) and exaggerates the centrality of his more "conservative" (and Foucauldian) desire to create a "paternal state" for purposes of regulating labor and "policing" and "coercing" the able-bodied, vagrant poor, see Schmidt, *Free to Work,* 57–63. Schmidt's more general, well-argued thesis is that there were several competing legal visions of free labor in the antebellum period. Tuckerman notably adopted strands from more than one of these visions.

29. This is not to deny that Chalmers's writings included attention to the moral failings of British capitalists; for his criticisms of factory conditions, see Brown, *Chalmers,* 202–4. Still, Chalmers's belief in the benefits of allowing markets to take their natural course entailed a general vindication of capitalists' activities and interests, and his overriding emphasis, like that of Malthus, remained the British laboring poor's moral and intellectual shortcomings and the social dangers of indulging these.

30. See Mark Robert Rank, *Living on the Edge: The Realities of Welfare in America* (New York, 1994); for the functions such stereotypes serve, see Herbert J. Gans, *The War against the Poor: The Underclass and Antipoverty Policy* (New York, 1995); David Turley notes some of the same tensions in Tuckerman's thought in "The Anglo-American Unitarian Connection and Urban Poverty," in *Charity, Philanthropy, and Reform: From the 1690s to 1850,* ed. Hugh Cunningham and Joanna Innes (New York, 1998), 235–36; Schwartz, *Fighting Poverty,* 8–18.

31. Tuckerman, *Wages,* 5–18, 37–38. Foreshadowing later thinkers who developed more explicit and systematic notions of structural unemployment, Tuckerman fastened on unemployment phenomena that represented something other than a cyclical phase of fluctuating business activity. Similarly, and despite his articulation of supply-and-demand shibboleths, he seemed in his discussions of pauperism and the laboring poor to downplay the self-correcting tendencies of the economy (Wach, "Philanthropy," 544). On Carey, see Benjamin J. Klebaner, "Poverty and Its Relief in American Thought, 1815–61," *Social Science Review* 38 (Dec. 1964): 385–95; James R. Gibson Jr., *Americans versus Malthus: The Population Debate in the Early Republic, 1790–1840* (New York, 1989), 272–88.

32. Tuckerman, *Elevation,* 64–79; for a different emphasis, see Wach, "Philanthropy," 544. Lynn Hollen Lees reemphasizes that English middle-class supporters of the New Poor Law were guided by the ideal of the "male-headed household, supported by male wages and female domestic labor" (*Solidarities of Strangers,* 144). Contrast, too, Tuckerman's ambivalence toward market forces and his accompanying doubts regarding the viability of an economically based "patriarchy" in many working-class households with Michael Meranze's Foucauldian-inspired characterization of elite antipathy to poor relief in Pennsylvania during the 1820s (*Laboratories of Virtue: Punishment, Revolution, and Authority in Philadelphia, 1760–1835* [Chapel Hill, N.C., 1996], 269–70). Tuckerman appears, in any case, not to have been among those American poor-law reformers who targeted various categories of poor women as especially undeserving of relief; on these, see Mimi Abramovitz, *Regulating the Lives of Women: Social Welfare Policy from Colonial Times to the Present* (Boston, 1989); Monique C. E. Bourque, "Virtue, Industry, and Independence: Almshouses and Labor in the Philadelphia Region, 1791–1860" (Ph.D. diss., Univ. of Delaware, 1995), 175–76.

33. Schmidt, *Free to Work,* 75, similarly notes Tuckerman's disregard for republican notions of virtue and freedom, although for purposes of making a different point from mine.

34. Tuckerman, *Principles,* 227–313.

35. Tuckerman, *Elevation,* 88.

36. As noted elsewhere, such appeals for an infusion of Christian love as a means of humanizing, and defending, free-market capitalism and its economic disparities were common among northern clerics and other public moralists (R. C. Waterston, *Christianity Applied to Cities: A Discourse Delivered at the Dedication of the Preble Chapel in Portland, October 29, 1851* [Boston, 1851], 3–4, 13–22). The abolitionist press, in its own efforts to elevate, and thereby vindicate, free-labor principles, similarly called for "the practical recognition of the Christian law of love, *in all the business relations of society.*" Much like Tuckerman, the *Philanthropist* insisted that this law provided "the only security for fair wages," the surest means, in particular (in contrast to impotent trade-union pressures) of curbing the tendency of employers to take advantage of the female labor surplus in seamstressing and other trades ("Young Women's Industrial Association," *Weekly Herald and Philanthropist,* March 19, 1845). In their sharp, religiously inspired criticisms of market processes and outcomes in the North, some prominent abolitionists, certainly, manifested a virtual anticapitalist sensibility, one that put them closer to James Freeman Clarke than to Tuckerman and many other public moralists; James L. Huston emphasizes this dimension of American abolitionism—the anticapitalist implications of its ethos of Christian brotherhood—in "Abolitionists, Political Economists, and Capitalism," *Journal of the Early Republic* 20 (Fall 2000): 487–521. However, other abolitionists (e.g., Joshua Leavitt), who were no less wedded to evangelical Protestant precepts, remained far more accepting of both significant economic discrepancies in the free states and the market processes that generated them. Notwithstanding abolitionists' recurrent criticisms of northern greed, excessive materialism, and other anti-Christian propensities, it seems questionable (contrary to Huston's suggestion) that there was a dominant ethos within American abolitionism favoring a fundamental transformation of prevailing economic and social arrangements in the free states; see also notes 70 and 74.

37. Tuckerman, *Elevation,* 81–82; Tuckerman, *Principles,* 301–2; Tuckerman, *Wages,* 38–41.

38. Howe, *Unitarian Conscience*, 250–52, 255. There is a firm line of continuity between Tuckerman's perspective—particularly his endorsement of both work-ethic norms and supply-and-demand principles—and the "liberal," "residual" welfare-state regime that the United States subsequently developed (Gosta Esping-Andersen, *The Three Worlds of Welfare Capitalism* [Princeton, N.J., 1990], 20–27).

39. Tuckerman, *Elevation*, 78–79, 167–68; Rothman, *Discovery of the Asylum*, 177.

40. Support for both these positions extended beyond Massachusetts. Despite his many agreements with Tuckerman regarding the plight of the female laboring poor, Mathew Carey was a prominent member of this first group. He opposed Pennsylvania's 1828 legislation banning almost all public outdoor relief on the grounds that many of the industrious poor, now deprived of their customary allowance by the Philadelphia guardians, had been reduced to begging. These peoples' aversion to becoming almshouse inmates should have been encouraged, in Carey's view, contrary to the effects of the action favored by Tuckerman and those in Pennsylvania (Carey, *Essays on the Public Charities of Philadelphia*, 5th ed. [1830], in *Miscellaneous Essays* [1830; rept. New York, 1966], 1:163–64; Benjamin J. Klebaner, "The Home Relief Controversy in Philadelphia, 1782–1861," *Pennsylvania Magazine of History and Biography* 78 [Oct. 1954]: 419; Priscilla Ferguson Clement, *Welfare and the Poor in the Nineteenth-Century City: Philadelphia, 1800–1854* [Rutherford, N.J., 1985], 74). For his criticism of Tuckerman's condemnation of the poor laws (and, indeed, of all "the Malthuses, the Seniors," and others "who so loudly disclaim against the poor rates"), see Carey, *Appeal to the Wealthy of the Land* (Philadelphia, 1833), 21–31. For references to the common argument that employment in the United States was available to all, a principal basis for blaming poverty on the personal failings of the poor, see Carey, *Public Charities*, 171; Klebaner, "Relief," 382–89. For Tuckerman's attempts to answer the group that used this argument and for his defense of the coordinated and efficient efforts of benevolent societies, see Tuckerman, *Elevation*, 77, 90–91; *Principles*, 124–25, 305–7.

41. The supplemental outdoor relief extended during this period was meager, whether offered by private agencies such as Tuckerman's or by state or local government overseers of the poor, and whether it was provided in the form of cash or noncash. Mathew Carey noted that in 1830 the relief extended to Philadelphia's 549 "out-door paupers" by its overseers averaged less than forty-seven cents a week. Of course, the recompense earned by this population was itself meager. Carey and Tuckerman reported that the seamstresses who benefited from home relief in Philadelphia and Boston could at best earn a dollar and a half a week from long hours of piecework. But that outdoor poor relief could therefore comprise a significant proportion of a household's income is not in itself proof that all such relief generated the kind of disincentives and downward pressure on wages suggested by Tuckerman's critics. Smaller proprietors in the clothing trade, and most of all subcontractors who directly employed the seamstresses and other unskilled labor, were themselves living close to the bone; pressured by their own thin profit margins, they lacked the means if not the generosity of heart to appreciably raise the rates they paid these workers were all supplemental aid foreclosed to the latter. As for many of the recipients of such relief, a variety of circumstances—lack of job skills, old age or disease, responsibilities for disabled or otherwise dependent family members—severely restricted their ability to move either occupationally or geographically out of glutted labor markets. For the elderly seamstresses who worked out of their homes, outdoor poor relief provided some minimal

security against starvation, not a disincentive to finding better economic opportunities. Still, there were grounds for the complaints of Tuckerman and others that the greater ease of obtaining public or private assistance in Boston and other urban centers contributed to their overstocked labor markets by attracting certain kinds of would-be paupers. These included indigent immigrants from abroad and male day laborers from the country's interior who had been thrown out of employment during the winter months (Mathew Carey, *A Plea for the Poor,* 7th ed. [Philadelphia, 1837], 5–14; Carey, *Appeal,* 19–20; Carey, *Public Charities,* 154, 167; Tuckerman, *Wages,* 14; Tuckerman, *Elevation,* 65–83). For the implications that agricultural-rural seasonal unemployment and migration to American cities had for urban wage levels in the mid-nineteenth century, see Earle, *Geographical Inquiry,* 180–88.

42. Quote from an 1837 memorial from the Philadelphia Guardians of the Poor to the Pennsylvania legislature, in Klebaner, "Controversy," 420. This memorial, like most such criticisms of outdoor relief's pernicious effect on the poor, directed most of its fire against compulsory public assistance. Still, Tuckerman was sensitive to the hostility that such criticisms could also carry for the voluntary relief that he championed; see also William Howe, *An Address before the Society for the Prevention of Pauperism* (Boston, 1849), 10–11.

43. George R. Boyer, *An Economic History of the English Poor Law, 1750–1850* (Cambridge, 1990); Peter Wood, *Poverty and the Workhouse in Victorian Britain* (Wolfeboro Falls, N.H., 1991), 64–66. It was not only the critics to Tuckerman's right who observed that private as well as public relief could depress or at least impose a cap on wage levels. Mathew Carey noted in 1830 that Philadelphia's Provident Society "originated in the purest motives of benevolence" not merely to supplement the wages of poor seamstresses but to furnish them with the entirety of their employment in the winter season, "when work from the [private] tailors slackens." But the less than subsistent minimum wage of 12½ cents per day paid out by the society, Carey explained, came to be regarded as "the general standard . . . a most serious evil — almost enough to countervail all the advantages resulting from the society." As a dogged champion, however, of both public and private relief that would alleviate employers' "grinding the faces of the poor," and as one who denied that assistance of either kind fostered "idleness and dissipation" in more than a small proportion of cases, Carey presented a solution to this wage-capping effect quite different from that of the most moralistic, unyielding critics of private charitable activities. He urged the Provident Society not to cease its interventions in the labor market but rather to raise its wages. Even if this meant giving work to fewer women, such a policy would set "a laudable example" that "would probably be followed by some of the tailors" (Carey, *Public Charities,* 181–94).

44. Robert J. Steinfeld, "Property and Suffrage in the Early American Republic," *Stanford Law Review* 41 (Jan. 1989): 352–65; Nancy F. Cott, "Marriage and Women's Citizenship in the United States, 1830–1934," *American Historical Review* 103 (Dec. 1998): 1453. For the early nineteenth-century reasoning that rejected elective rights for legally "independent" female wage earners — unmarried women and widows — see Jacob Katz Cogan, "The Look Within: Property, Capacity, and Suffrage in Nineteenth-Century America," *Yale Law Journal* 107 (Nov. 1997): 485. Skin color proved no less than gender a critical mediating factor: in the majority of antebellum states, the free black males who demonstrated their economic autonomy — their capacity to do without public assistance — similarly failed either

to acquire or to retain the voting and other rights that this autonomy brought to white males in the early nineteenth century.

45. Tuckerman, *Wages,* 46; Schmidt, *Free to Work,* 74–75.

46. Gertrude Himmelfarb, *The De-Moralization of Society: From Victorian Virtues to Modern Values* (New York, 1995), 131.

47. Steinfeld, "Property and Suffrage," 365–70. This countertendency toward reinforcing older patterns of social stratification is slighted in such studies as Shklar, *American Citizenship,* 86–98.

48. Yet antislavery, free-labor discourse, blending such themes as the power and the parasitism of large southern slaveholders, came increasingly to attack these slaveholders as "tyrant paupers."

49. In comparison with his pronouncements on pauperism, Joseph Tuckerman's published criticisms of modern chattel slavery were both rare and mild, notwithstanding his private aversion. Possibly Tuckerman did not wish to antagonize the Boston commercial and industrial interests that were proslavery in sympathy and upon which his urban missionary efforts financially depended. Family sensibilities were also involved; his second wife was the daughter of a West Indian planter (Tuckerman, *Elevation,* 173; Tuckerman, *Principles,* 256; Howe, *Unitarian Conscience,* 280–313; McColgan, *Tuckerman,* 223, 259). Channing (1780–1842) publicly spoke out against slavery only after a long period of hesitation. But although he could never bring himself to endorse either the militant rhetoric or the uncompromising solutions of radical abolitionists, his diagnosis of the moral and intellectual evils of slavery was identical to theirs. Channing grew up in Newport, Rhode Island, and graduated from Harvard College. He started out as a liberal Congregationalist, but under the leadership he assumed in 1803, Federal Street Church in Boston became the most important institutional center for the Unitarian religion outside of Harvard during the early nineteenth century. Channing's family fortune was consolidated by his marriage to his first cousin. As his antislavery views grew in intensity and visibility, he became increasingly estranged from his congregation.

50. Channing, *Slavery* (1835), rept. in *The Works of William Ellery Channing* (Boston, 1896), 709–19.

51. Haskell, "Capitalism," 107–60.

52. Indeed, to the extent that Channing exemplified the period's "romantic racialism" (and was to this extent not color-blind), he believed that members of the black race possessed innate, superior moral and Christian capabilities that rendered their victimization by slavery especially tragic (Channing, *Slavery,* 720–71; George M. Fredrickson, *The Black Image in the White Mind: The Debate on Afro-American Character and Destiny, 1817–1914* [New York, 1971], 105–8).

53. Channing, *Slavery,* 710.

54. For one early political-economic indictment of chattel slavery that anticipated Channing in extolling the "mental anxieties" to which only free laborers could be truly subject, see James Anderson, *Observations on Slavery; Particularly with a View to Its Effects on the British Colonies, in the West-Indies* (Manchester, Eng., 1789), 33–34.

55. For reference to the hopelessness and paralyzing fear of starvation that afflicted English day laborers, see Mill, *Principles of Political Economy,* 285–86.

56. Elizabeth B. Clark, "'The Sacred Rights of the Weak': Pain, Sympathy, and the Culture of Individual Rights in Antebellum America," *Journal of American History* 82 (Sept. 1995): 463–93; Karen Halttunen, "Humanitarianism and the Pornography of Pain in Anglo-American Culture," *American Historical Review* 100 (April 1995): 303–34; Karen Sanchez-Eppler, *Touching Liberty: Abolition, Feminism, and the Politics of the Body* (Berkeley, Calif., 1993); Stanley, *Bondage to Contract,* 17–35; Adam Jay Hirsch, *The Rise of the Penitentiary: Prisons and Punishment in Early America* (New Haven, 1992), 38–39, 104.

57. Channing, *Slavery,* 711–12. Because these sexual and other physical abuses undermined slave family structure, Stanley's illuminating *Bondage to Contract* may exaggerate the abolitionist tendency (23–27) to fixate only on female slaves as the victims of such abuses (Diana Paton, "Decency, Dependence, and the Lash: Gender and the British Debate over Slave Emancipation, 1830–34," *Slavery and Abolition* 17 [Dec. 1996]: 163–84). In contrast to Stanley and others, James L. Huston insists that radical abolitionists' (and by extension, Channing's) reaction of shock and abhorrence to slave whippings can somehow be divorced from their location in northern middle-class culture ("The Experiential Basis of the Northern Antislavery Impulse," *Journal of Southern History* 56 [Nov. 1990]: 609–40). For ex-slaves' own sense of the ways in which American bondage had sought to animalize them, see Mia Bay, *The White Image in the Black Mind: African-American Ideas about White People, 1830–1925* (New York, 2000), 127–43.

58. However, Theodore Dwight Weld and other abolitionists at times did highlight slaves' material deprivations when they castigated the profit-maximizing greed, as well as the barbarity and depravity, of slaveowners (Leo P. Hirrel, *Children of Wrath: New School Calvinism and Antebellum Reform* [Lexington, Ky., 1998], 142–44).

59. For the conflict between northern prostitution and antislavery ideology, in both the antebellum and postbellum periods, see Stanley, *Bondage to Contract,* 218–63.

60. Channing to Elizabeth Palmer Peabody, Sept. 1840, in Peabody, *Reminiscences of Rev. Wm. Ellery Channing, D.D.* (Boston, 1880), 415.

61. Channing, *Slavery,* 704, 720; Channing, "Remarks on the Slavery Question. In a Letter to Jonathan Phillips, Esq." (1839), in *Works,* 793; see also Garrison's reply to James Mitchell, in "The Poor of England," *Liberator* (Boston), Jan. 9, 1846.

62. Lasch, *Revolt of Elites,* 63n.

63. See here, in addition to Channing's above observations, his "Remarks on Slavery Question," 796. I draw here from the distinction between exploitation and humiliation made in Avishai Margalit, *The Decent Society,* trans. Naomi Goldblum (Cambridge, Mass., 1996), 222.

64. Voss, *American Exceptionalism,* 31.

65. Glickstein, *Concepts of Free Labor,* 56, 72. Because of his distaste for these particular capitalist tendencies, as well as because of the idealist, moral nature of the authority he lent market forces and the formal right of self-ownership, Channing's contribution to the legitimation of the capitalist system of production would seem more that of a "traditional" intellectual than an "organic" one, to borrow from Antonio Gramsci's elucidation of hegemonic cultures (Quintin Hoare and Geoffrey Nowell Smith, eds., *Selections from the Prison Notebooks of Antonio Gramsci* [New York, 1971], 328–76; Raymond Williams, "Base and Superstructure in Marxist Cultural Theory," *New Left Review,* no. 82 [Nov.–Dec. 1973]: 3–16; Eagleton, *Ideology,* 119–21; see also Peter S. Field, *The Crisis of the Standing Order: Clerical Intellectuals and Cultural Authority in Massachusetts, 1780–1833* [Amherst, Mass., 1998], 5–7).

66. Schlesinger criticized Channing's privileging of the "internal reform" of the "laboring classes" as designed to delegitimize working-class grievances against the "business community": "The work of Channing in sabotaging the liberal impulses of his day . . . has never been properly appreciated" (*The Age of Jackson* [Boston, 1945], 146, 271–73; see also Jack Mendelsohn, *Channing: The Reluctant Radical* [Boston, 1971], 203–5; Glickstein, *Concepts of Free Labor*, 191–92, 437; Channing's letter to Peabody, *Reminiscences*, 415).

67. Haskell, "Capitalism," 111–12. Haskell appears to qualify some of his claims in Haskell, "Convention and Hegemonic Interest in the Debate over Antislavery: A Reply to Davis and Ashworth," in Bender, *Antislavery Debate*, 237–40, 251.

68. For one such attack on the doctrine of overpopulation in "political economy," see Channing, *Lectures on the Elevation of the Labouring Portion of the Community* (Boston, 1840), 54–58; see also *Memoir of William Ellery Channing* (Boston, 1848), 2:74–79.

69. Channing was, for example, a strong supporter of child factory-labor legislation in Massachusetts.

70. C. B. Macpherson, *The Political Theory of Possessive Individualism: Hobbes to Locke* (Oxford, 1962), 263–70. Like some other Republicans, Abraham Lincoln invoked the notion of American exceptionalist class fluidity, in tandem with the life cycle, to uphold traditional stigmas attaching to waged labor as a permanent individual condition: there is something morally deficient, he noted, in poor northern youth—those "penniless beginners"—who fail over time to rise out of waged economic dependence. Channing's attitudes toward such dependence were more ambiguous given his greater revulsion toward success values that recognized manual-labor employments generally as stepping-stones to society's higher "ranks." Yet even Channing's faith in the intrinsic dignity of (free) manual-labor employments—their compatibility with the full development of human intellectual faculties—was tempered by his concern over the stultifying effects of manufacturing division of labor (Lincoln, "Address before the Wisconsin State Agricultural Society," Sept. 30, 1859, in *The Collected Works of Abraham Lincoln*, ed. Roy Basler [New Brunswick, N.J., 1953], 3:477–82; Channing, *Elevation*, 10, 12, 15). Eric Foner argues that Republicans like Lincoln, following various labor leaders, articulated the "classical republican" conception of liberty, which rested on economic independence. Abolitionists, in contrast, embraced the distinct "liberal" conception of liberty, highlighting the value of formal self-ownership apart from real access to economic opportunity. Yet the mythology of American exceptionalist class fluidity was not absent from the abolitionist rebuttals of the wage-slavery critique made by northern labor radicals; William Lloyd Garrison, Wendell Phillips, and Joshua Leavitt, among others, invoked that mythology at different times to affirm the fairness of existing economic discrepancies in the free states. And as suggested, the vision of Lincoln and other leading Republican politicians contained a healthy dose of professional, liberal capitalist success values; if their speeches and writings often extolled "republican" economic independence per se, they nevertheless did not share Channing's disapprobation of upward mobility out of the ranks of artisan proprietors and freehold farmers altogether (Foner, "Liberty in the Age of Emancipation," in *Liberty/Liberté: The American-French Experience*, ed. Joseph Klaits and Michael H. Haltzel [Washington, D.C., 1991], 101–2; Michael J. Sandel, *Democracy's Discontent: America in Search of a Public Philosophy* [Cambridge, Mass., 1996], 172–81).

71. Hollis, "Anti-Slavery," 305.

72. Engerman and Eltis, "Economic," 273; Engerman, "Introduction," 20.

73. Josiah Conder, *Wages or the Whip: An Essay on the Comparative Cost and Productiveness of Free and Slave Labor* (London, 1833), 1, 2, 91. However, Seymour Drescher argues that the absolute confidence exhibited by Conder in free labor's economic superiority was not in fact shared (at least with respect to the West Indies) by many of his antislavery contemporaries (Drescher, "Abolitionist Expectations: Britain," in *After Slavery: Emancipation and Its Discontents,* ed. Howard Temperley [London, 2000], 41–66).

74. For recent emphasis on the biblical moral economy of many American abolitionists, see Huston, "Abolitionists, Political Economists, and Capitalism," 487–521. In distinguishing this moral economy from the economic liberalism of classical economists, Huston, as suggested earlier, somewhat overstates American abolitionists' hostility toward market processes and outcomes. Like Channing, certain abolitionists recognized market forces as compulsory and as at least indirectly "coercive" yet embraced these as ennobling for the legally free laborer. Huston additionally exaggerates abolitionists' "constant disgust at commercial and manufacturing activity" (517): some were inspired to extoll such activity out of their belief that much of it (including factory work) was higher forms of enterprise, ones that were incompatible with slave labor.

75. Channing, *Emancipation* (1840), in *Works,* 828–32.

76. Ibid., 832; John Stuart Mill, "The Negro Question," *Fraser's Magazine* 41 (Jan. 1850): 25–51.

77. Channing, *Emancipation,* 830.

78. Channing, "An Address Delivered at Lenox, on the First of August, 1842, Being the Anniversary of Emancipation in the British West Indies," in *Works,* 916.

79. In ways, however, Channing's remarks paralleled the shifting defenses of British West Indies emancipation made by certain British abolitionists, who in the late 1830s and early 1840s countered the 30–40 percent decrease in West Indies sugar production with references to various beneficial effects accruing from the ex-slaves' developing consumer appetites (Seymour Drescher, "Free Labor vs. Slave Labor: The British and Caribbean Cases," in Engerman, *Terms of Labor,* 73).

80. Engerman and Eltis, "Economic," 285–88; Stanley L. Engerman, "Coerced and Free Labor: Property Rights and the Development of the Labor Force," *Explorations in Economic History* 29 (Jan. 1992): 1–29.

81. Charles Stephenson, "'There's Plenty Waitin' at the Gates': Mobility, Opportunity, and the American Worker," in *Life and Labor: Dimensions of American Working-Class History,* ed. Stephenson and Robert Asher (Albany, 1986), 81, 89; Eric Foner, *Nothing but Freedom: Emancipation and Its Legacy* (Baton Rouge, La., 1983), 15–57. Because wage-earning opportunities outside the home relaxed the constraints of patriarchal authority and increased their economic independence, white female wage earners may not have shared to a like degree an antipathy for wage-earning status (Jean Matthews, "Race, Sex, and the Dimensions of Liberty in Antebellum America," *Journal of the Early Republic* 6 [Fall 1986]: 282–84). However, historians may have overstated the antipathy for this dependent status even among white male workers, particularly among those wary of the economic risks of self-employment.

82. See, in addition to Conder's pamphlet, Charles Stuart, *The West India Question: Immediate Emancipation Would Be Safe for the Masters* (London, 1832), 42. Yet even in many of these antislavery writings the more negative strand of free-labor ideology—that under-

scoring the free wage laborer's superior exploitability—remained unstated, subordinate, and something that many of the authors in question would have in fact disclaimed. It was left to the Anglo-American critics of wage slavery, such as the *Northampton Democrat* discussed later, to highlight this strand and exaggerate its significance in the abolitionist ideological arsenal.

83. Clifford Geertz, *The Interpretation of Cultures* (New York, 1973), 201.

84. Even William Lloyd Garrison could be more unequivocal than Channing in condemning unjustly low wages, while still defending the wage system itself from the attacks made by northern labor radicals ("Free and Slave Labor," *Liberator,* March 26, 1847).

85. An exception is John Ashworth, *Slavery, Capitalism, and Politics in the Antebellum Republic* (Cambridge, 1995), 186.

86. Sven Beckert finds that even by 1860 only a minority of New York City's business and professional elite had shifted its allegiance to the Republican Party (*The Monied Metropolis: New York City and the Consolidation of the American Bourgeoisie, 1850–1896* [Cambridge, 2001], 84–97).

87. John P. Diggins, "Comrades and Citizens: New Mythologies in American Historiography," *American Historical Review* 90 (June 1985): 626–28; William E. Gienapp, "The Myth of Class in Jacksonian America," *Journal of Policy History* 6:2 (1994): 252, and "Ahistorical History," ibid., 277–81; Seymour Martin Lipset and Gary Marks, *It Didn't Happen Here: Why Socialism Failed in the United States* (New York, 2000), 15–21. Alternatively, such historians often maintain that northern critics of wage slavery, insofar as they were truly radical, were a tiny minority, marginalized from the mainstream of American workers (Gienapp, "Myth of Class," 251–52, 278–81; Peter D. McClelland, *The American Search for Economic Justice* [Cambridge, 1990], 38–43).

88. Lipset and Marks, *Didn't Happen,* 21.

89. Somewhat more problematically, John Ashworth argues that such an anticapitalist aversion also typified mainstream Democratic Party ideology (*"Agrarians" and "Aristocrats": Party Political Ideology in the United States, 1837–1846* [London, 1983]).

90. In this second anticapitalist criticism, that highlighting the often oppressive and degrading nature of the compulsions driving waged laborers, northern radicals were joined by George Frederick Holmes and other southern proslavery conservatives who were ideologically unreceptive to the first anticapitalist theme. Holmes and like-minded commentators were among the strongest defenders of a social hierarchy in which assorted "mental labor" occupations enjoyed the greatest material and status rewards.

91. "Freedom of the Public Lands," *Northampton Democrat,* Jan. 26, 1847. During this period such land-reform leaders as Lewis Masquerier contributed to the paper, which was edited and published by J. E. Thompson.

92. This reform mentality was famously satirized by Charles Dickens as the "telescopic philanthropy" practiced by Mrs. Jellyby in *Bleak House;* for an extreme version of the criticism, see the polemic by the Kentucky writer Henry Field James, *Abolitionism Unveiled! Hypocrisy Unmasked! and Knavery Scourged!* (New York, 1850); for a modern-day version, see the "revisionist" history, Michael A. Hoffman II, *They Were White and They Were Slaves: The Untold Story of the Enslavement of Whites in Early America* (Dresden, N.Y., 1991).

93. See, for example, Eileen Boris and Angelique Janssens, "Complicating Categories: An Introduction," in *International Review of Social History* 44, supp. 7 (1999): 1–13.

94. There were, undeniably, many wage-slavery and white-slavery attacks on abolitionist priorities in which antiblack prejudice and antipathy were manifestly more in evidence than was the case with the *Northampton Democrat*. Whatever the racial attitudes of northern labor and land reformers, the fact that their wage-slavery critiques commonly included the *Northampton Democrat*'s insistence that market-based coercion and exploitation entailed the sexual degradation of northern white working-class females renders problematic abolitionists' claim (one seemingly endorsed by David Roediger) that the labor reformers were only focused on "narrowly material concerns" (Roediger, "Race, Labor," 179). The validity of the labor-reform parallels between female chattel slaves and female wage slaves is a separate question.

95. Marc W. Steinberg, "Talkin' Class: Discourse, Ideology, and Their Roles in Class Conflict," in *Bringing Class Back In: Contemporary and Historical Perspectives,* ed. Scott G. McNall, Rhonda F. Levine, and Rick Fantasia (Boulder, Colo., 1991), 261–84. Garrison indeed perceived the editorials from the *Northampton Democrat* as hostile borrowings, placing them in the *Liberator*'s "Refuge of Oppression" section ("Black Slavery and White Slavery," *National Anti-Slavery Standard,* Aug. 5, 1847).

96. That the remuneration of many mid-nineteenth-century slaves was in fact neither guaranteed nor fixed—hence the abstract and somewhat tenuous nature of the argument being made by antislavery voices like Channing—has become increasingly evident in a growing body of scholarly work, pointing to a considerable diversity in slave conditions and earning patterns.

97. [Solon Robinson], "Negro Slavery at the South," Sept. and Nov. 1849, in Robinson, *Solon Robinson, Pioneer and Agriculturist: Selected Writings,* ed. Herbert Anthony Kellar (Indianapolis, 1936), 2:265, 276.

98. Evans, "To Gerrit Smith," July 24, 1844.

99. Ibid.

100. "The Wilmot Proviso," *Northampton Democrat,* May 11, 1847.

101. An example even more blatant than Solon Robinson's contribution is Alabama senator Jeremiah Clemens's bemoaning in 1850 of the "slavery" afflicting New England's female factory workers. For the resentment provoked in one of these workers by Clemens's remarks, see Nancy P. Healey, "Letter to J. Clemens from a Factory Operative," *National Era,* Oct. 17, 1850.

102. Middle-class and upper-middle-class antebellum Americans who remained Old School Presbyterian, Episcopalian, or Catholic tended to be particularly hostile not only to the abolitionist attacks on southern slavery but also to the labor and utopian socialist movements that criticized prevailing social and economic arrangements in the free states.

103. Appleby, *Inheriting the Revolution,* 5–6, 56–80, 144; Gienapp, "Myth of Class."

104. Even modern American popular attitudes toward capitalism, material success, and related issues of distributive justice remain diverse, multidimensional, and ambiguous, despite the availability of public opinion polling and the like (Jennifer L. Hochschild, *What's Fair? American Beliefs about Distributive Justice* [Cambridge, Mass., 1981]; Hochschild, *Facing Up to the American Dream: Race, Class, and the Soul of the Nation* [Princeton, N.J., 1995]; James R. Kluegel and Eliot R. Smith, *Beliefs about Inequality: American Views of What Is and What Ought to Be* [New York, 1986]; Michele Lamont, *The Dignity of Working Men: Morality and the Boundaries of Race, Class, and Imagination* [New York, 2000]).

105. Dirk Hoerder's remark regarding immigrant attitudes is to the point: "With access to letters from emigrant to friends and kin describing living and working conditions after migration, emigration researchers never fell for the now-outmoded U.S. discourse strategies of unlimited opportunities, the openness of the one-and-only frontier society, or American exceptionalism" (Hoerder, *AHA Perspectives* 34 [Feb. 1996]: 10).

106. For a good sense of the degree to which land-reform sheets like the *Northampton Democrat* spoke to the concerns of artisans as well as other workingmen in the eastern states, see Jamie L. Bronstein, *Land Reform and Working-Class Experience in Britain and the United States, 1800–1862* (Stanford, Calif., 1998), 162–85.

107. Richard Stott, "Artisans and Capitalist Development," *Journal of the Early Republic* 16 (Summer 1996): 257–71; Donna Rilling, *Making Houses, Crafting Capitalism: Builders in Philadelphia, 1790–1850* (Philadelphia, 2001).

108. John K. Brown, *The Baldwin Locomotive Works, 1831–1915: A Study in American Industrial Practice* (Baltimore, 1995); Huston, *Securing the Fruits,* 107–24.

109. "The Clothing Trade," *Hunt's Merchant's Magazine* 21 (Jan. 1849): 116; Wilentz, *Chants Democratic,* 121–22.

110. George Grantham, "Economic History and the History of Labour Markets," in *Labour Market Evolution: The Economic History of Market Integration, Wage Flexibility, and the Employment Relation,* ed. Grantham and Mary MacKinnon (London, 1994), 7.

111. Stuart M. Blumin, *The Emergence of the Middle Class: Social Experience in the American City, 1760–1900* (Cambridge, 1989), 75–76. As some historians prefer to emphasize, in a few trades like tailoring these developments in the early nineteenth century in fact only contributed to a process of craft erosion and journeymen immiserization and unrest that was well under way by the end of the previous century. There is certainly no intent here to idealize conditions and relationships in preindustrial artisanal workshops (Glickstein, *Concepts of Free Labor,* 50).

112. Richard A. Epstein, "Imitations of Libertarian Thought," in *Problems of Market Liberalism,* ed. Ellen Frankel Paul, Fred D. Miller Jr., and Jeffrey Paul (New York, 1998), 421.

113. Wilentz, *Chants Democratic;* William H. Sewell Jr., *Work and Revolution in France: The Language of Labor from the Old Regime to 1848* (Cambridge, 1980).

114. The Berkshire system, whereby employers introduced low-priced unskilled helpers into iron foundries during the 1850s, notably illustrated both these processes (Fogel, *Without Consent or Contract,* 358–59).

115. Some economic historians are reconsidering their older finding that the wages of skilled workers increased relative to those of unskilled laborers in the antebellum period. Stagnation in skilled wages likely reflected the devaluation of various artisanal skill premiums and the related competitive labor-market pressures referred to in the text, even if it was wages in unskilled occupations that might plausibly seem to have been most directly depressed by the heavy influx of Irish immigrant common laborers (Margo, *Wages and Labor Markets,* 155–56, 180; Ferrie, *Yankeys Now,* 182–83). Richard Stott suggests that the surge of journeymen protests in the 1820s and 1830s reflected the degree to which industrialization actually empowered such workers by removing the inhibitions imposed on an earlier generation of journeymen and apprentices by the family-based structure of the small preindustrial shops (Stott, "Artisans," 270). This argument slights the extent to which the protesting journeymen were animated by a sense of their impotence—by their inability to

prevent craft entrepreneurs and other capitalists from undermining artisan skills by subdividing work processes and tapping into pools of cheap and "dishonorable" labor.

116. Richard A. Easterlin, "Will Raising the Incomes of All Increase the Happiness of All?" *Journal of Economic Behavior and Organization* 27 (June 1995): 35–47; Bruce Laurie, "'Spavined Ministers, Lying Toothpullers, and Buggering Priests': Third Partyism and the Search for Security in the Antebellum North," in Rock, *American Artisans,* 98–106.

117. Bruce Laurie, Theodore Hershberg, and George Alter, "Immigrants and Industry: The Philadelphia Experience, 1850–1880," in *Immigrants in Industrial America, 1850–1920,* ed. Richard L. Ehrlich (Charlottesville, Va., 1977), 130–35; Lindstrom, review of "Special Issue on Capitalism." An indeterminate number of "debased" journeymen also became employers and supervisors of sweated labor.

118. Sokoloff and Villaflor, "Market for Manufacturing Workers," 30–31; Goldin and Margo, "Wages, Prices, and Labor Markets," 69. As discussed in the Introduction, Robert William Fogel has notably challenged the more roseate conclusions that other economic historians have drawn from indexes of real daily wages; see also Margo, *Wages,* 4, 144.

119. Green, *Artisans to Paupers,* 68–71.

120. Karl Marx, *The Economic and Philosophic Manuscripts of 1844,* ed. Dirk J. Struik, trans. Martin Milligan (New York, 1964), 117–18; George Catephores, "Marxist Alienation: A Clarification," *Oxford Economic Papers* 24 (July 1972): 133 n. But see also chapter 4's discussion of George Henry Evans.

121. Philadelphia's House of Refuge was founded in 1828 by Quakers who disapproved of the city's practice of incarcerating juvenile vagrants with adult criminals in prisons (Clement, *Welfare and the Poor,* 123–24; Negley K. Teeters, "The Early Days of the Philadelphia House of Refuge," *Pennsylvania History* 27 [April 1960]: 165–87; Meranze, *Laboratories of Virtue,* 254, 279–92).

122. "House of Refuge," *Mechanics' Free Press,* Oct. 18, 1828.

123. Clement, *Welfare and the Poor,* 124.

124. Ibid., 123–24; Rothman, *Discovery of the Asylum,* 261.

125. Ava Baron, "An 'Other' Side of Gender Antagonism at Work: Men, Boys, and the Remasculinization of Printers' Work, 1830–1920," in *Work Engendered: Toward a New History of American Labor,* ed. Baron (Ithaca, N.Y., 1990), 47–69; Joseph F. Kett, *Rites of Passage: Adolescence in America, 1790 to the Present* (New York, 1977), 146–49. It also remains possible that Simon was one of the larger and more "respectable" manufacturers whom he characterized in his piece as similarly opposed to the Refuge's intended labor policies.

126. Christine Stansell notes that in New York City journeymen belonging to the cordwainer and other trades with a "strong tradition of family-based production" and ones in which "a rigid sexual division of labor protected men from female competition" tended to be more supportive of wage-earning women's presence and own organizational efforts in those trades (Stansell, *City of Women,* 142).

127. Here the language of domesticity that skilled workers shared with capitalists could obscure different values and ideological objectives. Eric Lott observes that "radical workingmen's masculinist opposition to women's labor outside the home resisted rather than capitulated to bourgeois norms [of respectability], since workers thought the very necessity of female wage work was evidence of the class oppression they protested" (Lott, *Love*

and Theft: Blackface Minstrelsy and the American Working Class [New York, 1993], 196; Stansell, *City of Women,* 138–39). Simon's diatribe has interesting particularities. Prominent among the groups he cited as most immediately threatened by undercutting from the unskilled Refuge "vagrants" were "virtuous" "young girls" who currently earned $3 a week in trades, much of which went to the support of "aged parents." Simon exhibited no antagonism to such employment and evidently did not regard these particular female workers as constituting a dishonorable threat to the livelihood of Philadelphia's skilled male mechanics. But Simon denounced the threat posed by the Refuge to these independent female laborers as only "the first step to set in operation an enemy to our mechanics," and here he did exemplify that "manly" mentality of the period which prioritized the protection of skilled male artisan labor.

128. Walter Hugins, *Jacksonian Democracy and the Working Class* (Stanford, Calif., 1960), 155–61; for interpretations of skilled artisans' nativism, see Michael Feldberg, *The Philadelphia Riots of 1844: A Study of Ethnic Conflict* (Westport, Conn., 1984), 41–77.

129. For the continuing protests of Philadelphia mechanics against labor competition emanating from the House of Refuge and for the assurances from the institution's directors in 1830 that they were indenturing the boys to rural masters to "obviate the evil of competition," see Dennis Clark, "Babes in Bondage: Indentured Irish Children in Philadelphia in the Nineteenth Century," *Pennsylvania Magazine of History and Biography* 101 (Oct. 1977): 480–81. The House of Refuge's female inmates appear from the first to have been almost exclusively bound out as domestic servants (Meranze, *Laboratories of Virtue,* 283).

130. Voss, *American Exceptionalism,* 46–52; Cynthia S. Shelton, *The Mills of Manayunk: Industrialization and Social Conflict in the Philadelphia Region, 1787–1837* (Baltimore, 1986), 126.

131. This is a variation of one of the standard American exceptionalist arguments that the ethnic divisions encouraged by continuing immigration have made it particularly difficult to unionize and otherwise unite the American workforce. Historians also have noted, however, that the growth of the major antebellum umbrella labor organization, the National Trades' Union (NTU), to a peak membership of 300,000 by 1836 (between one-fifth and one-third of all urban workers) reflected a broadening of the labor movement to include some of the unskilled elements previously scorned and excluded. Kim Voss observes that "'half-trained,' sweated, and immigrant journeymen were welcomed in some trades as journeymen became more radicalized in the course of the movement." Yet despite this broadening solidarity, Voss concludes, the NTU's "inclusiveness did not generally extend too far beyond the ranks of the skilled" (Voss, *American Exceptionalism,* 30).

132. Jacques Rancière, "The Myth of the Artisan: Critical Reflections on a Category of Social History," in *Work in France: Representations, Meaning, Organization, and Practice,* ed. Steven Laurence Kaplan and Cynthia J. Koepp (Ithaca, N.Y., 1986), 329.

133. As earlier suggested, skilled workingmen had little desire to make working-class wives and other females more industrious in the sense of being economically self-supporting and independent. Their overriding vision was that of a working-class home sustained by men's wages and women's domestic activities.

134. The conviction that the putatively unrespectable components of the laboring population should be induced to be industrious was significantly residual, bearing a preindustrial, and even a precapitalist, history, though Simon and others, it should be equally

emphasized, were affirming the validity of this notion within a nineteenth-century early industrial-capitalist context (Joel Feinberg, "Economic Justice," in *Ethics in Perspective,* ed. Karsten J. Struhl and Paula Rothenberg Struhl [New York, 1975], 420–29).

135. For the workingmen's movement as an early advocate of welfare rights, see Elizabeth Bussiere, *(Dis)Entitling the Poor: The Warren Court, Welfare Rights, and the American Political Tradition* (University Park, Pa., 1997), 24–46.

136. Evans to Gerrit Smith, *Working Man's Advocate,* July 6, 1844; Walsh's editorial on "Moses G. Leonard and His Prison and Poor-House Project of Preying upon the Working Classes," in his New York newspaper, *Subterranean,* Dec. 19, 1846.

137. "Moses G. Leonard."

138. Wilentz, *Chants Democratic,* 327–35; Ignatiev, *How the Irish,* 77–79.

139. However, economic depression and adverse economic changes also induced skilled workingmen to join communitarian enterprises (Carl J. Guarneri, *The Utopian Alternative: Fourierism in Nineteenth-Century America* [Ithaca, N.Y., 1991], 6–67).

140. Richard Ashcraft, "Liberal Political Theory and Working-Class Radicalism in Nineteenth-Century England," *Political Theory* 21 (May 1993): 249–72; Bronstein, *Land Reform.*

141. Thus here as elsewhere I dissent from the "entrepreneurial" view that the literature of the Working Men's parties and the trade unions of the 1820s and 1830s added up to nothing more than the desire to democratize commercial and early industrial capitalism through the removal of "law-created privilege." This literature's expressed aversion to labor commodification and its accompanying articulation of the anticapitalist labor theory of value, while neither consistently nor unequivocally maintained, suggest that the mechanic members of New York City's Working Men's Party, along with other skilled artisans, were animated by more than the "desire for equal opportunity to become capitalists themselves" (Hugins, *Jacksonian Democracy,* 220, 222; more recent statements of the entrepreneurial position include Gienapp, "Myth of Class," 252, and "Ahistorical History," 277–81; Diggins, "Comrades," 626–28; Gronowicz, *Race and Class Politics,* 49–50).

142. Haskell, "Convention," 206.

143. Here, for example, I find unpersuasive Gertrude Himmelfarb's criticisms of the "social control" thesis as applied to Victorian England's working classes (*De-Moralization,* 22–33). Closer to my own view is Robert Gray, *The Labour Aristocracy in Victorian Edinburgh* (Oxford, Eng., 1976), 1–6; see also note 20 for my comments on Joel Schwartz, *Fighting Poverty with Virtue;* and chap. 4, 116–17.

144. In contrast to my own formulation here for the United States, Abercrombie and his coauthors characterize internal divisions within the British working classes as a completely alternative and a more credible explanation for mid-Victorian stability in Britain than any possible embourgeoisement of the nation's labor aristocracy (Nicholas Abercrombie, Stephen Hill, and Bryan S. Turner, *The Dominant Ideology Thesis* [London, 1980], 124).

145. Raymond Williams, *Marxism and Literature* (Oxford, Eng., 1977), 114. For other elements within artisans' (and other workers') producer ideology that "pointed toward accommodation [with the dominant culture] as well as resistance," see T. Jackson Lears, "The Concept of Cultural Hegemony: Problems and Possibilities," *American Historical Review* 90 (June 1985): 575–76; for a parallel insistence that Antonio Gramsci "located the

workings of ideological hegemony" in the "confusion and frustration" of the "subordinate population" rather than in the "absolute domination" of its thought, see Jonathon Glassman, *Feasts and Riot: Revelry, Rebellion, and Popular Consciousness on the Swahili Coast, 1856–1888* (Portsmouth, N.H., 1995), 18–19.

146. James A. Geschwender, "Race, Ethnicity, and Class," in *Recapturing Marxism: An Appraisal of Recent Trends in Sociological Theory,* ed. Rhonda F. Levine and Jerry Lembcke (New York, 1987), 145. Capitalists experienced their own competing pressures with respect to the barriers between more expensive and cheaper labor created by labor-market segmentation. On the one hand, the more immediate, profit-maximizing interests of craft entrepreneurs and other antebellum employers induced them to disregard such barriers and utilize cheaper labor sources, even to the point of directly replacing skilled journeymen in their enterprises with "half-trained" juveniles or immigrants. Yet the interests of capitalists as a class, in the antebellum as in other periods, commonly lay in observing certain forms of labor-market segmentation—most notably racially based ones that divided and weakened the working class as a whole even as they also conformed to the prejudices of dominant workers.

147. Earl Lewis, "To Turn as on a Pivot: Writing African Americans into a History of Overlapping Diasporas," *American Historical Review* 100 (June 1995): 784; Ignatiev, *How the Irish.*

148. "The same class of vagabonds who mob abolitionists, would as readily mob . . . the aristocracy could they do it with the same impunity" (an 1838 article from Philadelphia's *Colored American,* quoted in Lott, *Love and Theft,* 263).

149. Robin D. G. Kelley, "An Archaeology of Resistance," *American Quarterly* 44 (June 1992): 292–98; Noel Ignatiev, "The Paradox of the White Worker: Studies in Race Formation," *Labour/Le Travail* 30 (Fall 1992): 233–40.

150. Suggestive of this complexity was the frequency of intermarriage among African-American males and Irish women who resided in one of New York City's poorest areas (Graham Hodges, *Slavery, Freedom, and Culture among Early American Workers* [Armonk, N.Y., 1998], 122–50).

151. For acknowledgment, at least with respect to gender, of the limitations of existing working-class whiteness scholarship, see David Roediger, "What If Labor Were Not White and Male? Recentering Working-Class History and Reconstructing Debate on the Unions and Race," *International Labor and Working-Class History,* no. 51 (Spring 1997): 79; Roediger, "The Pursuit of Whiteness: Property, Terror, and Expansion, 1790–1860," *Journal of the Early Republic* 19 (Winter 1999): 588.

152. Benjamin B. Ringer and Elinor R. Lawless, *Race-Ethnicity and Society* (New York, 1989), 27. Peter Pringle, a New York City African American who had been "a waiter, hostler, and boot-black," noted at midcentury that "the mass of us are menials . . . because we choose rather to follow menial occupations than to contend with negro-hating apprentices and journeymen, in shops, or to contend with the negro-hating indisposition to give work to a black mechanic" ("The Way It Is Exactly," *Frederick Douglass' Paper,* April 22, 1853, quoted in Leslie Maria Harris, "Creating the African-American Working Class: Black and White Workers, Abolitionists and Reformers in New York City, 1785–1863" [Ph.D. diss., Stanford Univ., 1994], 217).

153. George M. Fredrickson, *Black Liberation: A Comparative History of Black Ideologies in*

the United States and South Africa (New York, 1995), 27; see also Charles W. Mills, *The Racial Contract* (Ithaca, N.Y., 1997), 137–38.

154. See, for example, Roediger, *Wages of Whiteness,* 26, 67, 104.

155. In view of the objectively limited foundation for such fears, and extending the scapegoat thesis noted in the text, one scholar has characterized "the myth of black competition" as "a cover story" for northern artisans' and other white workers' "precipitous descent in the class structure" (Eric Lott, "'The Seeming Counterfeit': Racial Politics and Early Blackface Minstrelsy," *American Quarterly* 43 [June 1991]: 241–42). Lott does not distinguish here between the artisans who did experience skill dilution and proletarianization and the common laborers (notably many of the famine Irish) whose experience in the United States was more problematically one of such class decline; see also Allen, *Invention of the White Race,* 194.

156. W. J. Rorabaugh, *The Craft Apprentice: From Franklin to the Machine Age in America* (New York, 1986), 160–85; Mark Voss-Hubbard, "The Amesbury-Salisbury Strike and the Social Origins of Political Nativism in Antebellum Massachusetts," *Journal of Social History* 29 (Spring 1996): 565–90; Bruce Levine, "Conservatism, Nativism, and Slavery: Thomas R. Whitney and the Origins of the Know-Nothing Party," *Journal of American History* 88 (Sept. 2001): 474–75. If only because of the preexisting presence of many native blacks—both some skilled, predominantly free black artisans and a mass of slaves employed in menial labor—the influx of Irish and other immigrants into southern cities introduced its own dynamics of economic competition. This also might encompass rivalry with southern-born white workers; for differing patterns, see Tommy L. Bogger, *Free Blacks in Norfolk, Virginia, 1790–1860: The Darker Side of Freedom* (Charlottesville, Va., 1997), 53, 63–84; Christopher L. Tomlins, "In Nat Turner's Shadow: Reflections on the Norfolk Dry Dock Affair of 1830–1831," *Labor History* 33 (Fall 1992): 494–518; Michele Gillespie, *Free Labor in an Unfree World: White Artisans in Slaveholding Georgia, 1789–1860* (Athens, Ga., 2000), 157–71; Christopher Silver, "A New Look at Old South Urbanization: The Irish Worker in Charleston, South Carolina, 1840–60," *South Atlantic Urban Studies* 3 (1974): 141–72; Randall M. Miller, "The Enemy Within: Some Effects of Foreign Immigrants on Antebellum Southern Cities," *Southern Studies* 24 (Spring 1985): 30–53; Christopher Phillips, *Freedom's Port: The African American Community of Baltimore, 1790–1860* (Urbana, Ill., 1997), 195–202.

157. For the "increasing fragmentation and hierarchical ordering of distinct white *races*" in mid-nineteenth-century American culture, see Jacobson, *Whiteness of a Different Color,* 41; see also Dale T. Knobel, *Paddy and the Republic: Ethnicity and Nativity in Antebellum America* (Middletown, Conn., 1986), 165–82; Eric Kaufmann, "American Exceptionalism Reconsidered: Anglo-Saxon Ethnogenesis in the 'Universal' Nation, 1776–1850," *Journal of American Studies* 33 (Dec. 1999): 437–57.

158. Similarly, one might ask how much their racial self-definition as white entered into male workers' conceptualizations of female waged laborers as naturally weak and servile. Did male workers perceive such women to be in some basic sense nonwhite? Gregory L. Kaster does not draw this conclusion, but it would seem to be a possible implication of his claim that the discourse of "organized white male workers . . . equated manliness and whiteness." Kaster does provocatively argue that for such workers whiteness itself was "constructed out of profound gender as well as racial anxieties and the interplay between

them" (Kaster, "Labour's True Man: Organized Workingmen and the Language of Manliness in the USA, 1827–1877," *Gender and History* 13 [April 2001]: 45).

159. For similar criticism of the whiteness–labor history scholarship, see Eric Arnesen, "Up from Exclusion: Black and White Workers, Race, and the State of Labor History," *Reviews in American History* 26 (March 1998): 164; a forum involving Arnesen and other scholars, entitled "Whiteness and the Historians' Imagination" and forthcoming in *International Labor and Working-Class History*, no. 60 (Fall 2001), promises to advance the debate; see also Ava Baron, "On Looking at Men: Masculinity and the Making of a Gendered Working-Class History," in *Feminists Revise History*, ed. Ann-Louise Shapiro (New Brunswick, N.J., 1994), 155–57; A. T. Lane, *Solidarity or Survival? American Labor and European Immigrants, 1830–1924* (New York, 1987), 15–32. The negative reference groups referred to in the text bore their own identity-shaping animosities, apart from Irish immigrants' well-known negrophobia; see Jay Rubin, "Black Nativism: The European Immigrant in Negro Thought, 1830–1860," *Phylon* 39 (Fall 1978): 193–202; and, for the antagonisms of white working-class females in the garment and other industries to competition from cheap immigrant labor, see Jean Gould Hales, "'Co-Laborers in the Cause': Women in the Ante-Bellum Nativist Movement," *Civil War History* 25 (June 1979): 120–23.

160. For the deeply rooted nature of nineteenth-century artisans' notions of the exclusivity of their skills—notions in which all the major categories of biology (gender, age, race/ethnicity) figured—see Ben Maddison, "Labour Commodification and Skilled Selves in Late-Nineteenth-Century Australia," *International Review of Social History* 43 (Aug. 1998): 265–86. With reference to female wage labor, Sally Alexander notes, "Whereas for men the threat of [such] cheap labor means *loss* of employment, status, and skill, to women workers [themselves] their cheapness represents *lack* of independence, status, and skill" (Alexander, "Women, Class, and Sexual Differences in the 1830s and 1840s: Some Reflections on the Writing of a Feminist History," in *Culture/Power/History*, ed. Nicholas B. Dirks, Geoff Eley, and Sherry B. Ortner [Princeton, N.J., 1994], 292). I include the adjective *ostensible* to denote that it was no more these groups' objective skill deficiencies than it was their past disassociation from skilled crafts, together with their continued conceptualization as low-status (based largely on the physiological differences underscored by Maddison and others), that stimulated antebellum artisans' continued disdain.

3. "Buy Cheap, Sell Dear"

1. Greeley, *Hints toward Reforms, in Letters, Addresses, and Other Writings* (1850; 2d ed., New York, 1853), 364–65. Pierre Vergniaud was a French lawyer and leader of the Girondists, guillotined in 1793; Lajos Kossuth was a Hungarian patriot prominent in the "Year of Revolutions" (1848).

2. Ibid., 7, 8, 40, 272–91, 366.

3. Henry E. Hoagland, "Humanitarianism (1840–1860)," in John R. Commons et al., *History of Labour in the United States* (New York, 1921–35), 1:601–7.

4. "Capital and Labor," *Tribune*, Jan. 24, 1855.

5. For Greeley's criticisms of the wage cutting engaged in by Boston's master tailors, see "Tailors' Strike in Boston, Mass.—The German Tailors of New-York," ibid., Aug. 21, 1849. Greeley's evenhandedness formed the basis of the hostile interpretation of him as

effectively antilabor, "a 'safe' radical" in the words of Arthur M. Schlesinger Jr. (*Age of Jackson*, 296); see also Glyndon Van Deusen, *Horace Greeley, Nineteenth-Century Crusader* (1953; rept. New York, 1964); Norman Ware, *The Industrial Worker, 1840–1860: The Reaction of American Industrial Society to the Advance of the Industrial Revolution* (1924; rept. Chicago, 1964), 21–22. More recent studies generally have presented more sympathetic interpretations of Greeley's positions on capital-labor conflict.

6. Bray quoted in Thompson, *People's Science*, 95. I am here characterizing the thrust of Greeley's antebellum writings on political economy and American society. Just as his clash with Democratic "demagogues" like Orestes Brownson induced some of Greeley's most Whiggish defenses of social and economic conditions (as in his intermittent praise of the Waltham-Lowell factory system for providing employment opportunities that elevated American women), so he elsewhere, above all in his exchanges with more conservative commentators, himself ventured into the labor radical-exploitation territory favored by a Brownson or John Bray. Greeley also grew more socially conservative during the 1850s and thereafter.

7. "Capital and Labor," *Tribune*, Aug. 21, 1849; see also "Strikes — First Principles," ibid., April 13, 1853.

8. The premium that Greeley attached to this differential-reward system prompted his expression of distaste for the radical versions of the labor theory of value favored by Bray and others — despite his conviction that the market and prevailing status values over-esteemed the contributions of particular occupations (lawyers and other professionals) while undervaluing those of others (freehold farmers) (Glickstein, *Concepts of Free Labor*, 222; Iver Bernstein, *The New York City Draft Riots: Their Significance for American Society and Politics in the Age of the Civil War* [New York, 1990], 169–72).

9. Appleby, "Vexed Story."

10. Lears, "Cultural Hegemony," 569.

11. Donald N. McCloskey, *The Rhetoric of Economics* (Madison, Wis., 1985), 25. Resonating with my argument is Paul Krause's discussion of the "paradoxes of American labor" for a later period (*The Battle for Homestead, 1880–1892: Politics, Culture, and Steel* [Pittsburgh, 1992], 252–66); see also Rex Burns, *Success in America: The Yeoman Dream and the Industrial Revolution* (Amherst, Mass., 1976), 91–123; William R. Sutton, *Journeymen for Jesus: Evangelicals and Artisans Confront Capitalism in Jacksonian Baltimore* (University Park, Pa., 1998), 307–8.

12. For similar remarks by Greeley, see "The Wrongs of Labor — the Remedy," *Tribune*, Aug. 20, 1849. Greeley moderated his critical characterization in the revised edition of *Hints*, referring approvingly to the fact that since the publication of the original essay, Pittsburgh ironworkers were showing signs of awakening to the value of "practical Association" (366 n). Throughout the free states a number of developments, including the influx of German artisan emigrants carrying a heritage of democratic socialism, for a time in the 1850s did stimulate increased working-class receptivity to labor cooperatives and other alternatives to capitalist forms of enterprise; see Bruce Levine, *The Migration of Ideology and the Contested Meaning of Freedom: German-Americans in the Mid-Nineteenth Century* (Washington, D. C., 1992), 11–13.

13. Hobsbawm, *Labouring Men*, 344–45; Gary J. Kornblith, "The Artisanal Response to Capitalist Transformation," *Journal of the Early Republic* 10 (Fall 1990): 315–21; Gerald N.

Grob, *Workers and Utopia: A Study of Ideological Conflict in the American Labor Movement, 1865–1900* (Evanston, Ill., 1961), 8–10; Ware, *Industrial Worker,* 227.

14. Diggins, "Comrades," 626–28; Diggins, *On Hallowed Ground: Abraham Lincoln and the Foundation of American History* (New Haven, 2000), 222–30; quote from journeymen printers at a mass organizing meeting, in Address to National Convention of Journeymen Printers, 1850, in Baron, "An 'Other' Side," 52.

15. Glickstein, *Concepts of Free Labor,* 492.

16. James C. Scott, *Domination and the Arts of Resistance: Hidden Transcripts* (New Haven, 1990).

17. Scott, *Domination,* 90, 91. Timur Kuran criticizes Scott's thesis on Gramscian grounds: "Scott confuses resistance to an oppressor with [complete] cognitive autonomy from the oppressor's ideology" (Kuran, *Private Truths, Public Lies: The Social Consequences of Preference Falsification* [Cambridge, Mass., 1995], 175); for a more detailed critique which similarly argues that Scott's insistence on the absence of Gramscian hegemony reflects an excessively narrow definition of that hegemony, see Timothy Mitchell, "Everyday Metaphors of Power," *Theory and Society* 19 (Oct. 1990): 545–77; see also Tom Brass, *Towards a Comparative Political Economy of Unfree Labour: Case Studies and Debates* (London, 1999), 257–58, 272. With primary reference to underdeveloped societies, Amartya Sen extends the notion of economically induced lassitude and suggests a scenario quite different from Scott's hidden transcript: "In situations of persistent adversity and deprivation, the victims do not go on grieving and grumbling all the time, and may even lack the motivation to desire a radical change of circumstances" (Sen, *Inequality Reexamined* [Cambridge, Mass., 1992], 6).

18. Scott, *Domination,* 92.

19. Hoare and Smith, *Prison Notebooks of Antonio Gramsci,* 206–78, 333; John Gaventa, *Power and Powerlessness: Quiescence and Rebellion in an Appalachian Valley* (Urbana, Ill., 1980), 1–32; Joseph V. Femia, *Gramsci's Political Thought: Hegemony, Consciousness, and the Revolutionary Process* (Oxford, Eng., 1981), 33–50; Lears, "Cultural Hegemony," 570.

20. Charles W. Mills, *Blackness Visible: Essays on Philosophy and Race* (Ithaca, N.Y., 1998), 26. However, Mills also endorses what he characterizes as Marx's own view: that notwithstanding ideological hegemony from above, membership in the working classes and the material constraints that this entails do confer an "epistemic advantage" in seeing through the "illusions" of the capitalist system (30–31).

21. Adam Przeworski, *Capitalism and Social Democracy* (Cambridge, 1994), 136–48.

22. Eagleton, *Ideology,* 35–36; Abercrombie et al., *Dominant Ideology Thesis,* 11–15; for a defense of Gramsci in response to Abercrombie et al., see Goran Therborn, "The New Questions of Subjectivity," in *Mapping Ideology,* ed. Slavoj Zizek. (London, 1995), 172–76.

23. Glassman, *Feasts and Riot,* 17–18.

24. In her elaborations of an early nineteenth-century popular culture of enterprise (extending into the antebellum period), Appleby is particularly insistent, contra Gramscian and other Marxist perspectives, that ordinary Americans' normative attachment to market-capitalist arrangements was as well placed as it was pervasive — i.e., they instinctively recognized that these best suited their interests.

25. Nevertheless, with respect to actual experiences, my own position remains that the narratives of Appleby and like-minded historians understate the casualties of American

market-capitalist developments—e.g., the number of wage-earning and other ordinary white males (not to speak of laboring women and blacks) who might well have experienced lesser exploitation and derived greater benefits under some form of alternative economic arrangements.

26. In addition to Diggins, "Comrades," 626–28, and Appleby, "Vexed Story," see Gienapp, "Myth of Class," 232–59, and "Ahistorical History," 277–81. In his exchange here with Gienapp over Charles Sellers, *The Market Revolution: Jacksonian America, 1815–1846* (New York, 1991), Iver Bernstein accepts Gienapp's characterization of many Americans as "invincibly optimistic" about the expanding antebellum American economy, but he remains more attuned to attitudes that fell short of a wholehearted and normative commitment to market-capitalist, acquisitive individualism (Bernstein, "Moral Perspective and the Cycles of Jacksonian History," 260–71). The short quotes in the text are from McClelland, *American Search*, 38–43, another discussion that too readily infers the many's positive endorsement of market-capitalist arrangements from the absence on their part of overt radical objections to those arrangements. Although he is primarily addressing a later period, Howard Kimeldorf's comments are to the point: "How do we know that American workers were ever 'so conservative' or, for that matter, enamored of capitalism and utterly lacking in class consciousness? Most such claims rest on little more than inference" (Kimeldorf, *Battling for American Labor: Wobblies, Craft Workers, and the Making of the Union Movement* [Berkeley, Calif., 1999], 8); see also Michael Merrill, "Putting 'Capitalism' in Its Place: A Review of Recent Literature," *William and Mary Quarterly*, 3d ser., 52 (April 1995): 324–26; Bruce Laurie, "'We Are Not Afraid to Work': Master Mechanics and the Market Revolution in the Antebellum North," in Bledstein and Johnston, *The Middling Sorts*, 52; Seth Rockman, "The Unfree Origins of American Capitalism," paper presented at the Library Company of Philadelphia Program in Early American Economy and Society Inaugural Conference, "The Past and Future of Early American Economic History: Needs and Opportunities," April 20–21, 2001, on Library Company of Philadelphia-PEAES website; and Michael Mann, "The Social Cohesion of Liberal Democracy," *American Sociological Review* 35 (June 1970): 423–39.

27. Lester C. Thurow, *Generating Inequality: Mechanisms of Distribution in the U.S. Economy* (New York, 1976), 40–41. For a somewhat different perspective, stressing the "potentially inconsistent" nature of the beliefs of modern-day ordinary Americans regarding American economic opportunity and inequality, see Kluegel and Smith, *Beliefs about Inequality*, 11–12.

28. This is also to recognize that even the strongly normative attachment to market-capitalist arrangements of individuals who most conspicuously benefited from those arrangements was not completely free of ambivalences and self-doubts; see Tamara Plakins Thornton, *Cultivating Gentlemen: The Meaning of Country Life among the Boston Elite, 1785–1860* (New Haven, 1991).

29. But see Sean Wilentz, "The Rise of the American Working Class, 1776–1877," in *Perspectives on American Labor History: The Problem of Synthesis,* ed. J. Carroll Moody and Alice Kessler-Harris (DeKalb, Ill., 1989), 115.

30. This is not to suggest that radical anticapitalist alternatives altogether failed to be put forward; for the 1850s, see note 12; for the post–Civil War period, see Messer-Kruse, *Yankee International.*

31. Allen Buchanan also refers to the "competitive egoistic barriers" among the prole-tariat that impede them from engaging in concerted anticapitalist revolutionary action, although his particular concern is one that is heavily debated among Marxist scholars: the free-rider problem and the failure of Marx's theory of revolutionary motivation to address it adequately (Buchanan, "Revolutionary Motivation and Rationality," in *Marx, Justice, and History,* ed. Marshall Cohen, Thomas Nagel, and Thomas Scanlon [Princeton, N.J., 1980], 272–78).

32. Michael Walzer, *Spheres of Justice: A Defense of Pluralism and Equality* (New York, 1983), 102; Margaret Jane Radin, *Contested Commodities* (Cambridge, Mass., 1996), 48. In fact, Gree-ley elsewhere applied the same double standard to some of these most desperate female workers themselves. Such was the ubiquity in antebellum society of the self-aggrandizing "Buy cheap, sell dear" imperative that "the overworked or underpaid" female milliner or bookfolder herself invariably followed it in her purchase of goods and services. "She never thinks of asking whether the manufacturer or merchant can really afford to sell his fab-rics she buys at the price she pays for them." And "if she buys, as a general rule, wher-ever she can cheapest," Greeley rhetorically asked, "how can she expect to sell otherwise?" Here, as in his observations on the striking iron puddlers, Greeley looked to a "radical social reconstruction" that would "place the complex relations of human beings on a different basis—the basis of Absolute Right." While expressing faith that such recon-struction "ultimately" will be accomplished, Greeley (with his days as an enthusiast of Association now well behind him) added that the means "we do not begin to compre-hend." He concluded this piece by embracing (as Henry Ward Beecher and many of his contemporaries were doing) a more modest and short-term solution to the problem of subsistence female wages, although one that faced considerable obstacles of its own: put-ting supply-and-demand forces to work in these workingwomen's favor by allowing them to "compete freely in employments now monopolized by men" (untitled editorial, *Tribune,* July 10, 1858).

33. John Majewski, "A Revolution Too Many?"—review of Stokes and Stephen Con-way, *Market Revolution,* in *Journal of Economic History* 57 (June 1997): 476–80; Winifred Barr Rothenberg, *From Market-Places to a Market Economy: The Transformation of Rural Massachu-setts, 1750–1850* (Chicago, 1993); Edward J. Perkins, "The Entrepreneurial Spirit in Colonial America: The Foundations of Modern Business History," *Business History Review* 63 (Spring 1989): 160–86; Richard Lyman Bushman, "Markets and Composite Farms in Early America," *William and Mary Quarterly,* 3d ser., 55 (July 1998): 351–74; Deborah A. Rosen, *Courts and Commerce: The Formative Period of American Legal Practice* (Columbus, Ohio, 1997), 74–92.

34. E. J. Hobsbawm, *Industry and Empire: An Economic History of Britain since 1750* (New York, 1968), 195; P. S. Atiyah, *The Rise and Fall of Freedom of Contract* (Oxford, Eng., 1979), 221–34.

35. Atiyah, *Freedom of Contract,* 232. Above all, the Tory-romantic and allied critiques tar-geted what some scholars have characterized as the theological utilitarianism of Thomas Malthus's *Essay on the Principle of Population* (1798) and the providential sanction that it pro-vided free-market processes. This the critiques of the time interpreted as singularly wrong-headed and callous—and in fact irreligious—for its attacks on the moral failings of the English poor, their right to procreate, and their right to poor relief. Yet Malthus blunted

some of his harshest and grimmest assessments in subsequent editions of the *Essay,* and Southey and other anti-Malthusians themselves became highly critical of the old Poor Law. Donald Winch comments on the ironies involved in Malthus, above all others, being held responsible by both contemporary critics and some later scholars for the "de-moralisation" of political economy, the process by which political economy was "supposedly divorced from moral considerations and made subordinate to impersonal economic forces" (Winch, *Riches and Poverty,* 5–6, 243–44, 288–322).

36. Richard Grassby, *The Business Community of Seventeenth-Century England* (Cambridge, 1995), 51. The differences among these perspectives were as important as their commonalities. Thus a Tory distaste for the cash nexus and its expression in rapid commercial and industrial development often reflected less an animus against capitalism per se than a desire to reinvigorate England's aristocratic ways. And in calling for the reassertion of old values, such as traditional Christianity or feudalism, as an antidote to atomizing economic developments and their ratification by political economy, upper-middle-class paternalistic perspectives hardly shared the plebeian, working-class attachment to the importance of trade unions. For the amorphous rubric of "paternalism" within which some of the anticommercial perspectives fell, see David Roberts, *Paternalism in Early Victorian England* (London, 1979); Kim Lawes, *Paternalism and Politics: The Revival of Paternalism in Early Nineteenth-Century Britain* (New York, 2000), 96.

37. On Macaulay as a self-conscious spokesman for England's middle-class Whigs, see John Clive, *Macaulay, the Shaping of the Historian* (New York, 1973), 496–97; for Macaulay's ridicule of the jeremiads launched by Southey and others against Victorian economic development and orthodox political economy, see Humphrey House, *All in Due Time* (London, 1955), 96–97. Modern neoclassical economists have invoked Macaulay in their own dismissals of criticisms of "a competitive economic system" (George J. Stigler, *The Economist as Preacher and Other Essays* [Chicago, 1982], 29).

38. Although he does not argue that larger English industrial employers, specifically, found the cash nexus morally repugnant, Patrick Joyce has emphasized (against Hobsbawm and other historians, and against the "Gradgrindian stereotype" created by Dickens) that these employers' "mental constructions" were as much distinguished by paternalist impulses toward their workers (and not simply for narrowly self-serving economic reasons) as they were marked by a bourgeois liberal individualist devotion to the cash nexus (Joyce, "Work," in *The Cambridge Social History of Britain, 1750–1950,* ed. F. M. L. Thompson [Cambridge, 1990], 2:168–69); see also, for diversity in English middle-class ideological outlooks, R. J. Morris, *Class, Sect, and Party: The Making of the British Middle Class, Leeds, 1820–1850* (Manchester, Eng., 1990), 318–25.

39. This central argument has been supported by many other historians who do not necessarily share the optimistic Hartwell-Ashton view of the Industrial Revolution; see, in addition to the previous note, John Seed, "Unitarianism, Political Economy, and the Antinomies of Liberal Culture in Manchester, 1830–50," *Social History* 7 (Jan. 1982): 24–25, where Seed observes that Carlyle's "social critique" of the cash nexus "simply gave a form to what was already common knowledge among the liberal intelligentsia in towns like Manchester: that market relations backed up by coercion were inadequate to maintain existing relations of production and had to be reinforced by cultural hegemony. . . . There were indeed Gradgrinds enough but liberal culture was stronger, more resilient and more diver-

sified than that"—it was forced to be through its confrontation with major social crises.

40. R. M. Hartwell, *The Industrial Revolution and Economic Growth* (London, 1971), 381–82; T. S. Ashton, *The Industrial Revolution, 1760–1830* (1948; rept. London, 1970), 92, 110–12. For another more complex picture of Victorian social ideologies, insisting on the existence of a range of frequently overlapping kinds of laissez-faire individualism and collectivism with a view toward refuting the "false" antithesis between the two drawn by Dicey (and others), see Harold Perkin, *The Structured Crowd: Essays in English Social History* (Sussex, Eng., 1981), 57–69; there is a large literature on the related debate over whether Tory-philanthropic, Whig political, or Benthamite reform impulses played the most basic role in the origins of the British welfare state.

41. "Legislation for the Working Classes," *Edinburgh Review* 83 (Jan. 1846): 86–92, rept. in *The Working Classes in the Victorian Age,* vol. 2, *Urban Conditions, 1839–1848.* Workingmen and other proponents of the factory acts were more impressed by the "slavery" that factory masters were able to impose on their operatives in the absence of such regulatory legislation—most conspicuously on more naturally vulnerable and "dependent" women and juvenile operatives, but also on adult male operatives. For the shifting emphases within the short-time movement's discourse of "factory slavery" as it achieved some of its earlier "patriarchal" goals for women and children, see Robert Gray, *The Factory Question and Industrial England, 1830–1860* (Cambridge, 1996), 21–47; see also Joseph Persky, "Wage Slavery," *History of Political Economy* 30 (Winter 1998): 627–51.

42. "Charities, Noxious and Beneficent," *Westminster Review,* n.s., 3:1 (1853): 64–65, rept. in *Poverty in the Victorian Age: Debates on the Issue from 19th Century Critical Journals,* vol. 3, *Charity, 1815–1870* (Hants, Eng., 1973); Geoffrey Finlayson, *Citizen, State, and Social Welfare in Britain, 1830–1990* (Oxford, Eng., 1990), 1–18, 90–93.

43. Atiyah, *Freedom of Contract,* 233.

44. Himmelfarb, *De-Moralization of Society,* 143–44, 254. The "humanizing" constraints imposed on what Himmelfarb characterizes as Britain's "industrial-capitalist-bourgeois revolution" may have derived chiefly from the persistent hegemony, both political and cultural, of its landed aristocracy, at least according to some historians. In his recent study of the evolving linguistic and political construction of the British middle class during this period, Dror Wahrman furthermore casts a skeptical eye on the "purportedly objective" underlying social foundations of that class altogether. Yet it is less clear that Wahrman denies the influence within early Victorian society of the commercialism and other values and behavioral traits that Robert Southey and others associated with the middle classes, because Wahrman also endorses the view that members of the dominant landed elite were themselves imbibing "strong allegedly 'bourgeois' drives" by the late eighteenth century (Wahrman, *Imagining the Middle Class: The Political Representation of Class in Britain, c. 1780–1840* [Cambridge, 1995], 376, 379). Poststructuralist engagements in the internal dynamics and self-referential qualities of language, and in the non-"documentary" character of "first-rate texts" especially, can illumine Marx's thought while exhibiting little interest in such positivist questions as whether Marx was more right than otherwise about the trajectory of social relationships and behavior under early industrial capitalism (Dominick LaCapra, *Rethinking Intellectual History: Texts, Contexts, and Language* [Ithaca, N.Y., 1983], 268–77, 325–46).

45. Louis Hartz, *The Liberal Tradition in America* (New York, 1955), 51–52; Wahrman, *Imagining,* 372–73.

46. "Democracy: The Pathfinder," *Tribune,* May 10, 1843; "Industrial Anarchy," ibid., May 18, 1843; "The Importance of a Christian Basis for the Science of Political Economy," ibid., March 2, 1844; Greeley, *Essays Designed to Elucidate the Science of Political Economy* (Boston, 1870), 24, 161–69. Scholars who characterize the early nineteenth-century attacks on the cash nexus as attacks on liberalism are therefore understating the ideological ferment and complexities of the period; they miss species of liberals like Greeley who joined conservatives (Carlyle) and radical socialists (Marx) in criticizing the cash nexus (Thomas A. Spragens Jr., "Communitarian Liberalism," in *New Communitarian Thinking: Persons, Virtue, Institutions, and Communities,* ed. Amitai Etzioni [Charlottesville, Va., 1995], 47). This is also to suggest that scholars remain hopelessly divided in their understandings of such constructs as liberalism, perhaps most of all for the early nineteenth-century United States. This is so even if historians generally agree that Whigs and Democrats offered broadly distinctive visions of the optimum nature and pace of American economic development. One recent survey of party ideology thus insists that Whiggery's "neo-mercantilist," "statist" agenda disqualified it as truly liberal, while the Democracy's "civic republican" impulses similarly disqualified it (John Gerring, *Party Ideologies in America, 1828–1996* [Cambridge, 1998], 118, 172); compare with the claim that "Democrats and Whigs were different kinds of liberals," in Major L. Wilson, "The 'Country' versus the 'Court': A Republican Consensus and Party Debate in the Bank War," *Journal of the Early Republic* 15 (Winter 1995): 643; see also, on the variants of the republican and liberal "traditions," Julie M. Walsh, *The Intellectual Origins of Mass Parties and Mass Schools in the Jacksonian Period* (New York, 1998), 1–41.

47. Novak, *People's Welfare,* ix, 7, 12–16, 95, 112.

48. Ibid., 22–23.

49. Morton J. Horwitz, *The Transformation of American Law, 1780–1860* (Cambridge, Mass., 1977), 161.

50. Novak, *People's Welfare,* 23; James T. Kloppenberg, "The Theory and Practice of American Legal History," *Harvard Law Review* 106 (April 1993): 1338–39.

51. Greeley himself would likely have been less resolutely "materialist" than Horwitz in accounting for the demise of "intrinsic value" in legal developments. As indicated earlier with regard to the market imperative, he refrained from assigning particular agency to capitalists or any other group of economic interests.

52. This was one implication of the earlier attacks on the "myth of laissez-faire" made by Louis Hartz and Oscar and Mary Handlin. In their so-called Commonwealth studies, as Novak suggests, the state was a liberal capitalist, promotional engine whose interventionism was strongly compatible with economic individualism and a self-aggrandizing imperative (*People's Welfare,* 85–86, 284); on similar compatibilities between state intervention and economic liberalism in nineteenth-century England (but with a more critical perspective than the Commonwealth studies), see Polanyi, *Great Transformation.*

53. Massachusetts, *Senate Documents* for 1868, no. 21, "Report of the Hon. Henry K. Oliver, Deputy State Constable, Specially Appointed to Enforce the Laws Regulating the Employment of Children in Manufacturing and Mechanical Establishments," 23. Mary Blewett identifies the factory agent and millowner as either Jefferson or Richard Borden (Blewett, *Constant Turmoil,* 38–39); for intensifying market-capitalist pressures and an atten-

dant "Devil take the hindmost" ethos brought to bear on another category of laboring people, see Way, *Common Labour*.

54. See Johnson, *A Shopkeepers' Millennium: Society and Revivals in Rochester, New York, 1815–1837* (New York, 1978), for the erosion of paternalistic work relationships that attended the decline of Rochester's small preindustrial shops, with their family-based structure.

55. Albert O. Hirschman similarly remarks, "The most plausible explanation for the eclipse of the *doux-commerce* thesis" (the pre-nineteenth-century thesis that an expanding capitalist market economy had beneficial effects on social relations) "is that it became a victim of the Industrial Revolution" (Hirschman, *Rival Views of Market Society and Other Recent Essays* [New York, 1986], 117).

56. The cultural salience of this self-maximizing competitive free-market ethos notwithstanding, there remained, as noted elsewhere, fundamental respects in which truly free competition and equality of opportunity were qualified, both ideologically and practically, in the antebellum United States.

57. Adrzej Walicki, *Marxism and the Leap to the Kingdom of Faith* (Stanford, Calif., 1995), 103–9. For, however, an interpretation emphasizing Simmel's more negative views of the depersonalizing effects of the "boundless market," see Viviana A. Zelizer, "Beyond the Polemics on the Market: Establishing a Theoretical and Empirical Agenda," *Sociological Forum* 3 (Fall 1988): 620–21.

58. On the growth of mutual-benefit and other voluntary associations during the early nineteenth century, see the essays by Mary P. Ryan and by Gerald Gamm and Robert D. Putnam in the *Journal of Interdisciplinary History* 29 (Spring 1999). Among the studies stressing gender differences, finding that rural farm wives were particularly resistant to market-individualist, self-maximizing values and pressures, see Nancy Grey Osterud, *Bonds of Community: The Lives of Farm Women in Nineteenth-Century New York* (Ithaca, N.Y., 1991), 222–27; for the argument that the antimarket attitudes of nineteenth-century American women (particularly middle-class women) were limited by their tendency to find domestic enrichment and personal expressiveness in expanding consumerism, see Lori Merish, *Sentimental Materialism: Gender, Commodity Culture, and Nineteenth-Century American Literature* (Durham, N.C., 2000), 134; see also Catherine E. Kelly, *In the New England Fashion: Reshaping Women's Lives in the Nineteenth Century* (Ithaca, N.Y., 1999), 62; Karen V. Hansen, *A Very Social Time: Crafting Community in Antebellum New England* (Berkeley, Calif., 1994), 10–32; for emphasis upon how antisocial market-capitalist pressures stimulated offsetting kinship and then wider community bonds within England's industrial laboring population, see Jane Humphries, "Class Struggle and the Persistence of the Working-Class Family," *Cambridge Journal of Economics* 1 (Sept. 1977): 241–58.

59. Mark Granovetter, "Economic Action and Social Structure: The Problem of Embeddedness," in *The Sociology of Economic Life,* ed. Granovetter and Richard Swedborg (Boulder, Colo., 1992), 53–81; Granovetter, "The Old and the New Economic Sociology: A History and an Agenda," in *Beyond the Marketplace: Rethinking Economy and Society,* ed. Roger Friedland and A. F. Robertson (New York, 1990), 89–112. Seemingly supportive of Granovetter's sociological position is historian John Majewski's argument that a spirit of "possessive communitarianism," grounded primarily in local kinship ties and constituting a

kind of middle-ground between antimarket communitarianism, on the one hand, and naked, market-oriented self-interest, on the other, governed economic transactions in many early nineteenth-century rural communities (Majewski, "Possessive Communitarianism and the Growth of Markets in Rural America, 1790–1840" [unpub. paper in my possession]); see also Thomas Bender, *Community and Social Change in America* (New Brunswick, N.J., 1979), 110–17; Robert E. Lane, *The Market Experience* (Cambridge, 1991), 217–19. As Granovetter notes in his second essay cited above (96), most economists (and some economic and other historians of the United States as well, he might have added) share his view that the transition from earlier to modern societies "did not much change the level of embeddedness"; where they differ from him is in their position that this level is insubstantial in both. Although Granovetter and other modern economic sociologists depart from Karl Polanyi's developmental perspective, their even greater argument remains with the "undersocialized" neoclassical economic view that such noneconomic motives as the search for approval, status, and power are "irrational" and incidental to more narrowly economic ones.

60. Haskell, "Capitalism," and Haskell, "Convention," 107–60, 200–259. Haskell does not posit that the emergent market-driven, contractual cognitive style was hostile to all or even most forms of human oppression that continued to exist throughout the nineteenth century. Indeed, he emphasizes that this cognitive style retained a much older formalist orientation that restricted its "widening of causal horizons"—that rendered it relatively insensitive to the substantive involuntariness of more circumstantially grounded forms of oppression (e.g., wage slavery as distinct from chattel slavery). In this particular sense his model does not contradict those (including myself) who would underscore the degree to which the capitalist market imperative generated and tolerated inequality and exploitation in the nineteenth century.

61. See, for example, Bertrand de Jouvenal, "The Treatment of Capitalism by Continental Intellectuals," in *Capitalism and the Historians,* ed. F. A. Hayek (Chicago, 1954), 100–101. However, such arguments are not confined to historians strongly identified with the "optimistic" school; see Hugh Cunningham's insistence that the emergence and spread of a new humane sensibility that viewed the British child laborer as "a victim and a slave . . . cannot be explained simply by the argument that the industrial revolution had intensified child labour" (Cunningham, *The Children of the Poor: Representations of Childhood since the Seventeenth Century* [Oxford, Eng., 1991], 51).

62. Here I am quoting, and partially dissenting from, Norman McCord's attack on the "lop-sided" criticisms that E. P. Thompson and other British Marxist historians directed against social relationships in early nineteenth-century industrial England (McCord, "The Poor Law and Philanthropy," in *The New Poor Law in the Nineteenth Century,* ed. Derek Fraser [London, 1976], 89, 96, 105–10); for essays similarly expressive of the "optimistic" view of the Industrial Revolution, see R. Hartwell et al., *The Long Debate on Poverty: Eight Essays on Industrialisation and "the Condition of England"* (Surrey, Eng., 1972).

63. For one study illustrating the decreasing success with which communal institutions in the mid-nineteenth century were able to restrain the economic individualism of an emergent rural bourgeoisie, see Susan E. Gray, *The Yankee West: Community Life on the Michigan Frontier* (Chapel Hill, N.C., 1996). Other scholars have stressed how, even as certain kinds of voluntary associations checked community instability and atomism, they were

yet most highly valued by members for their capitalist functionalism—for enhancing their individual opportunities for upward social mobility (Don Harrison Doyle, *The Social Order of a Frontier Community* [Urbana, Ill., 1978], 156–93). In *Bowling Alone: The Collapse and Revival of American Community* (New York, 2000), Robert Putnam only cursorily engages the question of a dialectical tension between the cash-nexus effects of early nineteenth-century market capitalism and the presence of voluntary associations and other forms of "social capital" and "civic engagement" (282).

4. Further Social Constructions of the Market Mechanism, Economic Justice, and Competitive Hierarchy

1. "Strikes. No. V," Boston *Pilot,* May 28, 1853; "Strikes. No. XIII," ibid., July 23, 1853. In at least some cases the *Pilot* was conceivably describing a relatively short-term attitudinal phenomenon. Workingmen's jealousy toward those who rose out of their ranks may have lessened over time as they adapted to their lack of comparable success by downscaling their occupational preferences; for "adaptive preference formation," see Jon Elster, *Sour Grapes: Studies in the Subversion of Rationality* (Cambridge, 1983), 109–24.

2. "Strikes. The Ten Hour System. No. IV," *Pilot,* May 21, 1853.

3. "Strikes. No. XIII," ibid., July 23, 1853. Although the *Pilot* harbored no affection for militant labor movements led by "demagogues," this editorial went on to make the argument that such upward mobility, far rarer in Old World societies like England, imposed a particular disadvantage on America's laboring classes in their confrontations with predatory capitalist interests: "It is certain that by the continued rise of these men, the ranks of workingmen lose an immense amount of talent, skill and determination which they cannot afford to lose." Here the *Pilot* anticipated Selig Perlman and other commentators who similarly identified the fluidity of the American class structure as one of American capitalism's major stabilizing forces.

4. I am not only referring here to the more obvious ways, as in the inheritance of uneven material resources, in which white males, including "poor" ones, did not in fact start out with equal chances to rise. The antebellum creed is also intellectually deficient by the more sophisticated and rigorous standards of "fair equality of opportunity" established by John Rawls and other modern philosophers of justice, by which not only intelligence and talent but individual preferences and effort (including the industry, sobriety, and other time-honored character virtues invoked by the *Pilot* and other antebellum commentators) themselves emerge as natural or at least as family-derived and socially determined endowments.

5. See also the untitled editorial in *Tribune,* June 17, 1856.

6. Social mobility also could encourage attitudinal phenomena other than either the egoistic jealousy of individuals left behind or the loss of fellow feeling by those who rose, although these other configurations might be no more conducive to the building of collective working-class consciousness. With respect to late nineteenth- and early twentieth-century industrial America, John Higham notes, "The immigrants tended to identify not with a downtrodden class but with exemplars of success among their own people" (Higham, *Send These to Me: Immigrants in Urban America* [New York, 1975], 24).

7. National Trades' Union, "Report of the Committee on Trades' Unions," Nov. 1836, in *A Documentary History of American Industrial Society,* ed. John R. Commons et al. (1910; rept. New York, 1958), 6:295; see also James Maginnis, of Lockport Protection, No. 1, "An Address Delivered before the Annual Convention of the State of New York and Protections 24 and 50, at Auburn," June 15, 1848, in *Mechanic's Advocate* (Albany), July 8, 1848; Greg Kaster, "'Not for a Class'? The 19th-Century American Labor Jeremiad," *Mid-America* 70 (Oct. 1988): 125–39.

8. "The Dignity of Labor," *Voice of Industry* (Lowell, Mass.), July 23, 1847.

9. The editor of the *Voice* was William F. Young. For the "at least implicitly anticapitalist" antagonism toward employers and other "idle rich" that Young shared with other New England workers and labor-reform activists in this period, see Jama Lazerow, *Religion and the Working Class in Antebellum America* (Washington, D.C., 1995), 177.

10. "Dignity of Labor"; see also L. A. Hine, "The Rich—the Poor," *Herald of Truth* 1 (Feb. 1847): 110, 121; Stephen Simpson, *The Working Man's Manual: A New Theory of Political Economy* (Philadelphia, 1831), 70.

11. "Under our present system . . . the landless laborer is completely at the mercy of the capitalist" ("The Condition of Labor," *Working Man's Advocate,* Oct. 4, 1845).

12. Conkin, *Prophets of Prosperity,* 256.

13. Freyer, *Producers versus Capitalists.*

14. Gary J. Kornblith, "Self-Made Men: The Development of Middling-Class Consciousness in New England," *Massachusetts Review* 26 (Summer–Autumn 1985): 467.

15. John Barkeley Jentz, "Artisans, Evangelicals, and the City: A Social History of Abolition and Labor Reform in Jacksonian New York" (Ph.D. diss., City Univ. of New York, 1977), 134–35.

16. Studies of localities where wage earners (for the most part journeymen rather than semiskilled factory workers) clung more persistently to the belief that their economic interests coincided with those of their employers—that both were producers working in tandem—include John S. Gilkeson Jr., *Middle Class Providence, 1820–1940* (Princeton, N.J., 1986); Brian Greenberg, *Worker and Community: Response to Industrialization in a Nineteenth-Century American City, Albany, New York, 1850–1884* (Albany, 1985); Carol N. Toner, *Persisting Traditions: Artisan Work and Culture in Bangor, Maine, 1820–1864* (New York, 1995).

17. Hartz, *Economic Policy,* 195–96. In contrast to Hartz, Mike Davis faults the early labor movement for being all too inclusive in its concept of the legitimate workingman (Davis, *Prisoners of the American Dream: Political Economy in the History of the U.S. Working Class* [London, 1986], 14).

18. Theophilus Fisk, "Capital against Labor," *Nineteenth Century: A Quarterly Miscellany* 1 (1848): 240; "Prospectus," *Working Man's Advocate,* Oct. 31, 1829; "Reply" of Evans, ibid., April 3, 1830.

19. "The Problem of the Age," *Fall River Mechanic* (Mass.), Sept. 29, 1844; Peter S. Roberts, "The Response of American Labor to the English Industrial Experience" (M.A. thesis, Columbia Univ., 1971), 47–48.

20. A few years later Evans would reconsider his position with respect to "the majority of merchants." The value of their exchange functions, he now suggested, had been negated by their ability to profit disproportionately from these. The unjust material "dis-

parity" that elevated merchants above "the majority of mechanics" (at present "crowded together in miserable hovels") was ipso facto proof to Evans that the interests of the two groups could hardly be "identical," and that the former could scarcely be included among society's useful workingmen ("'Best Friends,'" *Working Man's Advocate,* Sept. 20, 1834).

21. For one Marxist typology, see Erik Olin Wright, "Rethinking, Once Again, the Concept of Class Structure," in Hall, *Reworking Class,* 41–72.

22. Letter from "A Mechanic" to Evans, *Working Man's Advocate,* April 3, 1830; see also the earlier letter from "A Mechanic" in the March 27 issue. William Heighton, one of the leading American popularizers of Ricardian socialism, agreed with this correspondent's apparent assessment insofar as he designated small merchants and shopkeepers as a separate category of "the working or wealth-producing class": these "official" laborers played a "useful and necessary" role in the distribution and exchange of products created by the "productive" class of manual laborers (Heighton, *An Address to the Members of Trade Societies, and to the Working Classes Generally* [Philadelphia, 1827], 8).

23. Letter of April 3, 1830.

24. Remarks of Evans, who specified that ex-mechanics, as well as any others once engaged in "some *useful* occupation," might nonetheless forfeit their right to such confidence and respect if "we find that the system of speculation which is inseparable from almost every occupation in life, in the state of society as we find it, has perverted the finest feelings of their nature" and induced them, too, "to ape the aristocratic airs of those who, in consequence of the same system of speculation, were *born* to enjoy, or rather vegetate on, the labor of others, without laboring themselves" ("Reply," *Working Man's Advocate,* March 27, 1830). Evans was here responding to "Mechanic"'s advice that he steer clear of radical "agrarian laws," and also that he not "spurn every man who does not labor with his own hands, or who wears a ruffled shirt; many of whom have labored with their own hands, as you do now."

25. "Of the Origin and Progress of the Working Men's Party in New York," *Radical,* Jan. 1842; Foner, *History of the Labor Movement* 1:136.

26. For Evans's disagreements with his more radical fellow Working Man Thomas Skidmore, see Martin J. Burke, *The Conundrum of Class: Public Discourse on the Social Order in America* (Chicago, 1995), 89–91; Wilentz, *Chants Democratic,* 201–8.

27. "Reply" of Evans, April 3, 1830.

28. Wilentz, *Chants Democratic,* 15–17, 252–53. One can specify other circumstances that constrained the radical class-conscious edge of the protests of Evans and other workingmen. However, in arguing for the moderating role played by the workingmen's eighteenth-century republican political assumptions, Victoria C. Hattam slights the early nineteenth-century social and economic developments that I describe here (Hattam, "Institutions and Political Change: Working-Class Formation in England and the United States, 1820–1896," in *Structuring Politics: Historical Institutions in Comparative Analysis,* ed. Sven Steinmo, Kathleen Thelen, and Frank Longstreth [Cambridge, 1992], 172–76).

29. Michael Merrill and Sean Wilentz, "Introduction," in *The Key of Liberty: The Life and Democratic Writings of William Manning, "a Laborer," 1747–1814,* ed. Merrill and Wilentz (Cambridge, Mass., 1993), 60; Huston, *Securing the Fruits,* xxi.

30. Huston, *Securing the Fruits,* xxi.

31. Ibid., xxi, 12, 26–27, 75–76, 264. Some decades later Abraham Lincoln evidenced the willingness of other Republicans to differentiate labor from capital explicitly and to categorize the latter as merely the fruit of accumulated labor. Yet avowing the primacy of (manual) labor hardly led Lincoln, any more than these others, to categorize entrepreneurs and professional men like himself as parasites on the body politic. Did these not, to the contrary, remain workers in their own essential ways, individuals who contributed to the creation of wealth either by providing valuable expertise or by furnishing employment opportunities and maximizing the productivity of those manual laborers whom they employed? For Lincoln to have concluded otherwise would have been tantamount to endorsing those more stringent versions of the labor theory of value that denied the legitimacy of capitalist profit and professional remuneration (Mandel, *Labor: Free and Slave,* 156–59; Heather Cox Richardson, *The Greatest Nation of the Earth: Republican Economic Policies during the Civil War* [Cambridge, Mass., 1997], 16–22).

32. This is my conclusion, rather than necessarily the one drawn by Huston in *Securing the Fruits;* for my further questioning along these lines of Huston's treatment of consensus, see my review in the *Journal of the Early Republic* 18 (Winter 1998): 728; see also Paul G. Faler, *Mechanics and Manufacturers in the Early Industrial Revolution: Lynn, Massachusetts, 1760–1860* (Albany, 1981), 30–38. In England and to a lesser extent in the United States, discord over whether the supposed "mental labor" functions performed by professionals and capitalists constituted true labor was complicated by long-contested distinctions, within both mainstream and radical political-economic circles, between productive and unproductive labor (Claeys, *Machinery, Money;* Conkin, *Prophets of Prosperity,* 25).

33. Quotes from inaugural meeting of the Central Industrial Council of New York City, June 6, 1850, in Neufeld, "Realms of Thought," 21; editorial response to letter from "An Inquirer," *Mechanic's Advocate,* Nov. 4, 1848. For the impact of the Revolution in sensitizing journeymen to exploitation, see Robert J. Steinfeld, "The *Philadelphia Cordwainers'* Case of 1806: The Struggle over Alternative Legal Constructions of a Free Market in Labor," in *Labor Law in America,* ed. Christopher L. Tomlins and Andrew J. King (Baltimore, 1990), 32–35. Ronald Schultz, however, suggests that the radical labor theory of value and the militant journeymen trade unionism of the early nineteenth century were only slightly more developed variations on the equal-rights outlook held from a much earlier date by Philadelphia's workingmen (Schultz, *The Republic of Labor: Philadelphia Artisans and the Politics of Class, 1720–1830* [New York, 1993]).

34. For Marx's criticisms of some of these principal justifications for capitalist profit (e.g., profit as reward for management, "abstinence," or risk), see Ziyad I. Husami, "Marx on Distributive Justice," in Cohen et al., *Marx, Justice, and History,* 63–66; Robert L. Meek, *Studies in the Labour Theory of Value* (London, 1973), 121–200. For a controversial insistence on early nineteenth-century English radicals' limited understanding of industrial-capitalist exploitation, see Gareth Stedman Jones, *Languages of Class: Studies in English Working-Class History* (Cambridge, 1983), 90–178. As Robert Gray suggests, Stedman Jones's antimaterialist, "anti-Marxist" emphasis on the role of language in shaping the understanding of Chartist and other oppositional movements coexists with a distinctively Marxist tendency to devalue the class consciousness of such movements by evaluating them in terms of Marxism's own very demanding standards (Gray, "The Deconstruction of the English

Working Class," *Social History* 11 [Oct. 1986]: 373). See, however, Neville Kirk, *Labour and Society in Britain and the USA* (Hants, Eng., 1994), 1:93, 134, for another critique of Stedman Jones's analysis that insists on the impressive degree to which Chartists and other early nineteenth-century Anglo-American labor movements approached Marx's standards and developed a class consciousness that in fact did root exploitation in the sphere of production and the labor process, rather than merely in exchange and distribution; but see also David McNally, *Against the Market: Political Economy, Market Socialism, and the Marxist Critique* (London, 1993), 220–21.

35. A given account of economic exploitation that drew on the labor theory of value in a particular way (e.g., John Bray's) might prove no less radical than another account (e.g., Thomas Hodgskin's) that rested more squarely on the notion of the worker's right to his entire product but which also (compared to other anticapitalist accounts) defined "productive worker" quite broadly (Andrew Reeve, "Thomas Hodgskin and John Bray: Free Exchange and Equal Exchange," in Reeve, *Modern Theories of Exploitation*, 30–52). Ironically, one of the most radical early nineteenth-century American commentators, Thomas Skidmore, was appreciably less receptive to all forms of the labor theory of value, anticapitalist or otherwise. In any of its versions, Skidmore argued, the labor theory of value sought falsely to establish the uncompromising legitimacy of individual property rights. Such rights should be considered neither natural nor absolute but at best conditional, owing to their socially destructive tendencies. In Skidmore's elaborate utopian blueprint for America beginning with New York, popularly elected government would confiscate an individual's property upon his or her death and redistribute it on an equal basis to citizens who had just reached their maturity of eighteen years of age (this ongoing process was to follow the initial wholesale confiscation and redistribution of property held by New Yorkers within the state). In a sense Skidmore's scheme fell short of the higher communist ethics expressed by Marx and other early European socialists. By those ethics, every member of society, regardless of contribution to the social product, would enjoy a comfortable subsistence. Skidmore appeared not to accept such a principle, noting that "there is no occasion to question the general truth of the observation" that "he who would not work *ought* to starve." Prevailing social and economic arrangements were deficient, in his view, largely because they permitted the wrong people to starve; currently it was the producing masses who toiled and perished to support society's "DRONES." Despite the significant communal aspects of his blueprint, then, Skidmore would also allow for the operation of legitimate differences in individual talent and industry, and just as some citizens would prosper and acquire greater wealth in the years between maturity and death, others who were less productive might well suffer declining fortunes. Such inequalities did not trouble Skidmore because he recognized them to be temporary as well as legitimate; under his anti-inheritance provisions, they were not passed on to future generations. Skidmore, moreover, seemed confident that his implemented blueprint in time would remove all manifestations of long-standing social and political oppression, and that its retention of private property rights — its qualified incorporation of the labor theory of value — would not preclude the eventual emergence of the same egalitarian conditions favored in communist schemes. These were conditions in which "there shall be no lenders, no borrowers; no landlords, no tenants; no masters, no journeymen; no Wealth, no Want" (Skidmore, *The Rights of Man to Property!* [New York, 1829], 5–46, 79–80, 137–38, 241, 386;

Huston, *Securing the Fruits,* 291; Wilentz, *Chants Democratic,* 185; Burke, *Conundrum of Class,* 87–88; Conkin, *Prophets of Prosperity,* 239).

36. This is not to suggest that such labor organizations abandoned in a widespread or clear-cut way more long-standing emphases upon currency manipulations and the distribution and exchange of products in the marketplace as the source of the plundering of society's "true" producers.

37. Wilentz, *Chants Democratic,* 242; see also Sutton, *Journeymen for Jesus,* 310; John Rule, "The Property of Skill in the Period of Manufacture," in *The Historical Meanings of Work,* ed. Patrick Joyce (Cambridge, 1987), 107–14.

38. Wilentz, *Chants Democratic,* 231–32; David Brody, *In Labor's Cause: Main Themes in the History of the American Worker* (New York, 1993), 31–33.

39. Brody, *Labor's Cause,* 32–33.

40. Report of John Farrel, National Trades' Union, Convention of 1834, in Commons et al., *Documentary History* 6:205.

41. Ibid.

42. Huston, *Securing the Fruits,* 269–70; Glickman, *Living Wage,* 27. To Glickman's recognition here that the "consumerist" critique of wage slavery did not, in fact, entirely supplant the "producerist" critique in the late nineteenth century, I would therefore add that both coexisted within various discourses during the first half of the century.

43. For particular emphasis on low earnings and "unequal exchange" between capitalists and wage earners as the result of the "asymmetrical" and "disciplinary" power of the wage relationship, see Reddy, *Money and Liberty,* 91–96, 222. Reddy's emphasis recalls the criticisms made by many of the early nineteenth century's more progressive thinkers (see the Introduction's discussion of James Freeman Clarke). But in proceeding to argue that wage-labor agreements are only one of many forms of disciplinary "exchange asymmetries," Reddy less persuasively repudiates class altogether as a viable conceptual category.

44. See the series "Employer and Employed," in *Mechanic's Advocate,* Sept. 3, 11, 18, 1847; see also Sutton, *Journeymen for Jesus,* 311; Faler, *Mechanics and Manufacturers,* 177–78; on employer underselling and wage reductions in England, see Iorwerth Prothero, *Radical Artisans in England and France, 1830–1870* (Cambridge, 1997), 132; Stedman Jones, *Languages,* 122; Noel Thompson, *The Market and Its Critics: Socialist Political Economy in Nineteenth-Century Britain* (London, 1989), 71–75.

45. *Address of the Mechanics and Laborers, Assembled in Convention at Boston, October 16, 1844, to Their Fellow Mechanics and Laborers throughout the United States,* rept. in the *Herald of Freedom,* Nov. 1, 1844; Ware, *Industrial Worker,* 204–6; Guarneri, *Utopian Alternative,* 297–98; Teresa Anne Murphy, *Ten Hours' Labor: Religion, Reform, and Gender in Early New England* (Ithaca, N.Y., 1992), 153–54.

46. Kaster, "'Not for a Class'?"

47. If the *Address* recognized Old World societies and their laboring conditions as pernicious countermodels, some British radicals—Owenite socialists in particular—perceived the United States as itself a kind of countermodel—as the extreme apotheosis of selfish competition and "untrammeled *laissez-faire*" (Gregory Claeys, *Citizens and Saints: Politics and Anti-Politics in Early British Socialism* [Cambridge, 1989], 155). Certain American labor reformers, notably the American Owenites and Associationist socialists, tended to share

this view. But other reformers, closer to the Locofoco Democratic tradition, were more inclined to see true laissez-faire and naturally self-adjusting markets as part of the solution rather than as part of the problem.

48. In an example that was not extreme, one of Philadelphia's leading small-producer, radical activists, Stephen Simpson, opposed extending a common-school education to female members of the producing, or any other, classes on the grounds that it tended to a "destructive equality" of the sexes; the female's education should be confined to the home and should conform to her naturally "passive" disposition and duties (Simpson, *Working Man's Manual,* 206–9).

49. Holly Hanson, "'Mill Girls' and 'Mine Boys': The Cultural Meanings of Migrant Labour," *Social History* 21 (May 1996): 178.

50. The operatives' putative moral degradation and its causes were especially ambiguous themes. Thomas Dublin notes that some critics of factory conditions at Lowell and elsewhere "may have felt that mill employment made farmers' daughters less fit for marriage — not because they had been exploited and worn down by their work in the mill but because they had become citified and uppity." Linked to this belief was the perception (which had some substance) that the factory women were spending their earnings on themselves rather than sending them back home in fulfillment of their more socially acceptable supportive family role. While the majority of male reformers who attended the 1844 convention were, in their hostility to the factory system, overwhelmingly drawn to the exploitation scenario, a number likely shared something of the other criticisms as well, just as even Orestes Brownson may have when he remarked in his famous essay of 1840 that "the great mass [of operatives] wear out their health, spirits, and morals, without becoming one whit better off than when they commenced labor" (Brownson, quoted in Dublin, *Transforming Women's Work,* 110–11).

51. Murphy, *Ten Hours,* 46–56, 136–50, 191–215; see also the National Trades' Union, "Discussion of the Condition of Females in Manufacturing Establishments," Sept. 1834, in Commons et al., *Documentary History* 6:217–24, in which John Commerford, a New York cabinetmaker and a leading radical member of the city's General Trades' Union, expressed the rather modest hope that the "miserable [female] victims" employed in the nation's manufacturing establishments come to receive "a fair equivalent for their services" out of capitalist profits (221).

52. *Address of the Mechanics and Laborers.* Whatever the patriarchal nature of actual practices in the Owenite and Associationist experimental communities, their literature's critiques of existing capitalist arrangements tended to be pronouncedly more inclusive with respect to women and women's employments than were the trade-union critiques; on the mixed record of New York City's journeymen unionists during the 1830s, see Stansell, *City of Women,* 137–44; Wilentz, *Chants Democratic,* 248–51; Voss, *American Exceptionalism,* 46–52; on the reluctance of carpenters and other male artisans in New England to include "dependent," and largely female, factory workers in their campaigns for labor reform in the 1830s and 1840s, see Murphy, *Ten Hours,* 136–50; see also Mary H. Blewett, *Men, Women, and Work: Class, Gender, and Protest in the New England Shoe Industry, 1780–1910* (Urbana, Ill., 1988), 65–66.

53. Lazerow, *Religion,* 197–213.

54. The *Address*'s anticapitalist critique is also a hodgepodge of telltale emphases. For example, just as the gendered phrasing of the labor theory of value most closely reflects the reform perspective of male artisans, so the references to the "utter isolation" of the "present system of labor" originate from the Associationist contingent.

55. On the distinction made by some of Evans's radical contemporaries between "honorable" master craftsmen and "dishonorable," nonproducing employers or accumulators, see also Bruce C. Laurie, *Working People of Philadelphia, 1800–1850* (Philadelphia, 1980), 77–78.

56. Amartya Sen, "The Moral Standing of the Market," in *Ethics and Economics,* ed. Ellen Frankel Paul, Jeffrey Paul, and Fred D. Miller Jr. (Oxford, Eng., 1985), 15.

57. Ibid., 14–17; Allen E. Buchanan, *Ethics, Efficiency, and the Market* (Totowa, N.J., 1985), 51–53. Buchanan notes the possible inconsistencies between these two basic promarket arguments, as well as other of their shortcomings.

58. The Whig arguments, made by the likes of Daniel Webster and Edward Everett, were often popularizations of the more technical defenses of capitalist enterprise and profits that run through the literature of early nineteenth-century political economy.

59. Sen, "Moral Standing," 16–17. The difficulties in measuring individuals' inputs in the production process and basing individual rewards on these—as distinct from the market principle of linking individuals' rewards for work to the market-determined value of their output—resurface in the continuing debates over the viability of market socialism.

60. Huston, *Securing the Fruits,* 266–67.

61. For a defense of these entrepreneurial qualities, see Israel M. Kirzner, *Discovery, Capitalism, and Distributive Justice* (Oxford, Eng., 1989); a somewhat alternative defense is James M. Buchanan and Victor J. Vanberg, "The Market as a Creative Process," *Economics and Philosophy* 7 (Oct. 1991): 167–86. His own recoil from the radical anticapitalist versions of the labor theory of value led Horace Greeley to cite the spectacular productive contributions of such inventors and entrepreneurs as Richard Arkwright, as well as the example of the engineer who leveled a railroad to save ten thousand days' work in building it (Greeley, "Counsel to Boys. No. IV—Choosing a Vocation," *Little Corporal: An Original Magazine for Boys and Girls, and for Older People Who Have Young Hearts* 5 [July 1867]: 24).

62. Although Whigs trumpeted a large role for government in matters of economic development, they characteristically denied that such activities distorted natural market forces.

63. Bertrand de Jouvenal, *The Ethics of Redistribution* (1952; rept. Indianapolis, 1990), 47.

64. For a modern restatement of the argument warning of the economic and social costs of disregarding entrepreneurial incentives, see Henry Phelps Brown, *Egalitarianism and the Generation of Inequality* (Oxford, Eng., 1988), 10.

65. David Miller, *Social Justice* (Oxford, Eng., 1976), 119.

66. Huston, *Securing the Fruits,* 357–59; Hovenkamp, *Enterprise and American Law,* 189–92, 221–25.

67. "Reply" of Evans, April 3, 1830.

68. "I am of Jefferson's opinion, that great cities are great nuisances, and that there ought to be a considerable vacant space between all houses" (Evans, "To the Working Men of the U.S.," *Radical,* Feb. 1841).

69. Bronstein, *Land Reform,* 121; see also Charles W. McCurdy, *The Anti-Rent Era in New York Law and Politics, 1839–1865* (Chapel Hill, N.C., 2001), 172–73, 207–10.

70. Joseph Dorfman, *The Economic Mind in American Civilization, 1606–1865* (New York, 1956), 2:684; see also Pessen, *Most Uncommon Jacksonians,* 179–80; Bronstein, *Land Reform,* 42–43.

71. Edward J. Balleisen highlights a comparable disinclination to be independent proprietors among some antebellum mercantile clerks and other white-collar salaried employees. However, Balleisen also appears to accept as culturally overpowering the perception that the condition of wage-earning manual workers was inevitably one of servile dependence; he suggests that white-collar employees' very ability to contrast their more genteel working conditions with those of factory operatives and journeymen contributed to their acceptance of their own permanent subordination (Balleisen, *Navigating Failure,* 213–19).

72. "To the Working Man of the United States," Jan. 1841; see also "Mr. Alling's Report on Land Reform," *National Reformer* (Rochester), Oct. 19, 1847. Reeve Huston reaches a similar conclusion regarding the views of Evans's fellow land reformer Thomas Devyr: "He insisted that wage labor would be beneficial once land was guaranteed to all" (Huston, "Land and Freedom: The New York Anti-Rent Wars and the Construction of Free Labor in the Antebellum North," in Arneson, Greene, and Laurie, *Labor Histories,* 31; see also Helene Sara Zahler, *Eastern Workingmen and National Land Policy, 1829–1862* (New York, 1941), 35–36. Although Evans had more confidence than contemporary utopian socialists did in the possibility of nonexploitative, fair competition in a nonsocialist society, he was not the enthusiast of economic competition under governmental laissez-faire that William Leggett and other Locofoco Democrats were. The arguments for land reform that Evans pitched at big-city wage earners appear, in any case, to have had limited effectiveness. At least in New York City in the 1840s, support for National Reform remained relatively weak among the trade unions and working masses (Wilentz, *Chants Democratic,* 341–42; Blumin, *Emergence of the Middle Class,* 125, 348).

73. Recent economic historians minimize both the actual existence of land monopoly and the negative consequences of land speculation (e.g., its creation of permanent tenant farmers) in nineteenth-century America; for a review that finds some validity in the older, more critical view of land policy held by Evans and like-minded historians, see Jon Gjerde, "'Roots of Maladjustment' in the Land: Paul Wallace Gates," *Reviews in American History* 19 (March 1991): 142–53.

74. Iorwerth Prothero suggests that plebeian radicals in mid-nineteenth-century England may have turned to land reform for reasons similar to Evans's (*Radical Artisans,* 139–40).

75. I use the term *free market* in a loose sense here, because as legal and other historians now stress, Jacksonians hardly less than Whigs supported the basic state role of establishing and enforcing a legal framework, the "background operating rules," for economic transactions, even as they frequently contested, along with other early nineteenth-century Americans, the interpretation of particular rules (John T. Nockleby, "Two Theories of Competition in the Early 19th Century Labor Cases," *American Journal of Legal History* 38 [Oct. 1994]: 457). I would also refer again to the period's overridingly limited sense, shared by Jacksonians, of what true equality of opportunity entailed.

76. Ashworth, *"Agrarians" and "Aristocrats,"* 24–29; Lawrence Frederick Kohl, *The Politics of Individualism: Parties and the American Character in the Jacksonian Era* (New York, 1989), 186–227; Richard B. Latner, "Preserving 'the Natural Equality of Rank and Influence':

Liberalism, Republicanism, and Equality of Condition in Jacksonian Politics," in *The Culture of the Market: Historical Essays,* ed. Thomas Haskell and Richard Teichgraeber III (Cambridge, 1993), 189–231. Latner argues that Whigs shared the Jacksonians' "egalitarian assumptions" and their fear of "excessive inequality of condition" (225). He accordingly slights the mainstream Whig insistence on the significant differences in natural capacities and tastes among individuals and the role that these inevitably (and constructively) played in building a diverse, civilized society, one that included substantial economic and social disparities.

77. Left-liberal philosophers, one might generalize, hold both beliefs; right-libertarian ones only the first. The influential starting point for discussion remains John Rawls, *A Theory of Justice* (Cambridge, Mass., 1971); see also James M. Buchanan, "Fairness, Hope, and Justice," in *New Directions in Economic Justice,* ed. Roger Skurski (Notre Dame, Ind., 1983), 69–70.

78. Pessen, *Most Uncommon Jacksonians,* 182–83; Faler, *Mechanics and Manufacturers,* 183–88.

79. For Evans's own formulation along these lines, see "White Slavery," *Radical,* March 1841.

80. Albert Brisbane, *A Concise Exposition of the Doctrine of Association,* 8th ed. (New York, 1844), 32–37. Brisbane and other Associationists maintained that their fundamental mode of eliminating the antagonism between "Capital and Labor" in the larger society was to unite these, by means of the joint-stock arrangement, "in the same hands." Many of the actual practices of the Association communities varied in their ratio of rewards, even as they consistently sought to elevate the status and increase the attractiveness of manual labor. Associationists' breakdown of rewards acknowledging the distinct contributions of capital and labor provoked criticisms from more radical reformers that their notions of distributive justice remained all too conventional; for Owenite critiques, see *Herald of the New Moral World* (New York), Feb. 4, 1841, in Commons et al., *Documentary History* 7:222 –23; and H. R. S., letter in "Correspondence," *Harbinger* 7 (Oct. 28, 1848): 203.

81. David Roediger argues that owing to the discord its presence wrought among northerners of progressive vision, slavery posed particular obstacles in the United States to "the development of a telling"—a "more straightforward"—critique of "wage slavery" (including, presumably, the development of anticapitalist versions of the labor theory of value). But one may doubt that the critiques of capitalist exploitation made since the 1820s by northern trade-union activists, utopian socialists, and the like were any the less (or more) telling than most of those developed in slavery-free Europe (because they commonly shared Ricardian socialist and other basic tenets). Nor did they appear to be any the less (or more) straightforward than many of the critiques of wage labor that emerged in postemancipation America (Roediger, *Wages of Whiteness,* 87; Roediger, "Race, Labor, and Gender," 186–87).

82. "From each according to his ability, to each according to his needs!" (Marx, *Gotha Program,* 117–20). For the argument that Marx viewed all principles of distributive justice, including the anticapitalist labor theory of value, as a function of the competition for scarce goods, and that such principles, accordingly, would cease to exist in the "higher phase" of communist society, see Allen E. Buchanan, *Marx and Justice: The Radical Critique of Liberalism* (Totowa, N.J., 1982), 57–59; see also Thomas Nagel, *Equality and Partiality* (New York, 1991), 99.

83. In his labor history of the period, Norman Ware describes the craft-labor movements of the 1850s as in fact more "aggressive" than those of the preceding decade, but he means something quite different in his use of the term. By at last abandoning at this time their preindustrial, and increasingly utopian, hopes of maintaining the old master-journeyman-like "community of interests" with their employers (and in thereby freeing themselves of the deleterious influence of middle-class intellectual dreamers like Greeley), America's industrial wage earners, Ware maintains, were able to move on to adopting a more realistic, more "aggressive" stance in relation to the capitalist class. By accepting the inevitable, that their labor was only a commodity, for which they must engage in continuous, negotiated struggle with antagonistic interests to get the best possible price, they were accommodating themselves to market capitalism's rules of the game and to their own attendant loss of status. As I indicated earlier, I find considerable truth in this interpretation emphasizing the relatively "limited" and "pragmatic" objectives of late antebellum trade-union ideology. But I do not share Ware's low opinion of middle-class visionary influences. And to the substantial extent that the more expansive pre-1850 labor-reform movements and impulses did, in their resistance to social and economic change, draw upon anticapitalist, radical versions of the labor theory of value, I believe that Ware's interpretation misleads by characterizing them as "defensive" (Ware, *Industrial Worker*, 198, 227; Louis M. Hacker, *The Triumph of American Capitalism* [New York, 1940], 266–79; for criticism of Ware's categories on different grounds, see Blewett, *Constant Turmoil*, 46–47, 74).

84. *Report of the Brotherhood of the Union*, in "Labor Movements," *Tribune*, Aug. 15, 1850. The Brotherhood was originally a Philadelphia-based fraternal organization, founded by the popular novelist George Lippard. By the early 1850s it had evolved into a national organization and quasi-labor movement that synthesized land reform, Fourierism, producers' cooperation, and other labor-reform impulses of the day (David S. Reynolds, *George Lippard* [Boston, 1982], 20); for other examples of inflammatory union rhetoric in this period, see Amy Bridges, "Becoming American: The Working Classes in the United States before the Civil War," in *Working-Class Formation: Nineteenth-Century Patterns in Western Europe and the United States,* ed. Ira Katznelson and Aristide R. Zolberg (Princeton, N.J., 1986), 175–86.

85. "Labor Movements — Fallacies," *Tribune*, Aug. 6, 1850.

86. Mullins, *Voice from the Workshop*, 8–10, 23–24, 29, 31.

87. Ibid., 8, 10; Stanley, *From Bondage to Contract*, 160–61.

88. Mullins, *Voice from the Workshop*, 8.

89. Ibid., 20, 3. One might argue, in view of his many unrestrained attacks on capitalists in this manifesto, that Mullin's occasional lapse into moderation is a better illustration of the intrinsic ambiguity of linguistic meaning than it is of any genuine equivocation in his attitude toward capitalist desert. But as indicated, Mullins also explicitly recognized the existence of fair-minded employers, and his choice of words seems to reflect his run-ins with particular foremen and employers, which he perceived as assaults by "tyrants" on both his material interests and his dignity (25–26).

90. "Labor and Competition," from "One of the Men," *Mechanic's Advocate,* Jan. 15, 1848.

91. Neal quoted in Huston, *Securing the Fruits,* 268; for skilled laborers' parallel retreat from the most anticapitalist versions of the labor theory of value in England, see Keith

McClelland, "Time to Work, Time to Live: Some Aspects of Work and the Re-formation of Class in Britain, 1850–1880," in Joyce, *Historical Meanings,* 188–90.

92. For one of the many adaptations of Hamilton's argument, and the evident exasperation of the labor press in addressing it, see letter from "An Inquirer" and the reply by the editor, *Mechanic's Advocate,* Nov. 4, 1848.

93. Robert Nozick, *Anarchy, State, and Utopia* (New York, 1974), 150–208; Sen, "Moral Standing," 1–8; Hal R. Varian, "Distributive Justice, Welfare Economics, and the Theory of Fairness," in *Philosophy and Economic Theory,* ed. Frank Hahn and Martin Hollis (Oxford, Eng., 1979), 134–54.

94. Skidmore, *Rights of Man,* 243, 359–67. Despite the boldness of his anti-inheritance proposals, Skidmore remained one with a good number of his radical contemporaries in a basic sense: in his foreshadowing of modern neo-Marxists like John Roemer who attach primary importance to the initial maldistribution of wealth and its coercive effects, as distinct from the capitalist production process itself, as the source of labor's exploitation (Roemer, *Free to Lose: An Introduction to Marxist Economic Philosophy* [Cambridge, Mass., 1988]). For this reason, too, Michael B. Levy has characterized Skidmore's anti-inheritance proposals as a form of "radical 'confiscatory' liberalism" because they left untouched the continuing operation of a capitalist labor market (Levy, "Liberal Equality and Inherited Wealth," *Political Theory* 11 [Nov. 1983]: 551); see also note 35.

95. Here I am drawing on some of the categories of European conservative discourse explored in Hirschman, *Rhetoric of Reaction.* The term *free-market elitist* is my own.

96. Malthus, *Principle of Population.*

97. Letter to the editor from "S. Carolina.—T. C.," New York *Daily Sentinel,* April 24, 1830. The letter's Malthusian attacks on the "needless" reproductive propensities and other vices of the laboring poor point to Cooper as its author. But although Cooper like Malthus rejected notions of natural human equality, he also became, in contrast to Malthus, a "southern partisan" who directed his "liberal utilitarianism" to the defense of black chattel slavery, emphasizing the importance of planter self-interest (Daniel Kilbride, "Slavery and Utilitarianism: Thomas Cooper and the Mind of the Old South," *Journal of Southern History* 59 [Aug. 1993]: 485; Burke, *Conundrum of Class,* 63–68).

98. Letter from T. C.

99. Buchanan, "Fairness," 63–64. Cooper in fact declared himself on the side of the workingmen in supporting the abolition of any laws "in favor of the rich, and bearing unjustly on the poor . . . laws favoring monopolies and corporations—giving privileges to one class from which others are excluded"—laws, in short, that create "unnecessarily artificial inequalities." Notwithstanding such Jacksonian Democrat–like pronouncements, Cooper clearly believed that the existing social order was already sufficiently fair, adding in his letter to the *Sentinel* that the leveling proposals to which he objected would "rob the industrious and his children of the accumulations of meritorious industry, voluntary deprivations, frugality, and foresight" (letter from T. C.). Here Cooper was drawing on both the antecedent-rights objections to Thomas Skidmore's plan and the American exceptionalist argument noted later in the text.

100. For an example of the Whig use of such arguments to deny the existence of a "hereditary aristocracy" in America, to discredit "demagogic" attacks on capitalist power and economic inequalities, and to insist on the unequaled "harmony" of interests between

employers and wage earners that the openness of American society encouraged, see H. G. O. Colby's address, *The Relations of Wealth and Labor,* Annual Address before the American Institute, Oct. 20, 1842, rept. in *The American Laborer: Devoted to the Cause of Protection to Home Industry* 1 (Nov. 1842): 233–38. The Whig theme here that it was the sons of the wealthy who were, above all, psychologically disadvantaged in the competitive race, just as the character of poor boys in America benefited from their early adversity, represents an interesting concession to the modern Rawlsian argument that industriousness and other dispositions are "undeserved" to the great extent that the individual acquires them from family and environment. The empirical accuracy of this Whig theme has been indirectly challenged by studies finding strong economic upper-class familial continuity across generations (Betty G. Farrell, *Elite Families: Class and Power in Nineteenth-Century Boston* [Albany, 1993]).

101. Blumin, *Emergence of the Middle Class,* 10.

102. O. A. B., "Rich and Poor."

103. Voss, *American Exceptionalism,* 31; Steinberg, "The Dialogue of Struggle," 505–41; Johnson, *Shopkeepers' Millennium;* Anthony F. C. Wallace, *Rockdale: The Growth of an American Village in the Early Industrial Revolution* (New York, 1978).

104. Sutton, *Journeymen for Jesus;* Lazerow, *Religion.*

105. For the role that frugality and like values played in some Jacksonian Democrats' hostility to the entrepreneurial spirit, see William Gerald Shade, *Banks or No Banks: The Money Issue in Western Politics, 1832–1865* (Detroit, 1972), 174, 198; James Roger Sharp, *The Jacksonians versus the Banks: Politics in the States after the Panic of 1837* (New York, 1970), 181–87, 321–25. For one Associationists' partial attribution of manual labor's "debasement" to capitalist "cunning," see "What Is the Reason? 'How Much Land and Property, and I Have None!'" *United States Magazine and Democratic Review* 16 (Jan. 1845): 24. For the tensions within middle-class prescriptive literature itself regarding the more unscrupulous behavioral attributes conducive to success in early nineteenth-century business, see Roberts, *American Alchemy,* 30–31, 45–46. Revulsion against the bastardization of traditional Christian virtues and against competitive individualism run wild may have assumed its most poignant expression within the northern black communities whose members were most patently excluded from equal participation in the capitalist market's competitive race. As much as any group of white Americans, and as one means of overcoming race prejudice, prominent free black leaders and their press rhetorically honored Anglo-American norms, including thrift, frugality, and other individual, self-improvement virtues. Yet African Americans in the North may have also developed a relatively strong commitment to "a spirit of mutuality" and "communal advancement" because they interpreted the discrimination that they suffered, no less than the enslavement of blacks in the South, as an expression of white greed and opportunism—as proof of the distortions that a predatory race could impose on admirable Christian qualities (Freeman, "The Educational Wants," 118–19; Carol Buchalter Stapp, *Afro-Americans in Antebellum Boston* [New York, 1993]; Leonard I. Sweet, *Black Images of America, 1784–1870* [New York, 1976]; Patrick Rael, "The Lion's Painting: African-American Thought in the Antebellum North" [Ph.D. diss., Univ. of California, Berkeley, 1995]; Bay, *White Image*). However, one might also hypothesize that in the case of the most impoverished antebellum free blacks, it was no such active ideological revulsion to white values and practices but rather sheer deprivation and

demoralization that served most of all to blunt their individualist economic aspirations and their acquisitive and competitive drives; for analysis of today's Third World poor along these lines, see Sen, *Inequality Reexamined*, 150.

106. For the comparably limited workings of top-down ideology in mid-Victorian England, see John Saville, *1848: The British State and the Chartist Movement* (Cambridge, 1987), 226.

107. For a social-psychology discussion of "split consciousness perspectives" which supports the conclusion that "the stability of the stratification order" in modern-day capitalist societies "results more from self-canceling beliefs among the working class than from uncritical belief in its legitimacy," see James R. Kluegel et al., "Accounting for the Rich and the Poor: Existential Justice in Comparative Perspective," in *Social Justice and Political Change: Public Opinion in Capitalist and Post-Communist States*, ed. Kluegel, David S. Mason, and Bernd Wegener (New York, 1995), 206; see also Richard Della Fave, "Toward an Explication of the Legitimation Process," *Social Forces* 65 (Dec. 1986): 477.

108. See here the suggestive remarks in Neufeld, "Realms of Thought," 131–32.

109. Lears, "Cultural Hegemony," 582, 586.

110. Yet as Lester Thurow's remarks suggest, even some of these may have been ambivalent to the degree that they accorded significant legitimacy to market-capitalist arrangements that they deemed less than ideal.

111. John Patrick Diggins, *Thorstein Veblen: Theorist of the Leisure Class* (Princeton, N.J., 1999), 107–8.

112. Roediger, *Wages of Whiteness;* Ignatiev, *How the Irish Became White.*

113. Richard Stott, *Workers in the Metropolis: Class, Ethnicity, and Youth in Antebellum New York City* (Ithaca, N.Y., 1990), 160, 249–50.

114. Eric Foner, *Politics and Ideology in the Age of the Civil War* (New York, 1980), 24.

115. Ibid.

5. George M. Weston and Slave Labor: Free Labor, Gresham's Law, and Antebellum Cultural Anxieties

1. William S. Barry, House of Representatives, *Cong. Globe*, 33d Cong., 1st sess., *App.*, April 27, 1854, 616; see also the more extended postbellum arguments in Robert L. Dabney, *A Defence of Virginia, (and through Her, of the South,) in Recent and Pending Contests against the Sectional Party* (1867; rept. New York, 1969, 275–389. Richard Yates, Illinois congressman, was a free-soil Whig and a founder of the Republican Party.

2. George M. Weston, *Southern Slavery Reduces Northern Wages* (Washington, D.C., 1856).

3. Gresham's law was the term suggested in 1858 by Scottish economist Henry D. Macleod for the principle that when two coins are equal in debt-paying power but unequal in intrinsic value, the one of lesser intrinsic value tends to regulate the value of the whole currency and drive the other out of circulation—or, as the principle came to be briefly characterized: "Bad money drives out good." Macleod attributed the principle's discovery to the London merchant and Crown financial agent Sir Thomas Gresham in 1558, although it in fact appears to have been stated well before Gresham's time.

4. George Opdyke, *A Treatise on Political Economy* (New York, 1851), 330.

5. Smith, *Wealth of Nations,* 184, 488–89; Jean-Baptiste Say, *A Treatise on Political Economy* (1803), 6th Amer. ed. (1836), tr. C. R. Prinsep (New York, 1964), 206–8.

6. Weston, *Wages,* 5; Weston, *The Progress of the Slavery in the United States* (Washington, D.C., 1857), 228. Inspired by the federal census data of 1850, antislavery arguments attesting to southern economic backwardness and poverty became a torrent by the late antebellum years, although American commentary expressing Adam Smith's economic indictment of slavery was hardly absent from the earlier part of the century (Joshua Michael Zeitz, "The Missouri Compromise Reconsidered: Rhetoric and the Emergence of the Free Labor Synthesis," *Journal of the Early Republic* 20 [Fall 2000]: 447–86).

7. See Mill, *Principles of Political Economy,* 253. Adam Smith himself, as Seymour Drescher underscores, was not oblivious to the "ubiquity of bound labor" that existed in the face of the "optimality" that he claimed for free labor. In explanation of this paradox, Smith included in the *Wealth of Nations* certain qualifications to his "general axiom" of free labor's economic superiority. Still, many abolitionists subsequently found it easy to overlook these qualifications in a selective reading of the *Wealth of Nations.* Lewis Gray notably criticized Smith "and his followers" both for exaggerating the inefficiency of slave labor in an "extractive economy" and for concluding too much—its alleged relative costliness and unprofitability—from that inefficiency. Gray was perhaps the first modern historian to emphasize how slave labor, at least plantation slave labor in the Old South, could attain a superior cheapness and competitive advantage over free-labor enterprises (Drescher, "Free Labor vs. Slave Labor," 57–58; Gray, "Economic Efficiency and Competitive Advantages of Slavery under the Plantation System," *Agricultural History* 4 [April 1930]: 332–47). Weston was among the antebellum antislavery commentators who anticipated Gray in recognizing slave labor's ability to undersell white labor in the disposal of products. There were still earlier ones who, without departing from the antislavery orthodoxy that the slaveholder's lash was an ineffective labor incentive, shared Weston's position that plantation slave labor was no more expensive than America's well-remunerated white free labor, Adam Smith notwithstanding. Rarer were the antislavery commentators who could bring themselves to conclude explicitly, on the basis of the slaveholder's high profits, that the lash and the fear of the lash—brutish bodily pain—might indeed be highly effective labor incentives. Following Smith, most antislavery commentators believed that what they regarded as antithetical to the more civilized drives that rightfully animated all human beings (regardless of race) must also be inferior from a political-economic standpoint (Weston, *Wages;* Weston, *Progress,* 223–30; Davis, *Slavery and Human Progress,* 250–58; Robert William Fogel and Stanley L. Engerman, *Time on the Cross: The Economics of American Negro Slavery* [Boston, 1974], 2:184–90). Proslavery writers mounted a far more general challenge to the staple of antislavery political economy—the ineffectiveness of the lash. They did so primarily on racialist grounds, insisting on the inability of blacks to respond effectively and reliably to free-market labor incentives—e.g., "The only principle which controls them [America's black slaves] is the principle of fear . . . from apprehension of bodily pain" ("British Reviewers and the United States," *Southern Quarterly Review* 13 [Jan. 1848]: 200).

8. Weston, *Progress,* 234, and also: "It does not seem to be yet agreed, which of the two kinds of labor is now the cheapest; and the facts we observe are apparently contradictory" (223). William H. Seward was among those who anticipated Weston during the Senate

debates over the Compromise of 1850. In his "higher law" speech of March 11, Seward argued that slave labor was less productive than free white labor everywhere, in "even tropical climates" as well as "northern countries." Yet in rebuttal of Daniel Webster, Seward also insisted that slave labor's superior cheapness meant that it could and would go anywhere if permitted, especially in "all new countries" where "labor is in quick demand. . . . there is no climate uncongenial to slavery" (Seward, in *The Works of William H. Seward,* ed. George E. Baker [New York, 1853], 2:79).

9. At the same time, some southern proslavery commentators took particular pains to deny that free wage laborers were invariably cheaper than southern slaves. One of the more insistent endorsements by a proslavery writer of the "superior economy" and profitability of continuous slave labor, most of all in "new countries, and wherever labor is scarce and dear," was Edmund Ruffin's tract *The Political Economy of Slavery* (Washington, D.C., 1857?), 3–29. Ruffin partially reached his conclusions by returning to the mid-eighteenth-century pre-Smithian, mercantilist view that many if not most laboring people—whatever their race—naturally lacked the essential motivation of higher classes to develop the refined wants characteristic of civilized societies. Conceding the free laborer's superior efficiency when he did work, Ruffin insisted that under conditions of labor scarcity, where free workers were paid more than subsistent wages, their labor (unlike the slave's) would not be continuous: "self-interest" would encourage their laxity and idleness, not greater industriousness and productivity. Ruffin's conclusions remained more commonplace for his own time with respect to the behavior of free white laborers earning a bare subsistence wage in older, more densely populated European societies (and increasingly in New England as well). With both northern labor reformers and other southern proslavery writers, he held that the "pressure of want" driving such "class" slaves was indeed a more "potent" work incentive than the slaveholder's whip. But for all white wage slavery's superior cheapness, Ruffin also indicated, it could never flourish in the South, much less in the yet more "tropical climates" of Central and South America that were ripe for "African" slavery's reintroduction. Only the "negro," he claimed, "can safely labor in these most fruitful regions of the earth." Ruffin thus joined other proslavery commentators in grounding an economic defense of black slavery in the circumstances of the South: at least for southern staple-crop enterprises, situated in warm latitudes uncongenial to hard labor by free whites, compulsory black servitude was more productive and less expensive than any form of free labor could be.

10. Possibly the first critique of Robert W. Fogel and Stanley L. Engerman's claims for slavery's productive efficiency along these lines was by an intellectual, rather than an economic, historian: Thomas Haskell, in some essays of 1974, rept. in *Objectivity Is Not Neutrality: Explanatory Schemes in History* (Baltimore, 1998), 31–56. But Stanley L. Engerman has underscored to me that high demand did not in itself ensure that all cotton producers would do well. The slave system had to be able to respond with sufficient productive efficiency in order for high demand to be met. "One productive process," Robert W. Fogel notes, "is said to be technically more efficient than another if it yields more output from the same quantity of inputs" (Fogel, *Without Consent or Contract,* 72–73). While insisting that the gang system and other attributes of plantation slave labor rendered it relatively efficient in this productive or technical sense, Fogel also distinguishes a second, allocative standard of efficiency: planters' ability to shift their slaves and other capital resources from

place to place in order to exploit opportunities to increase their profits. It was the efficiency of antebellum southern slavery in this allocative sense—and planters' attendant responsiveness to the worldwide demand for cotton textiles—that Haskell appeared to be acknowledging in his own critique of Fogel and Engerman. Northern antislavery commentators like George Weston tended to ignore slavery's possible allocative efficiency and to explain slave labor's profitability solely in terms of slaveowners' capacity to screw down labor costs to offset their bondspeople's productive inefficiency.

11. There is, particularly, a growing literature on the "internal economy" in which slaves were able to engage, although some scholars resist the notion that such a network could have conferred bondsmen with meaningful agency. There is also the related question of how much such an internal economy may have worked to the benefit of masters. Recent scholarship continues to suggest that industrial and urban slaves in the Old South possessed greater economic leverage and/or social autonomy than most rural field hands, whatever the latter's engagement in an internal economy.

12. O. Nigel Bolland, "Proto-Proletarians? Slave Wages in the Americas: Between Slave Labour and Free Labour," in *From Chattel Slaves to Wage Slaves: The Dynamics of Labour Bargaining in the Americas,* ed. Mary Turner (Bloomington, Ind., 1995), 143. With respect to northern antebellum society, the findings of labor and social historians over the last several decades have generally indicated that free-labor ideology painted an overly roseate picture of conditions and opportunities for even white male wage earners, in both rural and urban areas. As Bruce Laurie notes, there were "several forms" and shades of "early free laborism," Whig and Democratic, in the 1830s. These also extolled northern economic opportunity but without the pointed antisouthern, antislavery dimension that marked the Republican Party's "ideology of mature free labor" (Laurie, *Artisans into Workers: Labor in Nineteenth-Century America* [New York, 1989], 51–56, 94).

13. Weston, *Wages,* 5; Weston, *Progress,* 229–32. Two decades later a California Senate committee would conceptualize in nearly identical terms the threat that the cheap labor of Chinese immigrant "serfs" posed to the interests and very identity of the state's free white laborers (Benjamin B. Ringer, *"We the People" and Others: Duality and America's Treatment of Its Racial Minorities* [New York, 1989], 603); for the antebellum roots of anti-Chinese "pollution" anxieties in California, see Robert G. Lee, *Orientals: Asian Americans in Popular Culture* (Philadelphia, 1999), 9.

14. Say, *Treatise,* 206–8. Despite his own assertions of slavery's economic inferiority, Say also insisted here, against Adam Smith, on slave labor's superior cheapness, to which he attributed individual masters' "exorbitance of profit" (206–7). During an important phase of the movement to abolish slavery in the West Indies, Say was directly challenged by British writer Adam Hodgson, who quoted Smith and others in support of the view that slavery indeed entailed greater expenses and generated less profit "than the labour of free men." In his response to Hodgson, Say claimed to have retreated from his earlier position, stating his faith in the progressive force and ultimate triumph of antislavery. But such expressed faith did not necessarily contradict Say's thesis as to slavery's debilitating "contagion." It was precisely the often uneasy coexistence of these two themes that also marked the later writings of Weston and Frederick Law Olmsted (Hodgson, *A Letter to M. Jean-Baptiste Say, on the Comparative Expense of Free and Slave Labour,* including "Letter from J. B. Say to the Author," March 25, 1823, 2d ed. [London, 1823], 25, 60).

15. Weston, *Progress,* 222, 234, see this entire chapter for Weston's fuller questioning of the various Malthusian arguments, advanced by George Tucker, Henry Clay, and others, which predicted that intensifying population pressures would increase free wage labor's relative cheapness and attractiveness for employers, eventuating in slave labor's extinction. Northern labor reformers who found the existing magnitude of American "wage slavery" alarming enough shared Weston's revulsion for this antislavery modus operandi (William J. Young, "The Prospect before the Working Classes," *Tribune,* Dec. 13, 1850). Some of the Malthusian arguments placed less emphasis on the expanding population of free laborers within or outside the slave states than on a projected surplus of the slaves themselves and the consequent economic burden for slaveowners (Spengler, "Population Theory in the Ante-Bellum South," 360–89).

16. For northern perceptions of the specifically political threats that slavery and the "slave power" posed to the "fragile republic," see Michael F. Holt, *The Political Crisis of the 1850s* (New York, 1978), 151–52.

17. This is not to deny that an accommodation to individual acquisitiveness, prosperity, and "luxury" distinguished the "liberal republicanism" of Madison and other Founders from ancient republicanism, and that they may have placed their faith more in institutional arrangements than in the citizenry's possession of a genuinely self-denying and self-sacrificing virtue to preserve their republic. The resultant tensions within late eighteenth-century American republican thought continue to draw scholarly debate.

18. Fredrickson, *Black Image,* 154–55; James D. Bilotta, *Race and the Rise of the Republican Party, 1848–1865* (New York, 1992), 376, 419–22; Weston, *Progress,* 33, 131.

19. Weston, *Progress,* 243.

20. As indicated in the Introduction, Achille Murat, among others, made a similar argument in the 1830s with respect to the actual enslavement of blacks in the United States.

21. Sidney George Fisher, *The Laws of Race, as Connected with Slavery* (Philadelphia, 1860), 22; Fredrickson, *Black Image,* 142–47, 154–59.

22. Lawrence Bobo, James R. Kluegel, and Ryan A. Smith, "Laissez-Faire Racism: The Crystallization of a Kinder, Gentler, Antiblack Ideology," in *Racial Attitudes in the 1990s: Continuity and Change,* ed. Steven A. Tuch and Jack K. Martin (Westport, Conn., 1997), 16–41; Carol Horton, "Liberal Equality and the Civic Subject: Identity and Citizenship in Reconstruction America," in Ericson and Green, *Liberal Tradition,* 126–27. Horton's larger argument is that such ascriptive inegalitarian outlooks as antislavery "phylogenetic liberalism" were part and parcel of the American "liberal tradition," rather than distinct from and inherently incompatible with it (136).

23. Here Sidney George Fisher's own racist views deviated from Weston's. Fisher insisted in 1860 that whether free or slave, blacks could not flourish in more temperate climates—ones in which the "more energetic," superior white man was able to "obtain a footing as a laborer"—so that such measures as the repeal of the Missouri Compromise must remain a hollow victory for the South. The climatic determinism that informed Fisher's "natural laws of race" also separated him from Weston, Olmsted, and other free-soil Republicans on the slavery contagion issue: Fisher attributed the degeneration of whites in the "extreme South" not to the effects of slavery but rather to their unsuitability for working and residing in "uncongenial" and "unhealthy" near-tropical conditions, ones for which blacks alone were suited (Fisher, *Laws of Race,* 25–43).

24. Weston, *Wages,* 1, 6–7.

25. Eugene D. Genovese, *The Slaveholders' Dilemma: Freedom and Progress in Southern Conservative Thought, 1820–1860* (Columbia, S.C., 1992), 57.

26. See, for example, "A Statistical View of the Colored Population of the United States—From 1790 to 1850," *Anglo-African Magazine,* May 1859, 141–43.

27. William W. Freehling, "The Divided South, Democracy's Limitations, and the Causes of the Peculiarly North American Civil War," in *Why the Civil War Came,* ed. Gabor S. Boritt (New York, 1996), 133–38. In contrast to Freehling, Weston ignored in his address the tensions over slavery existing between masters in the lower South and those in the middle and border states of the South, and he seems here to have regarded the "slave drain" out of Virginia and the upper South generally as evidence of the system's continuing strength and viability there (Weston, *Wages,* 6–7). But in *Progress of Slavery* Weston also expressed confidence in slavery's disappearance from the northernmost slave states, owing to both political and economic considerations, "at a period not distant" (234–35, 240–42).

28. Weston rejected the antebellum versions of these arguments (*Progress,* 167).

29. Harry V. Jaffa, *The Crisis of the House Divided: An Interpretation of the Issues in the Lincoln-Douglas Debates* (New York, 1959), 394–95.

30. Weston was more inclined in *Progress* than in his address to accentuate the economic inflexibility and occupational limitations of black slavery.

31. Weston, *Wages,* 5. Although abolitionists of the 1830s and 1840s generally subordinated economic to moral and religious themes, some did anticipate the warning of Weston and other Republicans that slave labor threatened growing numbers of free laborers with underselling. In its own earlier effort to draw the support of northern workers to their cause, so that "we should hear of no more [antiabolition] mobs in New-England," the *Liberator* quoted a letter "from a gentleman in Philadelphia" noting that cotton yarn manufactured by Virginia slaves was now selling in Philadelphia "at a lower price, than yarn of equal quality can be afforded when the laborer receives a just remuneration for his toil." The *Liberator* jumped on this bit of information: "Will the 'WORKING-MEN' of New England be content with such wages as will enable their employers successfully to compete with those whose laborers are slaves, receiving no compensation beyond a bare subsistence and which costs the employer a sum not exceeding eight cents a day?" ("The Working-Man," *Liberator,* Dec. 20, 1834). However, other antislavery voices that followed Adam Smith on the economic deficiencies of slave labor were adamant that such deficiencies rendered it incapable of mounting a serious challenge to free labor in manufacturing and other enterprises, which required, in their view, both substantial skill and a decent "motive" on the part of the laborer. As the *Philanthropist* argued, southern slavery certainly damaged "the interests of the free States." But the fear that "Free Labor . . . will be degraded, and impoverished" by slave-labor competition in more "complex" pursuits rested on the "utterly groundless" assumption that slave labor would be "cheaper" and "just as available" in these pursuits. True, "what naked brute force can accomplish, without the informing energy of Intellect, or the necessity of contrivance—and where this brute force may be drawn out under terror of the lash—that Slave-labor may effect. Hence, you may raise cotton, and sugar, and rice, with Slaves." But, the *Philanthropist* stubbornly insisted, "you cannot *farm* with them,—for then they cost more than they are worth,—much less can you manufacture with them" ("Slave-Labor and Free Labor,"

Weekly Herald and Philanthropist, Aug. 16, 1844). This abolitionist position anticipated the more confident and triumphal dimension of Republican free-labor ideology. But it also clashed with that ideology's more alarmist dimension, on particular display in Weston's address, which saw economic vulnerability in free labor's very superiority.

32. Weston, *Wages,* 3–4.

33. Ibid., 3.

34. Ibid., 5.

35. Weston, *Progress,* 221–22.

36. Weston, *Wages,* 3. Southern proslavery voices could share Weston's logic, if not his point of view. Noting that the South's slaves were increasing in "fearful ratio" and warning that their confinement to staple production must ultimately result in overproduction and declining market prices for staples as well as slaves, E. Steadman urged a regional commitment to slave-based manufacturing enterprise. Expansion in this area, he added, would attract white immigrants to the South, enabling it to maintain the equilibrium of the races, and would also establish the South's economic independence (*A Brief Treatise on Manufacturing in the South* [Clarksville, Tenn., 1851], 11–23).

37. With the material well-being of white factory workers in the North in mind, the Democratic paper *Pennsylvanian* in a sense endorsed Weston's pronouncements as to the gravity of the threat of slave-labor competition when it characterized as wrongheaded the efforts of "Black Republicans" like Weston to block slave labor's geographic expansion. Preventing slavery's movement into new agricultural regions in the territories would only stimulate slaveowners to find industrial uses for their expanding slave labor force within the South, thereby exacerbating one of the very tendencies which Weston warned against in his address: "Instead of being as they now are, the great consumers of the products of the mechanics and manufacturers of the North, they [the slaves] will become their rivals, and then supersede them in the markets of the world" ("Aims and Tendencies of Black Republicanism—No. 5," *Pennsylvanian* [Philadelphia], Sept. 1, 1856).

38. Thomas L. Clingman of North Carolina combined several of the stock themes in warning that penning up an expanding slave population eventually would prove calamitous for northern manufacturing workers as well as for the South's white laborers and the slaves themselves (speeches in House, *Cong. Globe,* 30th Cong., 1st sess., *App.,* Dec. 22, 1847, 45, and 31st Cong., 2d sess., *App.,* Feb. 15, 1851, 209, but see also 210). Other southerners saw few dangers in slavery's geographical confinement and warned that its territorial expansion in fact would lead to a damaging drain of slaves out of the South. Thomas Dew and Chancellor Harper earlier had underscored the South's long-term capacity to absorb a much denser slave population, and throughout the antebellum period there were southern proslavery voices (some of whom were involved in the movement to reopen the African slave trade) who also dismissed Malthusian fears of a potential black excess by invoking—as Weston did on a less triumphant note—the "self-protecting power against over-population existing in slave countries" (such dismissals were apart from the proslavery boasts that southern society likewise discouraged white overpopulation) ("Professor Dew on Slavery," *The Pro-Slavery Argument* [Philadelphia, 1853], 467–71, 484–89; "Harper's Memoir on Slavery," ibid., 25–26, 82–85; L. C. B., "The Country in 1850. Or the Conservatism of Slavery," *Southern Literary Messenger* 22 [June 1856]: 438; R. E. C., "The Problem of Free Society," pt. 2, ibid., 27 [July 1858]: 12–13). As Major L. Wilson understandably

concludes, there was considerable ideological disagreement and confusion within the ante-bellum South (as there was among antislavery northerners) regarding the applicability of Malthusian reasoning to the territorial expansion issue (Wilson, "The Controversy over Slavery Expansion and the Concept of the Safety Valve: Ideological Convulsion in the 1850s," *Mississippi Quarterly* 24 [Spring 1971]: 136–38). Still, from the late 1840s the con-tinued natural growth of the slave population generated growing apprehensions among some of slavery's warmest defenders, and one encounters increasingly frequent slavery-expansionist arguments rooted in the black race's ostensible lack of "all prudential restraint"; see the speeches of James McDowell of Virginia, House, *Cong. Globe,* 30th Cong., 2d sess., *App.,* Feb. 23, 1849, 216–17, and Joseph R. Underwood of Kentucky, Sen-ate, ibid., 1st sess., *App.,* July 25, 1848, 1168. William Barney dismisses southern warnings of a future slave surplus "as tinged with paranoia" while still recognizing it as the increas-ingly dominant position in the South (*The Road to Secession: A New Perspective on the Old South* [New York, 1972], 65–70). Northern proslavery voices for their part sympathized with such southern population concerns: the New York *Daily News* attacked Republican free-soil "fanatics" like Weston as "wretched . . . Malthusians who, by confining the slave . . . would exterminate the race" ("The Well Being of the African Race," *Daily News,* July 14, 1856); see also "Humanity and Freesoilism," New York *Weekly Day Book,* Sept. 27, 1856.

39. Weston, *The Poor Whites of the South* (n.p., 1856), 7.

40. Weston, *Wages,* 7.

41. Weston's vagueness as to time frame partially reflected the gradual operation of the soil erosion and other processes on which he pinned much of his hopes for slavery's growing "dearness" and ultimate disappearance from the United States. His gradualism also reflected aversion for immediate abolitionism's insensitivity to "vast pecuniary inter-ests" (Weston, *Progress,* 220–44). Weston's penchant for engaging in vague long-term prog-nostications made him no different from many of his contemporaries, including the proslavery voices who warned of the eventual penning up of a surplus slave population and demanded additional slave territory on this grounds.

42. Weston, *Wages,* 3, 5.

43. Similarly, in terms that were hardly complimentary to the South's enslaved blacks, Weston argued thusly in favor of their emancipation: "The truth is, the peculiar moral and intellectual conformation of the negro, which renders it so easy to enslave him, and which makes him so little dangerous as a slave, makes it safe to liberate him" (Weston, *Progress,* 244).

44. Weston, *Wages,* 7.

45. Foner, *Politics and Ideology,* 28.

46. Weston, *Progress,* 221. Weston was here challenging the notion that the increase of the free laboring population would lead to slavery's extirpation by eventuating in sur-plus—that the wages of free laborers would fall to such levels as to render their services less costly in the South. But aside from the fact that he considered this particular labor-cheapening scenario to be as undesirable as it was unlikely, Weston was also conveying his exceptionalist sense that increased population density was, more happily yet, failing to depress wages and generate widespread immiserization and unemployment in the free states. For one political leader who did regard population pressures and "surplus labor" in the free states as more immediate problems than Weston did and accordingly embraced

slavery's exclusion from Kansas and other territories as a way of preserving these regions as a "refuge" for existing and potential, virtual wage slaves from the North, see the speech of former Kansas governor A. H. Reeder, "The Danger of the Republic," rept. in *Tribune,* Sept. 22, 1856.

47. William Dusinberre suggests that the coercive powers wielded by slaveholders in various contexts may have pushed their slaves into being highly productive even as they remained "inefficient" (*Them Dark Days: Slavery in the American Rice Swamps* [New York, 1996], 136).

48. Despite his general assurances that blacks would "gradually disappear" from the South with slavery's eradication, Weston entertained the possibility that the system of slavery and contact with black slaves might have so "debauched, demoralized, and degraded" the mass of southern whites by this point that the whites would have lost all of their "natural superiority"; consequently it was they who would "run the risk of being expelled by the negro" (Weston, *Progress,* 244–45). The theme of Weston and other northern free-soilers as to a degrading and debilitating cultural osmosis, or pollution, also may have encompassed implicit anxieties that through competition with black labor, southern non-slaveholding whites actually lost some of their "whiteness." Some of the recent scholarship highlighting the social construction of race points to such anxieties, even as other portions of this scholarship suggest that there was a quite different (though not necessarily contradictory) dominant perception within the Old South itself: that to be considered truly white there, one had to own slaves (Scott L. Malcomson, *One Drop of Blood: The American Misadventure of Race* [New York, 2000], 296–302; Walter Johnson, *Soul by Soul: Life inside the Antebellum Slave Market* [Cambridge, Mass., 1999], 90).

49. Aside from the spatial and market proximity to slave labor that he primarily blamed for the degradation of southern nonslaveholding whites, Weston also invoked the southern states' neglect of the educational and other "civilized" needs of this population (Weston, *Poor Whites,* 3).

50. Weston, *Progress,* 231, 48. The fact that Weston dismissed the competitive economic threat posed by free blacks in the North suggests that he regarded the fundamental source of contagion and degradation for free white laborers to be their close market and spatial proximity with chattel slaves, rather than proximity with blacks per se. In 1832 Thomas R. Dew had agreed that in moral character and productivity, "free labor, by association with slave labor [i.e., by working alongside it in the same "occupation"] must inevitably be brought down to its level, and even below it." Although many later defenders of slavery argued differently, Dew nonetheless steered such Gresham's law contagion themes in proslavery directions. He used these first to justify Virginia's need for an ample supply of slaves and then to warn that emancipation without the removal of its infectiously "indolent" blacks would be the worst possible policy for the state ("Professor Dew on Slavery," in *Pro-Slavery Argument,* 363–66, 443–44). Antislavery commentators for their part generally insisted, against Dew, that the multitude of southern white farmers and laborers — and not merely those working in "association" with bondsmen — were already infected and debased by slavery. Yet some remained closer to Dew than to Weston on the Virginian's second point. Francis P. Blair Jr. thus feared that the continued presence of ex-slaves and other free blacks in the United States would "deteriorate" the "superior" white race (through modes of contact extending beyond amalgamation) (Blair, "The Destiny of the

Races of This Continent," lecture rept. in *Tribune,* Feb. 1, 1859). Other antislavery commentators even more vehemently rejected Weston's distinction between free and enslaved blacks: his insistence that only bondsmen constituted a serious economic contaminant and threat to free white labor. Speaking against the influx of blacks, regardless of legal status, into California, one delegate to the state's constitutional convention of 1849, O. M. Wozencraft, insisted that the "admixture" of the black population into the "political economy" of the United States acted as a "foreign, poisonous substance." Wozencraft's characterization of free blacks in the northern states did not differ appreciably from Weston's. As "dead weights in society," they constituted only a marginal competitive danger to northern white labor even as they imposed significant social costs as criminals and paupers. But in California's mines and other enterprises, Wozencraft warned, free blacks would undergo some perverse reinvigoration and emerge as formidable wage slaves. Because, after all, they were "so well adopted for servitude," blacks in California would become the "tool of the capitalist," who would use these "living laboring machines" to establish monopolies. Similar in some respects to Weston's free-soil perspective and deviating from it in others, Wozencraft's amalgam of antislavery, racist, and antimonopoly themes stands as further illustration of the variety that differing contexts and agendas were capable of producing (Wozencraft quoted in *Report on the Debates in the Convention of California, on the Formation of the State Constitution, in September and October, 1849,* ed. J. Ross Browne [Washington, D.C., 1850], 49–50).

51. Mary Douglas, *Purity and Danger: An Analysis of Concepts of Pollution and Taboo* (1966; rept. London, 1989), 3.

52. From his own emphasis upon the economic disadvantages of slave labor, Olmsted was less inclined than Weston even to acknowledge its profitability for individual slaveholders. He maintained that whatever the nature or size of their enterprise, slaveholders would earn greater profits by employing a force of undebased, well-motivated free wage laborers, be they black or white. In developing his own thesis of demoralizing cultural osmosis to explain the prolonged dominance of a system of production he regarded as not merely wasteful and inefficient but also relatively unprofitable for slaveholders themselves, Olmsted also parted company with North Carolina's Daniel R. Goodloe, his collaborator on *The Cotton Kingdom.* Goodloe did not deny that the system of slavery demoralized and debased free white laborers in the South. But he (like many economic historians today) mostly attributed its dominance to the draining monopolistic powers over capital resources maintained by agricultural slavery, above all by the cotton culture and the larger planters. More than Olmsted, Goodloe agreed with Weston's position that "the indolence and thriftlessness of unpaid [slave] labor" did not prevent it from being cheap and highly profitable for the slaveholders who enjoyed this monopoly. Goodloe also believed that apart from the booming state of slave economies in the Southwest, Olmsted slighted the degree to which the domestic slave trade sustained the slave system's profitability even in the border states. Yet the fundamental point of view, to which all three commentators fully subscribed, should not be lost sight of: whatever the specific reasons, the slave system exercised a devastating impact upon southern commercial and industrial development (Goodloe to Olmsted, Feb. 23, 24, March 1, 8, 1861, Frederick Law Olmsted Papers, Library of Congress; Schlesinger, "Editor's Introduction," *Cotton Kingdom,* xxviii–xxxi; [Goodloe], *Inquiry into the Causes Which Have Retarded the Accumulation of Wealth*

and Increase of Population in the Southern States [Washington, D.C., 1846]; Olmsted, *A Journey in the Seaboard Slave States in the Years 1853–1854* [1856; rept. New York, 1904], 2:232; Louis S. Gerteis, *Morality and Utility in American Antislavery Reform* [Chapel Hill, N.C., 1988], 154–65).

53. Olmsted, *Cotton Kingdom*, 90.

54. Olmsted, *Back Country*, 300.

55. Ibid., 302.

56. Olmsted, *Seaboard* 1:233–35, 332; see also Olmsted's letters from the South to the *New-York Times*, March 30, April 20, 1853, Jan. 26, Feb. 13, 1854; Schlesinger, "Introduction," xlviii–liii. In his antebellum published accounts, and more extensively in later unpublished writings, Olmsted described how slaveholders themselves, from the wealthiest on down, exhibited this "barbarizing" tendency. Olmsted was virtually obsessed with exploding the notion that black slavery had enabled southern society to attain a degree of civilization and refinement unknown in the free states.

57. Olmsted, *Seaboard* 1:211–12; see also Susan-Mary Grant, *North over South: Northern Nationalism and American Identity in the Antebellum Era* (Lawrence, Kans., 2000), 98–108.

58. For example, Lawrence T. McDonnell generalizes that southern nonslaveholding whites—the "folk" whom Olmsted broadly characterized as a "'dead peasantry,' 'unambitious, indolent, degraded, and illiterate'"—"probably lacked resources more than gumption" (McDonnell, "Work, Culture, and Society in the Slave South, 1790–1861," in *Black and White Cultural Interaction in the Antebellum South,* ed. Ted Ownby [Jackson, Miss., 1993], 131). For a critical assessment of the capitalist and "orientalist" imperatives that, in tandem with his conventional northern bourgeois beliefs regarding domestic arrangements and space, encouraged Olmsted to elide—and misconceive as white trash—the industrious non- and small slaveholding yeoman families of South Carolina's Low Country, see Stephanie McCurry, *Masters of Small Worlds: Yeoman Households, Gender Relations, and the Political Culture of the Antebellum South Carolina Low Country* (New York, 1995), 39–42, 72–75; see also Charles C. Bolton, *Poor Whites of the Antebellum South: Tenants and Laborers in Central North Carolina and Northeast Mississippi* (Durham, N.C., 1994), 4–41. "Republican" themes that recent scholarship has brought to bear on antebellum southern society have also tended to undermine Olmsted's perspective: "Plain folk, who were long seen as without ambition, are now seen as demonstrating a healthy aversion to the soulless capitalist market" (Edward L. Ayers, "What We Talk about When We Talk about the South," in Ayers et al., *All over the Map: Rethinking American Regions* (Baltimore, 1996), 72.

59. Thaddeus Stevens, House, *Cong. Globe,* 31st Cong., 1st sess., *App.,* Feb. 20, 1850, 142; Eric Foner, *Free Soil, Free Labor, Free Men: The Ideology of the Republican Party before the Civil War* (New York, 1970), 17–18; John Majewski, *A House Dividing: Economic Development in Pennsylvania and Virginia before the Civil War* (Cambridge, 2000), 150–67.

60. Olmsted likened the effects of slavery in Norfolk, Virginia, to a "deadly enervating pestilence" in his April 28, 1853, letter to the *Times.* And like Weston, he insisted that slavery generally demoralized and enervated not merely those free laborers employed in the same task or enterprise with slaves but also those "men working on their own account" in slave society. Yet Olmsted was not oblivious to social complexities that impelled him to qualify his general view occasionally. He admitted to seeing "industrious white men at the South, I have seen many, and seen them side by side with slaves. There are incentives to industry acting counter to this influence of slavery, which in certain situations can not

fail to be in some degree effective, for there is probably no country in the world where nature offers a better reward for intelligent labor than in some parts of the slave States" (Olmsted, *Back Country,* 302).

61. Against the free-soil insistence on slavery's debilitating and degrading influence, proslavery commentators, moreover, commonly defended not merely the respectability of whites who toiled in physical proximity to slave labor. Many included in their defense the small masters and the nonslaveholding whites who worked alongside slaves in the sense of being cooperatively engaged with them, often in performance of the same agricultural or manufacturing labor (the "menial" employments for which black slaves alone allegedly were suited were a different matter, although their attempts to elaborate this "mudsill" category occasioned various difficulties for proslavery polemicists). For one such attack on the "unfounded" antislavery "prejudices" of the Stevenses, the Olmsteds, and the Westons that formed part of his defense of the Kansas-Nebraska Act, see the Senate speech of George W. Jones, Iowa Democrat and a former slaveowner, *Cong. Globe,* 34th Cong., 1st sess., *App.,* April 16, 1856, 408–9; for an earlier rebuttal of the same antislavery "slanders," see the House speech of Richard H. Stanton of Kentucky, ibid., 31st Cong., 1st sess., March 11, 1850, 500; see also Mississippi's Albert Gallatin Brown, in Senate, ibid., 33d Cong., 1st sess., *App.,* Feb. 24, 1854, 230. New York's rabidly racist, proslavery newspaper editor John Van Evrie similarly rejected the "absurd notion" that "it degrades a white man to work alongside of a negro 'slave,'" although he also complained—with some exaggeration—that in the North there was "almost universal" acceptance of the notion, even among "Democratic editors and orators" ("Working Men and 'Slave' Labor," *Day Book,* Nov. 1, 1856). The objections of Van Evrie and others to the antislavery "simplications" of an Olmsted or Weston had a long lineage (perhaps as long as antislavery free-soil ideology itself): they were, for example, made during the Missouri Compromise crisis of 1819–21 by Virginia's Philip P. Barbour. Similar disclaimers of slave labor's degrading effects on the character and enterprise of proximate free white working people were also echoed by later historians—see Frank Owsley, *Plain Folk of the Old South* (1949; rept. Chicago, 1965), 2, and Robert R. Russell, "The Effects of Slavery upon Nonslaveholders in the Ante-Bellum South," *Agricultural History* 15 (April 1941): 112–26; see also Timothy James Lockley, *Lines in the Sand: Race and Class in Low Country Georgia, 1750–1860* (Athens, Ga., 2001), 29–30. Nor is it clear from one recent study of antebellum southern white artisans (Georgia's) whether these as a group were any the less enterprising or fared worse in terms of property and social mobility than northern craftsmen confronted by more extensive industrial deskilling and proletarianization (Gillespie, *Free Labor in an Unfree World,* 127–37). Finally, it remains possible that, northern antislavery claims notwithstanding, slavery and its influence bore only limited responsibility for antebellum southerners' lack of enterprise and aversion for hard work, such as these were; compare C. Vann Woodward, *American Counterpoint: Slavery and Racism in the North-South Dialogue* (Boston, 1964), 32–33, with Grady McWhiney, *Cracker Culture: Celtic Ways in the Old South* (Tuscaloosa, Ala., 1988), 45–46.

62. Weston, *Progress,* 231; Weston, *Wages,* 5.

63. I am referring primarily to Eric Foner's characterization of Republican free-labor ideology in *Free Soil, Free Labor.* But I also dissent from William E. Gienapp's different position regarding the party's late antebellum ideological thrust: "The belief that free labor

could not compete with slavery . . . was distinctly subordinate to other [Republican] concerns." Weston's orientation may well have been more political economic than that of most Republican commentators. Nonetheless, the economic anxieties that he as well as other of these commentators expressed cannot be neatly separated from what Gienapp does assign central importance to: the party's fears of the slave power's aristocratic, oligarchic designs on the "republican" liberties of northern whites (Gienapp, "The Republican Party and the Slave Power," in *New Perspectives on Race and Slavery in America,* ed. Robert H. Abzug and Stephen E. Maizlish [Lexington, Ky., 1986], 69–70).

64. Isaac Toucey, speech, *Cong. Globe,* 33d Cong., 1st sess., *App.,* March 3, 1854, 318.

65. To elaborate on northern Democratic attitudes: Toucey and other northern Democrats, following Illinois senator Stephen A. Douglas, insisted that among the most decisive determinants of whether a given community incorporated black chattel slavery were factors of "climate and soil." Because these "natural" factors largely determined slavery's profitability, they were in turn inexorably reflected in the popular will. They were reflected in the "democratic" sentiments of the white local majority that, exercising its moral right to community self-governance, "voted" slavery "up or down," along with other domestic institutions. This northern Democrat abstract formula of congressional nonintervention, or "popular sovereignty," in the territories contained undoubted flaws, both ethical and practical. But whatever these were, the formula's dollars-and-cents premise resolved itself into the two basic arguments in response to Republican free-soilism. (1) Federal action banning slavery would prove as unnecessary as it was offensive to southern sensibilities; free labor's victory was secure. This was owing to the conditions of climate and soil in the remaining territories, as well as because of other competitive advantages enjoyed by a free-labor economy (e.g., the superiority in numbers, ease and speed of migration, and overall energy of white farmers and wage earners committed to a free-labor system). (2) The expansive United States, encompassing many local communities, in any case had thrived on a "diversity" of institutions and arrangements. Black slave labor had contributed its part to American ascendancy just as it had not appreciably impeded the life chances of nonslaveholding whites in the South. My discussion in this chapter is mostly concerned with the Gresham's law–like anxieties that led Republicans like Weston to resist and attack the first of these Democratic arguments—the argument that played up the "natural limits" and impediments to slavery's expansion. But with respect to the second, "diversity" argument of Douglas and his followers, one may note what had become by the late 1850s the standard antislavery Republican response, in this instance curtly offered by Horace Greeley: "Men in South Carolina require different clothing, with somewhat different food, from men in Massachusetts; not different 'Institutions'" (untitled editorial *Tribune,* July 13, 1858). For the northern Democrat diversity perspective and the insistence that there was no natural, fundamental "antagonism" between North and South, see "The Slave-holding Aristocracy," Maine *Age* (Augusta), March 16, 1858 (ironically, this was the paper that Weston had edited back in the early 1840s). In an insightful discussion of the ideological distinctions between Republicans and northern Democrats, John Ashworth underscores the Republicans' more enthusiastic acceptance of free waged labor (usually coupled with an exaltation of upward-mobility opportunities in the free states) as a driving force behind their free-soilism and fixation on the slave power. Ashworth, however, seemingly misses the relevance of the two north-

ern Democratic themes accentuated above (Ashworth, "Free Labor, Wage Labor, and the Slave Power," in Stokes and Conway, *Market Revolution*, 141–42; see also Michael A. Morrison, *Slavery and the American West: The Eclipse of Manifest Destiny and the Coming of the American Civil War, 1844–1861* [Chapel Hill, N.C., 1997], 122–23, 143–48).

66. Weston, *Progress*, 231.

67. Ibid., 33–34, 234. See Seward's March, 11, 1850, Senate speech for one sample of his dualism. Seward noted that slavery observed no natural limits to its expansion, and that its expansion, encouraged by slave labor's cheapness, was driven by powerful economic and political interests — thus the desirability of state legal measures to exclude slavery from new territories. Yet, foreshadowing his "irrepressible conflict" speech of eight years later (and like some of his northern Democratic critics), Seward went on to suggest the ultimate irrelevance of such legal mechanisms: "I feel assured that slavery must give way, and will give way, to the salutary instructions of economy, and to the ripening influences of humanity; that emancipation is inevitable, and is near; that it may be hastened or hindered" (Seward, *Works of Seward* 1:87).

68. Foner, *Free Soil, Free Labor*, 53; Gunja SenGupta, *For God and Mammon: Evangelicals and Entrepreneurs, Masters and Slaves in Territorial Kansas, 1854–1860* (Athens, Ga., 1996). Weston's *Progress*, published in the year following the address, more fully expresses the optimistic side of his free-labor ideology; it exudes a stronger air of confidence that the superior system of free labor will win out, securing by its economic strengths the gradual displacement of slave labor everywhere in the nation. Frederick Law Olmsted, for his part, was pessimistic about the success in the foreseeable future of antislavery enterprises that depended on altering the social attitudes of southern poor whites and restoring their productive and competitive capability. He believed that the only way to eventually extinguish slavery was to ring the slave states with free farm communities that would "however slowly, move up upon & drive back slavery" (Olmsted to Samuel Cabot Jr., June 29, 1857, in *The Papers of Frederick Law Olmsted*, ed. Charles E. Beveridge and Charles Capen McLaughlin, 2 [Baltimore, 1981]: 433).

69. Francis P. Blair Jr. of Missouri, in House, *Cong. Globe*, 35th Cong., 1st sess., March 23, 1858, 1283–84; for an earlier statement of the antimonopoly theme by a political abolitionist, see "All Territory Acquired by the General Government Belongs to the Free Laboring Classes of the Country," *National Era*, Nov. 18, 1847. In applying the antimonopoly theme in antislavery, antisouthern directions — in making the shift from the attack on the northern money power to the southern slave power — Blair was preceded by other Jacksonian Democrats, as well as by the political abolitionists. Prior to this time, such Jacksonians as William Leggett had commonly supported slaveholders' right to their human property within the slave states by at the least implying that slaveholders had acquired this property without the benefit of governmental "exclusive legislation." But those Jacksonian Democrats and others who from the mid-1830s on targeted slaveholders as monopolists argued not merely that the slave power sought to extend its baleful influence within the national government. They also increasingly insisted that slaveholding planters were able to retain their human property — keep themselves afloat — "only by borrowing and buying on credit" from the northern monopolists of governmental privileges, from the "financiers and merchants, who had gained their own profits by plundering the wealth of northern farmers and workingmen" (Sean Wilentz, "Slavery, Antislavery, and Jacksonian

Democracy," in Stokes and Conway, *Market Revolution,* 212; Wilentz, "Jacksonian Abolitionist: The Conversion of William Leggett," in *The Liberal Persuasion: Arthur Schlesinger, Jr.,
and the Challenge of the Liberal Past,* ed. John Patrick Diggins [Princeton, N.J., 1997], 89–90).

70. Kennebec *Journal* (Maine), quoted in "'The Slave-holding Aristocracy.'"

71. Such ambiguity might be extended to urban slaveholders who employed slaves solely
as domestic servants rather than for income-generating purposes.

72. "Slavery and the Future," *Tribune,* May 27, 1854; James L. Huston, "Property Rights
in Slavery and the Coming of the Civil War," *Journal of Southern History* 65 (May 1999):
267–77. In his discussion of the Weston–free-soil theme that slave-labor competition—
competition from "property rights in people"—inexorably depressed wages and debased
free laborers, Huston perhaps overemphasizes the specter of slavocratic monopoly as a
component of such anxieties.

73. Seymour Drescher notes that "even at the height of abolitionist influence, . . . there
never seems to have been a moment when faith in free labor superiority reigned uncontested in Britain, including among the abolitionist leadership" (Drescher, "Free Labor
vs. Slave Labor," 85). Drescher's emphasis is upon the nagging, if usually recessive, perception within British antislavery circles that black bondage remained a rational and profitable response to free-labor-scarce, quasi-tropical, and staple agricultural conditions within
the Americas. That perception also contributed something to the comparable lack of total
faith in free-labor superiority manifested within United States antislavery circles. But there
remained important differences between the British and the United States contexts. By
the nineteenth century black slaves, first, were to an overwhelming degree physically absent
and geographically distant from the British mainland. Second, there appears never to have
been much thought that the slaves of the British West Indies would or could be deployed
in raising crops or manufacturing items directly competitive with those produced by
Britain's free laborers. Absent from the British case, in other words, was the proximity of
both the slaves themselves and the slave-labor market that might fuel anxieties over the
cultural contagion and economic debasement of free white labor, precisely those anxieties
that tempered the confidence of Weston and other American antislavery commentators
in slavery's inexorable disappearance from the United States.

74. Beyond his focus on slavery's tendency to infect and weaken free labor, Olmsted
was among those who cited the "fraud and violence" employed by the supporters of
Kansas's Lecompton Constitution in partial explanation of how slavery, with all its "eco-
nomical disadvantages, can take possession of any country, to the exclusion or serious
inconvenience of free labor" (Olmsted, *A Journey through Texas* [1860; rept. New York,
1969], xvi–xx).

75. Hammond's mudsill speech of March 1858 was especially rich in the flurry of celebratory portraits of the northern social order that it provoked from Republican senators.
However, a few of these portraits, such as that by Ohio's Benjamin F. Wade, were less
glowing than others. These noted the discomfiting presence in the North of the Irish and
other "offscourings" of the Old World—those social elements that contributed to the
viciousness of New York and other large cities and that, not coincidentally, were also perversely Democratic in their allegiance; see *Cong. Globe,* 35th Cong., 1st sess., for speeches
by Hannibal Hamlin (March 9 and 11, 1858, 1005–7, 1025–27), Zachariah Chandler (March
12, 1093), Wade (March 13, 1113), and Henry Wilson (*App.,* March 20, 169–74).

76. The analogous southern proslavery position, emerging in the wake of the favorable Dred Scott ruling and Stephen Douglas's efforts to salvage popular sovereignty through the Freeport doctrine, was the demand for a territorial slave code that would secure slavery's existence in the face of hostile community sentiment. Proslavery and antislavery commentators alike commonly subscribed to the view that the first (i.e., territorial) decisions made with respect to slavery were the crucial ones. If given the advantage of a foothold in a Kansas or Nebraska, slavery would become culturally ingrained and institutionalized and for all practical purposes was there to stay. But existing above and beyond this belief (which Lincoln notably articulated) was the free-soil fear that free labor simply could not compete with slave labor under most any circumstances.

77. One could include, among the examples of this late antebellum antislavery responsiveness, something like Olmsted's observation that "it is the first duty of those who think Slavery wrong to remove to the utmost all such excuse for it as is to be found in the occasional hardships and frequent debasement and ignorance of the laboring class in free communities." The North could help end slavery by "making the best possible use of free labor, by demonstrating that the condition of the laborer is *not* necessarily a servile one; that the occupation of the laborer does *not* necessarily prevent a high intellectual and moral development, does not necessarily separate a man from great material comfort" (Olmsted, *Seaboard* 2:58; Yeoman [Olmsted], "The South. Letters on the Production, Industry and Resources of the Southern States. Number Forty-Eight—The Last," *Times*, Feb. 13, 1854). In fact, however, by the late antebellum years proslavery challenges were inducing relatively few specimens of the self-scrutiny that characterized these particular remarks of Olmsted's. As the Republican congressional rebuttals of Hammond's mudsill thesis tended to exemplify, and as Olmsted himself illustrated on other occasions, the "responsiveness" of antislavery, antisouthern commentators more often took the form of a rather uncritical affirmation of the values and opportunity structure of the northern free-labor social order. On the rise of northern nationalism, see Grant, *North over South*.

6. Convict Labor, Free Labor, and Gresham's Law

1. Weston, *Wages*, 6.

2. For the neglected nineteenth-century metaphor of "debt slavery," see Scott A. Sandage, "Deadbeats, Drunkards, and Dreamers: A Cultural History of Failure in America, 1819–1893" (Ph.D. diss., Rutgers Univ., 1995), 122–30.

3. Weston was not alone among antislavery commentators in invoking the convict-labor issue to underscore the more momentous incompatibility of slave with free labor; see the warning that the Kentucky abolitionist Cassius Clay directed in 1845 at mechanics in his state who had petitioned against state prison industry competition (*The Writings of Cassius Marcellus Clay*, ed. Horace Greeley [1848; New York, 1969], 234). The *Pennsylvania Freeman* also foreshadowed Weston's use of analogies to stimulate antislavery action. Unlike abolitionists who minimized the deployment of "inferior" slave labor in manufactures as a potential competitive threat to northern enterprises, the *Freeman* warned that "the availability of slave labor for manufacturing has not yet been tested, we believe. If it can be successfully employed, it will be sorely at the expense of the free laborers of the North.—What will our political declaimers and statesmen—who are crying ever for a

protection to American working-men from a ruinous competition with the low-priced labor of Europe—say to exposing them to a worse competition with the *stolen* labor of the South? . . .Where are the men who have made an outcry against the competition of the labor of convicts in the penitentiaries with honest mechanics and manufacturers?" ("Slave Labor vs. Free Labor," rept. in *Emancipator,* Oct. 27, 1847).

4. Rothman, *Discovery of the Asylum,* 246–47. Contract labor was one outgrowth of the acceptance of ("silent") congregate-labor practices during the early nineteenth century— the distinguishing feature of the Auburn system. Beyond their promise as a source of reve-nue, growing numbers of penal reformers and elected officials came to endorse these practices (in conjunction with each inmate's isolation in a cell at night) as a more effec-tive means of disciplining and rehabilitating prisoners than the alternative system of con-tinuous solitary confinement, which included daily labor in the individual's cell (the Pennsylvania system). Nonetheless, there were early nineteenth-century commentators who insisted that any such endorsements of congregate prison labor for its supposed reha-bilitative value amounted to mere rationalizations of the profit motive; see the *Report on the Penitentiaries of the United States* (1835; Montclair, N.J., 1969), 24–25, by the British observer William Crawford.

5. Hirsch, *Rise of the Penitentiary,* 97–98; Glen A. Gildemeister, *Prison Labor and Convict Competition with Free Workers in Industrializing America, 1840–1890* (New York, 1987), 127–64; Orlando F. Lewis, *The Development of American Prisons and Prison Customs, 1776–1845* (1922; Montclair, N.J., 1967), 130–46; W. David Lewis, *From Newgate to Dannemora: The Rise of the Penitentiary in New York, 1796–1848* (Ithaca, N.Y., 1965), 178–200, 260–67; Hugins, *Jackson-ian Democracy,* 155–61; Georg Rusche and Otto Kirchheimer, *Punishment and Social Structure* (1939; rept. New York, 1968), 127–30. The last book is an influential comparative Marx-ist study that interprets the rise and persistence of the contract-labor system in the north-ern states as a function of free-labor shortages that prevailed there during the early Industrial Revolution. Such an explanatory emphasis cannot by itself readily explain the intense opposition of free workers to the contract system, which the study also acknowl-edges. A more recent Marxist interpretation, by Rosalind P. Petchesky, also runs into dif-ficulty in accommodating this opposition, although it characterizes the emergence of the contract system more as a preventive check on the "rebelliousness" of free workers than as a response to their numerical scarcity. Petchesky holds that the system was intended from the first not merely to inure convicts themselves in the ways of industrial work rhythms and productivity but to "discipline" free workers as well. She further claims that as an early form of industrial "subcontracting," contract convict labor did indeed suc-cessfully "remind" craft and other free workers of their replaceability and actually dis-couraged protest movements and strikes throughout the United States for most of the nineteenth century. But although free-labor opposition to contract prison competition may indeed have been generally unsuccessful during this period, that opposition was unde-niable and oftentimes intense—the contract system hardly checked its emergence (Petch-esky, "At Hard Labor: Penal Confinement and Production in Nineteenth-Century America," in *Crime and Capitalism: Readings in Marxist Criminology,* ed. David F. Greenberg, rev. ed. [Philadelphia, 1993], 595–611; see also Christopher Adamson, "Toward a Marx-ian Penology: Captive Criminal Populations as Economic Threats and Resources," *Social Problems* 31 [April 1984]: 435–56; Mark Colvin, *Penitentiaries, Reformatories, and Chain Gangs:*

Social Theory and the History of Punishment in Nineteenth-Century America [New York, 1997], 13–17; William G. Staples, *Castles of Our Conscience: Social Control and the American State, 1800–1985* [Cambridge, 1990], 26–42).

6. This is not to deny that at certain places, workers (both native and foreign-born) who belonged to trades that had never been especially skilled might also oppose convict labor. Along with their efforts at unionization, these workers' protests against prison industry might thus be seen as an attempt to construct a craft community, rather than to defend one. I am indebted to Howell Harris for underscoring this point to me with reference to the opposition waged by New York's iron molders against Sing Sing Prison's contract labor in the 1860s; see also Gildemeister, *Prison Labor,* 144–45, 175–85; Greenberg, *Worker and Community,* 143–60.

7. Gildemeister generalizes that convict laborers generally totaled less than one-tenth of 1 percent of the workingmen in New York and other states (Gildemeister, *Prison Labor,* 140). A New York Senate committee reported that in 1834 thirty-two industries employed 1,311 convicts, against a total of 125,000 mechanics in the state. Carl N. Degler notes that as of September 1860 in New York's two state prisons, 940 of Sing Sing's 1,238 convicts (most but not all of these being male) and 722 of Auburn's 853 prisoners were on contract (in response to the restrictive labor legislation of the 1830s and 1840s, convict labor at the newer Dannemora State Prison was devoted to noncompetitive iron manufacture and did not involve private contracting). These Sing Sing and Auburn figures might be set against the much larger one of 176,885 males (and additionally, the 53,227 females) who, according to the U.S. census of 1860, were employed in some manufacturing capacity in New York State. In this as in earlier years, the numbers who actually made their living in one of the "mechanic" trades most directly affected by convict-labor competition were less than this manufacturing total, though the incomplete data for the antebellum period and the ambiguities inherent in the category "mechanic" make it unlikely that the precise numbers can be determined (*Documents of the Senate of the State of New York* [hereafter *DS*] [1834], vol. 2, no. 114, p. 2; Degler, "Labor in the Economics and Politics of New York City, 1850–1860" [Ph.D. diss., Columbia Univ., 1952], 144 n). For a proposed specific breakdown of the employments in which male and female inmates of Sing Sing were to be contracted out around this time, see *New York State Assembly Documents* (hereafter *DA*) (1859), vol. 4, no. 172; see also Wilentz, *Chants Democratic,* 133; Lewis, *Prisons,* 146; Lewis, *Newgate,* 260–62.

8. Gildemeister, *Prison Labor,* 159.

9. Petchesky, "Hard Labor," 603–4.

10. Lewis, *Newgate,* 187; Hugins, *Jacksonian Democracy,* 161.

11. Lewis, *Prisons,* 134–35; Paul Robert Eisenhauer, "Organizing Discipline: Prison Organization and Penal Theory in 19th Century New York" (Ph.D. diss., Univ. of Pennsylvania, 1988), 106–8.

12. Minority report, *DA* (1835), vol. 4, no. 330, p. 15.

13. "We find that the injury [inflicted by "the present mode of employing convicts"] is spreading and increasing in magnitude—that trade after trade is being broken up, and that if not checked, its ultimate effect will be to force the well disposed laborer to perpetrate crime so that he may procure employment and a home in the prisons of the different States" (meeting of New York City mechanics, *DA* [1842], vol. 4, no. 65, p. 71). In fact, for

coopering and some other trades, contract-labor competition did assume more serious proportions in the latter part of the nineteenth century (Gildemeister, *Prison Labor,* 185–95). William Leggett, the New York journalist and Jacksonian proponent of laissez-faire principles, weighed in against the "state prison monopoly" but on yet more restricted grounds. "We believe that the *practical evil* of state prison competition on any mechanic class is . . . exceedingly and almost incalculably light," and he furthermore suggested, in contrast to the mechanics meeting quoted above, that it would continue to be so in the future, however much "demagogues" claimed otherwise. Nonetheless, Leggett agreed that state prison labor was odious and objectionable as *"principle,"* for it violated the "cardinal object of Government," which was "the equal protection of all citizens" (New York *Evening Post,* April 28, 1835, rept. in *Democratick Editorials: Essays on Jacksonian Political Economy by William Leggett,* ed. Lawrence H. White [Indianapolis, 1984], 315–18).

14. "Address and Resolutions of the Convention of Mechanics of New York State Held in Utica, Aug. 20, 1834," rept. in "Mechanic Convention," *Niles' Register,* Sept. 20, 1834. Quotations from Austin Baldwin, *DA* (1842), vol. 4, no. 65, p. 101; 1823 memorial of New York mechanics, quoted in Gildemeister, *Prison Labor,* 130; standing committee report, *DA* (1841), vol. 5, no. 186, p. 7; minority report, *DA* (1837), vol. 3, no. 169, p. 2; Lewis, *Newgate,* 190; see also Lewis, *Prisons,* 134–36, for a judicious assessment of many of these imputed evils, one that is generally supportive of the mechanics' position.

15. See letter from W on "The State Prison Question," *Tribune,* Nov. 6, 1841, in response to the argument made by one defender of New York's state prison system (Z. Y. X.) that society's felons, as well as its "virtuous" members, were "entitled" to labor. Unlike other opponents of contract convict labor, W did not respond by denying compulsory labor's moral value and its therapeutic benefits for the convict. For W there remained more compelling moral reasons to oppose contract convict labor, whatever "pecuniary advantage" it brought to the state. Virtuous men—those outside of prisons—did not, he explained, "work for the sake of labor merely." In fact, "the *reward* of labor is the inducing cause," and it was this reward which was being denied by the system that placed the labor of "convicts and felons . . . in competition with that of the honest man." In reducing that reward below "a fair average equivalent for services rendered," the state prison system "ruined" and demoralized New York's mechanics, thereby actually encouraging vice and committing "both a private injury and a public wrong." Individuals like Z. Y. X. with whom W was taking issue were not, for their part, necessarily unqualified enthusiasts of existing contract convict-labor practices. But they maintained that the ultimate result, if not the absolute intent, of a successful mechanic crusade of opposition would be to return convicts to a state of unwholesome and inhumane confinement without labor (Z. Y. X., "Thoughts on the State Prison System," and "Thoughts on the State Prison System. No. II," ibid., Sept. 23, Oct. 20, 1841).

16. "A Mechanic," *Working Man's Advocate,* March 12, 1831; "Mechanics' State Convention," *New York State Mechanic* (Albany), Dec. 11, 1841; mechanics state convention, *DA* (1842), vol. 4, no. 65, p. 61. Partly because New York and other northern states had a strong tradition of building state penitentiaries during the early nineteenth century, a contract system rather than a total lease system came to prevail there. Under the lease system employers exercised far greater autonomy with respect to security, maintenance, amount and type of labor, and conditions of confinement. Under the contract system contractors

divided these and other responsibilities with the state, a formula that followed from the fact that the labor of the prisoners generally remained within state prison walls. There was also a state account system, in which the prisons provided the raw materials and exercised more control over the labor regimen. Like total leasing, the state account system was less prevalent than the contract system during the antebellum period (Gildemeister, *Prison Labor*, 29–38).

17. Letter to Charles Humphrey, *DA* (1834), vol. 4, no. 352, pp. 47–48.

18. "Penitentiary Labor in Albany!!!" *Mechanic's Advocate*, Sept. 11, 1847.

19. Wilentz, *Chants Democratic*, 233. It "is no fancied picture . . . that the employers could compel them [the 'honest' cordwainers seeking a 'more equitable remuneration'] to stand out til starvation and desolation would stare them in the face, or cause them to work at such wages as their avarice may prescribe" ("Report of the Society of Journeymen Cordwainers of Philadelphia, Relative to Prison Labor," March 1836, in Commons et al., *Documentary History* 5:53–56).

20. "A Mechanic"; see also mechanic petitions, *DA* (1834), vol. 4, no. 352; Onondaga and Albany mechanic conventions proceedings, *DA* (1842), vol. 4, no. 65, pp. 64, 65, 71.

21. William G. Roy, *Socializing Capital: The Rise of the Large Industrial Corporation in America* (Princeton, N.J., 1997), 44; "A Mechanic." As a meeting of Rochester mechanics claimed, "Under the present prison system, we find the State virtually entered upon the arena of competition with the individual, and enabled by its superior power to crush entirely, or drive from his occupation the honest unaided mechanic, who has devoted the best years of his life to the acquisition of the knowledge essential to the practice of his vocation" (*DA* [1842], vol. 4, no. 65, pp. 63–64); see also "Mechanics' State Convention." Supportive members of a New York Assembly committee similarly characterized the underselling achieved by prison goods as an evil resulting from the "direct and arbitrary interference of an institution established by a government" (minority report, *DA* [1835], vol. 4, no. 330, pp. 12–13).

22. In the period before the emergence of large-scale corporations, workingmen and others were not generally confronted with the dilemma of assessing the competitive fairness and the threats to the economic and political liberties of ordinary Americans that inhered in enterprises wielding monopolistic powers without the benefit of explicit government-granted privileges.

23. For the related argument that Jacksonian labor activists in fact were quite accepting of judicial conspiracy rulings that would restrain their own combinations so long as the state, in consistent fashion, also more vigorously moved to check employers' collective and "monopolistic" actions and to otherwise offset previous "antilabor," "antirepublican" government intervention, see Victoria C. Hattam, *Labor Visions and State Power: The Origins of Business Unionism in the United States* (Princeton, N.J., 1994), 83–105. For a partial dissent from Hattam's quid pro quo interpretation, one that argues that precisely because Jacksonian labor activists saw workers as the most republican, legitimate members of the community, they remained resistant to governmental constraints upon labor's collective activity, see Tomlins, *Law, Labor, and Ideology*, 155–56.

24. Wilentz, *Chants Democratic*, 241; Lewis, *Newgate*, 189; Hugins, *Jacksonian Democracy*, 155–56; "Report of the State Prison Commissioners," *Working Man's Advocate*, Feb. 21, 1835; Roy, *Socializing Capital*, 73; for the willingness of Whig-Republicans as well as Democrats

to intermittently embrace anticorporate and antimonopoly small-producer rhetoric, see Freyer, *Producers versus Capitalists*, 35.

25. Remarks of James Hall, who for six years had been engaged in the Sing Sing marble quarries. Hall insisted along these same lines, with respect to the state-supported underbidding for stone cutting practiced by the contractors, that "the objections have not been raised against the right, but the mode of this competition." Because the Sing Sing marble workshops operated under disadvantages with regard to transportation and other matters, the establishment of competitive market conditions, in Hall's view, would place independent stone-cutting employers and their journeymen in a favorable position (*DA* [1833], vol. 3, no. 199, pp. 36–37).

26. Rochester mechanics meeting, *DA* (1842), vol. 4, no. 65, p. 63.

27. *DS* (1834), vol. 2, no. 114, pp. 2–5; see also report, *DA* (1834), vol. 4, no. 352, p. 12. A year earlier the Whig textile magnate and politician Nathan Appleton offered a similar definition of monopoly in rebuttal of the free-trade argument that existing protective-tariff legislation conferred monopoly privileges upon New England's cotton industry: "A monopoly is an exclusive privilege. What exclusive privilege attaches to a business which is open to every individual in the United States?" (Appleton, quoted in Huston, *Securing the Fruits*, 247).

28. *DS* (1834), vol. 2, no. 114, pp. 2–5.

29. *DS* (1841), vol. 2, no. 54, pp. 4–8. This particular argument—marketplace competition that injured some was justifiable because of the multitudinous (consumer) interests it benefited—could cut both ways. Only one year later the competition that promoted "the best interests of trade" was invoked by Chief Justice of Massachusetts Lemuel Shaw in his landmark decision *Commonwealth v. Hunt*, decriminalizing trade unions and "normalizing" them, in David Brody's words, as "economic actors" in an "enterprising society" (Brody, "Free Labor, Law, and American Trade Unionism," in Engerman, *Terms of Labor*, 223–26). Still, neoclassical economists have utilized the New York Senate committee's notion of consumer interests to discredit Marxist and other left-leaning notions of capitalist economic exploitation (George J. Stigler, *Essays in the History of Economics* [Chicago, 1965], 270–71).

30. *DS* (1841), vol. 2, no. 54, pp. 4–8. This report provoked a contrary response from William H. Seward, New York's liberal Whig governor. Seward insisted that there was indeed a distinct mechanic interest, just as there was a farming interest, a commercial interest, etc., and that it was the state's mechanics, not its lawyers, doctors, merchants, or farmers, who were disproportionately injured by existing prison practices. Seward rejected the demand of some of the most extreme critics that convicts be returned to an older barbaric and "horrible" system of solitary confinement without labor. With more moderate critics, he looked instead to rechanneling convict labor into enterprises in which the state's mechanics were not engaged, including silk manufacture, mines, and public works. All of these proposals, however, had their own disadvantages (*DS* [1841], vol. 3, no. 91, pp. 2–8).

31. Dunham in *DA* (1834), vol. 4, no. 341, pp. 4, 4–16. Dunham described himself as first a mechanic who had been employed in the construction of Auburn Prison in 1816 and then as a master builder, contractor, and officer at the prison (p. 2).

32. One informed source estimated the total number of mechanics in New York State to be 125,000 (minority report, *DA* [1835], vol. 4, no. 330, p. 15).

33. Dunham in *DA* (1834), vol. 4, no. 341, pp. 14–16.

34. The senate committee report of 1841 offered statistics from the Auburn State Prison in demonstration of "how small a portion, comparatively, of the products of convict labor, in fact, come in competition with the manufactures of the State, except the immediate neighborhood of the prison" (*DS* [1841], vol. 2, no. 54, pp. 11, 8–20). For another characterization of convict-labor competition as largely illusory, see standing committee report, *DA* (1841), vol. 5, no. 186, p. 9. Aside from endorsing Dunham's view that the products produced in New York's state prisons were "trifling" in quantity and inferior in quality, this document added the argument that they were often shipped out of New York and did not damage the state's manufacturing enterprises for this reason. This argument, however, failed to address the point that some of these enterprises also sought to sell their products out of state. For one of many disputes over the number of "honest" mechanics and the particular trades in New York State that were affected by state prison labor, see the exchange between Cato, "The State Prison Question," and Horace Greeley, in *Tribune*, Oct. 22, 1841. In his report of 1886 on convict labor, U.S. Commissioner of Labor Carroll D. Wright generalized the ratio of productivity between convict labor and free labor to be two-thirds (Gildemeister, *Prison Labor,* 126).

35. See the mechanic proceedings in *DA* (1842), vol. 4, no. 65, pp. 60–72.

36. Baldwin, ibid., p. 100.

37. Adam Smith for one, however, experienced growing doubts that cheapened commodities, as one result of the technical superiority of the division of labor, specifically redounded to the benefit of wage-earning laborers. His increased recognition that manufacturing capitalists did not necessarily share their higher profits with their workers ran alongside his separate criticisms of the intellectually degrading effects of detailed manufacturing division of labor upon workmen. For discussion of these issues, including Smith's apparent failure to recognize the operatives' degradation and demoralization as a possible obstacle to their productivity, see James Bernard Murphy, *The Moral Economy of Labor: Aristotelian Themes in Economic Theory* (New Haven, 1993), 151–64. Smith's multiple and even contradictory claims presaged the complex realities of manufacturing division of labor as it evolved in both old and new industries during the eighteenth and nineteenth centuries—realities that carried implications for both work skills and product quality. As Austin Baldwin hinted, manufacturing division of labor under capitalism could create and increase skills while simultaneously narrowing their sphere of activity, culminating in products of superior quality. Prison industries themselves, however, hardly provided the best examples of such tendencies.

38. Baldwin, *DA* (1842), vol. 4, no. 65, pp. 100–101.

39. For suggestive parallels with British attitudes, see Adrian Randall et al., "Introduction," in *Markets, Market Culture, and Popular Protest in Eighteenth-Century Britain and Ireland,* ed. Randall and Andrew Charlesworth (Liverpool, Eng., 1996), 1–24.

40. Minority report, *DA* (1835), vol. 4, no. 330, p. 13.

41. B. C. True, "State Prison Labor," *New York State Mechanic,* Jan. 28, 1843; see also mechanics' proceedings, *DA* (1842), vol. 4, no. 65, pp. 60–72.

42. Roy, *Socializing Capital,* 277.

43. Responding to one correspondent who, following Auburn agent Dunham, had claimed that the labor of state prison inmates was compulsory, "and consequently the least

possible amount is performed," Horace Greeley sided with Austin Baldwin on the productiveness, and hence the competitive threat, of that labor: "Prison laborers have few idle days or hours; there is hardly a drone in the hive; their energies are not diverted; and they are frequently stimulated by a stipulated payment for overwork, having a regular day's work allotted to them. We do not believe any population of 5,000 does so much work as [the 1,500 inmates of] our two State Prisons" (Cato, "Question," and Horace Greeley's response). And as the New York Senate committee report of 1841, discussed above, suggests, there were always some defenders of the contract system who, in contrast to Dunham, shared the view of adversaries like Baldwin and Greeley that convict labor might well approach or even surpass free labor in work performance and productivity. During their tour of American prisons in 1831, Tocqueville and Beaumont interviewed the supervisor for one contractor who oversaw thirty convicts in an Auburn Prison tool shop. Paralleling in his views some of the commentary on southern slave labor, this man was "convinced that . . . through the fear inspired in them by the whip [which was liberally applied at Auburn to maintain discipline] . . . in the course of a year more work is obtained from a prisoner than from a free labourer"—this despite the fact that the contractor paid out an average of only thirty cents per day for each of these inmates, compared to the twenty dollars a month minimum that men "at liberty" would earn for the same work (George W. Pierson, *Tocqueville in America*, abridged by Dudley C. Lunt [1938; rept. Garden City, N.Y., 1959], 132–33); for the stint and overwork reward system that prison wardens and contractors developed during the early nineteenth century to further stimulate convict productivity, see Gildemeister, *Prison Labor*, 101–25; for tensions between the use of such profit-maximizing incentives and the coexisting reform vision of convict rehabilitation through punitive incarceration, see Larry Goldsmith, "'To Profit by His Skill and to Traffic on His Crime': Prison Labor in Early 19th-Century Massachusetts," *Labor History* 40 (Nov. 1999): 439–57.

44. Those who minimized free labor's fragility—such as the northern Democrats discussed in chapter 5—were hardly more disposed to deny essential distinctions between free and chattel-slave labor.

45. Baldwin, *DA* (1842), vol. 4, no. 65, p. 102.

46. "A Mechanic"; Lewis, *Prisons*, 136, 143.

47. "State Prison Labor," New York *Plebeian*, rept. in *New York State Mechanic*, May 27, 1843. However, one defender of the system, Auburn agent Dunham, himself claimed in 1834 that not over one in twenty of the convicts received at Auburn had been mechanics when convicted. He did this for purposes of underscoring the time and effort that contractors were obliged to make in training convicts, in partial explanation of why they were not paying the state too little for their prison labor (*DA* [1834], vol. 4, no. 341, 13–14). But seven years later, when the focus of the debates had shifted, a different report in defense of the contract system more typically insisted that substantial numbers of men were entering Auburn as mechanics. In responding to this claim, the dissenting minority report preferred to emphasize the "new" trade skills that these convicts too were learning in prison, contrary to the best interests of the "honest" mechanics on the outside (minority report, *DA* [1841], vol. 7, no. 286, pp. 5–6).

48. For discussion of this issue, see standing committee report, *DA* (1841), vol. 5, no. 186, pp. 9–11, and also minority report, ibid., vol. 7, no. 286, pp. 5–6.

49. Taking the side of the workingmen critics, the minority report cited in the preceding note accordingly characterized the defense of even the limited training of convicts as a damaging admission (p. 5); see also Syracuse mechanics proceedings, *DA* (1842), vol. 4, no. 65, p. 63; Wilentz, *Chants Democratic,* 133, 237. By the 1870s and 1880s, the ongoing subdivision of labor experienced by crafts and the growing acceptance of the notion that the day of the complete craftsman had passed were encouraging a quite different defense of the narrow training of contract convicts. Rather than justifying such training for its failure to make convict laborers competitive threats to true craftsmen, advocates of the contract system now favored the argument that convicts who acquired only a narrow expertise were no different from tradesmen on the outside and for this reason were well prepared for reentry into society (Gildemeister, *Prison Labor,* 93, 228).

50. Lewis, *Prisons,* 138.

51. Lewis, *Newgate,* 194.

52. Both the 1835 and the 1842 acts exempted from their prohibitions the employment of convicts in the manufacture of articles principally imported from abroad. Such manufacture was accepted in all quarters as noncompetitive with the enterprise of New York's free mechanics.

53. "What Shall Be Done" and "State Prison Labor," *New York State Mechanic,* April 27, 1843; True, "State Prison"; report, *DA* (1842), vol. 4, no. 65, pp. 40–41, 62–64; see also report, *DS* (1843), vol. 3, no. 99. This last document reported that at present 450–500 of the convicts in the state's prisons were still being illegally employed by contractors, in violation of the most recent law of 1842 (p. 3); see also Lewis, *Newgate,* 193–97; Eisenhauer, "Organizing Discipline," 105–24.

54. Lewis, *Newgate,* 190, which I am quoting here, does not fully capture the scope of this grievance.

55. Mechanic proceedings, *DA* (1842), vol. 4, no. 65, p. 61.

56. Buffalo mechanics and manufacturers, *DA* (1834), vol. 4, no. 352, p. 26.

57. "Mechanics' State Convention"; True, "State Prison"; report, *DA* (1834), vol. 4, no. 352, p. 9.

58. Albany mechanics resolutions, *DA* (1843), vol. 6, no. 156, pp. 1–3.

59. "Mechanics' State Convention"; "A Mechanic"; Onondaga mechanics proceedings, *DA* (1842), vol. 4, no. 65, p. 64; Lewis, *Prisons,* 135.

60. Rothman, *Discovery of the Asylum,* 103–5.

61. Albany mechanics proceedings, *DA* (1842), vol. 4, no. 65, p. 72.

62. Response of A. S. Pond, *DA* (1842), vol. 4, no. 65, p. 73; see also report, *DA* (1834), vol. 4, no. 352, pp. 7–8; "Penitentiary Labor in Albany!!!" Some commentators largely attributed the actual recidivism and eventual recommittals of discharged convicts to their misguided decision to settle in New York and other cities. With their opportunities for engaging in vice and crime, the "atmosphere" of these environments proved particularly "dangerous" for individuals of so "feeble" a state as the released convict (Francis Lieber, "Translator's Preface," in Gustave de Beaumont and Alexis de Tocqueville, *On the Penitentiary System in the United States and Its Application in France* (1833), trans. Lieber [Carbondale, Ill., 1964], 16–18). There were, however, other commentators who minimized the recidivism; see Rev. John Luckey, *Life in Sing Sing, As Seen in a Twelve Years' Chaplaincy* (New York, 1860), 369–70.

63. Onondaga mechanics proceedings, *DA* (1842), vol. 4, no. 65, p. 66; Gildemeister, *Prison Labor,* 129; Lewis, *Newgate,* 190–92.

64. "Address and Resolutions of the Convention of Mechanics of New York State Held in Utica," 1834. Beaumont and Tocqueville noted that the Pennsylvania and Auburn systems shared the principle of isolation, one of discouraging all communication among prisoners, given the prisoners' tendency to "boast" of their "misdeeds" to one another. Among the major points on which advocates of the two systems disagreed was whether Auburn's incorporation of silent congregate labor during the day, whatever the practice's economic and other advantages, could approximate the all-important condition of isolation achieved by continuous solitary confinement (Beaumont and Tocqueville, *Penitentiary System,* 55–58, 198). Mechanic critics, as the aforementioned Address illustrates, were among those who insisted that the "present" (Auburn) system "has but little tendency to prevent crime, or reform criminals," largely because its prisoners could not be effectively "isolated"—prevented from conversing and conspiring together—"while suffered to work together." Congregate work arrangements, by such reasoning, helped explain why the virtuous character of manual labor was so largely subverted within the prisons—why the contemptible disposition of many convicts instead tended to transform labor into something contemptible.

65. Karen Halttunen suggests that the antebellum belief "in the contaminating powers of influence owed much to the popular pseudoscience of mesmerism and to the miasmic theories of the cholera epidemics that swept the United States in 1832 and 1849" (Halttunen, *Confidence Men and Painted Women: A Study of Middle Class Culture in America, 1830–1870* [New Haven, 1982], 5). But it is arguable that the appeal achieved by these pseudosciences and theories was itself more symptom than cause of underlying beliefs about influence and contagion.

66. Ibid., 4–15. As noted, Francis Lieber was among the commentators who extended this antiurban theme to the precarious situation of the discharged convict. That urban sensationalist literature and its theme of psychological influence contributed something to mechanic anxieties over convict labor does not mean that the parallels were exact. Although, for example, mechanics complained of their exposure to the corrupting example of ex-convicts who entered their workshops and communities, urban sensationalist literature, as T. Jackson Lears notes, earmarked as most susceptible to seduction and corruption those "free-floating urban youth (male or female)" who had been "disencumbered" from their rural family and community ties (Lears, *Fables of Abundance: A Cultural History of Advertising in America* [New York, 1994], 60–61).

67. "Address and Resolutions of the Convention of Mechanics of New York State Held in Utica," 1834; Paul Rozin and Carol Nemeroff, "The Laws of Sympathetic Magic: A Psychological Analysis of Similarity and Contagion," in *Cultural Psychology: Essays on Comparative Human Development,* ed. James W. Stigler, Richard A. Shiveder, and Gilbert Hendt (Cambridge, 1990), 205–32.

68. Although skilled master mechanics, at least, might themselves be considered part of the middle class, many of them, it bears repeating, were at best only tenuously so. The marginal middle-class status of such master craftsmen reflected not merely their deteriorating economic circumstances but also the fact that they often continued to perform some of their workshops' manual labor. In the early nineteenth century, as in earlier periods,

ages-old prejudices limited the social standing attainable by anyone who worked with his hands, even at skilled labor, for a living. Such master craftsmen should be distinguished from the larger, more successful masters—the respectable employing manufacturers or craft entrepreneurs—who had relinquished all manual labor to others in their employ, and who in many cases owed their prosperity to their willingness to utilize low-cost labor and other skill-degrading innovations, commonly through out-of-shop contracting. If declining small master-employers and aggrieved journeymen at times expressed notions of middle-class respectability in their bitter criticisms of prison and other cheap labor competition, thriving nonmanual masters had reasons of their own to even more consistently endorse bourgeois character virtues; they frequently characterized themselves as progressive businessmen who increased the productiveness of the mechanic trades and advanced the interests of all belonging to them; for a cogent discussion, see Blumin, *Emergence of the Middle Class,* 134–36; see also Wilentz, *Chants Democratic,* 115–16, 271–86; Glickstein, *Concepts of Free Labor,* 3–4, 303–7.

69. In the early twentieth century, according to one scholar, organized labor developed a more sympathetic attitude toward the convicts themselves even as it retained workers' long-standing sense of convict labor as threatening and unfair economic competition. Moved by the enlightening influence of the prevailing penology of their period, unions largely discarded antebellum labor's "moral prejudice" against convicts and came to embrace both the redeemability of the convict and the argument that the contract system also "exploits the *prisoner,* and prevents or hinders *his* best interests" (Henry Calvin Mohler, "Convict Labor Policies," *Journal of the American Institute of Criminal Law and Criminology* 15 [May 1924–Feb. 1925]: 572–73). Antebellum defenders of New York's prison system commonly made an issue of the mechanic critics' lack of sympathy and sensitivity for the convicts' plight Z. Y. X., "Thoughts, No. II"; report, *DS* (1841), vol. 2, no. 54, pp. 2–4.

70. Seneca mechanic proceedings, *DA* (1842), vol. 4, no. 65, p. 67.

71. Albany mechanic proceedings, ibid., p. 72.

72. Mechanic state convention proceedings, ibid., pp. 61–62.

73. Syracuse mechanic proceedings, ibid., p. 63; minority report, *DA* (1837), vol. 3, no. 169, p. 2; "Address and Resolutions of the Convention of Mechanics of New York State Held in Utica," 1834; "Prison Mechanics," *Workingman's Organ,* rept. in *Mechanic's Advocate,* March 18, 1848. To this position that mechanics carried an unjust burden, critics sometimes added the argument that because the great majority of prison inmates were serving sentences for crimes against property, and because their imprisonment made property more secure, it should be the more privileged and propertied classes that bore the financial burden of their support (Second Resolution of the State Convention of Mechanics, quoted in Z. Y. X., "Thoughts, No. II."

74. See E. G. B., "The State Prison Question," *Tribune,* Oct. 4, 1841. Yet there were some individuals who took seriously the idea of redirecting the energies of state prison inmates into the study of "law and divinity" ("Convict Labor," *Worcester Evening Budget,* rept. in *Mechanic's Advocate,* Feb. 11, 1847).

75. In 1845 even the socially humane Dorothea Dix claimed of Sing Sing's inmates that "coming, as they chiefly do, from the city of New York," they were "the most corrupt, the most degraded, most desperate class of prisoners in any prison north of Mason and Dixon's line" (Dix, *Remarks on Prisons and Prison Discipline in the United States,* 2d ed. [Phila-

delphia, 1845], 16). But as W. David Lewis suggests, Dix's perceptions, like those of other observers, were colored by the antiurban and nativist prejudices of the day (Lewis, *Newgate,* 143).

76. Governor Seward made the same appeal in his support for prison-labor reforms that would redress mechanic grievances (*DS* [1841], vol. 3, no. 91, pp. 7–8).

77. For reference to some of these difficulties, see Z. Y. X., "Thoughts, No. II." Spokesmen for the "immediate interests of Labourers" who were employed on "our Public Roads" also made clear their resistance to any such redeployment of convicts, whatever support skilled mechanics lent such proposals (resolutions of a mass meeting of the Laborers' Union Association of New York City, Sept. 15, 1843, quoted in Commons et al., *Documentary History* 8:225).

78. Shklar, *American Citizenship,* 67.

79. Even under the contract system, however, most mid-nineteenth-century state prisons at best broke even financially, and New York's penitentiaries frequently produced a deficit (Gildemeister, *Prison Labor,* 62).

80. Andrew Skotnicki, *Religion and the Development of the American Penal System* (Lanham, Md., 2000), 30–115. John Luckey, Sing Sing's chaplain during the late antebellum period, berated the pro-mechanic legislation already enacted for its morally pernicious impact on contractors and convict laborers alike: "The contractor being forbidden by law to make those wares which are the most *saleable,* is compelled to harden his heart against his own generous impulses, or suffer loss in his business"; he was consequently that much more inclined to drive his workforce to the breaking point (Luckey, *Life in Sing Sing,* 50–51).

81. New York's controversial "Report of the Commissioners Appointed under the 'Act concerning State Prisons," in *DA* (1835), vol. 2, no. 135, particularly infuriated workingmen for its vindication of many existing practices, largely because they expected more from one of the three commissioners, the trade-union activist Ely Moore. The investigative report did make greater concessions than other defenses of the prison labor system. It guardedly agreed, with respect to the issue of economic competition, that in the case of "*some articles,* and to *some extent,*" the complaint against convict labor was "well founded." It also acknowledged that "mechanics are more exposed to the association of discharged convicts," and that such association was "both degrading and dangerous to persons of good character." But the report also rejected as "unfounded and illusory" the complaint that "the occupation of mechanics in general is degraded in the public estimation" by teaching mechanical trades to convicts (p. 13). For more unequivocal defenses of prison industry, see report, *DS* (1834), vol. 2, no. 114, pp. 2–4; report, *DA* (1841), vol. 5, no. 186, pp. 5–17; report, *DS* (1841), vol. 2, no. 54, pp. 1–12; Hugins, *Jacksonian Democracy,* 158–59.

82. *New York State Mechanic,* Jan. 7, 1843, quoted in Commons et al., *Documentary History* 8:245.

83. One of these sympathetic observers, Orlando Lewis, thus agrees with some of the mechanics' contemporary adversaries that they "side-stepped a responsibility that was at least partly theirs" in failing to offer a feasible alternative to the contract system. "They wanted all competition abolished, and did not care primarily what happened to the convicts or to the State" (Lewis, *Prisons,* 143, 332; see also Hirsch, *Rise of the Penitentiary,* 100–105).

84. See minority report, *DA* (1841), vol. 7, no. 286, p. 8.

85. For one labor sheet's begrudging satisfaction with the law of 1842 that brought partial relief to New York's mechanics, see "Convict Labor in Ohio" and "Sing Sing Prison and Convict Labor," *Mechanic's Advocate*, Feb. 11, 1847. For the indifferent economic success of the new Dannemora State Prison in Clinton County, despite skilled labor's enthusiastic support for the project, see Lewis, *Newgate*, 198–200, 259–63. Their decline notwithstanding, the same mechanic complaints regarding contract convict labor did persist into the 1850s; see Proceedings of the New York State Industrial Legislature, Sept. 1851, in Commons et al., *Documentary History* 8:322–23.

86. Herkimer mechanics proceedings, *DA* (1842), vol. 4, no. 65, p. 68.

87. Report, *DS* (1841), vol. 2, no. 54, p. 2.

88. The Senate committee report cited in the previous note remarked (p. 7) that convicts "are not well qualified for the learned professions" and left it at that. In a more loquacious, and possibly facetious, vein, another defender of New York's prison system remarked that "if the convict were taught the law whilst in prison, he would only come out the more accomplished rogue; and as no one would employ him, desperation would drive him to crime of perhaps more extensive injury, than that for which he first suffered. — Were he taught medicine, why it would only be increasing the number of quacks" (Z. Y. X., "Thoughts[, No. I]"). Much more so than Dorothea Dix, quoted above, Elam Lynds, who was possibly the most instrumental figure in the founding of the Auburn system, would have found particularly laughable the notion of preparing convicts for the liberal professions. Lynds informed Tocqueville and Beaumont that prisons "are filled with coarse beings, who have had no education, and who perceive with difficulty ideas, and often even sensations." Lynds's regime as Auburn's warden in the 1820s was distinguished by the severity of its punishments, and he shut down a school on Sunday for the younger prisoners on the grounds that educated convicts in fact posed a greater rather than a lesser danger to society (Beaumont and Tocqueville, *Penitentiary System*, 164; Lewis, *Prisons*, 95). Yet the notion of educating convicts for one of the learned professions remains less bizarre than one might suppose, if only because the educational preparation requisite for entering one of these in the early nineteenth century was far less rigorous and extended than it was to become subsequently.

89. Francis P. Blair Jr., House, *Cong. Globe*, 35th Cong., 1st sess., March 23, 1858, 1284.

7. The "Pauper Labor" of the Old World, Free Labor, and Gresham's Law

1. Baldwin, *DA* (1842), vol. 4, no. 65, p. 102; Greenberg, *Worker and Community*, 143–60; "Penitentiary Labor in Albany!!!", *Mechanic's Advocate*, Sept. 11, 1847; Stephen A. Klips, "Institutionalizing the Poor: The New York City Almshouse, 1825–1860" (Ph.D. diss., City Univ. of New York, 1980), 340–42.

2. James Brewer Stewart, "The Emergence of Racial Modernity and the Rise of the White North, 1790–1840," *Journal of the Early Republic* 18 (Summer 1998): 182.

3. Owing to the provisions of the state's gradual emancipation act, black chattel slavery itself was hardly a distant memory in Jacksonian New York; its last vestiges were not abolished until 1827 (and still later in neighboring states).

4. None of the antebellum contract-labor data that I have seen for Auburn and Sing Sing include racial breakdowns.

5. For relevant figures for Auburn and Sing Sing, see Crawford, *Report on the Penitentiaries,* Appendix, 27–35; *Thirteenth Annual Report of the Board of Managers of the Prison Discipline Society,* of Boston (1838; rept. Montclair, N.J., 1972), 40–42; Gildemeister, *Prison Labor,* 72–80.

6. Conceivably, too, hostility to northern blacks, including African-American convict laborers, was most of all tempered in the case of that minority of white artisans and tradesmen who formed part of the abolitionist constituency in the 1830s and 1840s, and who remained relatively distanced from any developing white supremacist consensus. Were, however, the mechanic participants in the protests against state prison industry among the artisans who remained most sympathetic to abolitionism and the plight of northern blacks (prison inmates or otherwise)? No study to my knowledge has explored such a connection.

7. *DA* (1834), vol. 4, no. 352, p. 26.

8. "State Prison Monopoly," *National Magazine and Industrial Record,* Sept. 1845, 356.

9. *DS* (1841), vol. 2, no. 54, p. 9.

10. During their peak protests over prison industry, in the 1830s and 1840s, mechanics for their part sometimes insisted that slave labor was the lesser threat: "This species of competition [convict labor] has been compared sometimes with that between free and slave labor, which is said to be very unequal, but which is far more advantageous to the free than this competition to the mechanic, for the slave is to be supported both in helpless infancy and declining age; whereas the convict usually both commences and ends his labor as an apprentice or journeyman to the state, in the prime vigor of manhood" ("Address and Resolutions of the Convention of Mechanics of New York State Held in Utica," 1834).

11. Weston, *Wages,* 2.

12. Ibid.

13. Ibid. Interestingly, Weston, a former Democrat, here endorsed anxieties that historians more closely associate with the rival Whigs, the party of the "protective" tariff.

14. Ken Cole, John Cameron, and Chris Edwards, *Why Economists Disagree: The Political Economy of Economics,* 2d ed. (London, 1991).

15. Richard C. Edwards, "Economic Sophistication in Nineteenth Century Congressional Tariff Debates," *Journal of Economic History* 30 (Dec. 1970): 802–38; Huston, *Securing the Fruits,* 236–51; Jonathan J. Pincus, *Pressure Groups and Politics in Antebellum Tariffs* (New York, 1977); Joanne Reitano, *The Tariff Question in the Gilded Age* (University Park, Pa., 1994); David C. Colander and A. W. Coats, eds., *The Spread of Economic Ideas* (Cambridge, 1990).

16. Untitled editorial, *Champion of American Labor,* May 8, 1847; see also Samuel S. Busey, *Immigration: Its Evils and Consequences* (1856; rept. New York, 1969), 77–82; Dale T. Knobel, *"America for the Americans": The Nativist Movement in the United States* (New York, 1997), 133.

17. Economic historians disagree over the actual extent to which antebellum immigration reduced wages and economic opportunities for native-born artisans and other workers. A recent quantitative study concludes that skilled workers in eastern urban centers were the only group upon which antebellum immigration had an appreciable negative economic impact (Ferrie, *Yankeys Now,* 182–83).

18. Alan M. Kraut, *Silent Travelers: Germs, Genes, and the "Immigrant Menace"* (New York, 1994). Kerby A. Miller notes that although there was also present "an Irish-American

Catholic bourgeoisie" that had grown in absolute numbers, "it composed at midcentury an increasingly small minority within a peasant-proletarian mass that was feared and stigmatized by the native middle classes" (Miller, "Class, Culture, and Immigrant Group Identity in the United States: The Case of Irish-American Ethnicity," in *Immigration Reconsidered: History, Sociology, and Politics,* ed. Virginia Yans-McLaughlin [New York, 1990], 109–10).

19. Their own experience of European conditions did not invariably lead immigrants themselves to reject in toto the dominant stereotypes. One German-born farmhand in Cincinnati, Ernst Stille, objected to the exaggerated trumpeting of American economic rewards and opportunity in which the anti–Old World, alarmist "pauper labor" literature commonly engaged. He thus deplored the "boastful and imprudent letters" written by some of his own countrymen; these enticed individuals who were already "well off in Germany" to come to the United States—where conditions were in fact "so varied"—with unrealistic dreams of becoming rich. Yet Stille himself sounded another common immigrant theme in granting some validity to the Old World "pauper labor" representations. He noted that the one and only group of people "who are really happy" in the United States "are those who were used to hard work at Germany" but even "with toil and great pains could hardly even earn their daily bread" there (Stille to "friends and relatives," May 20, 1847, in *News from the Land of Freedom: German Immigrants Write Home,* ed. Walter D. Kamphoefner, Wolfgang Helbick, and Ulrike Sommer, trans. Susan Carter Vogel [Ithaca, N.Y., 1992], 85).

20. Central Committee of the Home League, in "Anniversary of the Home League," *American Laborer* 1 (Sept. 1842): 179–80.

21. Scholars generalize that nineteenth-century western European nations, as in the case of England under the New Poor Law, scaled back statutory outdoor-relief provisions for the able-bodied and (in many cases) working poor, although expanding voluntary charity, including the working classes' own organizations, took up part of the slack (Stuart Woolf, *The Poor in Western Europe in the Eighteenth and Nineteenth Centuries* [London, 1986], 88–90; Peter Mandler, ed., *The Uses of Charity: The Poor on Relief in the Nineteenth-Century Metropolis* [Philadelphia, 1990]).

22. In suggesting that the late nineteenth-century labor movement was the sole or primary source in defining an "American standard of living," Lawrence B. Glickman neglects this earlier history of Whig-sponsored tariff proposals that party spokesmen argued were essential to protecting high American wages and the comfortable subsistence they provided (*A Living Wage,* 159).

23. In explaining England's capacity to undersell other European nations whose labor was even more low-cost, Horace Greeley invoked London's advantage as the world's commercial center("The Independent and Free Trade," *Tribune,* Feb. 12, 1856; see also "Free Trade and the New Tariff," *National Magazine and Industrial Record* 3 [Sept. 1846]: 349).

24. Conkin, *Prophets of Prosperity,* 290; Daniel Walker Howe, *The Political Culture of the American Whigs* (Chicago, 1979), 113–14.

25. David Waldstreicher, *In the Midst of Perpetual Fetes: The Making of American Nationalism, 1776–1820* (Chapel Hill, N.C., 1997), 6.

26. Horace Greeley, *Protection and Free Trade: The Question Stated and Considered* (New York, 1844), 13.

27. Michael Hudson, *Economics and Technology in 19th Century American Thought* (New York,

1975), 195. Colton notably offered different, sometimes contradictory protectionist arguments in his writings, at one point, for example, locating the primary threat to American industry in British capital rather than British labor. In addition, Colton did occasionally acknowledge that a nation whose labor was free, independent, fairly compensated, and well motivated might possess "inherent" productivity and competitive advantages over countries "where labor is not free." But such an insight did not, for him, at all vitiate American free labor's need for protection from its debased foreign pauper rivals. Rather, the antiabolitionist Colton used the insight to explain why protection would most of all benefit the South, which was dependent on a form of labor that he characterized as more costly yet no more physically effective than Europe's "forced" pauper labor: "If, therefore, American free labor requires protection against foreign pauper labor, much more does American slave labor require it" (Colton, *Public Economy for the United States* [1848; rept. New York, 1969], 309). Needless to say, many of Colton's antislavery contemporaries believed that tariff protection for the South's slave economy was hardly the most appropriate response to slave labor's inferior productivity and relative costliness ("Slave-Labor and Free Labor," *Weekly Herald and Philanthropist,* Aug. 16, 1844). On protectionists' common slighting of the productivity-differential issue, see also George Benjamin Mangold, *Labor Argument in the American Protective Tariff Discussion* (1908; rept. New York, 1971), 106–7. For the European genesis of the high wage–productivity concept and its use against eighteenth-century mercantilist thought, see Douglas A. Irwin, *Against the Tide: An Intellectual History of Free Trade* (Princeton, N.J., 1996), 154–60.

28. Henry Clay, speech of Sept. 1842, quoted in Alfred E. Eckes Jr., *Opening America's Market: U.S. Foreign Trade Policy since 1776* (Chapel Hill, N.C., 1996), 24.

29. For one of the many American antislavery examples of this linkage, designed to appeal to the economic self-interest of slaveholders, see John G. Palfrey, *Papers on the Slave Power* (Boston, 1846), 67–68.

30. Furniss, *Position of the Laborer;* Coats, *Economic Thought,* 63–117; for additional attention to nuances, variations, and contradictions within mercantilist and other eighteenth-century wage doctrines, see David A. Baugh, "Poverty, Protestantism, and Political Economy: English Attitudes toward the Poor, 1660–1800," in *England's Rise to Greatness, 1660–1763,* ed. Stephen Baxter (Berkeley, Calif., 1983), 63–107; Richard C. Wiles, "The Theory of Wages in Later English Mercantilism," *Economic History Review,* 2d ser., 21 (Aug. 1968): 113–26; John Hatcher, "Labour, Leisure and Economic Thought before the Nineteenth Century," *Past & Present,* no. 160 (Aug. 1998): 96–115; Cosimo Perrotta, "The Preclassical Theory of Development: Increased Consumption Raises Productivity," *History of Political Economy* 29 (Summer 1997): 295–319; Bruce C. Baird, "Necessity and the "Perverse' Supply of Labor in Pre-Classical British Political Economy," ibid. (Fall 1997), 497–517.

31. Industriousness and work intensity are not synonymous with work efficiency, but here Smith drew no distinction: "The wages of labour are the encouragement of industry, which, like every other human quality, improves in proportion to the encouragement it receives. . . . Where wages are high, accordingly, we shall always find the workmen more active, diligent, and expeditious, than where they are low" (Smith, *Wealth of Nations,* 81). Smith's influential advocacy of high wages, while broadly anticipating such modern-day

concepts as that of efficiency wages, did not truly constitute a theory of wages. It also appears in a chapter that, as Mark Blaug observes, is "a compendium" of quite different, and often contradictory, wage theories. And while insisting that the "greater part" of workmen responded to a "liberal reward" with increased industriousness, Smith did not entirely repudiate older leisure-preference notions: that "a little more plenty than ordinary may render some workmen idle, cannot well be doubted" (ibid., 80–82; Mark Blaug, *Economic Theory in Retrospect* [Cambridge, 1985], 44–46; Patricia H. Werhane, *Adam Smith and His Legacy for Modern Capitalism* [New York, 1991], 150; Andrew, *Philanthropy and Police*, 140–43; John Sekora, *Luxury: The Concept in Western Thought, Eden to Smollett* [Baltimore, 1977]), 125–28; stressing Smith's ideological affinities with David Hume is Marshall, "Scottish Economic Thought," 309–21, and Marshall, "Luxury, Economic Development," 631–38; see also George A. Akerlof and Janet L. Yellin, eds., *Efficiency Wage Models of the Labor Market* [Cambridge, 1986]).

32. For criticisms of this prevailing neoclassical economic emphasis, see Michael Perelman, *The Pathology of the U.S. Economy: The Costs of a Low-Wage System* (London, 1993), 199–202; see also Morris Altman, *Human Agency and Material Welfare: Revisions in Microeconomics and Their Implications for Public Policy* (Boston, 1996); and Altman, *Worker Satisfaction and Human Performance* (Armonk, N.Y., 2001).

33. Given his concurrent criticisms of the "Buy cheap, sell dear" market mechanism (see chap. 3), Greeley found much more problematic than more conservative Whigs did the existing harmony of interests between capital and labor in the United States. There, as in Europe, the "natural" harmony between capital and labor—the harmony that should and could exist between these—waited upon an underlying transformation of the market mechanism, even as American workers remained materially better off than their European counterparts.

34. Brown, *Hierarchy, History*, 14. Many Whigs extended this roseate view to take in such female workers as the young Lowell operatives.

35. Whigs, however, were generally unwilling to divest themselves of the legitimating authority of Smith as a progenitor of their positions on a variety of economic issues. They instead concentrated their fire on Ricardo, Malthus, and other principals of the "new school" of English political economy for, among other sins, deviating from Smith's original model. Notwithstanding that model's antimercantilist animus toward trade restrictions, Smith, such Whigs claimed, shared their own appreciation of the importance of home markets—of reducing the distance between consumer and producer; see, in addition to Henry Carey's books, an article that he likely wrote: "What Constitutes Real Freedom of Trade," *American Review* 12 (1850): 131–40, 228–40, 456–66; Conkin, *Prophets of Prosperity*, 281; Howard Horwitz, *By the Law of Nature: Form and Value in Nineteenth-Century America* (New York, 1991), 58–61.

36. Thaddeus Stevens, House, *Cong. Globe*, 32d Cong., 1st sess., *App.*, June 11, 1852, 745.

37. *The Tariff Question, or Protection and Free Trade Considered, in a Series of Articles. Addressed to the American Public. By a Mohawk Valley Farmer* (Utica, N.Y., 1852), 28; see also Colton, *Public Economy*, 87–108; "The Tariff and the Cotton Manufacture—Prices of Cotton," *Tribune*, Sept. 23, 1844; Carl William Kaiser Jr., "History of the Academic Protectionist–Free Trade Controversy in America before 1860" (Ph.D. diss., Univ. of Pennsylvania, 1939), 117.

38. T. De Scitovsky, "A Reconsideration of the Theory of Tariffs," *Review of Economic Studies* 9 (Nov. 1941): 89, 109.

39. James L. Huston, *The Panic of 1857 and the Coming of the Civil War* (Baton Rouge, La., 1987), 103; Mangold, *Labor Argument*, 66–108; Hudson, *Economics and Technology*, 46–50; for the support that Pennsylvania's iron and steel workers gave to protectionist reasoning, see James L. Huston, "The Political Response to Industrialism: The Republican Embrace of Protectionist Labor Doctrines," *Journal of American History* 70 (June 1983): 48–49.

40. John R. Commons, "Horace Greeley and the Working Class Origins of the Republican Party," *Political Science Quarterly* 24 (1909): 473, 487. Similarly, as Helene Sara Zahler notes, Whiggish and other elements of the antebellum "conservative press" never stated "a desire to keep wages down" as among their reasons for opposing the land-reform movement: "such frankness went out with Federalism" (Zahler, *Eastern Workingmen*, 74–75).

41. Hudson, *Economics and Technology*, 45–48; Mangold, *Labor Argument*, 46–59, 104, 107; Kaiser, "Academic Protectionist," 133–35.

42. For the insistence, contrary to such authorities as F. L. Taussig, that Henry Carey and other later Whigs continued to emphasize only a temporary need for tariff protection, in accordance with the old infant-industries theme, see Howe, *Whigs*, 119–20. The extent of Carey's deviation from earlier American protectionists remains ambiguous in view of his elaborate home-markets model, by which the United States was to enact free trade only after the nation's internal development had been achieved; see also Rodney J. Morrison, "Henry C. Carey and American Economic Development," *Explorations in Entrepreneurial History* 5 (Winter 1968): 132–43.

43. Andrew Stewart, House, June 11, 1848, rept. in Stewart, *The American System: Speeches on the Tariff Question and on Internal Improvements* (Philadelphia, 1872), 211. Calvin Colton similarly insisted: "Free trade would not bring up the rest of the world, in ameliorating the condition of the laboring classes, raising their wages to a fair value, and giving them freedom; but it would carry down the people of the United States to their level, in all particulars, political, social, moral, and physical" (Colton, *Rights of Labor*, 13).

44. Hudson, *Economics and Technology*, 52, 219–20; E. Peshine Smith, *A Manual of Political Economy* (1853; rept. New York, 1966), 27, 44; Joel Mokyr, "Dear Labor, Cheap Labor, and the Industrial Revolution," in *Favorites of Fortune: Technology, Growth, and Economic Development since the Industrial Revolution,* ed. Patrice Higonnet, David S. Landes, and Henry Rosovsky (Cambridge, Mass., 1991), 185–87.

45. Smith, *Manual*, 111, 106.

46. E. Peshine Smith, "The Law of Progress in the Relations of Capital and Labor," *Hunt's Merchant's Magazine* 26 (Jan. 1852): 42; Smith, *Manual*, 104; Hudson, *Economics and Technology*, 219–20.

47. See, aside from Smith's *Manual*, Colton, *Public Economy*, 310; Stewart, speech in House, Feb. 1, 1827, rept. in *American System*, 142.

48. For other nineteenth-century antecedents to modern nutrition and efficiency-wage models, linking higher wages, the improved physical condition of laborers, and increased productivity, see Ray Petridis, "Brassey's Law and the Economy of High Wages in Nineteenth-Century Economics," *History of Political Economy* 28 (Winter 1996): 583–606; see also Hudson, *Economics and Technology*, pt. 4; Huston, *Securing the Fruits*, 177–82; B. F. Kiker, "The Historical Roots of the Concept of Human Capital," in *Human Capital For-*

mation and Manpower Development, ed. Ronald A. Wykstra (New York, 1971), 2–24; see also, on today's working poor, Richard G. Wilkinson, *Unhealthy Societies: The Afflictions of Inequality* (London, 1998); for the distinctive high-wage, eight-hour-day theories of Ira Steward and other late nineteenth-century trade-union activists, favoring not increased worker productivity but rather expanded employment induced by greater employer efficiency, see Dickman, *Industrial Democracy,* 162–64.

49. Smith also held that protective tariffs would not strengthen the power of industrial capital relative to that of labor precisely because industrialists would find high wage levels to be in their own best interests (Smith, "Law of Progress," 31–42; Smith, "Protection vs. Free Trade," *Hunt's Merchant's Magazine* 25 [Nov. 1851]: 534–43).

50. Hudson, *Economics and Technology,* 215.

51. Greeley, *Protection and Free Trade,* 13.

52. For the highly partisan nature of congressional voting on the Walker tariff in 1846, see Joel H. Silbey, *The Partisan Imperative: The Dynamics of American Politics before the Civil War* (New York, 1988), 36–38.

53. Robert J. Walker, Treasury Report for 1847, rept. in *Cong. Globe,* 30th Cong., 1st sess., *App.,* Dec. 7, 1847, 14.

54. Ibid.

55. Treasury Report for 1848, rept., ibid., 2d sess., *App.,* Dec. 5, 1848, 14.

56. T. W. Hutchison, *On Revolutions and Progress in Economic Knowledge* (Cambridge, 1978), 40–43. In the notoriously difficult language in which he presented the inverse relationship between profits and wages, Ricardo himself invited the common perceptions that first, he was positing an inevitable conflict of interests between capital and labor, and second, that he was propounding a doctrine of low wages in the absolute sense.

57. Treasury Report for 1845, rept. in *Cong Globe,* 29th Cong., 1st sess., *App.,* Dec. 4, 1845, 10. From the perspective of a strong protectionist, Edward Stanwood offers a detailed analysis of Walker's economic views in *American Tariff Controversies in the Nineteenth Century* (1903; rept. New York, 1967), 2:44–69.

58. For an attack on Walker's arguments as not merely demagogic but also hypocritical, in view of the economic benefits that Walker, a southern slaveowning planter, derived from the exploitation of his own labor force, see the speech of Maine Whig Luther Severance, House, *Cong. Globe,* 29th Cong., 1st sess., *App.,* June 27, 1846, 705.

59. Ficklin, speech in House, ibid., July 1, 1846, 1056, 1060; for similar antiprotectionist arguments, see the speech of New Hampshire's Moses Norris, House, July 2, 1846, ibid., 927–28; "Pauper Labor," *Newburyport Advertiser,* rept. in *Northampton Democrat,* Oct. 6, 1846.

60. See also "American Labor," New Hampshire *Dover Gazette,* Dec. 23, 1848.

61. Dublin, *Women at Work;* David A. Zonderman, *Aspirations and Anxieties: New England Workers and the Mechanized Factory System, 1815–1850* (New York, 1992); Hannah Josephson, *The Golden Threads: New England's Mill Girls and Magnates* (New York, 1949).

62. Ficklin, *Cong. Globe,* July 1, 1846, 1057.

63. Norris, ibid., July 2, 1846, 928.

64. Ibid., 927.

65. Ibid.

66. "Pauper Labor," *Ohio Statesman,* quoted in the *Illinois Register* (Springfield), Sept. 25, 1846.

67. R. H. Kingsbury to Nathan Appleton, June 18, 1846, Nathan Appleton Papers, Massachusetts Historical Society.

68. "The Federal Whigs and the Laboring Classes," *Daily Plebeian,* Oct. 30, 1844.

69. "Let It Alone—Governing Overmuch—Injustice of a High Tariff—A Word of Warning to the Agriculturists," ibid., Feb. 7, 1844; Walker, Treasury Report for 1846, rept. in *Cong Globe,* 29th Cong., 2d sess., *App.,* Dec. 8, 1846, 10–11. For earlier Jeffersonian Republican views that similarly rooted the independence and dignity of American freeholders in their ability to market their agricultural surplus through an unrestricted foreign commerce, see Drew R. McCoy, *The Elusive Republic: Political Economy in Jeffersonian America* (New York, 1980).

70. This argument renders problematic Judith Goldstein's claim that antebellum "free-trade analysts had no theory about how increased trade would allow free labor to maintain high wages" (Goldstein, *Ideas, Interests, and American Trade Policy* [Ithaca, N.Y., 1993], 19.

71. Irwin, *Against the Tide,* 3–5, 217–20.

72. The turbulence of the global economy has produced such modern-day American protectionist diatribes against cheap foreign labor as Edward N. Luttwak, *The Endangered American Dream: How to Stop the United States from Becoming a Third World Country and How to Win the Geo-Economic Struggle for Industrial Supremacy* (New York, 1993); Patrick J. Buchanan, *The Great Betrayal: How American Sovereignty and Social Justice Are Sacrificed to the Gods of the Global Economy* (Boston, 1998); see also John Gray, *False Dawn: The Delusions of Global Capitalism* (London, 1998).

73. Irwin, *Against the Tide,* 89–98.

74. "Some Reflections of a Free-Trader," *Democratic Review* 18 (Feb. 1846): 138.

75. Hudson, *Economics and Technology,* 194–95.

76. "Reflections," 138.

77. Ibid., 138–40. To one of the free-trade arguments advanced in this excerpt from "Reflections," that individuals recognized their own best interests better than governments did, Whig protectionists had at least one standard response: the interests of the larger community—the public good—commonly remained distinct from, and even opposed to, the interests of private individuals ([William Burley Howes], *Protection and Free Trade* [Salem, N.J., 1846], 16; see also Michael A. Morrison, "Distribution or Dissolution: Western Land Policy, Economic Development, and the Language of Corruption," *American Nineteenth Century History* 1 [Spring 2000]: 1–33).

78. For one of Cobden's many expressions of free trade as an instrument of world peace, see "Free Trade. V" (Sept. 28, 1843), in *Speeches on Questions of Public Policy by Richard Cobden, M.P.,* ed. John Bright and James E. Thorold Rogers (London, 1903), 40. Even as they commonly attributed the intellectual prominence of free tradeism to the same hard-headed, predatory economic interests within England that drove the subsistence-wage doctrines of Malthus and Ricardo, antebellum American protectionists also sought to discredit free-tradeism as the impractical doctrine of dreamy-eyed idealists and philosophers ([Howes], *Protection and Free Trade,* 5).

79. Magnus Blomstrom and Bjorn Hettne, *Development Theory in Transition* (London, 1984).

80. Walker, 1848 Report, 13.

81. Ibid.

82. Ibid.

83. For Walker's expressed solicitude for the nation's "manufacturing classes," including the development of "new manufacturing towns and cities," see 1847 Report, 11–16; 1845 Report, 11.

84. Greeley, *Essays Designed to Elucidate*, 162–63; see also Stanwood's criticism of Walker's views in *Tariff Controversies* 2:59; Wolfgang F. Stolper and Paul A. Samuelson, "Protection and Real Wages," *Review of Economic Studies* 9 (Nov. 1941): 58–73.

85. Walker, 1848 Report, 13; 1845 Report, 11, 13; for relevant breakdowns of the antebellum labor force, see Stanley Lebergott, *Manpower in Economic Growth: The American Record since 1800* (New York, 1964), 510.

86. Primarily directed against the economic benefits enjoyed by northern, particularly New England, industrial capitalists, this class-oriented social-justice theme overlapped with another of the Democrats' antiprotectionist arguments. This was the accusation that tariff protection for the nation's finished manufactured goods plundered the southern states most of all. However, southern Democrat thought evidenced tensions on issues of trade. These were apparent on the question of whether protection for northern manufactures merely deepened and exposed the economic dependencies and vulnerabilities that were always present in a more exclusively agrarian rural economy, one that was technologically undeveloped and had relatively unskilled labor. George Fitzhugh was among the antebellum southerners who endorsed this notion of southern economic underdevelopment and deficiency. Here he anticipated modern critiques of "unequal exchange" and dependency between metropolis and periphery, as well as exhibiting some of the northern Whig appreciation for internal economic development and diversity. But Fitzhugh's perspective was not easily reconcilable with the orthodox comparative-advantage notion of complementary economies that many southern Democrats shared with other free-trade Americans. That notion held that free trade worked more or less equally to the mutual advantage of all participants (Joseph J. Persky, *The Burden of Dependency: Colonial Themes in Southern Economic Thought* [Baltimore, 1992], 1–3, 75–76).

87. Ashworth, *"Agrarians" and "Aristocrats"*; Howe, *American Whigs*; Major L. Wilson, *Space, Time, and Freedom: The Quest for Nationality and the Irrepressible Conflict, 1815–1861* (Westport, Conn., 1974).

88. F. W. Taussig, *The Tariff History of the United States*, 7th ed. (New York, 1892), 107, 109, 114. Some free-trade advocates, particularly independent and strongly antislavery voices outside the Democratic Party, accordingly criticized the Walker tariff for not going far enough. One such advocate, the *National Era*, denounced this supposedly "revenue-only" measure for overly taxing American consumers and, in the process, helping the Polk administration finance its loathsome war of "conquest" against Mexico. The Liberty Party's national platform for 1848 endorsed this argument, while claiming that the "*protective* feature" of the Walker tariff provided additional support for the territory-hungry "Slave Power" by bribing "the northern manufacturing capitalist" into supporting the war ("The President and Mr. Calhoun — the War and the Future," *National Era*, Dec. 23, 1847; Liberty Party platform, rept. in *Letters of James Gillespie Birney, 1831–1857*, ed. Dwight L. Dumond [1938; rept. Gloucester, Mass., 1966], 2:1049–51).

89. Participants in the antebellum trade debates discovered diverse intimate relationships between trade provisions and these other developments; for an example from the protectionist camp, predicting that the Walker tariff would have disastrous consequences for the nation's financial soundness, see Mohawk Valley Farmer, *Tariff Question,* 19–30.

90. Taussig, *Tariff History,* 108, 122. A recent technical study holds, contrary to Taussig, that tariff protection for cotton goods did provide valuable stimulation to domestic cotton manufactures throughout the 1820s and 1830s, when they remained unable on their own to withstand foreign competition. Mark Bils estimates that without such protection "about half of the industrial sector of New England would have been bankrupted"—this despite his recognition that New England's cotton-textile mills occupied a separate niche from England's, specializing as they were in the production of lower-quality goods (Bils, "Tariff Protection and Production in the Early U.S. Cotton Textile Industry," *Journal of Economic History* 44 [Dec. 1984]: 1033–45). On the moderate free-trade provisions of the 1846 tariff, which was essentially a revenue tariff, see also Eckes, *Opening America's Market,* 24–25; on the failure of the Walker tariff to confirm the worst predictions of the Whigs respecting its impact on home industry, see Michael F. Holt, *Political Parties and American Political Development from the Age of Jackson to the Age of Lincoln* (Baton Rouge, La., 1992), 214–36. Modern economic historians who agree with Bils that textile production in early nineteenth-century New England needed tariff protection from England do not all share his Whig-like emphasis on the wage differential as the primary element contributing to the British cost advantage. Some insist on the technological superiority of Lancashire's cotton mills, while others argue that the greater experience of the region's mule spinners actually made them more productive than New England's cotton spinners. This last interpretation would seem particularly dismissive of some of the general claims embedded in American pro-factory, Whiggish literature—e.g., that in great measure owing to their better wages, New England operatives (both male and female) were more intelligent and productive than their English counterparts; for a summary of the economic-history literature, see Winifred Barr Rothenberg, "The Invention of American Capitalism: The Economy of New England in the Federal Period," in *Engines of Enterprise: An Economic History of New England,* ed. Peter Temin (Cambridge, Mass., 2000), 100–103; see also on the continuing scholarly debates, Douglas A. Irwin and Peter Temin, "The Antebellum Tariff on Cotton Textiles Revisited," and C. Knick Harley, "The Antebellum Tariff: Different Products or Competing Sources? A Comment on Irwin and Temin," *Journal of Economic History* 61 (Sept. 2001): 777–805.

91. Eckes, *Opening America's Market,* xii.

92. Joseph A. Schumpeter, *History of Economic Analysis,* ed. Elizabeth Boody Schumpeter (New York, 1954), 10, 11, 337 n; Irwin, *Against the Tide,* 7.

93. For one of the exceptions to the prevailing view that poorly recompensed, low-cost labor was inferior in terms of the quantity and/or quality of its productive output, see Austin Baldwin's remarks on contract convict labor.

Some Elaborations and Conclusions

1. Some postmodern perspectives might argue that such cultural anxieties themselves are not truly recoverable and are of problematic existence, insofar as they are being con-

veyed through words whose meanings are intrinsically ambiguous and unstable. But I find such interpretations unpersuasive—or at least no more helpful than more conventional perspectives that have always cautioned against accepting at face value the sincerity and the depth of expressed anxieties; for the conclusion that "the destabilizing effects of postmodernism are only beginning to be noticed in the area of economics," see Jack Amariglio and David F. Ruccio, "Postmodernism, Marxism, and the Critique of Economic Thought," in *Why Economists Disagree: An Introduction to the Alternative Schools of Thought,* ed. David L. Prychitko (Albany, 1998), 237.

2. Marvin Meyers, *The Jacksonian Persuasion* (Stanford, Calif., 1957); Ashworth, *"Agrarians" and "Aristocrats";* for contrasting emphasis on the Democrats' Smithian desires for "freeing the economy," see Robert Kelley, *The Transatlantic Persuasion: The Liberal-Democratic Mind in the Age of Gladstone* (New York, 1969), 262–65.

3. "Free Labor and Protection," *National Era,* May 4, 1854. The paper's editor, Gamaliel Bailey, had long embraced many standard Democratic positions.

4. "Speech of the Hon. John C. Calhoun," ibid., July 20, 1848.

5. Hartz, *Liberal Tradition,* 198–99; Foner, *Free Soil, Free Labor,* 1–39; Howe, *American Whigs,* 279–81.

6. The opposition to state prison industry, although a staple of the Working Men's Party platforms of the Jacksonian period, failed to win the unequivocal support of either major party, at least in antebellum New York. Democrats in the state may have more consistently embraced a critical stance toward contract convict-labor practices as part of their rhetorical assaults on monopoly and unfair privilege, and conservative Whigs constituted the hard-core opposition to the mechanic petitions for abolition of those practices. But as indicated in chapter 6, these petitions also found a sympathetic voice among progressive Whigs like William Henry Seward and Horace Greeley.

7. Alexander Saxton, "Blackface Minstrelsy, Vernacular Comics, and the Politics of Slavery in the North," in *The Meaning of Slavery in the North,* ed. David Roediger and Martin H. Blatt (New York, 1998), 166; Alexander Saxton, *The Rise and Fall of the White Republic: Class Politics and Mass Culture in Nineteenth-Century America* (New York, 1990), 227–51. This is not to deny the existence of more racially egalitarian elements (less frequently originating from the Democratic Party) within the Republican coalition.

8. Fogel, *Without Consent or Contract,* 350–87; Levine, "Conservatism, Nativism, and Slavery," 474–75; Stephen E. Maizlish, "The Meaning of Nativism and the Crisis of the Union: The Know-Nothing Movement in the Antebellum North," in *Essays on American Antebellum Politics, 1840–1860,* ed. Maizlish and John J. Kushma (Arlington, Tex., 1982), 166–98.

9. One example was the former British Chartist Thomas Devyr, who became a leading participant in New York's land-reform and antirent movements after his arrival in the United States in 1840. For Devyr's bitterness over the distractions created by the growth of antislavery agitation, see "Letter of Thomas A. Devyr to Horace Greeley: Dedicated to the Reformers of New York State," newspaper clipping, Oct. 29, 1860, Greeley Papers, New York Public Library; Ray Boston, *British Chartists in America, 1839–1900* (Manchester, Eng., 1971), 44–62. The Jacksonian labor reformer Theophilus Fisk similarly protested in 1860 that free-soilism and abolition distracted northern workers from "their own grievous wrongs and intolerable oppressions" (Fisk quoted in Ashworth, "Free Labor, Wage Labor," 137); see also the attack on Massachusetts senator Charles Sumner that linked

his free-labor ideology with "'our legislators'" despicable conversion of "our prisons into manufacturing monopolies" (Mullins, *Voice from the Workshop,* 19).

10. There were, for example, the anxieties generated by employers' utilization of low-cost, tractable child labor in their factories and manufactories, most of all perhaps during the earlier phases of the Industrial Revolution in both England and the United States.

11. For an elite commentator who generally acquiesced to the reign of supply-and-demand market forces, see the discussion of Joseph Tuckerman.

12. Lebergott, "Pattern of Employment," 292.

13. The market revolution and the spread of wage labor helped generate attendant intellectual ferment and disagreement in early nineteenth-century northern courts regarding the precise contractual rights and obligations of employers and workers; for the competing, if still "bourgeois capitalist," legal constructions of free labor that developed in this context, see Schmidt, *Free to Work,* 57–111.

14. Most industrial outwork, both in England and the United States, was performed in the home. However, scholars of the garment and other trades where sweating predominated, operating from the premise that the most basic attribute of outwork in nineteenth-century capitalist economies was that it was work done under subcontract agreements, commonly include as outworkers many of the employees who congregated in garrets and other small workshops; for this and related issues, see Duncan Bythell, *The Sweated Trades: Outwork in Nineteenth-Century Britain* (London, 1978); James A. Schmiechen, *Sweated Industries and Sweated Labor: The London Clothing Trades, 1860–1914* (Urbana, Ill., 1984); Jenny Morris, "The Characteristics of Sweating: The Late Nineteenth-Century London and Leeds Tailoring Trade," in *Unequal Opportunities: Women's Employment in England, 1800–1918,* ed. Angela V. John (London, 1986), 95–121; Christine Stansell, *City of Women,* 106–25; Baron and Klepp, "Sewing Machine," 39; Dublin, *Transforming Women's Work,* 163–204.

15. Parson Lot [Charles Kingsley], *Cheap Clothes and Nasty* (London, 1850); Henry Mayhew, *London Labour and the London Poor* (1861–62; rept. New York, 1968), 4 vols.; see also Katrina Honeyman, *Women, Gender, and Industrialisation in England, 1700–1870* (New York, 2000), 88–91; Sally Alexander, *Women's Work in Nineteenth-Century London* (London, 1983), 30–33. Alexander adds that, in London at least, skilled women workers—those in the dressmaking and needlework trades—suffered from slopwork competition even more than did the male-dominated skilled trades (39).

16. Extensively documenting the various forms of slopwork organization and exploitation devices in the cabinet trade and other London trades, Mayhew argued that their general propensity for subdivision of labor and piecework encouraged "overcompetition," overproduction, and a highly uneven distribution of slopwork labor. All of these helped determine existing wage rates, as the overwork of some slopworkers came to mean the unemployment of others. There also followed Mayhew's general conclusion as to a vicious circle of "overwork" and "underpay" in the sweated trades, which he offered in rebuttal to the view that subsistent wages were a function of simple demand-and-supply forces (or absolute "surplus population") within the sweated trades (Mayhew, *London Labour* 2:327, 3:227; Eileen Yeo, "Mayhew as a Social Investigator," in *The Unknown Mayhew: Selections from the* Morning Chronicle, *1849–1856,* ed. Yeo and E. P. Thompson [New York, 1971], 70–77; and Mayhew's writings, ibid., 185–88, 363–88). For a critical view of Mayhew's analysis of low wages in the trades, see Karel Williams, *From Pauperism to Poverty* (London, 1981),

254–58; for description of comparable employments in New York City, see the series "Labor in New-York," *Tribune,* Aug. 1845–Jan. 1946—e.g., the Aug. 22 and 28 profiles of the "respectable" and dishonorable establishments in the city's bookbinding trade. One of the reporters who wrote this series, George Foster, subsequently included his findings in several books on antebellum New York, notably contributing to the developing genre of nonfictional urban sensationalism; see Foster, *New York Naked* (New York, 185?), 153.

17. "Labor and the Laborers: The Shoe Trade and Shoemakers of New-York," *Tribune,* May 27, 1853.

18. For Marx's demonstration that in mid-nineteenth-century England as well, "the heralded forces of capitalist competition were anything but the guardians of labor," see Botwinick, *Persistent Inequalities,* 87; see also Marx, "Appendix" (trans. Rodney Livingstone) to *Capital: A Critique of Political Economy,* trans. Ben Fowkes (New York, 1977), 1:381, 990; for the criticism made by John Stuart Mill and others that anticapitalist labor reformers had a one-sided notion of competition—that (regardless of what transpired in the sweated trades) such reformers ignored the general extent to which competition among employers to purchase the services of laborers acted to raise wages—see Dickman, *Industrial Democracy,* 91–92. Although not denying the existence of sex-based occupational segregation, some American middle-class commentary insisted that the difficulties of "exit" remained considerably of native-born females' own making. They could relieve their clustering in needlework and other sweated labor in the North if at least those who were not confined by domestic responsibilities to home-based outwork were willing to emulate Irish immigrant single females and overcome their distaste for better-paying domestic service, work that they reputedly rejected as beneath their dignity. Horace Greeley, among others, responded that whatever the available employment opportunities in domestic service, the distaste for such work was well justified: it did not offer a truly meaningful option for native-born working-class women. For a variety of reasons, too, many antebellum working-class females, native-born or otherwise, may have been unable to decisively exit waged work once they married, the domestic ideology of separate spheres notwithstanding. In fact, the plight of single seamstresses was exacerbated by the recurrent tendency of married women to reenter the labor market and sell their sewing skills when household income from other sources proved inadequate (Glickstein, *Concepts of Free Labor,* 180, 426–27, 432–33).

19. Anderson, *Observations on Slavery,* 8–9. In illustration of his dictum that higher wages encouraged greater industry, Adam Smith remarked that workmen who were "liberally paid by the piece" were "very apt to over-work themselves." Had he seen the inside of a nineteenth-century sweatshop, Smith might have concluded that overwork was hardly less common among pieceworkers who were not so well paid (Smith, *Wealth of Nations,* 81). For the related argument that Smith and other late eighteenth-century high-wage advocates had only male workers in mind—that gender bias was deeply embedded in their newer notions of work psychology—see Valenze, *First Industrial Women,* 138–39.

20. Tuckerman, followed by Carey's editorial comments, in Tuckerman, *Wages,* 37–38 n. Mayhew's investigations represented an elaborate working-out of the critical perspective that Carey brought here to Tuckerman's supply-and-demand argument; see also Sutton, *Journeymen for Jesus,* 165.

21. According to the federal census of 1860, one-quarter of New York City's labor force—25,000 women—worked in manufacturing, and two-thirds of these were employed in the clothing trades. Other sources reported far higher numbers (Stansell, *City of Women,* 108; Baron and Klepp, "Sewing Machine," 23). Twenty years earlier, by one estimate, women made up almost half of all American manufacturing workers when outworkers are included. However, for a variety of reasons, only a portion of these outworkers might be accurately characterized as sweated laborers (Christopher Clark and Nancy A. Hewitt, *Who Built America? Working People and the Nation's Economy, Politics, Culture, and Society* [New York, 2000], 1:390; Dublin, *Transforming Women's Work,* 36–37).

22. Stansell, *City of Women,* 261.

23. "Female Employment," *Tribune,* March 7, 1845. Here the *Tribune* attributed the seamstresses' "miserable pittance" not only to demand factors—the competitive pressures for cutting labor costs that faced the small manufacturers and contractors. It also blamed the oversupply of seamstresses in New York and other large cities, while adding the reform refrain that such an oversupply was itself largely a function of the discriminatory gender norms that limited demand for females in other employments; see also Stansell, *City of Women,* 110–13; Wilentz, *Chants Democratic,* 119–29. For a neoclassical economic acknowledgment of gender-based occupational crowding in England, see Joyce Burnette, "An Investigation of the Female-Male Wage Gap during the Industrial Revolution in Britain," *Economic History Review* 50 (May 1997): 261–62.

24. "Labor in New-York: No. XV. The Milliners," *Tribune,* Sept. 16, 1845; see also, on the rationale for the short-lived Shirt-Sewers' Association of New York, a cooperative store for needlewomen's products, "A Movement for the Shirt-Sewers," ibid., March 27, 1851, and "Annual Report of the Shirt Sewers and Seamstresses Union," ibid., March 22, 1853.

25. "The Clothing Trade," 116. *Hunt's* brief article, one of its "Mercantile Miscellanies," describes conditions in D. & J. Devlin, among New York's "largest and most enterprising clothing establishments" and one that was engaged in both a large wholesale and "a very extensive and fashionable" retail trade. The firm's cutters were among the aristocrats of the city's clothing trade. Some of the piece masters, or head cutters, those who distributed the work, drew anywhere from $25 to $150 per week. The firm's approximately 2,000 hands, "many of these supporting large families," earned from $3 up to $15 per week ("according to their skill, capacity, and promptness") sewing pieces together into the final product. The regular in-shop cutters, according to other sources, typically enjoyed wages in the upper end of this scale. The weekly earnings of the male tailors and other outwork hands ranged from around $9 down to the cited $3 minimum, although averages could drop considerably during hard times. Whatever the degree to which earning disparities in D. & J. Devlin might be seen as exploitative, *Hunt's* hardly intended an exposé of exploitation. Its perspective with respect to the scale of D. & J. Devlin, the extensive employment opportunities that it provided, and most of all, what it illustrated about New York as the supplier for approximately two-thirds the nation's clothing was completely congratulatory; for another favorable view of this firm, see William E. Devlin, "Shrewd Irishmen: Irish Entrepreneurs and Artisans in New York's Clothing Industry, 1830–1880," in *The New York Irish,* ed. Ronald H. Bayor and Timothy J. Meagher (Baltimore, 1996), 184–86; see also Stansell, *City of Women,* 264; Wilentz, *Chants Democratic,* 121–22; Feldman, *Fit for Men,* 113;

Michael Zakim, "A Ready-Made Business: The Birth of the Clothing Industry in America," *Business History Review* 73 (Spring 1999): 61–90.

26. "Labor and the Laborers: "The Needlewomen of New-York." *Tribune,* June 8, 1853. The first of the series, "The Shoe Trade and Shoemakers of New-York," appeared in the May 27 issue. In modern economic parlance the June 8 piece was suggesting that the needlewomen employed in these particular firms were earning less than the marginal value of their productive contributions. Piece-rate wages were generally lower for home-based, sweated outwork than they were for women employed in the centralized, "inside" facto-ries and workshops. Beyond the likelihood that the wage differential reflected the larger labor pool within which they competed, many of the most poorly paid outworkers were being penalized for enjoying the convenience of working out of their own households — i.e., they were being negatively compensated for their relative freedom from the clock dis-cipline and surveillance to which their better-paid factory counterparts were subjected. Mention should also be made of two studies that paint a more multidimensional picture of urban needlework and rural industrial-outwork enterprises in nineteenth-century America: they indicate that for skilled needlewomen and for those belonging to rural New England families that retained alternatives to wage labor, conditions were other than ones of unrelieved poverty and exploitation (Wendy Gamber, *The Female Economy: The Millinery and Dressmaking Trades, 1860–1936* [Urbana, Ill., 1997]; Dublin, *Transforming Women's Work*). Defenders of the Industrial Revolution, of which the early nineteenth-century sweated industries were certainly a part, are also inclined to emphasize that there was no previous "golden age" in which the "helpers, apprentices, and hired hands" employed in "pre-industrial mills, shops, and farms" enjoyed wages in amounts that were "visibly linked to the market value of a product" (Nathan Rosenberg and L. E. Birdzell Jr., *How the West Grew Rich: The Economic Transformation of the Industrial World* [New York, 1986], 182); for the relevance of theories of labor-market segmentation to exploitative wages, such as those paid antebellum seamstresses, see the essays in Frank Wilkinson, ed., *The Dynam-ics of Labour Market Segmentation* (London, 1981), esp. those by Ryan and by Rubery and Wilkinson.

27. "The Milliners," *Tribune,* June 16, 1854.

28. By a modern, less censorious economic perspective, the relatively inelastic nature of seamstresses' work output and quality (as indicated by this *Tribune* investigator, at least), together with low "turnover" costs (the minimal expense of acquiring and replacing seam-stresses in overstocked urban labor markets), suggests that the "cheap shops" were simply acting in a more rational manner than their "Christian" competitors when they failed to pay wages above the market rate (Andrew Weiss, *Efficiency Wages: Models of Unemployment, Layoffs, and Wage Dispersion* [Princeton, N.J., 1990]).

29. The plight of the English needlewomen, one scholar notes, was "the most popu-lar of all social themes" in the Victorian period (T. J. Edelstein, "They Sang 'The Song of the Shirt': The Visual Iconography of the Seamstress," *Victorian Studies* 23 [Winter 1980]: 183–210). On the distressed needlewoman as an embodiment of social anxieties regarding the position of single women, woman's work, and sexuality, see Rogers, "Good"; Catherine Gallagher, *The Industrial Reformation of English Fiction: Social Discourse and Narra-tive Form, 1832–1867* (Chicago, 1985), 130–36; for the specter of the mid-nineteenth-century French needlewomen, see Judith G. Coffin, *The Politics of Women's Work: The Paris Garment*

Trades, 1750–1915 (Princeton, N.J., 1996), 64–65. The relatively intimate size of many American urban and rural sweatshops, together with their decentralized locations, may have exacerbated oppressive surveillance and exploitation of the workers. But the same characteristics may have also impeded public recognition of such oppressiveness and exploitation, preventing such recognition from assuming even greater proportions by 1860. Without specific reference to sweated enterprises, James L. Huston suggests that the predominantly small-scale, "horizontal" nature of American industrial growth for most of the nineteenth century constrained public perceptions that particular industrial conditions were exploitative, as well as broad recognition of the fact that American economic inequality was both significant and growing during this period (Huston, *Securing the Fruits,* 124).

30. On the prevalent "craving desire for *cheapness*" in connection with the plight of the Victorian seamstress, see Christina Walkley, *The Ghost in the Looking Glass: The Victorian Seamstress* (London, 1981), 7–8.

31. As indicated in the Introduction, even such economic historians as Robert A. Margo who have adopted some of the pessimistic insights of labor historians retain this view of long-term real wage gains.

32. See such criticisms of Charles Sellers's assault on the market revolution as Appleby, "Vexed Story," and Daniel Walker Howe, "The Market Revolution and the Shaping of Identity in Whig-Jacksonian America," in Stokes and Conway, *The Market Revolution,* 259–81.

33. Sweated industries continue to flourish today, of course, serving various needs in the United States as well as less developed countries. But they are now conceptualized differently, if only because many of their conditions and operations now exist in violation of the minimum wage, health, and safety laws and other legal regulatory apparatus that developed over time precisely to check the unregulated excesses of their nineteenth- and early twentieth-century antecedents (Alejandro Portes, Manuel Castells, and Lauren A. Benton, eds., *The Informal Economy: Studies in Advanced and Less Developed Countries* [Baltimore, 1989]).

34. In noting that labor activists objected most clearly to a state double standard for capital and labor, one should, again, not overstate their embrace of competitive capitalism. As with the contract convict-labor issue, journeymen and other activists gave off mixed signals on their willingness to take their chances with a relatively unregulated market ethos as an equitable arbiter of their fortunes — as an acceptable form of economic discipline for both the buyers and sellers of labor power. Nor should one exaggerate early industrial capitalists' own embrace of "truly open competition," at least as it applied to their own enterprises (see chapter 1's discussion, centered around Barrington Moore Jr.'s remarks).

35. Suggestive here is John E. Crowley, *The Invention of Comfort: Sensibilities and Design in Early Modern Britain and Early America* (Baltimore, 2000), 143.

36. "Philosophy of Labor," *Chronotype.* As noted elsewhere, such exploitation scenarios carried common corollaries: that "starvation wages" acted over time to physically and spiritually wear down the hireling and erode his (or her) productivity, and that, largely owing to the unskilled or deskilled nature of his labor input in the context of crowded labor markets, the employer might then replace him at minimal effort and expense.

37. Smith, *Wealth of Nations,* 66–67.

38. For the fuller theoretical and economic context (e.g., spiraling living costs and declining real wages for British workers during the 1770s) within which Smith made his high-wage appeals, see Mathias, *Transformation of England,* 157–65; Hatcher, "Labour, Leisure," 98–102, together with the other sources cited in chap. 7, note 30. Michael Perelman argues that Smith "disapproved of low wages because they reinforced precapitalist norms of behavior," while he advocated high wages as a means of encouraging workers "to adopt middle-class aspirations" and recognize that their interests too would be served by the "harmonious functioning of the market." These arguments are less exceptional, and more convincing, than Perelman's further claims: that Smith "was thoroughly antagonistic toward the vast majority of the working class," and that his "solicitude" for its "well being" was altogether bogus (Perelman, *The Invention of Capitalism: Classical Political Economy and the Secret History of Primitive Accumulations* [Durham, N.C., 2000], 189–92).

39. Antebellum proslavery thought offered a different, racialist repudiation of the "utility of poverty" theme. New Orleans physician Samuel A. Cartright intoned that "free negroes will not work": they were no more responsive to free-market subsistence wages and the penalties of destitution than they were to the more generous levels of compensation animating free white workers' hope of improvement (Cartright, "How to Save the Republic, and the Position of the South in the Union," *DeBow's Review* 11 [July 1851]: 185).

40. However, such relevant phenomena as the reluctance of manufacturing firms to keep piece rates constant when output per worker rose, their consequent resort to "rate busting," and the reactive withholding of effort by their workers have been more extensively explored for later periods of American history, when piecework came into increasingly widespread use (Daniel Nelson, *Managers and Workers: Origins of the Twentieth-Century Factory System in the United States, 1880–1920,* 2d ed. [Madison, Wis., 1995], 44–47; David Montgomery, *The Fall of the House of Labor: The Workplace, the State, and American Labor Activism, 1865–1925* [Cambridge, 1987], 151–52).

41. Hatcher, "Labour, Leisure," 114–15. More generally, it would appear that workers, individually and collectively, have historically drawn on a wide range of values in deciding on their work effort, rather than making a narrowly strategic calculation of their individual interests; for discussion of the mechanisms, including worker norms and expectations, that generate labor effort within modern-day capital labor contracts, see Samuel Bowles and Herbert Gintis, "Contested Exchange: New Microfoundations for the Political Economy of Capitalism," *Politics & Society* 18 (June 1990): 178–81; and the responses, particularly Michael Burawoy and Erik Olin Wright, "Coercion and Consent in Contested Exchange," ibid., 252–63; see also Aage B. Sorensen, "Firms, Wages, and Incentives," in *The Handbook of Economic Sociology,* ed. Neil J. Smelser and Richard Swedberg (Princeton, N.J., 1994), 514; James A. Jaffe, *Striking a Bargain: Work and Industrial Relations in England, 1815–1865* (Manchester, Eng., 2000).

42. Richard Price, *Masters, Unions, and Men: Work Control in Building and the Rise of Labour, 1830–1914* (Cambridge, 1980), 132; Sidney Pollard, *The Genesis of Modern Management: A Study of the Industrial Revolution in Great Britain* (Cambridge, 1965), 190–91.

43. For the high-wage arguments made by Robert Owen and others on grounds of both worker productivity and worker purchasing power, see Dickman, *Industrial Democracy,*

84–86. In today's high-consumption societies, rising wag e rates and additional income may be a more negligible stimulant of labor productivity; for some of the issues from a left perspective, see Bowles and Gintis, "Contested."

44. On the continuing susceptibility of Britain's early industrial employers to the temptations of a cheap labor economy, see Hobsbawm, *Labouring Men,* 351–56; Pollard, *Genesis,* 189–93, 258–59; Michael Haynes, "Employers and Trade Unions, 1824–1850," in *British Trade Unionism, 1750–1850: The Formative Years,* ed. John Rule (London, 1988), 256–59; for some of these employers' corresponding propensity to avail themselves of penal sanctions (rather than pay higher wages) to elicit worker effort, see Steinfeld, *Coercion, Contract,* 70–72.

45. Philip C. Friese, *An Essay on Wages* (New York, 1853), 8–22, 26–32. Although Friese speaks generally of American "capital," the tariff-centered nature of his tract indicates that he has employers in the manufacturing trades most strongly in mind.

46. Ibid., 7.

47. Burritt, in his newspaper, *Bond of Brotherhood,* Oct. 1854, quoted in Merle Curti, *The Learned Blacksmith: The Letters and Journals of Elihu Burritt* (New York, 1937), 119.

48. A. L. Bayley, "To the Workingmen of Essex," *Essex Transcript,* rept. in *Herald of Freedom,* Oct. 23, 1846; "Slave vs. Free Labor," *National Era,* July 24, 1851. These commentaries are reprinted in *Northern Labor and Antislavery: A Documentary History,* ed. Philip S. Foner and Herbert Shapiro (Westport, Conn., 1994), 99–101, 83–86.

49. For southern proslavery ideology's resistance to acknowledging the "commodity property" character of chattel slavery that so outraged abolitionists, see Gregory S. Alexander, *Commodity and Propriety: Competing Visions of Property in American Legal Thought, 1776–1970* (Chicago, 1997), 211–40.

50. One need only, after all, refer to the thousands of Lynn, Massachusetts, shoemakers who struck in 1860 under complaints of their growing wage slavery to the shoe bosses. On the other hand, many of these workers may have also been persuaded that their economic plight, however rooted they recognized it to be in technological and other developments within their trade, could only be worsened by the successful aggressions of the southern slavocracy (e.g., the closing off of territorial "safety valves" to northern wage earners by slavery's expansion). In the state and national elections of 1860, the majority of male shoe workers voted Republican (Dawley, *Class and Community,* 82; Clark and Hewitt, *Who Built America?* 588).

51. Foner, *Politics and Ideology,* 24; Guarneri, *Utopian Alternative,* 380. In some cases the abandonment of radical views was only temporary, these reemerging after the Civil War's defusion of the threat from the southern slavocracy (Messer-Kruse, *Yankee International*).

Index

Abercrombie, Nicholas, et al., 276

Abolitionists, 3, 81; role of in legitimating northern capital-labor relationships, 78–79; focus on different commercial attribute of slavery than do Republicans, 227; attitudes of toward market forces and commercial and manufacturing enterprise, 264, 270; and American exceptionalism, 269; disagreements among regarding slave labor as threat to free labor, 307–8, 317–18; free-trade attacks of on Walter tariff, 337

"Abundance consciousness," 142

Adams, John, 148

Adaptation, phenomenon of, 231, 289

Address of 1844 of the New England Working-men's Association, 125–27, 128, 129, 296

Alexander, Gregory S., 346

Alexander, Sally, 279

Allen, Theodore W., 251

Allowance system, England, 61, 189, 260

Almshouse officials and anti-poor-law commentators, American, 42–45, 61–63. *See also* Tuckerman, Joseph

American exceptionalism, mythology of: consensus regarding, 2; and extrinsic rewards, 3; versions of, 4–5; and marginalized social groups, 5–6; and republican and liberal values, 6, 11; and supply-and-demand forces, labor-market segmentation, and nature of American economic competition, 8, 13–14, 55, 62–63; and expectations and anxieties, 8–11, 92; and "drudgery," 34; and British political economy, 38, 41–49; and negative labor incentives, 43, 222; and

Old World, 125; and republican traditions stigmatizing wage-earner status, 147–48; and contract convict labor, 168–69; free-trade Democrats and protectionist Whigs both wedded to, 190; and high-wage vein of British political economy, 222; and utility-of-poverty arguments, 223; and urban casual labor, 231; and English artisan traditions, 233–34; and Republican and abolitionist conceptions of liberty, 269; and skilled and ethnic divisions in labor force, 275. *See also* Gresham's law–like anxieties

American Fourierism. *See* Association

American Quarterly Review, 43, 62

American Revolution and Revolutionary era, 69, 122, 123, 125

American Unitarian moral philosophy, 64

Anderson, James, 267

Antiabolitionist mobs: and class frustrations, 93, 277

Antislavery political-economic orthodoxy, 144–46, 303, 316

Appleby, Joyce, 63, 104, 231, 281, 282

Appleton, Nathan, 126, 322

Arkwright, Richard, 296

Arnold, George, 43, 53, 249

Artisans: sense of entitlement and anxieties of, 9–10, 92; and relative versus absolute immiserization, 20, 84–85; declension and labor hardship model of, 84–87; and non-black unskilled, cheap others, 85–86, 88–93, 234; exclusivism and exclusionist shelters of, 89, 127, 234; and middle-class criticisms of unskilled and capitalist hegemony,

Index

Brooks Brothers, 218

Brotherhood of the Union, 299

Brownson, Orestes, 225, 237, 280; and exploitation, 20, 74; and Whig class-fluidity claims, 42, 139–40; on Lowell operatives' loss of health and morals, 295

Buchanan, Allen E., 283

Burawoy, Michael, 233–34

Burritt, Elihu, 226–27

"Buy cheap, sell dear" ethos, 99–101; and shibboleths of supply and demand and free competition, 57, 287; and eighteenth-century expressions, 106–7; and Anglo-American and diverse character of criticisms of, 107, 109–10; and industrial and urban capitalist components of market revolution, 112–13, 287; and Gresham's law–like anxieties, 215, 221; southern proslavery invocations of, 226. *See also* Gresham's law–like anxieties

Byllesby, Langton, 126

Capitalism, 101, 105, 137, 241, 272. *See also* Labor incentives, negative; Labor incentives, positive; Market revolution

Carey, Henry C., 195, 333; and Malthusian-Ricardian economy of scarcity, 42, 193, 196; and England's policy-setting elites, 190; and Democrats, 205; and Whiggish versions of wages-fund, 249; and "infant industries" argument, 334

Carey, Mathew, 67, 216, 227; rebuts Tuckerman in insisting on wage-lowering power of unscrupulous employers, 217, 226; as observer of sweated trades, 217, 218, 219, 220; and poor relief and seamstresses in Philadelphia, 265, 266

Carlyle, Thomas, 48, 253, 286; and idolization of work and work's instrinsic rewards, 31, 32; and British political economy, cash nexus, and laissez-faire, 107, 110

Cartright, Samuel, 345

Cash nexus: and public moralists, 31; and diverse sources of criticism of in England, 107, 284; and defenders of economic individualism in England, 108–9; checks upon in nineteenth-century America, 113, 114,

287–88. *See also* "Buy cheap, sell dear" ethos; Market revolution

Casual labor, 36, 231

Chadwick, Edwin, 60, 62

Chalmers, Thomas, 62, 64–65, 66, 68, 261, 263

Champion of American Labor, 187–88

Channing, William Ellery, 79, 87, 89, 254; and boundaries between free and unfree labor, 19, 270; ennobles wage laborer's negative incentives, 19, 71, 72–74, 78, 97; differences from both American exceptionalists and labor reformers, 19, 76, 79–80; and abolitionists, 19, 73–74, 76, 267; relative color blindness of, 72, 267; and high-wage economy and manual labor's instrumental value, 74, 222, 269; paradoxical full-blown market ideology of arising from his non-materialist preoccupations, 74–75, 78; as apologist for capitalist class interests and hegemony, 75–76, 78, 83; and economic attack on slavery, 76–78; shifting defenses of British Emancipation Act, 77, 270; and liberal-capitalist success values and Republican free-labor ideology, 230–31, 269; as "traditional" intellectual, 268; and scholarship on slaves' remuneration, 272

Channing, William Henry, 75

Chapin, Edward H., 253

Chartism, 91–92, 243, 292–93

Child labor, 269, 288, 340

Chinese in California, 305

Christian socialists, England's, 241

Chronotype (Boston), 36–38, 45, 47, 48, 250

Civil War, 2, 220

Clark, John Bates, 130

Clarke, James Freeman, 173, 216, 225, 264, 294; on labor-reform "cannot wait" argument, 15, 20, 237; male breadwinner–exploitation scenario and its corollaries, 16–18, 237, 239; on Channing's views of chattel slavery, 19, 238; and labor-reform condemnation of hunger and fear of poverty as capitalist labor incentives, 19, 22; and "let alone" principle and unhibited economic competition, 19–20, 237; and wage slavery, 21, 239–40; agreements with Associationists and Marx on exploitation and needs, 21, 26,

349

Index

Extrinsic rewards of manual labor (*continued*)
marginalized groups in North, 5–6; insistence on, 32, 244–45; failure of commentary to distinguish from intrinsic rewards, 32–33, 230–31; and middle-class attitudes toward physical labor, 34; bearing of on manual labor's social status, 34–35; premium on one kind (upward mobility) over another (consumer capabilities), 244–45

Factory women, New England: and mythology of American exceptionalism, 6; spending power of, 35; limited expectations of regarding wages, 126; perspective of compared with male labor reformers, 126–27, 246; and Democrats' antiprotectionist arguments, 199–200; and representations of Lowell mills, 220; supposed mortality of, 252; "Improvement Circles" of, 256; and Whigs, 333
Fall River, Mass., factory agent, 112, 113, 286
Farmers, 36, 215
Ferrie, Joseph P., 237–38, 330/
Ficklin, O. B., 199–201, 202, 208
Fisher, Sidney George, 148, 306
Fiske, Theophilus, 120, 339
Fitzhugh, George, 161, 337
Fogel, Robert W., 7, 8, 274, 304
Foner, Eric, 154, 160, 269, 313
Foster, George, 341
Foucault, Michael, 57, 243
Fraser, Nancy, 29
Fredrickson, George, 148
Free competition, 13, 57, 58–59, 112, 297. *See also* Supply and demand
Freehling, William W., 307
Free labor, northern, 9–10, 222, 238. *See also* American exceptionalism, mythology of; Artisans; Gresham's law–like anxieties
Free-labor ideology, 77–78, 146, 305. *See also* Northern nationalist, Republican free-labor ideology
Freeman, M. H., 231
Free-market incentives, 60–61, 62, 70, 222, 260, 261. *See also* Labor incentives, negative; Labor incentives, positive
Freeport doctrine, 317

Freyer, Tony, 321–22
Friese, Philip C., 225–26, 227, 346

Gans, Herbert J., 44, 250
Garrison, William Lloyd, 77, 261, 269, 271, 272
Geertz, Clifford, 78
German immigrants, 280
Gerring, John, 286
Gienapp, William E., 282, 313–14
Glassman, Jonathon, 276–77
Glickman, Lawrence B., 245–46, 294, 331
Godwin, William, 138
Goldin, Claudia, 233
Goldstein, Judith, 336
Goodloe, Daniel R., 311
Grampp, William, 247
Gramsci, Antonio, 99, 102, 103, 105, 268
Granovetter, Mark, 287–88
Gray, John, 126
Gray, Lewis, 303
Gray, Robert, 292
Greeley, Horace, 116, 119, 141, 173, 195, 196, 218; and debate with Raymond, 33–34; and Pittsburgh's striking iron-puddlers, 97–98, 280; as critic of "Buy cheap, sell dear" ethos, 97–99, 107, 109, 110–14, 123; Whiggery of, 98, 106, 333; and Association, 98; seeks middle course between capital and labor, 98, 280; and attributes of American capitalism, 99, 280; and divided mentality and opportunistic behavior of striking workers, 99–106, 115; and workers' double standard, 106, 115, 283; and social progress, 108; and anticapitalist labor theory of value, 133–34, 296; and pauper-labor argument, 191–92, 197; and free-trade comparative advantages argument, 207; and capitalist wage minimizing, 225; and land monopoly and supply and demand, 258; conflicting tendencies and evolution of his thought, 280; and women's occupational segregation, 283; and Horwitz, 286; and northern Democrat "diversity" argument, 314; on productiveness and competitive threat of New York convict labor, 324, 339; on London's economic advantage, 331; and domestic service in New York City, 341

Index

Republican free-labor ideology. *See* Northern
  nationalist, Republican free-labor ideology
Republicanism, 11, 12, 148, 177–78, 215
Republicans, 2–3, 79, 212–14, 317, 339. *See also*
  Northern nationalist, Republican free-labor
  ideology; Weston, George M.
Ricardian socialism, 125, 291, 298
Ricardo, David, 45, 207, 248–49, 336; and di-
  minishing returns, 39, 196, 247; and Smith's
  more optimistic views, 39–40, 193; dis-
  parate wage doctrines of, 56, 198, 335
Robinson, Solon, 82
Roediger, David R., 251, 272, 277, 298. *See also*
  Whiteness and whiteness/cultural studies
  scholarship
Roemer, John E., 237, 300
Rogers, Helen, 256
Romantic reform, 21
Rothman, David J., 164, 262
Roy, William G., 173
Ruffin, Edmund, 304
Rusche, Georg, and Otto Kircheimer, 318
Ruskin, John, 107, 108, 110, 111

Saville, John, 302
Say, Jean-Baptiste, 45, 147, 168–69, 305
Schlesinger, Arthur, Jr., 75, 179–80, 269
Schmidt, James D., 259, 263, 264, 340
Schneider, Eric C., 262
Schultz, Ronald, 292
Schumpeter, Joseph A., 209–10
Schwartz, Joel, 262
Scott, Donald M., 257
Scott, James C., 93, 94, 101–2
Scott, Joan W., 260
Seamstresses, 12; sentimentalization of, 52; and
  economic historians, 220–21; emergence of
  category, 253; genteel origins of a minority,
  255; and E. M. Powell, 256; wages of, 265;
  poor relief as work disincentive, 265–66;
  blamed for their own plight, 341; numbers
  of employed in New York City manufac-
  tures, 342; compared to other urban needle-
  work and rural outwork, 343. *See also* Carey,
  Mathew; Sweated labor; Tuckerman, Joseph
Second Great Awakening, 180
Seed, John, 284–85

Self-made man, creed of, 244
Sen, Amartya, 128–29, 240, 281, 301–2
Senior, Nassau, 40, 64, 70, 72, 249, 260; oppo-
  sition of to British moral economy, 50, 254;
  as co-author of Britain's Poor Law Com-
  mission *Report*, 60, 62; on positive and
  negative labor incentives, 63
Severance, Luther, 335
Seward, William H., 159, 304, 315, 322, 328, 339
Sewell, William H., Jr., 29
Shaw, Lemuel, 322
Shirt-Sewers' Association of New York, 342
Shklar, Judith N., 234, 267
Siegel, Reva B., 255
Simmel, Georg, 113, 287
Simon, 87–88, 89, 93, 178, 274, 275
Simpson, Stephen, 126, 295
Sing Sing State Prison, 166, 183, 184, 319, 322,
  327
Skidmore, Thomas, 131, 132, 137, 225, 293, 300
Skill, 26–27, 174, 279
Slater, Samuel, 126
Slave labor, southern, 36, 146, 246, 304–5
Slave power, 2, 9, 160–61, 315
Slavery (Channing), 19, 71
Smiles, Samuel, 64
Smith, Adam, 68, 203, 219, 224, 225, 250, 260,
  303, 305, 307; high-wage scenario, 39, 47,
  53, 192–93, 222, 223, 332–33, 341, 345; and
  employer combinations, 57, 223; and slav-
  ery, 145, 303; trade doctrines of, 187; and
  manufacturing division of labor and capi-
  talist profits, 323
Smith, John, 231
Smith, Peshine E., 195–97, 199, 224, 335, 346
Smithian socialism, 125
Snell, K. D. M., 261
Social Darwinism, 15
Solow, Robert, 263
Southern Slavery Reduces Northern Wages (Weston),
  143, 144
Southey, Robert, 107, 111, 284, 285
Spence, Thomas, 131
Stanley, Amy Dru, 254, 268
Stansell, Christine, 218, 274
Stationary state, 193
Steadman, E., 308

Index